The Post-Subcultures Reader

The Post-subcultures Reader

**Edited by
David Muggleton
and
Rupert Weinzierl**

Oxford • New York

First published in 2003 by
Berg
Editorial offices:
1st Floor, Angel Court, 81 St Clements Street, Oxford OX4 1AW, UK
838 Broadway, Third Floor, New York, NY 10003-4812, USA

Berg is an imprint of Oxford International Publishers Ltd.

Library of Congress Cataloging-in-Publication Data
The post-subcultures reader / edited by David Muggleton and Rupert
Weinzierl.— 1st ed.
        p. cm.
Includes bibliographical references and index.
        ISBN 1-85973-663-7 (cloth) — ISBN 1-85973-668-8 (paper)
    1. Subculture. I. Muggleton, David. II. Weinzierl, Rupert, 1967–
        HM646.P67 2003
        306.1—dc22

                                                    2003019624

British Library Cataloguing-in-Publication Data
A catalogue record for this book is available from the British Library.

ISBN 1 85973 663 7 (Cloth)
        1 85973 668 8 (Paper)

Typeset by JS Typesetting Ltd, Wellingborough, Northants.
Printed in the United Kingdom by Biddles Ltd, Guildford and King's Lynn.

www.bergpublishers.com

Contents

Contents

Contents

Contributors

David Bloustien is completing his doctoral thesis on Kathy Acker's Jewish literary identity at the University of Sydney, Australia. His research interests include punk, media and the avant garde, epidemiology, piratology, psychoanalysis, myth and Jewish cultural history.

Martina Böse is currently completing her doctoral thesis on 'cultural diversity' and exclusion in Manchester's night-time economy in the Department of Sociology at Manchester Metropolitan University, UK. Her main research interests are city cultures, work in the cultural sector, racism and exclusion. Publications include 'Manchester's Cultural Industries: A Vehicle of Racial Ex/Inclusion?' in F. Eckardt and D. Hassenpflug (eds), *Consumption and the Post-industrial City* (Peter Lang Publishers, 2003).

Andy R. Brown is Senior Lecturer in Media Communication at Bath Spa University College, UK. His research interests include popular music, media and niche consumerism, television and audience studies and racism and identity politics. He is currently researching the New Wave of British Heavy Metal (NWOBHM). Previous publications include, *Political Languages of Race and the Politics of Exclusion* (Ashgate, 1999).

Rhiannon Bury received her Ph.D. from the University of Toronto in 2000 and is now an assistant professor in the Department of Communication Studies at Wilfrid Laurier University in Waterloo, Canada. Her research interests centre on the processes of online identification and community-making among female media fans. She has published several articles on her work, including 'From a Room to a Cyberspace of One's Own: Technological Change and the Construction of Women's Social Space', in G. Currie and C. Rothenberg (eds), *Feminist (Re)Visions of the Subject: Landscapes, Ethnoscapes, Theoryscapes* (Lexington, 2002).

Dylan Clark teaches at the University of Colorado, Boulder, USA. In 2000 he completed his doctoral dissertation at the University of Washington, Seattle, on the topic of anarchism and punk in Seattle. As a 'rogue scholar' he continues to explore these areas and is interested in critically studying Whiteness, consumerism, and capitalism. He is currently in the process of editing an anthology to be titled *The Punk Reader*.

Contributors

Paul Hodkinson is Lecturer in Sociology at the University of Surrey, UK. He is author of *Goth: Identity, Style and Subculture* (Berg, 2002). In addition to the specific area of subcultural theory, his research interests are focused more broadly upon the relationship between media, commerce and collective forms of cultural identification.

Roman Horak is Associate Professor and Head of Sociology of Art and Culture at the Department of Aesthetics, Cultural Studies/Art Pedagogy, University of Applied Arts, Vienna, Austria. He is Associate Member of Staff at the International Centre for Sports History and Culture, De Montfort University, Leicester, UK, and member of the editorial board of the journal *Cultural Studies*. Main research interests are popular culture, ethnography, urban studies and the politics of cultural studies. Latest publications include *Die Praxis der Cultural Studies* (Loecker, 2002).

Rupa Huq is a lecturer at the School of Education, University of Manchester, UK, where she teaches on the leisure management and language, literacy and communication degrees. Her research interests include issues of ethnicity, youth and post-compulsory education for which she held a Leverhulme Special Research Fellowship from 2000-2002. Forthcoming publications include *Rethinking Youth Culture* (Routledge).

Richard Kahn is a Ph.D. student in the Social Sciences and Comparative Education division of the Graduate School of Education, University of California at Los Angeles (UCLA), where he is working towards a dissertation on 'Post-human' literacies that will map how humanistic notions of self have combined in the present with a social revolution in technology and the radicalization of nature. He is presently the chair of the Ecopedagogy wing of the new UCLA Paulo Freire Institute. He has publications forthcoming in the journals *Social Thought and Research* and *Democracy & Nature*. His Web site is http://getvegan.com.

Douglas Kellner holds the George Kneller Chair in the Philosophy of Education at UCLA, and is author of many books on social theory, politics, history and culture. He has recently published a book on the 2000 presidential election, *Grand Theft 2000: Media Spectacle and a Stolen Election* (Rowman & Littlefield, 2001); also *Media Spectacle* (Routledge, 2003), and *From 9/11 to Terror War: The Dangers of the Bush Legacy* (Rowman & Littlefield, 2003).

Gabriele Klein is Professor of Sociology at the University of Hamburg, Germany. Her main research interests are studies around movement (motion) and the body, the sociology of culture and arts, dance studies, gender studies and urban sociology. Recent publications include *Dance Theory Text* (Lit-Verlag, 2002) and *Electronic Vibration: Pop Culture Theory* (Rogner & Bernhard, 1999).

Louis Kontos is Associate Professor of Sociology at Long Island University, New York, USA. He has published in the areas of ethnography and critical theory, and is a co-editor of *Gangs and Society* (Columbia University Press, 2003).

Oliver Marchart lectures at the University of Basel, Switzerland, in the Department of Media Studies, and at the University of Vienna, Austria, in the Department of Political Science. His main research interests are political and cultural theory as well as art theory. He has published in various journals and is also co-editor, with Simon Critchley, of the forthcoming *Laclau: A Critical Reader* (Routledge).

David Muggleton, ex-bass player with the Street Sadists, was involved in the British punk rock scene of the 1970s. He is now Senior Lecturer in Sociology in the School of Sport, Exercise and Health Sciences at University College Chichester, UK. His research interests include sport, popular culture and subcultures. He is the author of *Inside Subculture: The Postmodern Meaning of Style* (Berg, 2000).

Doreen Piano is a Brittain Teaching Fellow at the Georgia Institute of Technology in Atlanta, USA. Her research interests focus on the intersection of subcultural studies, feminist studies, and rhetorical theory, particularly in the areas of technology and alternative media production. She has published a chapter titled 'Leaving Las Vegas: Reading the Prostitute as a Site of Abjection' in M. Brewer (ed.), *Exclusions of Feminist Thought: Challenging the Boundaries of Womanhood* (Sussex Academic Press, 2002).

Helen Reddington used to play bass in the punk band Joby and the Hooligans. She is now Senior Lecturer in Commercial Music at the University of Westminster, UK. Her main research interests are women and music technology, scenes and subcultures. She is also involved in song writing outside the commercial sphere - for purposes of communication, not cash 'n' glitz. Recent publications include 'Voxpop Puella' in *Digital Desires*, edited by Cutting Edge Women's Research Group (I.B. Tauris, 2000).

Geoff Stahl is currently completing a Ph.D in the Department of Art History and Communication Studies at McGill University, Canada. His research interests include cities and scenes, and images of the city as they inform musical practice. He has published on the Montreal scene in the journal *Public* (volume 22/23, 2001) and is currently co-editing *Night and the City: Reflections on the Nocturnal Side of Urban Life* (Verso, forthcoming).

Graham St John is a post-doctoral research Fellow in the Centre for Critical and Cultural Studies at the University of Queensland, Australia. His research interests are new youth counter cultures, the global techno-tribal movement, environmentalism and reconciliation. He has recently edited *FreeNRG: Notes From the Edge of the Dance Floor* (Common Ground, 2001), and *Rave Culture and Religion* (Routledge, forthcoming).

Toshiya Ueno, sociologist, critic and media theorist, is Professor in the Department of Expressive Cultures in Wako University, Japan. In the mid-1980s he was involved in a free pirate radio movement in Tokyo, and for the past three years has been a psychedelic-trance-techno DJ in Amsterdam, Zagreb and Tokyo. His main research area is the theory and politics of subcultures. Recent Japanese language publications include *Thinking Diaspora* (Chikuma Shobo, 1999); *Introduction to Cultural Studies* (Chikuma Shobo, 2000); and *The Practice of Cultural Studies* (Chikuma Shobo, 2002).

Angharad N. Valdivia is a research associate professor at the Institute of Communications Research at the University of Illinois, USA. She is the author of *A Latina in the Land of Hollywood* (University of Arizona Press, 2000), editor of *Companion to Media Studies* (Blackwell, 2003), and co-editor of *Geographies of Latinidad* (Duke University Press, forthcoming). Her research focuses on transnational multi-culturalist gender issues with a special emphasis on Latinas in popular culture.

Rupert Weinzierl holds a Ph.D. in political science and sociology from the University of Vienna, Austria, and currently lives and operates in that city as a freelance researcher in cultural studies. He is the author of *Fight the Power: A Secret History of Pop and the Formation of New Substreams* (Passagen-Verlag, 2000).

Theresa M. Winge holds a Bachelor degree in Apparel Design, and a Master of Liberal Studies degree, which focused on urban subcultures and chaos theory. Currently, she is pursuing a Ph.D. in the Design, Housing, and Apparel Department, at the University of Minnesota, USA. Her research interests include subcultural dress and sustainable design. Her diverse educational and practical experiences have allowed her to design unique fashions that have been presented in juried fashion exhibitions, both on runways and in galleries.

Part I
Introduction

What is 'Post-subcultural Studies' Anyway?
Rupert Weinzierl and *David Muggleton*

This reader investigates the changing relationship between youth cultural tastes, politics and music in today's so-called 'post-modern world' and, in so doing, provides a comprehensive introduction to the theoretical understanding and ethnographic practice of what has only recently come to be known as 'post-subcultural studies'. More specifically, it explores how we might retheorize and reconceptualize youth (sub)cultural phenomena on the shifting social terrain of the new millennium, where global mainstreams and local substreams rearticulate and restructure in complex and uneven ways to produce new, hybrid cultural constellations. Is it possible to work within the existing limitations of 'subculture', or has the concept exhausted its usefulness? Can attempts at reconceptualization adequately capture the experience of fragmentation, flux and fluidity that is central to contemporary youth culture? And to what extent does this involve the challenging of past theoretical and political orthodoxies about 'spectacular' subcultural styles? By addressing such questions through a wide variety of international case studies, this reader helps to chart the emergence of a new agenda for the study of youth.

The Origins of Post-subcultural Studies

Although the intellectual inspiration for the construction of this reader can be precisely located in a 'Post-Subcultural Studies' symposium held in Vienna in 2001,[1] the papers presented at that event were clearly drawing on debates that had been developing for some time within the world of academia and popular culture more generally. Indeed, the first published reference to the 'post-subculture' terminus can be traced back to at least Chambers (1987), although its use by

---

1. The symposium 'Post-Subcultural Studies: New Post-Subcultural Formations within Popular Culture and their Political Impact' was conceptualized by Rupert Weinzierl and held at The Depot, Museumsplatz, Vienna from 11–12 May 2001.

Polhemus (1996) and Muggleton (1997) is better known. Post-subculture, under-stood as a collection of published works, and thus a constructed field of study, is, however, a much more recent development.[2]

While a wide range of sources can be nominated for inclusion within this newly designated field there does appear to be a broad agreement on the selection of certain 'core' texts. The 'popular cultural studies' approach of Steve Redhead and the Manchester Institute for Popular Culture, is invariably represented (see, for example, Redhead 1990, 1993, 1995, 1997; Redhead *et al.* 1997), as are later works addressing 'post-modern' developments (for example Bennett 1999; Muggleton 2000) as well as Sarah Thornton's (1995) now seemingly indisp-ensable, Bourdieu-influenced, *Club Cultures*.[3] The thematic unity to be found amongst these and other, equally theoretically disparate, examples lies in their acknowledgement (either implicit or explicit) of the seminal 1970s British sub-cultural theory of the Centre for Contemporary Cultural Studies (CCCS) at the University of Birmingham as a revered, yet critical, benchmark against which to mark out and assess subsequent developments.[4]

At the risk of some simplification we might therefore suggest that post-sub-cultural studies tends to be equated with what is, generally, a post-CCCS position that has been gathering momentum and influence throughout the 1990s. As we argue in this reader, the era seems long gone of working-class youth subcultures 'heroically' resisting subordination through 'semiotic guerrilla warfare'. Both youth cultural activities and the research efforts in this field seem nowadays to reflect a more pragmatic approach compared to the romanticism of the CCCS, whose authors saw radical potential in largely symbolic challenges. While we argue that certain contemporary 'subcultural' movements can still express a

2. Chambers (1987: 9) uses the phrase 'post-subcultural styles' in the context of stylistic and musical eclecticism. Polhemus's (1996: 91) reference is to '"clubbing" as a post-subcultural phen-omenon'. Muggleton's (1997) essay is entitled 'The Post-subculturalist'. On the issue of post-subculture as a field of study see, for example, recent journal references to 'Post-subcultural Theory' (Martin 2002: 77-9) and '"post-subculturalist" or "clubcultures" strands of theory' (Wilson 2002: 377). But for 'official' recognition of a distinct post-subcultural perspective, can there be any more fitting authority than the University of Birmingham? For the 2002-3 academic year, the 'Youth, Culture and Society' course in the School of Social Sciences has a week on 'Post-Subcultural Theories: From Critique to Rejection'. See http://www.crees.bham.ac.uk/study/undergraduate/youth.pdf (accessed December 2002).

3. See the texts cited in the Martin (2002) and Wilson (2002) articles, the reading list for the above Birmingham course, and the outline of Carleton University's current 'Representing Youth' module for Fall 2002, where week five's topic is entitled 'Post-modern Youth: "Rave Off" and the End of the Century Party' http://www.carleton.ca/polecon/outlines/44551F02.html (accessed December 2002).

4. The four major texts that are arguably crucial in outlining the theoretical, political and methodological assumptions of CCCS subcultural theory are Hall and Jefferson (1976), Mungham and Pearson (1976), Willis (1978) and Hebdige (1979).

political orientation, the potential for style itself to resist appears largely lost, with any 'intrinsically' subversive quality to subcultures exposed as an illusion. Thus, while the analyses of the CCCS can still be regarded as pioneering scientific work, they no longer appear to reflect the political, cultural and economic realities of the twenty-first century.[5]

Within the post-subcultures field, two main strands can be identified, although these are neither wholly encompassing nor mutually exclusive, and some work may either fall outside of, or into, both positions. The first strand attempts to jettison the whole theoretical apparatus of the CCCS and establish a new framework for the analysis of contemporary subcultural phenomena. Whereas a decade ago Beezer (1992) had still felt confident in asserting the continuing 'intellectual hegemony' of the Gramscian-semiotic approach of the CCCS, we now appear to be in the advanced stages of the dissolution of this, once formidable, orthodoxy. Yet although the whole research agenda in this area has clearly shifted, heralding the emergence of new methodological, theoretical and substantive concerns, a new, dominant paradigm has yet to develop in place of the old. Three main contenders presented here that currently vie for theoretical supremacy are those based on the works of Pierre Bourdieu (1994), Judith Butler (1990, 1993) and Michel Maffesoli (1996).

We discuss each of these perspectives in more detail in a later section of this chapter. For now, we can note that the use of Bourdieu has been instrumental in introducing 'taste', 'distinction' and 'cultural capital' as important concepts for the analysis of youth culture, primarily through the work of Sarah Thornton (1995). These concepts are utilized further in Chapters 2, 3 and 10 of this reader. The application of Butler's work has led to a growing concern with performativity as a basis for comprehending the ongoing construction of subcultural identities. Chapters 3, 7 and 18 explore these themes in the contexts of both dance and online communities. Finally, Maffesoli has been enormously influential in establishing a post-modern framework for youth analysis that abandons modernist concerns with socio-structural identities in favour of a focus on the fluidity of a variety of nebulous 'tribal' formations. The legacy and limitations of such a Maffesolian position are demonstrated and debated in Chapters 5, 7 and 8.

If this first strand of post-subcultural studies presents an effective challenge to the theoretical orthodoxies of the CCCS, the second goes even further in rejecting outright any possibility of the continuing usefulness of the subculture terminus

---

5. The theoretical and methodological deficiencies of the CCCS texts should not be allowed to detract from their undoubted impact upon the formation of post-subcultural studies. Like Angela McRobbie, we would 'remind the reader of the great importance of these volumes and the extent to which they had both thoroughly influenced and helped to form [our] own outlook and views' (McRobbie 1991: xviii–xix).

itself. The result is a wrestling for a new conception more adequately disposed to capture the changing sensibilities and practices of post-subcultural formations. Armadeep Singh (2000) has conceptualized such contemporary youth groups as 'channels' or 'subchannels', Rupert Weinzierl (2000) refers to them as 'temporary substream networks', while Andy Bennett (1999), in what is currently perhaps the most well-known attempt at reformulation, has also drawn on the French socio-logist Maffesoli and called them 'neo-tribes'. Redhead (1997: x), on the other hand, has argued that '"clubcultures" is the concept, and global youth formation, which supplements "subculture" as the key to the analysis of the histories and futures of youth culture.'

As Hodkinson (2002: 23) has already commented on these shifts in terminology and theoretical frameworks, 'it is not readily apparent what to make of this remark-able plethora of concepts and explanations.' Some of this confusion can, however, be alleviated if we recognize that different concepts are often used to abstract different aspects of social reality. 'Clubculture', for example, can be employed substantively to refer to a designated set of 'tastes' that are consumed within specific spatial locations (for example, Thornton 1995: 3). 'Neo-tribe', however, is mainly used analytically (for example, Bennett 1999, 2000) to capture the sense of fluidity and hybridity in the contemporary urban club-scene, with all the theoretical post-modern implications that this carries. Once we appreciate that these different conceptualizations are not necessarily incompatible, it is possible to understand how, as Toshiya Ueno argues in Chapter 7, '"post-subcultural studies", implies a sort of "Urban Tribal Studies"', and why the terms subculture, club-culture and tribe or neo-tribe are all used, sometimes interchangably, to refer to the variety of youth cultural formations discussed in this reader.

The End of Subcultural Heroism

Critics of the 'heroic' CCCS model of subculture emphasize that the complexity and shifting nature of current youth cultural practices can no longer be explained with a framework that imputes to these forms a linear temporal logic. From the teddy boys of the 1950s, via the mods, rockers and skinheads of the 1960s, through to the punks that provided the raw material for Hebdige's (1979) work, the CCCS posited in modernist time the unfolding and subsequent swift demise of a success-ion of discrete, clearly identifiable youth subcultures. Whether or not this was ever an accurate portrayal of subcultural emergence and eventual incorporation,[6] the sheer diversity and plurality of current (sub)cultural styles, forms and practices presented and discussed in this reader bears testimony to its irrelevance for the

6. There are good theoretical and empirical reasons to suggest that it was not. See, for example, Osgerby (1992) Redhead (1993, 1997) and Muggleton (2000: Chapter 8).

twenty-first century. Without wishing to subscribe to all the tenets of a popular post-modernism, a world populated by bondage punks and anarcho-punks (Chapters 4 and 15), DiY-protest cultures (Chapter 5), techno tribes (Chapter 7), Modern Primitives (Chapter 8), Latino gangs (Chapter 9), new-wave metallers (Chapter 14) and net.goths (Chapter 19) has seemingly more resonance with Polhemus's (1994) 'supermarket of style' than with 1970s British subcultural theory.

Nor is it any more legitimate to attempt to explain the contemporary subcultural scene with a conception that assumes a homological unity of class-based practices, particularly one that 'imposes a hermeneutic seal around the relationship between musical and stylistic preference' (Bennett 1999: 599). As Bennett (2000) has gone on to show, it is common for members of a nebulous neo-tribal grouping to demonstrate their enthusiasm for a wide range of musical dance genres. In fact, according to Muggleton (2000: Chapter 4), this somewhat paradoxical expression of 'widespread tastes' in underground sounds is one tactic by which 'liminal' youth cultures attempt to accumulate subcultural capital (a term coined by Sarah Thornton), thereby maintaining distinction from other, more 'restrictive' (sub)-groups and claiming authenticity of identity. Ironically, it is precisely because certain musically oriented subcultures were unable to be contained within restrictive class-based homologies that the CCCS regarded them as *inauthentic* – politically conservative rather than radically resistant. But then 'popular music and "deviant" youth styles never fitted together as harmoniously as some subcultural theory proclaimed' (Redhead 1990: 25). In Chapter 14, Andy Brown examines the case of the heavy metal subculture, and draws on the above deficiency in the CCCS analysis to explain why the account of this musical genre 'in subcultural theory is, at best, marginal; at worst, simply "invisible"'.

Another area of criticism is that the subculture concept seems to be little more than a cliché, with its implications that both 'subculture' and the parent culture against which it is defined are coherent and homogenous formations that can be clearly demarcated. But contemporary youth cultures are characterized by far more complex stratifications than that suggested by the simple dichotomy of 'monolithic mainstream' – 'resistant subcultures'. The assumptions of the CCCS-theorists clearly neglected the numerous forms of 'osmotic' interaction between subcultural-related and other societal formations. This omission becomes particularly crucial in an increasingly globally interconnected world where ideas, styles, music, people, technology and capital circulate and collide in complex ways, and on a scale and with a speed previously unimaginable (Morley and Robins 1995). Here, the transgression of the subcultural-mainstream boundary appears to have two main implications for how post-subcultural forms of organization can differ politically from those theorized by the CCCS.

First, the explicitly political agenda of the CCCS – to discover forms of rebellion in working-class youth movements – led them to underemphasize the extent of subcultural participation in economic processes. Indeed, subcultures were theorized as rebelliously 'political' by virtue of their ritualistic resistance to capitalist incorporation (what the CCCS termed a 'magical' or 'imaginary' solution to social subordination). Yet commodity-oriented subcultures, such as bikers (Willis 1978), snowboarders (Humphreys 1997) and windsurfers (Wheaton 2000) have been living out consumerist ambitions since their very beginnings. Subcultures of today are also complicit in the (niche) marketing of their own identities. There is a vivid role for subcultural-related practices as an entrepreneurial engine for the new media, fashion and cultural industries, while many of these young producers themselves have subcultural origins (McRobbie 1989, 2002). Dylan Clark, in Chapter 15, refers to this process when he points out how 'subcultures may serve a useful function for capitalism by making stylistic innovations that can then become vehicles for new sales'.

Yet it is the very marketing of these signs of rebellion that politically radicalizes the Seattle punks of Dylan Clark's study. As Oliver Marchart argues in Chapter 6, the importance the CCCS placed on ritualistic resistance to economic incorporation effectively confined any notion of subcultural radicalism to the cultural rather than the political level of society (what Marchart terms the '"micro-politics" of everyday life'). But once freed from the trappings of a (now commodified) style that no longer has the power to shock, anarchist-punks are able to embrace a radical discourse and praxis that Marchart might regard as having the potential to become macro-political in scope. For the CCCS, authentic subcultures were those that preceded stylistic cooptation. For Clark, it is only following cooptation that subcultures come to realize 'the ultimate authenticity lies in political action'. As he puts it, 'the threatening pose has been replaced with the actual threat'.

A second point that allows today's youth formations to differ politically from the 'heroic' notion of subculture is their enormously heightened media awareness. A main criticism of the CCCS approach is its assumption of a 'media-free space', thus 'positioning subcultures as transparent niches in an opaque world as if subcultural life spoke an unmediated truth' (Thornton 1995: 119). This positioning not only veils the role that the media play in the subculture's own internal construction but it posits the media along with the forces of capital and commerce as instrumental in the eventual 'defusion and diffusion' of the subculture. By contrast, Thornton argues that various forms of media, through promoting (flyers), reviewing (music papers) and sensationalizing (tabloids), actually aid what are initially diverse and diffuse cultural fragments to cohere as recognizably defined subcultures, effectively emphasizing their rebellious status and prolonging their existence.

A rather benign contemporary example might be the long-standing gothic subculture, members of which are now heavy users of new media, particularly the Internet. As Paul Hodkinson demonstrates in Chapter 19, the Internet fulfils both an internally integrative and externally differentiating function for gothic identity. The virtual interactions of goths through online technology serve both to 'consolidate and strengthen' the boundaries that both internally define this subculture and render it distinct from other formations. But computer-mediated communications (CMCs) also provide enhanced possibilities for more encompassing and political forms of subcultural organization. In Chapter 20, Richard Kahn and Douglas Kellner emphasize how the anti-globalization movement is using the Internet to connect 'a diversity of movements into global solidarity networks' in order to advance its struggle. In a time when the political right is hegemonic in the West, and social democratic parties fit smoothly into the neo-liberal consensus, the anti-globalization movement is currently the only promising political project of the left.

The Post-heroic Phase of Subcultural Studies

Throughout the 1990s many youth researchers moved away from the semiotic approach of the CCCS theorists, returning to sociological research approaches informed by ethnographic and qualitative methodologies. Despite publishing just a single major study before leaving academia, one of the most influential of these researchers has been Sarah Thornton. Her (1995) ethnography of clubbing drew heavily on the work of Pierre Bourdieu who understands lifestyles (aesthetic attitudes) as a means of distinction from other classes. According to Bourdieu (1984) symbolic capital (signs of distinction like language or dress codes, and actions of distinction such as the symbolic consumption of music) is as important for social stratification as the accumulation of economic capital. In a further departure from the CCCS, however, Thornton does not attempt to map the resulting 'taste cultures' firmly back onto socio-structural variables like class.[7] Rather, her focus is on how clubbers use 'subcultural capital' (as she terms it) as an ideological resource through which to accrue 'hip' or 'cool' status – obtained through 'being "in the know"' about what is 'in' or 'out' on the subcultural scene (Thornton 1995: 11).

The important implication that arises from this is that subcultural capital is valuable by virtue of its exclusivity; hence, as new subcultural sounds and styles emerge they must be prevented from being continually coveted and appropriated by the 'mass'. In Thornton's study, subcultural capital is protected in this way by clubbers discursively defending the lines of demarcation that differentiate their 'underground' tastes from those of the 'mainstream' (1995: Chapter 3). This

---

7. As she argues, 'class . . . does not correlate in any one-to-one way with levels of youthful subcultural capital. In fact, class is wilfully obfuscated by subcultural distinctions' (Thornton 1995: 12).

attempt at demonstrating 'distinction' occurs through the construction of a commercialized subcultural or mainstream 'Other' as a symbolic marker against which to define one's own tastes as 'authentic'. In this way, Thornton is able to account for the *development* of subcultures, for the boundaries that distinguish them from the inauthentic and commercial are understood as porous and permeable, requiring constant policing through the on-going process of classifying and reclassifying certain tastes as legitimate. As she notes elsewhere (Thornton 1994: 192, n 46) this diachronic treatment contrasts favourably with the static portrayal produced through the homological analysis of the CCCS that seeks to identify cultural correspondences between different levels of a subculture (such as style, music, focal concerns) at a particular point in time.

Through her understanding of subcultures as constructed through rather than existing prior to media discourse – 'communications media create subcultures in the process of naming them and draw boundaries around them in the act of describing them' (Thornton 1995: 162) – Thornton also moves radically away from the CCCS conceptualization of subculture as a rigid, reified and realist entity, rooted in underlying class relationships (see Muggleton 2000: Chapter 2; Martin 2002). In so doing, she points to the possibility of what Evans (1997: 179) refers to as a 'flight from fixity' in subcultural studies. In a rather different way, the same potential can be found in the work of Judith Butler (1990, 1993). Butler's concern is to 'de-mask', in order to subvert, the apparent stability and 'naturalness' of gender and sexual identities. She theorizes gender not an aspect of one's identity by which one acts, but as itself an enactment that 'produce(s) that which it names' (Butler 1993: 225). In Butler's terms it is *performative*, having 'no ontological status apart from the various acts which constitute its reality' (1990: 139). Yet, while the ongoing repetition of these constitutive acts is constrained by pre-existent norms, it is always a *differential* rather than identical repetition, leading to the potential for a displacement, transformation or rewriting of gendered and sexual identities.

Viewed in this way, all such identities are profoundly unstable, and it is through parody in particular that the potential to subvert appears greatest. Butler's own (1990) example of parody is that of drag, which undermines the assumed essential reality and originality of gender and heterosexuality though its hyperbolic mimicry. Leblanc (2002) provides an example of how punk style can be employed as parodic 'performance' by which to undermine conventional notions of femininity. But Butler's arguments have most typically been applied to work on sexually transgressive subcultures, where the politics of performativity are discussed in relation to hypermasculine and hyperfeminine parodies of straight styles, namely the 'gay skinhead' and the 'lipstick lesbian', both of which first emerged during the 1980s and 1990s (Bell *et al.* 1994; Healy 1996). As Bell and his co-authors argue of these two styles, 'the excessive performance of masculinity and femininity within homosexual frames exposes not only the fabricated nature of hetero-sexuality but also its claim to authenticity' (Bell *et al.* 1994: 33). Thus gay skinheads are not mere fake copies of 'real' or 'original' 1960s and 1970s heterosexual, right-wing skinheads, precisely because all such identities are performative fabrications – 'fictions, copies' (Bell *et al.* 1994: 33).[8]

These different applications of the work of both Bourdieu and Butler have helped to establish a resolutely anti-essentialist approach to subcultural theory. Hence, Evans (1997: 181) can assert that *all* subcultural 'identities are not ontolog-ically distinct or pre-existent, but are bought into being, constructed and replayed through every day actions, dress, adornment and other cultural practices'. Both Bourdieu and Butler understand the body as culturally constructed and see this occurring through a notion of productive 'practice'; although for Bourdieu, it is through the 'habitus' that tastes are ritually installed and memorized within the body, manifesting themselves as physical dispositions (the bodily 'hexis'). Yet, while the work of Sarah Thornton has shown how cultural tastes and capital can be understood as fluid and dynamic, it is less easy to conceive of the habitus in this way (it is indicative that Thornton does not use the concept). Indeed, Lovell (2000: 28) refers to its 'durability', a point similar to that made by Gabriele Klein in Chapter 3 of this reader.

For Klein, the habitus suggests only the bodily reproduction and confirmation of social norms, whereas Butler's concept of performativity (as we noted above) offers the possibility of their subversion. Yet, for Butler, there is literally 'no body' outside of the ongoing practice of performative citation, and therefore no body 'memory' that 'enables the actor to cite'. For this reason Klein prefers to draw on Bourdieu's use of mimesis as an explanation for the practical embodiment of norms and tastes. Mimesis implies not only imitation, but also interpretation and new creation. It establishes 'the difference with respect to the original', as Roman Horak in Chapter 12 puts it. For Klein, then, mimesis mediates 'between the impressions of the inner and exterior worlds'. In a very different way, David Bloustien in Chapter 4 draws on psychoanalytical theory and punk's masochistic imagery of bondage-wear to posit the skin (or the 'epidermal') as the place that sutures the mind and body, and which mediates between interior (metaphysical) and exterior (physical) inscriptions of knowledge.

The emphasis on the fluidity and mobility of subcultures that we have so far been concerned to highlight can also be found, but linked to theorizations of post-modernity, in Michel Maffesoli's (1996) conception of a 'tribus'. With this terminus,

---

8. A failure of the viewer to read parody in this way is one reason why such subcultural examples as given by Bell *et al.* (1994) or Leblanc (2002) are rarely convincing.

Maffesoli describes new forms of sociality that can be understood as 'post-traditional'. Group identities, he argues, are no longer formed along traditional structural determinants (like class, gender or religion); rather, consumption patterns and practices enable individuals to create new forms of contemporary sociality – small-scale social configurations that operate beyond modernist class borders. The 'tribe' is also 'without the rigidity of the forms of organization with which we are familiar; it refers more to a certain ambience, a state of mind, and it is preferably to be expressed through lifestyles that favour appearance and "form"' (Maffesoli 1996: 98). Tribes do not therefore exhibit stable practices of inclusion and exclusion – they are integrative and distinctive at the same time. These new network socialities seem to encourage plural, fluid and part-time rather than fixed, discrete and encompassing group identities – individuals are able to flow between multiple signs of identity conceptions.

Although Maffesoli's argument is one of de-individualization, in the sense of a decline in the atomization of actors and the emergence of affective communities, the individualism of tribal participants is still rated much higher than with 'heroic', modernist youth subcultures, and it is possible to participate simultaneously in the activities of two or more such network socialities. The single members of these groups do not foster their community as a priority but use the group to satisfy their individual needs. Utopian ideas are mostly uninteresting for tribes because they are mainly oriented to the present. It is not difficult here to see why Maffesoli's concept, adapted as 'neo-tribe', has become an invaluable heuristic device for subcultural-related research (see Gore 1997; Malbon 1999; Bennett 1999, 2000). As Bennett (1999: 614) has argued, 'neo-tribalism . . . allows for the shifting nature of youth's musical and stylistic preferences and the essential fluidity of youth cultural groups'.

Heavily influencing post-modern interpretations of youth culture, Maffesoli's work has helped to overcome what Graham St John, in Chapter 5, has called the 'lumbering modernist paradigm' of the CCCS. But the post-modern reworking of youth cultural theory that draws on Maffesoli is now being opened up to criticism that suggests his work fatally underemphasizes the politically emancipative elements within youth culture. As we have already remarked, Maffesoli argues that tribal members rate their individual needs and satisfactions higher than group values and political utopia. While this ensures his theory can successfully account for the dispersed and diffuse contextual nature of youth cultural production and consumption, it manifestly fails as an adequate explanation of new forms of political youth cultural activism that have developed during recent years.

A similar point can be made about Sarah Thornton's (1995) work on club-cultures. As Gilbert and Pearson (1999) have pointed out, by drawing on Bourdieu's notion of cultural capital, Thornton breaks with the orthodox Gramscian model of the CCCS by which youth cultures are presumed to form in opposition to, and eventually become incorporated by, a dominant culture. Instead, as we have already seen, she is more concerned with elaborating the elitist hierarchies of tasteful distinction that operate *within* subcultures. By so doing, her work is able to dispense with the (inaccurate) assumption that such subcultures are 'inherently' resistant or oppositional simply by virtue of their positioning *vis-à-vis* a dominant cultural formation. Yet this mode of analysis effectively robs youth cultures of any macro-political dimension, for 'however "radical" a group may consider their particular practice to be, in truth they are merely trying to accumulate subcultural capital at the expense of the unhip' (Gilbert and Pearson 1999: 159-60).

In a time of furious youth protests from Stockholm to Genua, both the 'tribus' and 'cultural capital' conceptions have therefore begun to show their obvious limitations in their adaptations for youth cultural studies. As an antidote to this apoliticizing of youth cultural theory, Gilbert and Pearson, like Oliver Marchart in Chapter 6, recommend a return to a Gramscian-derived model of the social formation, but one that is more attuned to the *complexity* of hegemony theory as arguably intended in Gramsci's original writings. In particular, it is the work of Laclau and Mouffe (1985) that is commonly cited here as a way of allowing us to move from an 'inherently' radical notion of subculture, coupled to a monolithic conception of the dominant culture, to a position that recognizes the differentiation and multiplicity of points of power in society and the way that various cultural formations and elements articulate within and across these constellations of power in complex and non-linear ways to produce contingent and modificatory outcomes. Such a model dispenses with the theorization of subcultures as *either* oppositional *or* incorporated, and arguably brings us close to Hebdige's (1988: 35) rethinking of his original (1979) approach to CCCS subcultural theory, a reformulation in which 'the "subcultural response" is neither simply affirmation nor refusal'.

Party for Your Right to Fight – The Politicization of Youth Cultures

One focal point of subculture-related articulations and group representations has always been emancipation, albeit mostly expressed symbolically and within the cultural field. Historically, it has become clear that although 'heroic' subcultures were able to 'win space' for working-class interests, these gains were effectively limited to the cultural sphere. In fact, youth resistance through consumption rituals has been widely apolitical, at least from a macro-political point of view, contrary to the articulation of what we call the new 'post-subcultural protest formations' that are examined in this reader (see Chapters 5, 15 and 20). What was traditionally ascribed to subcultures in semiotic analysis was the idea of the *latent* political nature of their practices. By emphasizing only 'identity politics', both subcultural theory and the youth formations that it claimed to explain failed to develop a macro-political dimension. Thus, subcultural acts of resistance degenerated to little more than *Senseless Acts of Beauty* (McKay 1996).

But if the CCCS over-politicized youth formations, then post-modernist and other post-subcultural positions have been equally guilty of under-politicizing them. The assumption that youth cultures are mainly hedonistic, individualistic and politically disengaged, or are concerned only to assert their authenticity via the accumulation of subcultural capital, has been significantly undermined by the political activism and media visibility of new post-subcultural protest formations. According to Kahn and Kellner in Chapter 20, the mass protests of the anti-globalization movement have sought to show how global capitalism has resulted in 'intensified exploitation of labour, environmental devastation, growing divisions among the social classes and the undermining of democracy'.

As these changes wrought by capitalist globalization have intensified, one side effect has been the disappearance of many niches that subcultural-related formations used to occupy for themselves. Neo-liberal capitalism has destroyed many independent structures of production and distribution during recent years with the relatively frictionless integration of subcultural capital into the cultural industries. This has helped provoke the reaction by which some youth cultural formations attempt to directly oppose economic neo-liberalism, thus combining their particularist approaches with a universalist (anti-capitalist) dimension. Contrary to traditional left-wing political movements, these new protest formations use subcultural codes for their articulation but use them within the political (not only the cultural) field (Weinzierl 2000).

It should now be clear that we do not regard 'subculture', 'clubculture' or 'neo-tribe' as adequate conceptualizations by which to account for the overtly politicized agenda of new youth formations. It might be argued, however, that the CCCS authors were aware of the limitations of the subculture concept for explaining the political protest dimension of youth cultures; for they made a clear distinction between working-class subcultures, which resisted bourgeois hegemony through ritualistic means, and 1960s middle-class countercultures that, it was claimed, articulated a far more potent critique of capitalism. It was because of their position *within* the dominant culture that these countercultures were ably poised to 'become an emergent ruptural force for the whole society' (Clarke *et al.* 1976: 69). Yet we would caution against too hasty a transference of the 'counterculture' concept to the youth protest formations of today, for two reasons.

Firstly, we need to bear in mind the political and ideological divisions that existed within the counterculture. One of the most important of these was the distinction between radicals and hedonists (or the 'New Left' and the 'hippies'); for, as the CCCS authors themselves acknowledge, only the former were engaged in attempting to effect positive change through 'activist politics': the latter were more concerned to disengage *from* the political system by exploring 'alternative lifestyles'.[9] Secondly, in this era of 'class decomposition' and cultural hybridity, the strict distinction between middle-class radical countercultures and working-class 'heroic' subcultures is no longer tenable (Muggleton 2000; Chapter 8). In the context of late 1980s UK dance culture, for example, there has appeared 'an uneasy and drug-related syncretism of the most unlikely collections of youth: hoolies, hippies, crusties, casuals, and more besides' (Gilbert and Pearson 1999: 28). Arguing along similar lines, we would claim that certain contemporary hedonistic youth 'tribes' (such as rave and techno cultures) have, in some cases, 'crossed-over' with radical, politically motivated 'countercultures' and expressive, ecologically aware 'social movements' to create new forms of post-subcultural allegiances.

The main thesis of Graham St John, in Chapter 5, is that the new protest form-ations combine subcultural communications and (often post-Marxist) counter-cultural ideologies to produce 'carnivals of protest'. They use subculturally derived modes of articulation and identity generation but also engage macro-politically, operating ideologically and hedonistically at the same time. With their universalist dimension of anti-capitalism the youth cultural networks within the anti-global-ization movement have reached the moment of politicization when forms of cultural self-organization turn into overtly politicized 'anarchist bazaars'. Hence, these new protest formations differ considerably from historical countercultures because they are able to self-incorporate subcultural communication modes. And while they have in common with 'new social movements' an unconventional form of political participation, they differ from these movements by explicitly targeting the core of the global capitalist economy.

New protest formations like *Reclaim the Streets* and *Disobbedienti* (which include the former *Tute Bianche)* position themselves as antagonistic to the commodification of life in capitalist societies. They orientate themselves towards principles of ecological ethics and fight for standards of social justice. Like 'heroic subcultures' they define themselves *ex negativo* against a hegemonic parent culture (in their case against neo-liberal capitalism). But, contrary to 'heroic subcultures', such post-subcultural protest formations are both micro-politically and partially macro-politically effective – they favour politically visible 'direct action' over the

---

9. This is, incidentally, the reason why we would also reject the concept of 'new social move-ments' by which to account for post-subcultural protest formations. 'NSMs', as both Scott (1995) and Martin (2000) explain, are groups that can be mobilized around various types of humanitarian, citizenship and 'quality of life' issues (for example, gay and women's liberation groups, Black civil rights, anti-nuclear and 1960s student movements, animal rights and environmental protesters). Their membership is not class specific, nor are they primarily concerned with economic protest. Rather, in so far as they focus on both cultural and lifestyle politics, they can be regarded as 'post-material' in origin and orientation. These and other 'new movements attempt to bring about change though changing values and developing alternative life-styles' (Scott 1995: 17).

indirect strategy of expressing 'resistance' via style. They succeed in attracting widespread publicity for their opposition to the hegemony of economic neo-liberalism in Western democracies. With public attention directed towards the anti-globalization movement, (socio-cultural) relations of subordination in everyday life become publicly visible as (political) relations of oppression.

From a theoretical point of view the new protest networks can be approached with conceptions of radical democracy. Their articulation lies between the universal and the particular: each formation has its single-issue demands on the level of the particular but, on the level of the universal, all formations of the 'anti-globalization-movement' oppose the neo-liberal project of capitalist 'globalization' and advocate the increasing democratization of many areas of social life. With this combination of a universalist approach and heterogeneous particular demands, these oppositional groups live up to one of the central demands of the conception of a radical democracy: that 'universalism is not totally abandoned but particularized' (Mouffe, 1993: 13). That is to say, they:

> do not limit themselves to their particularisms (thus enclosing themselves within their own claims, as some forms of identity politics would do) but assume a much more universalist stance. Contrary to the universalist conception of 'actually existing' liberal democracy, however, radical democracy claims for the acceptance of difference and pleads for the common articulation of a plurality of particular interests and social antagonisms. (Marchart and Weinzierl 2002: 3)

The articulation of a universalist approach in the form of common ideological points of reference is necessary in order for post-subcultural protest formations to become macro-politically effective (together with a clear antagonism and a certain level of organization and collectivity). But this new form of universalism means a step away from the 'heroic' conception of subcultural 'identity politics'. As Oliver Marchart states in Chapter 6, 'by emphasizing cultural "micro-politics", what had previously been considered ordinary politics (the political field, or "macro-politics") was increasingly pushed out of focus'. It could therefore be a necessary next step for subcultural-related research to shift its focus back on the macro-political level, a task that some of our authors tackle in this reader.

Changes and Continuities

A number of chapters in this reader also attempt to discuss the implications of contemporary 'post-modern' changes for the ethnic structure and composition of new, post-traditional subcultural forms. Clearly, much has altered in this field since Hebdige's (1979: 45) attempt to construct 'a phantom history of race relations' upon 'the loaded surfaces' of White, working-class British subcultures. Two important subsequent and related developments are, first, the reterritorialization of global diasporic Black and Asian culture – styles, music, representations – in a distinctively post-colonial era; second, the actual physical movement of temporarily or permanently dispersed peoples and populations – migrants, casual workers, international students and so on – around the globe. As Wulff (1995: 10) has argued (in the context of an ethnic 'cross-cultural perspective') 'when it comes to globalization or transnational connections youth cultures are in the forefront of theoretical interest; youth, their ideas and commodities move easily across national boundaries, shaping and being shaped by all kinds of structures and meanings.'

One effect of the weakening of these national boundaries has been the emergence of strange and previously unknown transnational, cultural hybrids. A case in point is that of the Modern Primitives and their body modifications discussed in Chapter 8 by Teresa Winge. In its relocation of traditional (pre-modern) tribal, ethnic symbols to a modern, urban, White setting, it is argued that this subculture can be considered a peculiarly post-modern phenomenon. On the other hand, it is clear that more established cultural forms are still with us. In Chapter 9, Louis Kontos reports on the Latino urban tribe, The Latin Kings. While his intention is to provide a methodological and theoretical critique of previous research into delinquent gangs, he nonetheless establishes a line of continuity in post-subcultural studies that stretches back to the ethnographic research of the Chicago School.

The exploration of ethnically encoded hybridity is made an explicit theme of a number of chapters of this reader, through the examples of dance, music and style. In Chapter 10, Angharad Valdivia, like Kontos, provides a US case study of Latina/os, but does so through the example of Salsa as a transnational cultural form where local and global Latino influences mix and merge. Roman Horak writes in Chapter 12 on the importance of Black sounds – rap and hip-hop – and their relation to traditional East European 'folk' music in the lives of young second-generation migrants, in families from Turkey and the former Yugoslavia, who were either born in Vienna or came to Vienna at a very early age. Rupa Huq, in Chapter 13, also discusses rap, but in its French variant, set alongside the new UK Asian dance music and in a global, post-colonial context. In Chapter 11, meanwhile, Martina Böse focuses on style and its implications for the identity politics of Manchester based 'cultural practitioners' (DJs, club promoters and venue managers, music producers, flyer designers and media workers) who are mainly of Afro-Caribbean descent.

Yet Böse's aim in this chapter is to delve beneath the level of appearances to examine how both 'race' and class can be positioned in 'a revised analysis' of Black subcultural style. This is important, for in doing so she points to the continuing importance of *social* reference points for the construction of cultural identities. This provides a clear critique of post-modern formulations that regard culture as merely a kind of depthless, symbolic veneer that has either obscured socio-structural distinctions of class, gender and ethnicity or, in some stronger formulations, come to replace them (see Muggleton 2000: Chapter 3). But then, as all the above chapters have between them attempted to indicate, culture must be understood as embedded in social processes. Moreover, the liberal discourse of cultural hybridity and diversity as a lifestyle choice should not blind us to continuing economic, political and ideological inequalities. Nor can we ignore ongoing relationships of ethnic subordination and exploitation, for these help to sustain racialized representations of 'Otherness' upon which the hegemony of dominant groups rest.

Gender relations are also a significant field of both change and continuity within post-subcultural studies. With justified anger, female scholars have over the past fifteen years continued to challenge the male domination of both subcultural formations and related academic discourse (for example, Roman 1988; Miles 1997; Leblanc 2002). Such critiques can themselves be traced back to earlier work that emerged from writers who at some point were established within the CCCS and who sought to rectify what they saw as the masculinist bias in British subcultural theory that had led to an exclusive concentration on male styles and subcultures (for example, McRobbie 1980). An early response was to propose the notion of 'bedroom culture' as both an alternative to and explanation of girls' absence from male subcultures (McRobbie and Garber 1976). If male subcultures organize largely in the public sphere of the neighbourhood, then teenage girls are more likely to be engaged in a culture of pop 'fandom'- the buying of records, magazines and posters - that can be consumed and displayed within the private sphere of the home.

Yet this early feminist strand of the CCCS effectively confined girl's (sub)-cultural experiences to the domestic sphere of consumption, even if in later versions (for example, McRobbie 1984, 1991) these activities were more heavily overlaid with the gloss of 'resistance' and 'pleasure'. Moreover, its unintended legacy has been to 'marginalize' the position of women within subcultures insofar as subcultural theory continues to gauge 'core' resistance by members' commitment to masculine criteria – activity in the public sphere that revolves around non-commercialized cultural forms (Muggleton 2002). By contrast, both Helen Reddington and Doreen Piano, in Chapters 16 and 17 respectively of this reader, take the path of later, revisionist feminist work (for example, McRobbie 1993) in presenting women as central to subcultural practices of cultural production. Through interviews with female punk-practitioners, Reddington re-inscribes the presence of young women punk musicians into accounts of British subcultural history from which they had previously been excluded. Piano examines the influence of 'Third Wave' feminist practices on youth cultures as exemplified by the US riot grrrl subculture (see Kearney 1998). As Piano argues, 'riot grrrl helped enact a broad-based shift of women's subordinate position within punk subcultures from consumer or observer to that of producer.'[10]

Piano's chapter is also important for the way in which it examines how women in subcultures are able to empower themselves, personally and politically, through the production of various micro- and macro-media forms, including fanzines, tapes and Web sites. Also on the topic of gender and media communication, Rhiannon Bury, in Chapter 18, presents a qualitative study of the women-only online communities that arise around a private e-mailing list for fans of the popular sci-fi programme, 'The X-Files'. What is particularly interesting here is the way in which each of these chapters offers important correctives to some of the more excessive post-modern claims about the implosionary effects of 'media hyperreality'. Firstly, the organization of explicitly feminist modes of communication through DiY media networks suggests that proclamations of the 'death' of (resistant) youth culture (Redhead 1990) are, to say the least, premature. Secondly, Bury's claim that 'online communities are constituted along the faultlines of the gendered body' challenges assumptions about the liquidation of both corporeal and social identities in cyberspace.

Clearly, if the 'death of the social' has occurred, then the boundaries that establish subcultural identities have not disappeared. Instead, as Geoff Stahl argues in Chapter 2, they are 'continually shifting and being redrawn' through disputes over taste and sensibilities. This struggle to legitimate (sub)cultural capital takes place, moreover, not in some flattened-out plane of 'hyperreality', but in a stratified global economy where social groups engage in conflict over scarce economic, cultural and political resources. Thus, despite claims to the contrary, power still matters. Variables like class, gender and ethnicity continue to be an important factor influencing access to globally circulating technologies, goods, ideas, styles and fashions, while they also remain crucial in terms of the perceived legitimacy of the identities constructed from these resources, as Chapters 10 and 18 both illustrate. Indeed, as the overriding message of this reader indicates, while the modernist paradigm of the CCCS cannot explain the economic, cultural and political dynamics of contemporary subcultural movements, neither can an uncritical, unreconstituted post-modernism.

10. With the possible exception of certain dance related club/subcultures and all-female movements such as riot grrrl, this shift towards greater visibility and a more central, productive role for women does not necessarily mean that females in contemporary 'post-subcultures' are approaching a position of equality, in terms of either status or numerical participation, with that of their male counterparts (see, for example, Leblanc 2002).

References

Beezer, A. (1992), 'Dick Hebdige, *Subculture: The Meaning of Style*', in M. Barker and A. Beezer (eds), *Reading into Cultural Studies*, London: Routledge.

Bell, D., Binnie, J., Cream, J. and Valentine, G. (1994), 'All Hyped Up and No Place to Go', *Gender, Place and Culture*, 1 (1): 31–47.

Bennett, A. (1999), 'Subcultures or Neo-Tribes? Rethinking the Relationship between Youth, Style and Musical Taste', *Sociology*, 33 (3): 599–617.

Bennett, A. (2000), *Popular Music and Youth Culture: Music, Identity and Place*, Basingstoke: Macmillan.

Bourdieu, P. (1984), *Distinction: A Social Critique of the Judgement of Taste* (trans. Richard Nice), Cambridge MA: Harvard University Press.

Butler, J. (1990), *Gender Trouble: Feminism and the Subversion of Identity*, London: Routledge.

Butler, J. (1993), *Bodies that Matter: On the Discursive Limits of 'Sex'*, London: Routledge.

Chambers, I. (1987), 'Maps for the Metropolis: A Possible Guide to the Present', *Cultural Studies*, 1 (1): 1–21.

Clarke, J., Hall, S., Jefferson, T. and Roberts, B. (1976), 'Subcultures, Cultures and Class', in S. Hall and T. Jefferson (eds), *Resistance Through Rituals: Youth Subcultures in Post-War Britain*, London: Hutchinson.

Evans, C. (1997), 'Dreams that Only Money Can Buy . . . Or, the Shy Tribe in Flight from Discourse', *Fashion Theory: The Journal of Dress, Body and Culture*, 1 (2): 169–88.

Gilbert, J. and Pearson, E. (1999), *Discographies: Dance Music, Culture and the Politics of Sound*, London: Routledge.

Gore, G. (1997), 'The Beat Goes on: Trance, Dance and Tribalism in Rave Culture', in H. Thomas (ed.), *Dance in the City*, London: Macmillan Press.

Hall, S. and Jefferson, T. (eds) (1976), *Resistance Through Rituals: Youth Subcultures in Post-War Britain*, London: Hutchinson.

Healy, M. (1996), *Gay Skins: Class, Masculinity and Queer Appropriation*, London: Cassell.

Hebdige, D. (1979), *Subculture: The Meaning of Style*, London: Methuen.

Hebdige, D. (1988), *Hiding in the Light: On Images and Things*, London: Routledge.

Hodkinson, P. (2002), *Goth: Identity, Style and Subculture*, Oxford: Berg.

Humphreys, D. (1997), 'Shreadheads go Mainstream? Snowboarding and Alternative Youth', *International Review of the Sociology of Sport*, 32 (2): 147–60.

Kearney, M. C. (1998), '"Don't Need You": Rethinking Identity Politics and Seperatism from a Grrrl Perspective', in J. Epstein (ed.), *Youth Culture: Identity in a Postmodern World*, Malden MA: Blackwell.

Laclau, E. and Mouffe, C. (1985), *Hegemony and Socialist Strategy: Towards a Radical Democratic Politics*, London and New York: Verso.

Leblanc, L, (2002), *Pretty in Punk: Girls' Gender Resistance in a Boys' Subculture*, New Brunswick NJ and London: Rutgers University Press.

Lovell, T. (2000), 'Thinking Femimism with and against Bourdieu', in B. Fowler (ed.), *Reading Bourdieu on Society and Culture*, Oxford: Blackwell.

Maffesoli, M. (1996), *The Time of the Tribes: The Decline of Individualism in Mass Society*, London: Sage.

Malbon, B. (1999), *Clubbing: Dancing, Ecstasy and Vitality*, London: Routledge.

Marchart, O. and Weinzierl, R. (2002), 'New Urban Protest Formations and their Implications for Conceptions of Democratization and Participation in the European Union', unpublished working paper.

Martin, G. (2002), 'Conceptualizing Cultural Politics in Subcultural and Social Movement Studies', *Social Movement Studies*, 1 (1): 73–88.

McKay, G. (1996), *Senseless Acts of Beauty: Cultures of Resistance Since the Sixties*, London: Verso.

McRobbie, A. (1980), 'Settling Accounts with Subcultures: A Feminist Critique', *Screen Education*, 34: 37–49.

McRobbie, A. (1984), 'Dance and Social Fantasy', in A. McRobbie and M. Nava (eds), *Gender and Generation*, London: Macmillan.

McRobbie, A. (1989), 'Second-Hand Dresses and the Role of the Rag Market', in A. McRobbie (ed.), *Zoot-Suits and Second-Hand Dresses: An Anthology of Fashion and Music*, London: Macmillan.

McRobbie, A. (1991), *Feminism and Youth Culture: From Jackie to Just Seventeen*, Basingstoke: Macmillan.

McRobbie, A. (1993), 'Shut Up and Dance: Youth Culture and Changing Modes of Femininity', *Cultural Studies*, 7 (3): 406–26.

McRobbie, A. (2002), 'Clubs to Companies: Notes on the Decline of Political Culture in Speeded up Creative Worlds', *Cultural Studies*, 16 (4): 516–31.

McRobbie, A. and Garber, J. (1976), 'Girls and Subcultures: an Exploration', in S. Hall, and T. Jefferson (eds), *Resistance Through Rituals: Youth Subcultures in Post-War Britain*, London: Hutchinson.

Miles, C. (1997), 'Spatial Politics: a Gendered Sense of Place', in S. Redhead, D. Wynne and J. O'Connor (eds), *The Clubcultures Reader: Readings in Popular Cultural Studies*, Oxford: Blackwell.

Morley, D. and Robins, K. (1995), *Spaces of Identity: Global Media, Electronic Landscapes and Cultural Boundaries*, London: Routledge.

Mouffe, C. (1993), *The Return of the Political*, London and New York: Verso.

Muggleton, D. (1997), 'The Post-Subculturalist', in S. Redhead, D. Wynne and J. O'Connor (eds), *The Clubcultures Reader: Readings in Popular Cultural Studies*, Oxford: Blackwell.

Muggleton, D. (2000), *Inside Subculture. The Postmodern Meaning of Style*, Oxford: Berg.

Muggleton, D. (2002), *Some Notes Towards a Critique of Female 'Marginaliz-ation' in Youth Subcultures*, paper presented at 'Masculinities and Violence in Youth Micro-Cultures' conference, Kazan State Technological University, Kazan, Russia, 27–29 August.

Mungham, G. and Pearson, G. (eds) (1976), *Working Class Youth Culture*, London: Routledge & Kegan Paul.

Osgerby, W. J. (1992), '"One for the Money, Two for the Show": Youth, Consumption and Hegemony in Britain in 1945–70, with Special Reference to a South East Coastal Town', unpublished Ph.D. thesis, University of Sussex.

Polhemus, T. (1994), *Streetstyle*, London: Thames & Hudson.

Polhemus, T. (1996), *Style Surfing: What to Wear in the 3rd Millennium*, London: Thames & Hudson.

Redhead, S. (1990), *The End-of-the-Century-Party: Youth and Pop Towards 2000*, Manchester: Manchester University Press.

Redhead, S. (ed.) (1993), *Rave Off: Politics and Deviance in Contemporary Youth Culture*, Aldershot: Avebury.

Redhead, S. (1995), *Unpopular Cultures: The Birth of Law and Popular Culture*, Manchester: Manchester University Press.

Redhead, S. (1997), *From Subcultures to Clubcultures: An Introduction to Popular Cultural Studies*, Oxford: Blackwell.

Redhead, S., Wynne, D. and O'Connor, J. (eds) (1997), *The Clubcultures Reader: Readings in Popular Cultural Studies*, Oxford: Blackwell.

Roman, L. G. (1988), 'Intimacy, Labor and Class: Ideologies of Feminine Sexuality in the Punk Slam Dance', in L. G. Roman and L. K. Christian-Smith (eds), *Becoming Feminine: The Politics of Popular Culture*, London: Falmer Press.

Scott, A. (1995), *Ideology and the New Social Movements*, London: Routledge.

Singh. A. (2000), 'Live, Streaming Subculture', *Springerin*, 3: 17.

Thornton, S. (1994), 'Moral Panic, the Media and British Rave Culture', in A. Ross and T. Rose (eds), *Microphone Fiends: Youth Music and Youth Culture*, London: Routledge.

Thornton, S. (1995), *Club Cultures: Music, Media and Subcultural Capital*, Cambridge: Polity.

Weinzierl, R. (2000), *Fight the Power: A Secret History of Pop and the Formation of New Substreams*, Vienna: Passagen-Verlag.

Wheaton, B. (2000), '"Just do it": Consumption, Commitment and Identity in the Windsurfing Subculture', *Sociology of Sport Journal*, 17 (3): 254–74.

Willis, P. (1978), *Profane Culture*, London: Routledge & Kegan Paul.

Wilson, B. (2002), 'The Canadian Rave Scene and Five Theses on Youth Resistance', *Canadian Journal of Sociology*, 27 (3): 373–412.

Wulff, H. (1995), 'Introducing Youth Culture in its Own Right: The State of the Art and New Possibilities', in V. Amit-Talai and H. Wulff (eds), *Youth Cultures: A Cross Cultural Perspective*, London and New York: Routledge.

Part II
Post-subcultural Theory

–2–

Tastefully Renovating Subcultural Theory: Making Space for a New Model
Geoff Stahl

Subcultures represent noise (as opposed to sound): interference in the orderly sequence which leads from real events and phenomena to their representation in the media. We should therefore not underestimate the signifying power of the spectacular subculture not only as a metaphor for potential anarchy 'out there' but as an actual mechanism of semantic disorder: a kind of temporary blockage in the system of representation.

(Hebdige 1979: 90)

Subcultures as noise: a metaphor that possesses a deep, romantic and poetic resonance for many scholars. The heroic rhetoric of resistance, the valorization of the underdog and outsider, and the reemergence of a potentially political working-class consciousness are all embedded in discourses that have shaped the theorization of subcultures in the past twenty years. The work of Dick Hebdige and others connected with the Centre for Contemporary Cultural Studies (CCCS) at the University of Birmingham, through which these conceits evolved, remain a backdrop for many contemporary theories of subcultures. The sartorial splendour of teds, mods, rockers and punks became emblematic of a 'semiotic guerrilla warfare', which took objects from the dominant culture and transformed their everyday naturalized meaning into something spectacular and alien. Style became a form of resistance.

This discourse of style has outlasted many other aspects of the CCCS work, recuperated through recent attempts to situate subcultural practices within a post-modern milieu. In this context Baudrillard's implosion of meaning, the blurring of fantasy and reality through the aestheticization of everyday life and the supremacy of the image in an ocularcentric culture, have become tropes that consign sub-cultural practices to a narrow notion of spectacle. Social and cultural practices, condensed to mere processes of signification, are consequently viewed through theories inadequately predisposed to consider the complex intersection and layering of institutional, industrial, material, social, spatial and temporal dimensions and relations that facilitate and circumscribe a given social formation's operation.

The discussion that follows questions the efficacy of subcultural theory as it has been understood since the work of the CCCS rejuvenated an interest in the field. The spectacularization of subcultures offers ineffective descriptive tools and often obscures the complexity of current cultural practices that constitute, and are constituted by, the aleatory effects of a globalized cultural economy. The exploration of globalized cultural sensibilities and their coalescence into what will be denoted here as variegated and stratified taste cultures, requires a conceptual framework that is also amenable to describing reconfigurations of spatiality and their effect on social relations. Tastes, alongside dispositions, preferences and affinities, all systems of classification and organization (Bourdieu 1984), are deliberately amorphous terms denoting social activities and attitudes that influence, as much as they are influenced by, the spaces in which they reside. They suggest a rhetorical move away from rigidly vertical models that rely upon universals such as class, while enabling a nuanced examination of individual identity and group dynamics and how these are articulated (often unevenly) to large-scale, cultural arenas.

An emphasis on the specificities of local and regional cultures understood in a global setting, where spaces become sites fraught with competition, negotiation and accommodation occurring on multiple and intersecting planes, undermines any notion of a single determinant, often cast in essentialist terms (class, ethnicity, age, gender), which might exist as the overarching structuring principle of contemporary cultural practices, preferences and formations. The contexts that are most affected by globalization are the products of the circulation of ideas, texts, styles, and people around the globe, a process that has been elided in subcultural theory. The institutional and infrastructural mechanisms that enable this mobility have produced networks, circuits and alliances, all modes of communicative and community action, which traverse the globe. An analysis of their role in the creation of geographically dispersed audiences will be a central component of the following chapter.

Subcultural Theory Rethought

The work of the CCCS opened up a theoretical space that enabled a richer study of peripheral social formations and their cultural practices. Their examinations of the power differentials that structure contemporary culture created analytical tools that remain critical to any attempt to account for the myriad responses of subordinate(d) groups to structures of domination. There remain, however, a number of areas that are overtheorized, and others undertheorized, which question the continued relevance of their work. First, the discourse of style overemphasizes a symbolic response to exclusion, situating semiotic play with appropriated texts above that of the imaginative and concrete contexts in which cultural activity is enacted. The second criticism is that the creation of a subcultural Other, such as the media, the mainstream or the popular, elides the role each plays in the subculture's own internal construction (Thornton 1996; Grossberg 1994, 1997). Third, the emphasis on a linear model, such as class acting as the sole determinant in the origins of subcultural practices, marginalizes other factors such as age, gender and ethnicity, and consigns consideration of those factors to outside the purview of a model bound to a geographically specific notion of territory and 'winning space'.

The first criticism has been (somewhat awkwardly) rethought in the context of post-modernism; the latter criticisms have been highlighted by the effects of a globalized cultural economy. For the purposes of this discussion, there will be a cursory discussion of style below, while more stress will be placed on the latter criticisms as they offer more compelling responses to some of the problems subcultural theory poses. As the following chapter demonstrates, this is due, primarily, to the shifting parameters circumscribing the spaces where cultural practices are realized (the tension between local circumstances and global flows, or more specifically, between the dispersed and geographically disconnected sites of production and consumption); secondly, by the movement and mobility of ideas, objects, people and texts through that globalized cultural economy and its apparatuses (including computer-mediated communication technologies), undermining the notion of a single trajectory or determinant shaping individual identity and group affiliation.

As to the first criticism, attempts to reposition cultural studies alongside the vector of postmodernism offer little in the way of improvement. David Muggleton (1997) has extended those previous studies of subcultural practice, repositioning them in a post-modern milieu. Writing on the 'post-subculturalist' he places particular emphasis on style and the encroachment of the visual into the everyday. In the aestheticized setting of the quotidian there are no commodities left, just signs, the logical conclusion of a move away from use-value (authentic-modern) to exchange-value (manufactured-modern) and finally to the apotheosis of sign value (post-modern). Subcultural styles become simulacra, copies with no originals (Muggleton 1997: 196). Accordingly, there is no longer space for originality, as referents have been displaced or 'disappeared' and the 'real' reduced to the play of surfaces, an infinite series of signifiers signifying more signifiers. Creative practices such as fashion, art and music become depthless manifestations of post-modern pastiche, where any potentially radical politics (identity, resistance or otherwise) is thus erased. If there is no originality there is no authenticity:

Post-subculturalists no longer have any sense of subcultural authenticity where inception is rooted in particular sociotemporal contexts and tied to underlying structural relations. Indeed post-subculturalists will experience all the signs of the subculture of their choosing time and time again. Choosing is the operative word here, for post-subculturalists revel in the availability of subcultural choice . . . This is something that all post-subculturalists are aware of, that there are no rules, that there is no authenticity, no reason for ideological commitment, merely a stylistic game to be played (Muggleton 1997: 198).

Muggleton's account of current cultural practices focuses on rootlessness and play, where any hope for the ruptures that characterized the CCCS model of subcultural practice is seen as impossible. Cut adrift in a free-floating, inauthentic and valueless ether, post-subculturalists are interpreted as mindlessly genuflecting in awe at the post-modern, millennial sublime, where 'the trappings of spect-acular style are their right of admission to a costume party, a masquerade, a hedonistic escape into a Blitz Culture fantasy characterized by political indif-ference' (Muggleton 1997: 200). This formulation of post-modernism, framed by a cultural pessimism suggesting quietism, apathy, moral relativism, and the ability to occupy a multiplicity of subjectivities, obscures the effect that difference (structural and otherwise) and differential access to power have on producing meaningful contexts (and contexts of meaning) for cultural activity. The gravitation of individuals and groups to sites of emotional investment, whether they be imaginary or real, is evacuated of all meaning.

Almost as a pre-emptive corrective to this, Grossberg (1984, 1994) has more convincingly characterized the post-modern as a disarticulation of affect and ideology, where maps of meaning and mattering maps become disengaged and re-engaged in new places. Affect is a structured plane of effects (investment), which offers the possibility of agency (of acting willfully) and describes 'observable differences in how practices matter to, or are taken up by, different configurations of popular discourses and practices – different alliances (which are not simply audiences)' (Grossberg 1984: 228). Although affect waxes and wanes within everyday contexts, authenticity has not disappeared; it remains crucial to processes of differentiation, but has been modified in ironic fashion:

> Confronting the post-modern vector of everyday life produces an increasing tendency to stop in places (for example, taking on particular cultural identities or taking up forms of agency), while self-consciously questioning, limiting or perhaps even challenging the investment in them: authentic inauthenticity (indifference) is a popular logic that refuses to distinguish between the authentic and inauthentic, between boredom and terror – and a set of practices that celebrates the affectivity of investment while refusing to discrim-inate between different forms and sites of investment – as the only viable response to contemporary conditions (Grossberg 1984: 233).

Thus, contrary to Muggleton's proposed model, rules still exist within the spaces of everyday life, albeit in very provisional and ad hoc forms. The unequal exercise of power (and its uneven distribution) in any given context negates the claims that post-modern theory makes about a cultural levelling where boundaries disappear. Boundaries are continually shifting and being redrawn; the contexts of cultural activity are habitually reconstituted by the power relations and lines of continuity (traditions, mythologies, and the circulation of commodities) which cut through them.

Subcultures Tastefully Redone

Cultural production produces spaces that are dynamic sites of activity and include the continual reassertion and maintenance of boundaries enacted through processes of differentiation and distinction made by groups and individuals, all of which needs stronger consideration. Grossberg (1984, 1997) and Sarah Thornton (1996) have each challenged the CCCS's assessment of cultural practices unfolding in discrete, self-contained spaces, the former by problematizing the notion of the mainstream (in relation to the post-modern) and the latter by inserting the media into the very origins of subcultures. For Grossberg the mainstream, or more correctly the popular, exists as a social pastiche where fragments from the margins are incorporated and fragments of itself are excorporated back into the margins: 'a structured distribution of practices, codes and effects' (Grossberg 1997: 220). The intersection and overlap of margin and mainstream creates a space where practices of social and cultural differentiation unfold whereby the mainstream can no longer be seen as unified or monolithically 'Other'.

The researchers at the CCCS construed the media as a *post facto* response to subcultures, allowing them to see more 'uncontaminated homologies'. They saw the media as instrumental to the success of the dominant hegemony, an integral part of the apparatus (the control culture) which constructed punks as 'Other'. Subcultures were consequently theorized as 'transparent niches in an opaque world as if subcultural life spoke an unmediated truth' (Thornton 1996: 119). In contrast, Thornton suggests that the media (television, radio, magazines, zines, pamphlets, virtual media such as the Internet) are integral to the formation of subcultures, playing a significant role in both their origin as well as prolonging their lifecycle. The media exist as systems of communication critical to the circulation of ideas, images, sounds and ideologies that bind culture(s) together. Thornton reminds us that some media legitimate while others popularize, some preserve the esoteric while others are seen to sell out: 'As subjects of discussion and sources of infor-mation, media are deliberate and accidental determinants of cultural hierarchy' (Thornton 1996: 164). The media function in that latter instance as a central network for the movement and distribution through cultural and social hierarchies of what Thornton, borrowing from Bourdieu (1984) has called 'subcultural capital'. Various types of capital (cultural, economic, social, symbolic) are acquired and distributed according to a logic specific to the field in which they reside. Economic capital is distributed through the field of economics, educational capital through an educational field, and so forth. Fields (of cultural production, of economics, of education) are hierarchies structuring the social spaces where struggles over capital and various resources are played out. The overarching field, of which these narrower fields are subsets, is the field of power (Bourdieu, 1993). Cultural capital, a form of knowledge acquired through education and upbringing, is dispersed throughout the field of cultural production, where individuals and groups struggle to acquire and reinvest it to maintain social status.

Bourdieu's taxonomy of capital effectively describes the hierarchies of value and social status that underlie the (conscious and unconscious, subjective and objective) construction of individual preferences, tastes, and how they might then be articulated to, and by, social formations. As he puts it, 'taste, the propensity and capacity to appropriate (materially or symbolically) a given class of classified, classifying objects or practices, is the generative formula of life-style, a unitary set of distinctive preferences which express the same expressive intention in the specific logic of each of the symbolic subspaces, furniture, clothing, language or body hexis' (Bourdieu 1984: 173). The field of production, for example, could not exist if it were not for always already pre-existing tastes. It offers a universe of cultural goods, a range of stylistic possibilities from which individuals select the system of stylistic features constituting a lifestyle (Bourdieu 1984: 230). In contrast, by not considering the origins of style as a preference or predisposition, the CCCS never fully explained how style might become a 'uniform', a lifestyle replete with 'attitude'. For both Bourdieu and Thornton cultural capital can be embodied/objectified (style/lifestyle), the end result being the naturalization of preferences into what might be called second nature, the ability to make the 'right' choices. This is evidence of what Bourdieu calls the habitus: 'both the generative principle of objectively classifiable judgements and the system of classification of these practices. It is the relationship between the two capacities which define the habitus, the capacity to differentiate and appreciate these practices and products (taste), that the represented social world, i.e. the space of life-styles, is constituted' (Bourdieu 1984: 170).

Bourdieu (1993) states that the field of production is composed of two differing fields: the field of restricted production and the field of large-scale production. The former is germane to this discussion because it describes the 'negative existence' of this field in relation to the latter. Externally, the subfield of restricted production is opposed to the dominant economic order ('the mainstream'). Internally, the subfield of restricted production is structured by the opposition between what Bourdieu calls the 'consecrated avant-garde' and the 'avant-garde': an opposition between those who have the power to consecrate and those who are trying to acquire that power (newcomers). The activity within the field of restricted cultural production is more characteristically defined as production for producers. In this context, where market forces are integral to the formation of the field, notions of autonomy become paramount. Authenticity and selling out are terms that are frequently deployed to define and justify who or what might be in or out.

Bourdieu's notion of fields as 'spaces of possibles' emphasizes the contested and conflicted activities of individuals vying for positions and resources in several fields and given sites. In these differing contexts, his notion of accruing and investing various types of capital is most amenable to describing systems of exchange and distribution that are not reducible to a simple economism. The field of cultural production exists as a field of 'possible forces' that organizes and is organized by the agents operating within it:

> (and is) defined in the relationship between the structure of average chances of access to different positions (measured by the difficulty of attaining them and, more precisely, by the relationship between the number of positions and the number of competitors) and the dispositions of each agent, the subjective basis of the perception and appreciation of the objective chances (Bourdieu 1993: 64).

Dispositions and positions combine to form a sense of social direction that orients individuals within a given field. This 'direction' cannot be understood solely as linear. The work of CCCS, which often correlated a vertical model of class rather mechanically to culture to explain the cultural forms produced, fails to consider the effects of power differentials that function to quantitatively and qualitatively determine access to a given field (Bourdieu, 1993: 65). Bourdieu's model of fields, taste and habitus moves beyond a rigidly vertical description of cultural practices by theoretically enumerating the activities occurring within and between fields that are interrelated in more complex, mobile, non-linear and multi-dimensional ways than previously theorized.

Everything Flows

In order to maintain its currency (or cultural worth) cultural capital must flow through channels of communication, which themselves operate with, and are subject to, varying degrees of restriction. In globalized fields of cultural production and consumption these channels form part of a global infrastructure composed of networks of exclusion and inclusion, in which both state/institutional power is exerted (through cultural policy, protectionism, and so forth) and individuals who have strategically reinvested their capital, subcultural or otherwise, consolidate positions of power. These agents, or agencies, act as gatekeepers, cultural custodians and intermediaries who can oversee, evaluate, sanction, or consecrate (Bourdieu 1984), and thereby legitimize, certain cultural forms and practices. In this capacity, they operationalize discourses, such as those attached to notions of authenticity, constructing an (ideological) opposition between mainstream and margin that remains integral to the distinctions that differentiate individuals and their social groups from others (often in the same field).

Grossberg (1984) employs Bourdieu's notion of sensibility to describe the intersection of these discursive practices and human actors. Sensibilities 'empower cultural practices to work in certain ways, and they empower individuals to enact them in certain places. Sensibilities define the dialectical production of active audiences, everyday practices and productive contexts' (Grossberg 1984: 227). These productive contexts are interrelated with other contexts, not only by discursive practices since 'contexts are produced in the complex imbrication of discursive and nondiscursive practices, and so the sense in which contexts imply other contexts, so that each context implies a global network of contexts' (Appadurai 1996: 187).

If Grossberg overemphasizes the localized context, Appadurai more appropriately links interrelated and interdependent contexts to global processes. Appadurai speaks of mobility and mediation of both objects and ideas as having profound effects on the shape of contexts of production and consumption. New modes of communication and new means for distributing information assist the circulation of the various forms of capital, while simultaneously reconfiguring the contexts in which cultural production and consumption take place. Forms of knowledge such as cultural capital can also be subject to global forces, distributed according to the organizing principles of a given spatial configuration (Thrift, 1985). Because the political, social, economic and cultural transformations occurring on a global scale are necessarily fluid, chaotic, arbitrary and uneven, resulting from the institution of mobile and mobilizing forces, they run contrary to the assumptions of the CCCS paradigm where social movement is restricted to vertical ascent or descent. The movement and distribution of people, ideas, money and technologies through this global cultural economy takes hold in both the imaginations of individuals as well in concrete contexts. At the same time, the flow of commodities through these networks is subject, much like capital, to local restrictions that create differential access. Access to commodities determines the forms of experience that are possible in a given space, where it is important to note that 'spatial patterns cannot be said to interact, only the social objects present within one or more such spaces interact' (Urry 1995: 65). To avoid fetishizing the spatial, it remains critical to distinguish a given space from the flow of goods and objects through that space.

The entropy characterizing the distribution of goods, services, ideas, images, capital and people is contingent upon the structure of the spaces through which they flow. The sites where they come to rest can become places of conflict over access and distribution of these resources, a struggle organized according to indigenous social hierarchies. The intersection of social spaces and social relations shifts emphasis to the greater global contexts and the smaller local circumstances in which social and cultural activities unfold. Urry (1995: 66) suggests that 'there is no simple space, only different kinds of spaces, spatial relations or spatial-isations', where space is not neutral. Urry recalls Lefebvre's theoretical structure for the analysis of the production of space, which is composed of three elements: spatial practices, representations of space and spaces of representation (Urry 1995: 25). Spatial practices include individual daily routine as well as the concretization of zones and regions, through urban planning, etc. Representations of space include the forms of knowledge and practices that organize and represent space in particular forms. Spaces of representation include the imaginative construction of collectively experienced sites: 'These include symbolic differentiations and collective fantasies around space, the resistances to the dominant practices and resulting forms of individual and collective transgression' (Urry 1995: 25). It is this third element that has the most rhetorical force. Appadurai (1996) has suggested that within the processes of globalization there has been a notable return to the imagination persisting as a repository of nostalgia, engendering and preserving collective experiences constituted through mythology, and guaranteeing the promise of individual agency. The imagination 'has become an organized field of social practices, a form of work (in the sense of both labour and culturally organized practice), and a form of negotiation between sites of agency (individuals) and globally defined fields of possibility' (Appadurai 1996: 187).

All three of Lefebvre's spatial components accentuate the multiple layers that compose social spaces, themselves shaped by multiple vectors (economic, political), which can be enacted and engaged on a micro-level of individual imaginings and articulated to the macro-level of larger scale regional or global forces. Each vector simultaneously extends and limits the horizon of the imagination, the flow of ideas, capital and commodities. Neighbourhoods need reconsideration in the context of global scale forces:

> The capability of neighbourhoods to produce contexts (within which their very localizing activities acquire meaning and historical potential) and to produce local subjects is profoundly affected by the locality-producing capabilities of larger-scale formations (nation-states, kingdoms, missionary empires, and trading cartels) to determine the general shape of all the neighbourhoods within the reach of their powers (Appadurai 1996: 187).

'The neighbourhood' remains a powerful metaphor for the organization and lived spaces of contemporary cultures, illustrating connections between geographical area, physical structures and social organization. Neighbourhoods exist as productive contexts for subjectivities, where meaningful activity is initiated, enacted, performed and reproduced. This productive activity, however, often extends beyond the narrow confines of the neighbourhood and its kinship systems, making connections and finding affinities with neighbouring as well as distant contexts. A notion of neighbourhood that depends upon a territorial imaginary needs to reconsider, for example, the emergence of virtual neighbourhoods, electronically produced and connected spaces. New media such as the Internet build unique social links, creating conduits for the transmission of ideas, money and information, which in many ways also transform the lived spaces of neighbourhoods in which the participants live.

Virtually New Social Formations

The emergence of computer-mediated communications (CMC) systems and their effect on the intersection of social and spatial relations as well as notions of community is worthy of some consideration here. Every new development in technology has promised new forms of community and connectivity, forming spaces that will allow the free flowering of proper democratic exchanges and pluralistic togetherness, recapturing some form of gathering and interactivity that has since been lost. Surrounded by the rhetoric of prophecy, 'assumptions about technological change tell us what we believe the technology is supposed to do, which in turn reveals much about what we believe *we* are supposed to do' (Jones 1995: 27). The ascent of CMCs has also emphasized the distinctions drawn between what James Carey has called the view of communication either as 'transportation' or as 'ritual' (Carey 1992). Viewing communication as transportation tends towards explaining the domination of time and space through the transmission of signals (in the form of information, for example). It is a view tied to notions of control and power, a mastery of time and space through new, efficient and accelerated forms of dissemination. On a broader scale, it is a view still framed by discourses of frontierism, colonialism, mercantilism, expansionism: the desire for leaving behind older communities and creating new ones (Carey 1992: 16).

The ritual view of communication, in contrast, is still very much an overlooked way of conceptualizing social interaction and movement. It is, as Carey states, 'directed not toward the extension of messages in space but toward the maintenance of society in time; not the act of imparting information but the representation of shared beliefs' (Carey 1992: 18). Both Carey (1992) and Steve Jones (1995) – the latter employing these terms in discussing cyberspace and its relation to community – advocate this view of communication. In its evocation of a prelapsarian cultural moment it retains a connection between community, commoness, and communion that positions it as the desirable and proper directive behind communicative action (Carey 1992: 18). That desired action itself assumes a dramaturgical function as information becomes part of a socially sanctioned staging, the portrayal of 'an arena of dramatic forces and action' allowing sites for physical and imaginative enactments and performances (Carey 1992: 21). In its ritual mode communication becomes a powerful tool that organizes individual desires and dreams of belonging by representing a certain range of experiences, thereby offering the possibility for deep, affective investment.

However much the pursuit of this ritualistic notion of communication may appear as ideal, it is a particularly problematic and highly contested one. As Jones (1995) suggests, most discussion surrounding the emergence of new communities founded through computer-mediated interactions fails to consider the 'concomitant conceptualization of space and the social, the inquiry into connections between social relations, spatial practice, values, and beliefs' (Jones 1995: 23). In this sense, and without a greater examination of issues surrounding access, the recent analyses of virtuality and digitally connected individuals and groups shares common absences and elisions with certain aspects of subcultural analyses.

Both old and new communications technologies assist in connecting individuals, organizing them in various contexts as audiences and consumers. Given both the ritualistic and transportation view of communications and their effect on relations of time and space, any attempt to supply a cartography of consumption requires a provisional model of taste cultures which should no longer be understood as localized in any site-specific sense. Analyses of the flow of capital, information and people connected and mediated through communicative apparatuses that span the globe offer suggestive entry points into an account of the similarities that exist between dispersed consumers and their respective shared cultures. No longer hermetically sealed or self-contained, the spaces of culture should rather be understood as organized through a series of interconnections. Doreen Massey (1998) has suggested that cultures, specifically youth cultures, could be understood as a 'particular articulation of contacts and influences drawn from a variety of places scattered, according to power relations, fashion and habit, across many different parts of the globe' (Massey 1998: 124). Social relations are often constellations of temporary and *ad hoc* coherence embedded in a social space that is the product of relations and interconnections from the very local to the regional and transregional (Massey 1998: 125). The local structures (social and spatial) that determine the duration of these constellations as well as inflecting the reception and transmission of goods, images and people from distant contexts are interconnected through a series of networks. These networks (which are understood in this context in the 'transportation' mode of communication activity) function in the same capacity as networks of exclusion and inclusion, serving as channels for the transmission of people, ideas, objects and images that link one context and taste culture to another.

However, in their levels of sociality, participation and symbolic interaction these networks can be thought of in terms of ritual modes of communication, forging affective alliances or networks of empowerment (Grossberg 1984). They serve as links between dispersed individuals and groups that are neither geographically specific nor dependent upon face-to-face contact, existing instead as 'imagined communities'. Benedict Anderson (1992: 6) suggests three ways in which a community is imagined. First, though many of the members will never meet,

face-to-face with others, 'in the minds of each lives the image of their communion'. Second, this community is limited, because it has 'finite, if elastic
boundaries, beyond which lie other (communities)' (Anderson 1992: 7). Finally, it
is imagined because 'regardless of the inequality . . . that may prevail in each, the
(community) is always conceived as a deep, horizontal comradeship' (Anderson
1992: 7). Mass mediation, particularly electronic media and CMCs, enable these
imagined communities to transcend some of the limits of local, regional or national
space, activating what Appadurai (1996) has called a 'community of sentiment'.
Here, '(sentiment's) greatest force is in their ability to ignite intimacy into political
state and turn locality into a staging ground for identity, have become spread over
vast and irregular spaces as groups move yet stay linked to one another through
sophisticated media capabilities' (Appadurai 1996: 41). These mediations work
most heavily on the level of the imagination in which local subjectivity exists
as a 'palimpsest of highly local and highly translocal considerations', where
the imagination of individual agents is articulated to a larger social imaginary
(Appadurai 1996: 198).

Whether it be in contexts, neighbourhoods or communities (concrete or imagined, material or virtual), increasingly the quotidian rhythms of life are refracted
through the localized effects of these translocal forces. On the level of the everyday,
greater consideration must be given to how individuals operate within demarcated
spaces situated in a global cultural economy. Grossberg's (1984, 1997) work is
useful for mapping out the lines that distribute, place and connect cultural practices.
The everyday here is meant to convey a sense of a structured mobility, constructing
a space that includes 'specific forms and trajectories of movement (change) and
stability (agency)' (Grossberg 1997: 229). Although the field and habitus (which
share an affinity to 'structured mobility') are spaces shaped by these trajectories,
recast in a global framework, Bourdieu's terms cannot remain uncontaminated by
the changing shape of social spaces in this context. As Appadurai suggests, the
habitus, no longer simply a realm of reproducible practices and dispositons, has
instead become 'more an arena for conscious choice, justification, and representation' (Appadurai 1996: 44). As a schema for the appreciation and perception
of cultural goods, the habitus must be broad enough to incorporate the larger scale
social universe in which tastes and fields are subject and object of the glacial drift
of global forces.

Conclusion

I have outlined here a number of limitations of subcultural theory, particularly its
longstanding British variant. I have also offered a number of terms that fall outside
of the rhetoric of rupture, which otherwise highlight the tensions between the

continuities and discontinuites, the formal and informal structures, that link spatialized cultural practices, production and consumption. I have also made reference to post-modern theories that focus solely on a flattened cultural terrain permeated by undifferentiated signs, without consideration of either material practices or the concrete and imaginative organization of a given space. Both theoretical paradigms neglect the contextual variability that determines how, where and why social and spatial relations intersect in the places they do. No longer understood as being restricted to physically bounded sites, existing cultural and social formations exemplify the insinuation of cultural activity into global flows. The dispersal of consumer products, ideas and cultural idioms has to be framed in terms which can convey the local specificities of a given site as well as the globally defined determinations that inflect their seemingly asymmetrical appropriation and incorporation.

This framework would allow consideration of the vicissitudes of a global cultural economy and how they impinge on imaginative activity and material practice, and what shape they give to structures of feeling that adhere in both physical and imagined locales. It must move away from rigid, vertical and static models and enable a model that considers the articulation of individual to proximal group, illustrate how that latter group is articulated to distant groups, and finally show how the social agglomerations of different shapes and sizes enter into dialogue with their disparate counterparts. In many ways it must move beyond a valorization of the local as site of authentic relations and heterogeneous cultural production and the demonization of the global as abstract homogenizing juggernaut. In accounting for the dispersed and diffuse nature of contexts of production and consumption it would facilitate an examination of the distributive and connective functions of networks, alliances, circuits and conduits through which people, commodities, the myriad forms of capital, ideas and technology flow.

Providing an examination of the mechanics of solidarity illuminates the diverse forces circumscribing each one of these links, illustrating how these processes of exclusion and inclusion function to arrange social and cultural practices in complex, interrelated, arbitrary and opaque configurations. Cultural practices, whether dominant or subordinate, do not unfold in hermetically sealed or geographically discrete contexts. The parameters that define cultural practices, industries and institutions have been blurred, stretched, exploded, erased and redrawn through the complex and arbitrary effects wrought by the machinations of a globalized cultural apparatus. It is among the shifting origins and destinations of cultural production, distribution and consumption, that an analytic model more flexible than that offered by subcultural theory must be found to describe the elasticity and fluidity that confounds any notion of self-contained cultural practices.

References

Anderson, B. (1992), *Imagined Communities*, New York: Verso.

Appadurai, A. (1996), *Modernity At Large: Cultural Dimensions of Globalization*, Minneapolis MN: University of Minnesota Press.

Bourdieu, P. (1984), *Distinction: A Social Critique of the Judgement of Taste* (trans. R. Nice), Cambridge MA: Harvard University Press.

Bourdieu, P. (1993), *The Field of Cultural Production*, New York: Columbia University Press.

Carey, J. (1992), *Communication as Culture*, New York: Routledge.

Grossberg, L. (1984), 'Another Boring Day in Paradise: Rock and Roll and the Empowerment of Everyday Life', *Popular Music*, 4: 225–58.

Grossberg, L. (1994), 'Is Anybody Listening? Does Anybody Care?: On "The State of Rock"', in A. Ross and T. Rose (eds), *Microphone Fiends: Youth Music and Youth Culture*, New York: Routledge.

Grossberg, L. (1997), 'Re-placing Popular Culture', in S. Redhead, D. Wynne and J. O'Connor (eds), *The Clubcultures Reader: Readings in Popular Cultural Studies*, Malden MA: Blackwell.

Hebdige, D. (1979), *Subculture: The Meaning of Style*, New York: Routledge.

Jones, S. G. (1995), 'Understanding Community in the Information Age' in S. G. Jones (ed.), *Cybersociety: Computer-mediated Communication and Community*, Thousand Oaks CA: Sage.

Massey, D. (1998), 'The Spatial Construction of Youth Cultures' in T. Skelton and G. Valentine (eds), *Cool Places: Geographies of Youth Cultures*, New York: Routledge.

Muggleton, D. (1997), 'The Post-Subculturalist', in S. Redhead, D. Wynne and J. O'Connor (eds), *The Clubcultures Reader: Readings in Popular Cultural Studies*, Malden MA: Blackwell.

Thornton, S. (1996), *Club Cultures: Music, Media and Subcultural Capital*, Hanover NH: Wesleyan University Press.

Thrift, N. (1985), 'Flies and Germs: A Geography of Knowledge', in D. Gregory and J. Urry (eds), *Social Relations and Spatial Structures*, London: Macmillan.

Urry, J. (1995), *Consuming Places*, New York: Routledge.

3

Image, Body and Performativity: The Constitution of Subcultural Practice in the Globalized World of Pop

Gabriele Klein

The Field of Pop

> Pop is physical, sensual, of the body rather than the mind, and in some ways it is antiintellectual; let yourself go, don't think – feel.
>
> (Kureishi 1995: xix)

Pop culture is a cultural field that confronts hundreds of millions of people world-wide in their everyday lives. The sheer omnipresence of pop alone delivers enough reason for sociological attention. But this is not the only reason for sociological curiosity; pop is a cultural practice that has unfolded in an area of interactive tension between globalization and localization. This makes pop culture different from all other cultural fields, and is why pop culture is a well-suited field of examination for dealing with cultural globalization.[1] I use the term 'pop culture' to describe this area of tension between the globalized production of images and the local adaptation of these images. This area of tension is neglected by using terms like 'youth culture', 'youth subculture' or 'youth music culture', which are most commonly used in subcultural research and that deal with either production or reception. Pop culture, as I understand it, is not restricted to 'youth' but has become a phenomenon that overlaps generations; it can therefore be characterized as a cultural practice that seems to dissolve the borders between youth and youth-fulness.[2] Beyond that, pop culture is a very special cultural practice because it has always been based on an indissoluble interlocking of art and commerciality, a connection that has become a special issue for the art market since the 1980s. And finally, pop culture unfolds a social field that is not only dominated by men but is defined by a male pop discourse.

1. See, among others, Beck (1999), Featherstone (1990).
2. Think, on the one hand, of ageing popstars, like the Rolling Stones or Eric Clapton, and their fans – and on the other, Japanese pop culture for children, for example, Tamagotchis and Pokémons.

Today pop exists as an industry, as a culture and as a way of thinking (see Savage 1995: xxivf). In these threefold forms of appearance pop aims at contradictory goals. The pop industry is the most professional and most commercialized of all culture industries. Together with the film, radio and TV industries it forms the entertainment industry, and as part of this entertainment industry it is still a component of a permanent process of production, commercialization and exploitation. With the globalization of consumer markets and the digitalization of information streams, pop has become an important engine of the Western consumption machinery. Like Hollywood in the 1940s, it helps to spread to new markets like Eastern Europe, China or Russia the illusion of a world of glamour and the values of a society oriented towards individual consumption. In the Western world the pop industry has long since become an integrated part of everyday life and dominates it in the form of advertisements or radio-compatible pop music.

Pop as culture has its roots in the underground, in subcultural movements of Black youth, White gays or artistic avant-gardes. These are the roots of pop music; but pop as culture is far more than just music, even if these two terms are often used synonymously in recent pop discourse. In different historical periods pop as culture was always connected with alternative ways of experiencing the world. Because it has always had fluid boundaries, pop never became a static ideology. 'Pop is always transformation, dynamic movement. Cultural material and its social environments permanently re-shape each other in new forms while crossing fixed borders' (Diederichsen 1996: 38f). The central characteristic of pop, therefore, is the element of crossover, the permanent crossing of borders between low and high culture, the permanent change of place between the cultural fields. This continuous movement ensures that pop constantly changes its faces and meanings. Pop can be a subcultural movement but also part of a mass culture, artistic avant-garde or insignificant leisure-time activity.

Pop, as a way of living, makes its difference to popular culture especially explicit: pop as a way of living means a way of thinking and feeling, of living and also of dying – it is for this reason that the mystification of an early death is an important element of pop culture, from James Dean to Jim Morrison, Jimi Hendrix, Janis Joplin and Kurt Cobain. Pop is not only a (sometimes dangerous) way of living but also an instrument needed by the culture industry. 'Pop means always both: promise and betrayal' (Poschardt 1996: 101). Poschardt's statement indicates an important element of the pop discourse: pop has always been a medium of ideological conflict for the left. Even if pop culture is mainly an aesthetic phenomenon it has been politicized since at least the punk era.[3]

---

3. These strategies of politicization of the self and the other also happen with fun-oriented youth cultures like techno (see Klein 1999).

According to Bourdieu (1998) pop culture can be described as a cultural 'space' composed of a number of fields (different parts of pop culture). The unique element of the cultural space 'pop' that makes it different from all other cultural spaces is that it disposes of specific forms of capital. Scene-internal knowledge is, for example, as much a central and constitutive form of capital for pop culture as social capital (for example, whom you know through social networks). It is this specific capital of pop-cultural knowledge that is decisive for one's social standing within pop culture, rather than cultural capital as education, as in the field of art or legitimate culture (Thornton 1996).

The Global Circulation and Local Adaptation of Pop

The relationship between the production, distribution and adaptation of cultural objects and symbols plays a central role in each analysis of pop culture. How, for example, can it be explained that pop has different effects on everyday culture in Hong Kong than in Barcelona or New York? It took thirty years of theoretical discussion to rethink the relationship between cultural production and consumption. While the Frankfurt School's theories of the culture industry were developed in the 1940s (Horkheimer and Adorno 1947; Adorno 1981), it was more than thirty years later when Stuart Hall presented his 'encoding/decoding' model (Hall 1980). From a media theory perspective Hall developed the hypothesis that cultural products do not have to circulate as in a one-dimensional sender-receiver-model. Cultural production does not, therefore, presuppose determinate, fixed or clear-cut messages. Instead, the process of adaptation reflects the varied everyday life contexts of the people; each instance of adaptation therefore differs in potential from all others. This is also the reason why cultural globalization does not necessarily result in homogenization and standardization, or in a 'McDonaldization' of culture. On the contrary, globalized culture produces difference (Lash and Urry 1994; Robertson 1998) because of the different everyday life contexts of the consumers. Therefore the interaction of globalization and localization has to be considered when describing the circulation of pop cultural products. It is an expression of the relationship between homogenization and difference (Robertson 1998).

The process of adaptation of globalized pop cultural symbols is in itself again ambiguous. By adopting global elements, local practice can reproduce traditional, industrial and medially circulating pictures; but it can also become different and resistant to the global because of all the local contexts of adaptation. Within the process of the circulation of production and adaptation, pop images can be received in two fundamental ways: while media-effective pictures of mainstream pop can under certain circumstances subvert the everyday life of consumers, oppositional models of pop (such as punk) do not necessarily have subversive power. The question of whether globalized pop images can be relevant for consumers and influence their ways of living cannot be answered with analyses that look only at the aesthetics of production. The thesis of cultural studies, that adaptation only makes sense when the products and symbols are relevant for everyday life, is also insufficient because it neglects the questions relevant for the theoretization of the body: firstly, *how* pop cultural images are negotiated; secondly, if this negotiation process reproduces a globalized and industrially produced codex of norms or whether (and how) this codex can be transgressed.

The Performativity of Pop

The field of pop is itself structured by a relational structure of the connections between the different players: DJs, musicians, producers of music and video, publishers, music critics and promoters. They engage in what Bourdieu calls 'the game of art as art' (Bourdieu 1998: 354), a game of power over what legitimates pop as pop and what is of worth within the symbolic economies of the pop cultural field. These who play the most important roles in this game are the 'legitimate speakers' (Bourdieu 1990). They are legitimated by their social positioning in the pop cultural field and confirm this legitimation with the negotiation of 'aesthetic dispositions' – ways of reflecting upon pop and its modes of reception, all of which are generated within the logics of this game.

These considerations of Bourdieu make clear that the habitus-field theory can hardly encompass a transgression of a conventionalized codex of norms. The theoretical reason for this is that Bourdieu explains the generation of the cultural habitus by a process of conventionalization. According to him the habitus constitutes itself with the adaptation of the rules of the field, which are learned, embodied and updated by the acting people. With the process of habitualization, pop's codex of norms is transformed into aesthetic preferences that create difference in the form of categories of taste. Aesthetic judgements like, for example, the stated aesthetic inferiority of mainstream pop are permanently reconfirmed and consequently believed in. Thus, the pop cultural habitus creates a framework for the reproduction of the beliefs in the male world of pop. The illusion of the pop cultural taste is therefore being constantly reproduced in the habitus, and the dispositions for the field of pop are thereby developed. The habitus is generated via a codex of norms, and creates a body for this codex in which the rules of the pop cultural game are stored. The body is the place where practical knowledge is produced and practical sense is evoked. Bourdieu describes it as a storage place of a lived history. The body acts according to the rules given by the pop cultural field. But what enables the body to act? Another way of posing this question is: how is the update of the codex of norms effected in the practice of pop?

Embodiment: The Performative Becomes Effective

Bourdieu understands the actualization of norms as a process of convention-alization – a confirmation of structures. He explains it by the term *sens pratique* – a practical sense that he understands as a principle that generates reality with performative magic (see Audehm 2001) and shows itself in bodily action. The post-structuralist theory of Judith Butler (1993, 1997) on the other hand asks for both the success and failure of the actualization of a given codex of norms and uses a conception of performativity that is derived from linguistic theory.

Butler's conception of performativity means, on the one hand, the reality-generating power of (and through) bodily actions; on the other, she brings up the subject of the action-character of linguistic expression. In her book *Excitable Speech*, she examines the subject-constituting power of linguistic expression and discusses the possibilities and conditions of a subversive way of speaking (Butler 1997). She understands performativity not as a single or intentional act but as a permanently recurring and self-citing practice with which the discourse produces the effects that it designates (Butler 1997). It is the permanently recurring power of the discourse that creates what we call, for example, man or woman, Black or White. As she puts it, 'the doctor who receives the child and pronounces – "It's a girl" – begins that long string of interpellations by which the girl is transitively girled: gender is ritualistically repeated, whereby the repetition occasions both the risk of failure and the congealed effect of sedimentation' (Butler 1997: 49).

Butler shares the thesis of a reality-constituting power through the embodiment of a codex of norms with Bourdieu´s theory of embodiment of the habitus. Bourdieu describes the body as the storage place of a history. At the same time he under-stands it as an instrument and a scene of action where practical knowledge is produced and the belief in 'reality' is permanently reproduced. According to Butler the habitus theory of Bourdieu describes a silent form of performativity that is believed in and lived at the level of the body (Butler 1997: 219). Butler sees the possibility of 'another' way of speaking (since speaking as a physical act cannot be controlled completely), but Bourdieu´s habitus-field theory indicates the difficulty of breaking a codex of norms in social practice precisely because the habitus inscribes itself in the body in such a subtle way that the body reproduces the codex of norms.

Both authors do, though, term the cultural constitution of certain phenomena 'performative' to emphasize that they are not determined ontologically or biolog-ically but produced by cultural processes. This theory of constitution mainly refers to phenomena that are traditionally seen as 'natural' – for example, gender and sexual identities. Both Butler and Bourdieu orientate themselves to a way of think-ing that does not search for essentialist or biological explanations but emphasizes the meaning of social practices. Thus, the approaches of both Butler and Bourdieu are non-essentialist but do not deny the existence of phenomena. Both authors acknowledge social, sexual, gender and physical differences, yet interpret them not as ontological essence, biological characteristic or phenomenologically given but as schemata developed in social practices. The use of a model of performativity is helpful to bring out the double aspect of non-essentiality and existence via cultural foundation.

Whereas Butler calls cultural acts performative because they constitute identity with (not before) the act of negotiation, Bourdieu calls the so-called 'rites of installation' performative because they legitimize and naturalize social distinction. 'Rites of installation' inscribe qualities that are social inventions, and in such a way that they appear to be 'natural'. Whereas Butler's conception of performativity describes citation as actualization of a structure of norms and therefore also explains the local negotiation of global images, it cannot explain what enables the actor to cite. Butler's theory does not imply a conceptualization of 'memory', or that of a 'body-memory' that functions as a storage place of history, as a place of memory or a resort of knowledge. For this question Bourdieu's theory of habitualization delivers some ideas that need further consideration.

Habitualization as Mimetic Identification

With Butler's conception of performativity, citation can be understood as the actualization of a structure of norms and as a process of local negotiation of global images. It also delivers an explanation about how speakers in illegitimate social positions within the field obtain a 'voice' – how they become legitimated. Where does the performative knowledge come from that is so important for the process of adaptation and for the success of the performative action? Bourdieu´s theory of habitualization helps to answer this question. Bourdieu understands habitualizations as processes of socialization and he emphasizes that these bodily inscriptions are effected via mimesis. According to Bourdieu mimesis is the process with which the rules immanent to the context are embodied. My hypothesis is that this consideration only makes sense within the framework of a theory of performativity if mimesis is not understood as 'blind' imitation but as a process of construction – a process not only of imitation but also of a new creation.

The consideration that mimesis should be understood as a process of re-construction can be traced back to Viktor Zuckerkandl (1958) who, with reference to Aristoteles, assigned a double importance to mimesis. According to Zuckerkandl the dimensions of importance of mimesis are not only imitations or replicas but also representations of a new picture, 'a new process of generating in a new medium' (Zuckerkandl 1958: 226). With this he indicates the character of construction within the mimetic process.

Mimesis in its threefold function as imitation, representation and construction creates the basis for mediation between the impressions of the inner and exterior worlds. It comprises the ability to acquire an insight into 'reality' and to represent it sensually. With this process 'reality' enters the 'inner world' of the people and is constructed at the same time. This new 'reality' is a symbolic world whose existence is based on the activity of acting people. Mimesis means doing. It is a product of human practice and only gets its shape via people's actions.

Within the mimetic process, acting does not follow rational motives or intentions. In distinction to cognitive models of cognition and action, mimetic actions are executed with practical knowledge. Relying on Bourdieu's *sens pratique*, Gunter Gebauer and Christoph Wulf (1992: 431) describe this process as a provision of patterns of action that follow the cognition process. These patterns of action in their turn anticipate the next executions of action. Gebauer and Wulf, like Bourdieu, also present people as symbolic constructors of 'reality' with their conception of social mimesis. Thus, these symbolic worlds are again mimetic processes. Although mimetic processes find their starting point in the symbolic construction of the empirical world, they are not similar to it but interpret 'world' in a new way: mimesis means adaptation of another world. The mimetic reference provides things and actions with a new structure of meaning that is different from that of the world of proceedings.

It is the merit of Gebauer and Wulf that they placed emphasis on the social dimensions of mimesis. Mimetic processes take place not only in the field of the aesthetic but also in the field of the social. According to Wulf (1989: 113) their importance for the human sciences has seldom been recognized. Social and aesthetic dimensions are combined in mimetic processes. Mimesis is therefore a necessary precondition of the social, just as the aesthetic represents its condition of construction. For the very reason of its bonds with the aesthetic and social dimensions, mimesis can again become an important category for the analysis of everyday cultural practices, helping to describe how cultural adaptation is bodily executed. My hypothesis is that the process of adaptation becomes describable with the conception of mimetic identification, a process that does not just happen but is made.

With the conception of mimesis, embodiment becomes recognizable as a performative process. Mimesis mediates between the impressions of the inner and exterior world or, to put it in other words, between the body world and the social world. It comprises the ability to acquire an insight into 'reality' and to represent it sensually. With this process of adaptation the social is inscribed into the body and becomes habitualized. This means that mimetic identification does not imitate a given reality on the level of the body but produces a new reality. Mimetic identification does not only mean conventionalization in the form of a reproduction of a structure of norms but describes the performative process of new construction and contextualization. From this perspective the imitation of pop cultural images by consumers cannot simply be understood as an adoption of cultural industrial products at the cost of the authentic self. Globalized images can, rather, unfold their effectiveness by being duplicated mimetically and re-interpreted in a performative act of new construction by the consumers. If the performative negotiation of images succeeds, field-specific norms are extended in the process of mimetic identification. Popcultural practice can therefore not be described as a local representation of a global culture industry, but as a performative cultural practice. Pop does not exist if it is not produced and believed in – as an industry, as a culture and way of living.

(Translated by Rupert Weinzierl)

References

Adorno, T. W. (1981), 'Résumé über Kulturindustrie', in: T. W. Adorno, *Gesammelte Schriften, Volume 3*, Frankfurt am Main: Suhrkamp.

Audehm, K. (2001), 'Die Macht der Sprache. Performative Magie bei Pierre Bourdieu', in C. Wulf , M. Göhlich and J. Zirfas (eds), *Grundlagen des Performativen*, Weinheim: Juventa.

Beck, U. (1999), *Was ist Globalisierung?* Frankfurt am Main: Suhrkamp.

Bourdieu, P. (1990), *Was heisst Sprechen? Die Ökonomie des sprachlichen Tausches*, Vienna: Braumüller.

Bourdieu, P. (1998), *Die Regeln der Kunst*, Frankfurt am Main: Suhrkamp.

Butler, J. (1993), *Bodies that Matter: On the Discursive Limits of 'Sex'*, New York and London: Routledge.

Butler, J. (1997), *Excitable Speech: A Politics of the Performative*, New York and London: Routledge.

Diederichsen, D. (1996), 'Pop - Deskriptiv, Normativ, Emphatisch', in M. Hartges and M. Lüdke (eds), *Pop Technik Poesie. Die nächste Generation*, Reinbek: Rowohlt.

Featherstone, M. (ed.) (1990), *Global Culture: Nationalism, Globalization and Modernity*, London: Sage.

Gebauer, G. and Wulf, C. (1992), *Mimesis: Kultur - Kunst - Gesellschaft*, Reinbek: Rowohlt.

Hall, S. (1980), 'Encoding/Decoding', in S. Hall (eds), *Culture, Media, Language*, London: Hutchingson. First published 1973 as *The Television Discourse: Encoding and Decoding*, Centre for Contemporary Cultural Studies, Occasional Papers, No.7, University of Birmingham.

Horkheimer, M. and Adorno, T. W. (1947), *Dialektik der Aufklärung*, Frankfurt am Main: Fischer.

Klein, G. (1999), *Electronic Vibration: Pop Kultur Theorie*, Hamburg: Rogner & Bernhard.

Lash, S. and Urry, J. (1994), *Economies of Signs and Space*, London: Sage.

Kureishi, H. (1995), 'That's How Good it Was', in, H. Kureishi and J. Savage (eds), *The Faber Book of Pop*, London and Boston MA: Faber & Faber.

Poschardt, U. (1996), 'Hip-Hop-Kultur', *Kunstforum International*, 134: 100–1.

Robertson, R. (1998), 'Glokalisierung: Homogenität und Heterogenität in Raum und Zeit', in U. Beck (ed.), *Perspektiven der Weltgesellschaft*, Frankfurt am Main: Suhrkamp.

Savage, J. (1995), 'The Simple Things you see are all Complicated', in, H. Kureishi and J. Savage (eds), *The Faber Book of Pop*, London and Boston MA: Faber & Faber.

Thornton, S. (1996), *Club Cultures: Music, Media and Subcultural Capital*, Hanover NH: University of Wesleyan Press.

Wulf, C. (1989), 'Mimesis', in G. Gebauer and D. Kamper (eds), *Historische Anthropologie: Zum Problem der Humanwissenschaften heute oder Versuche einer Neubegründung*, Reinbek: Rowohlt.

Zuckerkandl, V. (1958), 'Mimesis', *Merkur*, 12: 225–40.

4

'Oh Bondage, Up Yours!' Or Here's Three Chords, Now Form a Band: Punk, Masochism, Skin, Anaclisis, Defacement

David Bloustien

One night I wandered into a rock-n-roll club named CBGB's . . . Boomp boomp boomp entered my feet. Boomp boomp boomp entered my head. My body split into two bodies. I was the new world. I was pounding. Then there was these worms of bodies, white, covered by second-hand stinking guttered-up rags and knife-torn leather bands, moving sideways HORIZONTAL wriggling like worms who never made it to the snake-evolution stage, we only reproduce, we say, if you cut us apart with a knife.

(Acker 1984: 120)

Torn clothes and bondage pants, pierced skin and leather clothing continue to be ubiquitous symbols of punk in the popular imagination, and there is certainly no lack of empirical evidence to locate the paraphernalia of masochism in punk design and cultural production. Musical genealogies of American punk performance often begin with the Velvet Underground (Henry 1989), a band whose name is taken from a masochistic text, and whose song 'Venus in Furs' invokes Sacher-Masoch's (1991) novel of the same title. In London, a decade later, it is Adam and the Ants who bring punk's masochistic imagery to the fore. Having abandoned his art-college thesis in rubber and leather fetishism, Adam introduced S/M into his stage performances with songs such as 'Whip my Valise' and 'Rubber People' (Home 1988; Sabin 1999). But what do bondage pants have to do with punk 'identity'? Is the correspondence between masochism and punk merely an accident of history?

Punk discourse is saturated with the language of both liberal humanism and dialectical materialism, the radically autonomous individual who resists uniformity and seizes the means of production. Described in this way, punk is merely the logical extension of a (Western) metaphysics of selfhood. Masochism, on the other hand, is first and foremost a psychoanalytic term, although Gilles Deleuze (1991) returns this to its original literary context. Essentially a fetish of the skin, maso-chism places physical sensation (the coldness of marble, the interdependence of pleasure and pain) above the metaphysical self. Through association, this extends to a fixation in both the literature and in practice of 'feelings' (self-fulfilling anxieties of abandonment), hair and clothing (leather and fur specifically), and the apparent negation of the self through slavery and contractional obligation. This means that psychoanalytic readings of masochism are not only determinist (in their most simplistic and least satisfying interpretation) but also 'superficial' and 'of the surface'. Masochism and punk may meet in punk performance but they appear to be philosophically incompatible. It is important to note that the perceived rift between masochistic fashion and punk identity is therefore a problem of method-ology and epistemology. For many, the question is not simply 'why did/do some punks wear bondage pants?' but 'is punk even quantifiable in this way?'

The purpose of this chapter is to reconcile the semiology of punk fashion, specifically the use of sado/masochistic imagery and fetish wear, with the anti-essentialist, anti-materialist arguments that have made themselves felt in normative (post-)subcultural theory. I would argue that subcultural studies needs to reclaim the superficial, or at least the epidermal, as its discursive domain. It is my contention that punk and masochism are two expressions of the same phenomenon, the defacement of the skin in its biological, psychological and sociological manifest-ations.

Epistemological Considerations: Interior and Exterior

There is a fundamental disparity between the 'true' inner self – the mind, soul or spirit – and one's physical body, which remains more or less constant throughout the history of Western thought (Grosz 1995). Appearances are deemed deceiving; the true self is concealed, rather than revealed, by the bodily self, and the skin in particular. This is especially germane when considered alongside the racist pseudo-sciences of the turn of the last century, such as phrenology or social Darwinism, which make simple correlations between a person's appearance and his or her biological or cultural essence. Indeed, the social hierarchies maintained by biolog-ical racism inevitably valorize the 'higher races' as spiritually and intellectually superior, while at the same time condemning the 'lower races' for their extreme physicality (Gilman 1991). The historical consequences of such discourses add a moral imperative to the metaphysical separation of 'true self' from 'bodily self'.

Moreover, it is the apparently superficial nature of masochism's presence in punk that frustrates a study such as this one. In the case of punk, identity is increasingly located anywhere *but* the eye of the beholder (Sabin 1999), for

> once you accept the fact that Sid and Siouxie wore swastikas because they *weren't* Nazis, the dresscode for the *truly* punk was clearly anything but pink hair, safety-pins and bondage gear. The only acceptable function of fashion was the overthrow (for all time) of the very metaphysics of 'fashion'. (Sinker 1999: 125, emphasis added)

This argument is phrased more strongly than most, but it marks out the sites of conflict between different approaches to punk. On the one hand, it is ridiculous to equate punk with 'the overthrow . . . of the very metaphysics of fashion'. Punk is most immediately identified as a set of stylistic and performative practices, not least by those who may wish to be a part of it. On the other, it is just as problematic to assert the presence of any one element in punk style, 'pink hair, safety-pins and bondage gear', as correlative with punk identity, and any attempt to grasp punk identity by its 'uniformity' is doomed to failure. This is particularly true in light of current research that seeks to drive a wedge between the more visible elements of subcultural identity and the values or pleasures that might be said to inform it (see Andes 1998).

Removed from the domain of appearances, punk ceases to be a style and instead becomes a group identity that, ironically, orients itself around radical individualism (Muggleton 2000). In its extreme form, this radicalism sometimes manifests as a social programme against corporate power, specifically those economic forces that are believed to compromise individualism (Traber 2001). In this sense, triage aesthetics and hastily photocopied fanzines are not the codified language of a clandestine community, nor are they an historically determined cross-fertilization of class and youth that seeks to reclaim the means of production, but the by-product of a do-it-yourself philosophy of cultural manufacture. The problem with this approach to subculture is that it is counter-intuitive and disingenuous; it risks lapsing into Platonic idealism, which is just as removed from the punk experience as that which it seeks to rectify. Although for many self-professed punks, the visible element may be less important than the values ascribed to it, such an approach can not explain subcultural affiliation except as a kind of spontaneous 'punk-nature' that wells up within the disenfranchised. There is no room for, as Andes (1998) puts it, 'growing up punk', whereby a subculturalist finds the conventions of punk useful as a framework for self-expression and self-becoming.

So we cannot do away with punk fashion in a study of punk identity, although we must recognize the awkward logic that sutures the two. This discord stems in part from what Elizabeth Grosz describes as a fundamental incompatibility between two species of bodily knowledge:

> The first conceives the body as a surface on which social law, morality and values are inscribed; The second refers largely to the lived experience of the body, the body's internal or psychic inscription. Where the first analyses a *social*, public body, the second takes the body-schema or imaginary anatomy as its object(s) . . . Where psychoanalysis and phenomenology focus on the body as it is experienced and rendered meaningful, the inscriptive model is more concerned with the processes by which the subject is marked, scarred, transformed, and written upon or constructed by the various regimes of institutional, discursive, and nondiscursive power as a particular kind of body. (Grosz 1995: 33)

It seems obvious that style and collectivizing, material practices exist in the social realm, whereas identity is a discourse of the interior. Of course, internally and externally inscribed knowledges of the body are rhetorical extremes, and Grosz's article is as much about shifting disciplinary walls as the lacunae between interior and exterior. Nonetheless, anthropological ethnography does not accord with Grosz's internally inscriptive model in the same manner that, say, ethological studies or clinical psychoanalysis might. Rather, a closer analysis reveals that in practice these orientations are reversed. 'Identity', as a mutable process by which one navigates and mediates the external world, is the subject of ethnographic research. Culture is therefore identity on a collective level. The subject of classical psychoanalysis is also 'identity', but identity as ego-formation (or 'ego-main-tenance') and how this manifests in (aberrant) social behaviour. Culture is the collective manifestation of identity. The difference between the two is subtle but significant.

Ethnographic testimony provides data for the analysis of the individual as part of a social network. By contrast, psychoanalytic case studies provide the researcher with information regarding the individual case and his or her self-inscription through the material base of the body, which is a given biological fact and informs all subsequent psychological development. The materiality of the body produces, rather than receives, knowledges of the social. The ethnographer looks for corresp-ondence within and between communities, the practising psychoanalyst attempts to correct aberrations of psychological development on an individual basis. Whereas the ethnographer participates in order to experience the social context of the subject's body, the practising psychoanalyst *provides a context for the subject* within which he or she (the subject) will be able to untangle the threads of his or her experience. In other words, we might say that classical psychoanalysis seeks objective knowledge of the interior subject, whereas anthropological ethnography seeks a subjective knowledge of the exterior object (or subject, in the Foucauldian sense of the word).

In most cases, and with good reason, the fruits of ethnographic research are removed from their psycho-biological bases, except where the body is understood as it is inscribed from without. The sociopolitical basis of cultural studies means that there is an overwhelming tendency to place subcultural identity within a discursive framework of social forces and external inscription. Conversely, the readerly, textual basis of French semiotics (after Barthes and before Baudrillard), as reinterpreted by the CCCS, locates style and socio-political practice firmly *within* the body of the subject.

Punk certainly lends itself to an external discourse of social struggle and ideological resistance. Although deviance plays an important role in the theoretical framework of the Chicago School, it is Dick Hebdige's use of punk as the exemplar of subcultural identity that has cements the 'subcultural' into a wider social dynamic of class conflict. The moral panics that surround punk's earliest appearances in the mass media and the subcultural resistance theory of Hebdige can be said to share a certain dialectical synchronicity. Both position punk as 'noise . . . interference in the orderly sequence' that governs high-culturally sanctioned mass communication (Hebdige 1979: 90). Accordingly, the 'sub' in subculture has come to signal the subaltern, rather than simply a smaller subset of a wider social grouping. Within this context, the more visible, stylistic practices of punk are read as iconoclastic and defiant when considered alongside 'mainstream' dress codes.

Psychoanalytic masochism belongs to the other kind of bodily inscription. Although masochistic desire can only be satiated or observed in the social realm of the exterior, it is generally assumed that this desire stems from a particular psychological state that inscribes the body from the interior. This then manifests on the exterior. So, the prevalence in sadomasochistic literature of leather and fur, particularly when worn over naked flesh, suggests a skin that has been flayed by a hunter and then turned into a garment (Anzieu 1989). Torn clothing and leather jackets, common signifiers of punk subculture, can thus be syncretized with the more functional trappings of masochistic sexuality, such as bruised skin and bondage pants. However, such a semiotic approach is no longer considered an appropriate methodology for subcultural analysis. In particular, it does not appear to privilege an internal discourse of the body at all. So far as any 'interior' world analysed through visual style is really a socially experienced one, rather than an objectified one, it is thus (in our terminology here) an exterior, rather than interior, analysis.

There is a contrary tendency in some contemporary texts to separate punk 'essence' out from its easily imitated physical manifestations. These texts tend to be written in a more testimonial or journalistic style located outside the traditional conventions of academic writing, and Mark Sinker's (1999) piece is an important example. I have already discussed the philosophical shortcomings of such an argument, but find it difficult to incorporate into my analysis here except to say that these texts might have more in common with the arguments put forward by the CCCS, principally Hebdige's thesis of diffusion, than it would first appear.

To summarize, it is difficult to explain the masochistic presence in punk style as having significant bearing on punk identity because of a basic incongruity between the interior and exterior realms within which punk operates. I now turn my attention to that metaphorical surface upon which interior and exterior knowledges of the body are etched – a surface that, like a translucent sheet of paper, is two sided yet not separable into two distinct halves. Reclaiming the superficial for subcultural analysis necessitates a psychosocial analysis of the skin and its various psychosocial manifestations.

Skin: Beyond Interiority and Exteriority

From an epidemiological perspective, the methodological and epistemological problem posed by the conflict between style and identity can be mediated through the same logic that gives meaning to the skin, as a psychosocial membrane that connects internal and external inscriptions of the body. As the site of both individuation and interpersonal communication, the skin is the primary locus of subcultural identity, the organ through which one tries to 'fit in and yet stand out' (Muggleton 2000: Chapter 4).

Drawing on ethological studies, psychoanalytic theory and his own experience as a practising psychoanalyst, Didier Anzieu links the development of the Ego to an infant's discovery of its own skin. He argues that the child experiences its skin as a two-sided envelope: the outer porous layer is protective and sensory whereas the smooth inner layer contains the body (Anzieu 1989). Together, the interior and exterior surfaces of the skin form a communicative interface between the interior and exterior worlds of the subject, between a perceived 'inner self' and the socially perceptive schema of the exterior (Anzieu 1989; Gell 1993).

This becomes more apparent when one considers the ways in which we manipulate our appearance in order to affect these transmissions:

> Decorating, covering, uncovering or otherwise altering the human form in accordance with social notions of everyday propriety or sacred dress, beauty, solemnity, status or changes in status, or on occasion of the violation or inversion of such notions, seems to have been a concern of every human society of which we have knowledge . . . the surface of the body seems everywhere to be treated, not only as the boundary of the individual as a biological and psychological entity, but as the frontier of the social self as well. (Turner 1980: 112)

Unlike our other sensory organs, we have relatively little control over how our skin functions. Skin covers the entire body, and so cannot be turned off in the same way that one's eyes can be closed or one's ears stopped up. Clothing, hair and body modification are the technologies through which one can take a measure of control over these functions of the skin. They are therefore as much implicated in the expression of agency and self-determination as they are rooted in social expectation and the accruement of cultural capital. Drawing on his experiences with the Kayapo in the Amazon Forest, Turner (1980) argues that body painting can perform the same social functions as casual and ceremonial dress (including cosmetics, coiffure, piercings and other related practices of body modification) in Western societies. By drawing attention to the limits of the physiological self, at the same time concealing those elements such as the genitals that are considered to reveal the pre-social or natural self, dress represents the skin in a way that the skin cannot possibly do on its own. Belonging in *both* the psychological and social worlds, the skin needs a synthetic buffer zone that will perform its exterior functions without inhibiting its interior processes.

Alfred Gell (1993) takes Anzieu's psychobiological arguments about skin, and projects them onto the social realm of body modification. In particular, Gell is interested in 'social reproduction', the way in which a culture reproduces itself across subsequent generations. He describes this process as a 'network of agentive relations' that is *not* a matter of mapping a Xerox copy of the self onto one's cultural offspring. Rather, social reproduction entails the adoption of the responsibilities of cultural reproduction by a new generation 'who have all the attributes (moral qualities, status attributes, possessions, titles etc.) they ideally should have' (Gell 1993). Whereas Anzieu is a psychoanalyst, Gell is an anthropologist. His breach of the interior/exterior divide may be termed anaclitic. In Freud's terminology, anaclisis ('reclining') refers to the attachment of the subject to an object-choice that that is reminiscent of his or her mother or father (Freud 1953). Structurally, this also provides psychoanalysis with a strategy for depicting psychic development as 'leaning back' on the physiological life it has left behind, without simply dissolving the distinction between them. This relationship is not exactly metaphoric, which would suggest an internal inscription, as it reflects a developmental progression that can be used to reconcile differences, rather than a static substitution intended to reveal similarities. Neither is anaclisis metonymic, as it is develops from tangible, sensory data, precluding the endless leap 'from signifier to signifier, without any reference to a signified' (Handelman 1982). Rather, psychic life is an *extension* of physical life, an 'increasing complexity in the service of the satisfaction of vital needs' (Anzieu 1989).

As psychic systems develop, they become increasingly abstracted from the physical systems upon which they are based, until that relationship is more one of structural resemblance than stimulus-response. There remain traces of connectivity (the distinction between the two sets of systems is never really complete), and so we are able to elaborate upon a psychic system with reference to the physiological phase of development in which it developed. The psychic and the physiological break off from each other into parallel discourses, except where pathologies of the psyche manifest physiological symptoms. The brain 'outgrows' the body, but never leaves it entirely.

The epidemiologies of Didier Anzieu (1989), Terence Turner (1980) and Alfred Gell (1993) map out a network of anaclitic relationships between the communal and the personal that befits the interrelation of style and individuality particular to subcultural identity. It will now be necessary to specify the ways in which punk and masochism are both specifically epidermal practices, and how individuation and collectivism might be allowed to exist simultaneously through the same medium.

Margins and Limits

A collective identity is something inherently sexual, in the manner theorized (if not abstracted) by Bataille (2001); it entails the transcendence (and loss) of the self into something transmissive and transgressive, both comforting as the womb and undesirable as death. Just as Acker's (1984) narrator is interpolated into the subterranean sub-urban through the resounding 'boomp boomp boomp' of the punk club, eliciting a confusion of subjectivity, the 'youth subculture'/'parent culture' dyad is fraught with anxieties over communal identity and radical autonomy. This manifests in two ways. The first is the abject or limit case, the identity that sits *on the skin*. Abject identities are radically individual, and therefore suit punk's meta-narrative of social autonomy. The other part of this dynamic entails a rending of that skin.

In Acker's (1984) text, punk and masochism are parallel gestures towards urban maggot-hood, a self-deprecating group identity that thrives in the subcultural compost beneath the veneer of civilization. Their horizontal, writhing gestures, ostensibly the ecstatic energies of a punk audience, also evokes the blind urgency of a sexual compulsion. This compulsion appears bestial, abhuman:

> the abject confronts us . . . with those fragile states where man strays on the territories of *animal*. Thus, by way of abjection, primitive societies have marked out a precise area of their culture in order to remove it from the threatening world of animals or animalism, which were imagined as representatives of sex or murder. (Kristeva 1982: 12–13)

The animalism of CBGB's punk patrons places them on the margins of social life, and necessarily so; no matter how mistaken its disavowal of commercialization, punk resists mass production. Blatant attempts to commodify the punk 'look', or even for an individual to adopt a particular style without sufficient authentication, risk spectacular failure. (This is despite the poverty of theories of subcultural commitment and authenticity as philosophical axioms.) Linda Andes, for example, notes that her informants 'not only said that they felt that punk was becoming trendy; they all said that this happened *after* they became involved, regardless of when that involvement took place within the history of the subculture' (Andes 1998: 219; emphasis in original).

By disavowing their own punk development, Andes's subjects are able to reinforce their 'innate' authenticity. Andes's model is simplistic in its linearity, and no doubt simplified for the forum in which it is published, but it makes the important point that commitment and authenticity are rhetorical modes used to demarcate punk as a cultural 'alternative'. However, as David Muggleton has pointed out, commitment and authenticity in this sense do not indicate 'an objective . . . subcultural stratification' of subcultural identity as a whole (Muggleton 2000).

Rather, these terms are used to differentiate between 'core' and 'marginalized' members of a particular subcultural community. What is significant about these terms is the way in which they are used to demonstrate one's marginality, or abjection, from a perceived cultural mainstream.

Social, political and biological abjection is an integral part of punk's (limited) public image, what Daniel S. Traber (2001) describes as the 'sub-urban' and its corresponding rhetoric of self-marginalization. Punk names itself as the waste and excrescence of the post-industrial world. Whether disaffected or angry at being excluded, punk youth seemingly place themselves outside the parent culture as 'Other'. However, the rhetoric of abjection is imprecise. Traber's White, privileged punks are able to slip into an 'authentic' sub-urban lifestyle, and therefore not really slip at all, precisely because their Californian Whiteness affords them a degree of social mobility. That is not to credit Whiteness with an essential malleability, but to bring the 'social conditions' of punk back to a tangible discourse of social embodiment. Ultimately, self-marginalization, 'silence[s] the marginal subject's own viewpoint on marginality. By proposing that they have joined a different cultural formation by adopting a certain lifestyle, punks further naturalize that subject position in a binary relationship to suburban life that is also (re)-naturalized. The power of Whiteness is recentered and buttressed as the norm' (Traber 2001: 54). My point is not that punk is inherently conservative or a magical solution to the problems of disenfranchisement but that the abject (or marginal) does not truly exist as *outside* the parent culture. Rather, it is as a limit case, or along the skin of the parent culture, that subculture operates.

In masochism, too, abjection is a performative practice. The sexualized ego is itself made abject, but seemingly in a way that threatens the ego's integrity:

> The function of individuation of the Self can only be accomplished through suffering both physical (the tortures) and moral (the humiliations); the systematic introduction of inorganic substances under the skin, the ingestion of repugnant substances (urine, the partner's excrement) reveal the fragility of that function; the distinguishing of his own body from those of others is constantly being put into question. (Anzieu 1989: 10)

Whereas punk appears to break away from the parent culture and posit itself as an 'Other', it seems that masochism seeks the submission of the self to the 'Other'. According to Deleuze (1991), however, the masochist invites the physical subjugation of his or her body in order to counteract his or her *moral* subjugation at the hands of the superego. Contradicting Freud, Deleuze argues that the masochist exorcizes his or her superego, rather than submitting to it, by bestowing it upon an external party. Thus at the end of *Venus in Furs*, Sacher-Masoch's protagonist 'cures' himself of his own morality and turns to beating women, rather than asking to be beaten by them (Deleuze 1991; Sacher-Masoch 1991).

Tears and Bruises

> The abject confronts us, on the other hand, and this time within our personal arch-
> aeology, with our earliest attempts to release the hold of *maternal* entity even before ex-
> isting outside of her, thanks to the autonomy of language. It is a violent, clumsy breaking
> away, with constant risk of falling back under the sway of a power as secure as it is
> stifling. (Kristeva 1982: 13)

As with authenticity and commitment, the desire to 'resist' must be maintained in
a comprehensive theory of subculture, more for its importance as an interior strategy
for making the punk body meaningful than for its ability to tell us about socio-
political 'reality'. Removed from hegemonic Marxism and incorporated into an
epidemiologically abject discourse, subcultural resistance becomes a necessary
condition of youth, as a catalyst for intergenerational cultural transmission.

Gell (1993) sees agency itself as pivotal to cultural reproduction – cultural
offspring must be social actors to fulfil their responsibilities. Without agency, the
parent culture stalls and dies. Ironically, this need for one's cultural offspring to
stand on his or her own two feet as an independent cultural agent can only be
achieved, in part, through rebellion, a refusal to submit to the will of that prior
generation. The rhetoric of death, struggle and apocalypse serve to mark out the
liminal spaces of the parent culture, scarifying the social epidermis to reify its
borders, not to rupture them.

In *The Skin Ego*, Didier Anzieu (1989) argues that it is through a tactile relationship with the parent that the child is imbued with a sense of security and the limits
of the self. The 'shared skin' of the mother-child dyad, prefigured by the womb,
provides the infant with comfort and support, in order to build the self-confidence
necessary for autonomous life, but it is also a constraint that prevents that autonomy from functioning effectively. As the child matures and seeks to forge a
separate identity to the 'mother', he or she must slowly tear away the imaginary
membrane that joins them. This process is painful and traumatic for both parties,
achieved only through continual recourse to the security of the shared skin.

Anzieu pathologizes sadomasochistic practice to a degree that is not helpful
here. What we *can* take from his work, however, is the perverse relationship
between sadomasochism and autonomy: masochism as the expression of a frustrated
will to autonomy, rather than a desire for submission, as one might presume. By
damaging or staining the skin, the self can hope to attain 'omnipotence in destruction'
(Anzieu 1989), thereby reclaiming it for the self (Rosenblatt 1997). Connections
may therefore be drawn between masochistic discourse and the ripped aesthetics
identified with the wider punk scene. This relationship is anaclitic, rather than
semiotic, and evinces a direct relationship between the radical individualism of
punk testimony and the group identity of punk social praxis.

In different contexts, punk fashion, as a popular form of epidermal defacement, can lend a synthetic toughness to one's skin – what Alfred Gell (1993) calls 'character armour', or provide a comforting blanket of familiarity. The primary biological functions of the skin are augmented by its scarification, as if through sympathetic magic. Knives, fragments and incisions predominate in Acker's (1984) description. The libidinal drives of the nightclub's patrons spill out from their wounds. Like worms, they can only reproduce 'if you cut [them] apart with a knife' (Acker 1984: 120). It is the cut, or rather the omnipresent threat of cutting inherent in scarification, that sutures punk into masochism and vice versa.

The distinction between an actual cut, and the threat of a cut, is an important one to make. In his reading of masochistic testimony and literature, Didier Anzieu (1989) emphasizes the importance of 'marking' the skin with a whip or brand, that the sensation felt by the skin be validated through a sense of visual permanency. The skin is injured by the lash in such a way as to reify its surface. Masochistic sexuality makes a fetish of the skin, infusing it with idolatrous power, and granting it an excess of visibility through tearing, bruising or piercing. Michael Taussig (1999) has observed this same process at work in the 'defacement' of public monuments and artworks, or in the explosive significance of cinematic montage and its symbolic presence in the motif of the ruptured eye. He writes, 'the statue barely exists for consciousness and perhaps is nonexistent – until it receives a shock to its being, provided by its defacement issuing forth a hemorrhage of sacred force. With defacement, the statue moves from an excess of invisibility to an excess of visibility' (Taussig 1999: 52). Following Taussig, defacement is not a process of obliteration, but of a sacrilegious/sacrificial scarification that draws attention to the surface of things, to the skin in all its communicative power.

The accoutrements of Punk – torn clothing, torn skin, fetish gear, leaking bodies, sharp hair, social aggression and an aesthetics of sensory indiscrimination – are a concerted attack on the psycho-biological skin, as much as the social skin. This scarification is part of the quest for radical autonomy, which operates on an individual and a communal level simultaneously. Through a defacement of the excrescences of the body, mirrored by a parallel scarification of the social structures and interstitial spaces within which it perceives itself to be located, punk enacts all the anxieties and pleasures of youth as a liminal condition caught between generations. The deployment of cut-up aesthetics, torn clothes and the trappings of masochism work in concert with the will to radical independence that saturates the punk ethos.

References

Acker, K. (1984), *Blood and Guts in High School, Plus Two*, London: Picador.

Andes, L. (1998), 'Growing Up Punk: Meaning and Commitment Careers in a Contemporary Youth Subculture', in J. Epstein (ed.), *Youth Culture: Identity in a Postmodern World*, Malden MA: Blackwell.

Anzieu, D. (1989), *The Skin Ego: A Psychoanalytic Approach to the Self*, New Haven CT: Yale University Press.

Bataille, G. (2001), *Eroticism: Death and Sensuality*, London: Penguin.

Deleuze, G. (1991), 'Coldness and Cruelty', in *Masochism: Coldness and Cruelty & Venus in Furs* (translated by J. McNeil), New York: Zone Books.

Freud, S. (1953), 'On Narcissism: An Introduction', in J. Strachey, A. Freud, A. Strachey and A. Tyson (eds), *The Standard Edition of the Complete Works of Sigmund Freud, Vol. 14*, London: Hogarth Press.

Gell, A. (1993), *Wrapping in Images: Tattooing in Polynesia*, Oxford: Oxford University Press.

Gilman, S. (1991), *The Jew's Body*, New York and London: Routledge.

Grosz, E. (1995), *Space, Time and Perversion: The Politics of Bodies*, St Leonards: Allen & Unwin.

Handelman, S. A. (1982), *Slayers of Moses: The Emergence of Rabbinic Interpretation in Modern Literary Theory*, Albany: State University of New York Press.

Hebdige, D. (1979), *Subculture: The Meaning of Style*, London: Methuen.

Henry, T. (1989), *Break All Rules! Punk Rock and the Making of a Style*, Ann Arbour MI: UMI Research Press.

Home, S. (1988), *Assault on Culture: Utopian Currents from Lettrisme to Class War*, London: Aporia Press and Unpopular Books.

Kristeva, J. (1982), *Powers of Horror: An Essay on Abjection*, New York: Columbia University Press.

Muggleton, D. (2000), *Inside Subculture: The Postmodern Meaning of Style*, Oxford: Berg.

Rosenblatt, D. (1997), 'The Antisocial Skin: Structure, Resistance, and "Modern Primitive" Adornment in the United States', *Cultural Anthropology*, 12: 287–334.

Sabin, R. (1999), 'Introduction', in R. Sabin (ed.), *Punk Rock: So What? The Cultural Legacy of Punk*, London and New York: Routledge.

Sacher-Masoch, L. von (1991), 'Venus in Furs', in *Masochism: Coldness and Cruelty & Venus in Furs* (translated by J. McNeil), New York: Zone Books.

Sinker, M. (1999), 'Concrete, so as to Self-Destruct: the Etiquette of Punk, its Habits, Rules, Values and Dilemmas', in R, Sabin (ed.), *Punk Rock: So What? The Cultural Legacy of Punk*, London and New York: Routledge.

Taussig, M. (1999), *Defacement: Public Secrecy and the Labour of the Negative*, Stanford CA: Stanford University Press.

Traber, D. S. (2001), 'L.A.'s "White Minority": Punk and the Contradictions of Self-Marginalization', *Cultural Critique*, 48: 30–64.

Turner, T. S. (1980), 'The Social Skin', in J. Cherfas and R. Lewin (eds), *Not Work Alone: A Cross-Cultural View of Activities Superfluous to Survival*, London: Temple Smith.

–5–

Post-Rave Technotribalism and the Carnival of Protest
Graham St John

This chapter assesses the applicability of Maffesolian thought to DiY technocultural youth formations. Through Michel Maffesoli's post-structuralism, contemporary society is characterized by voluntary, unstable and sensuous micro-cultures. These 'neo-tribes' are interconnected in a *network*, with each node representing a possible site of belonging for contemporary nomads, each achieving their fullest expression in the festal. In a growing body of youth research, especially dance culture (or 'clubculture') research conducted in the UK, 'neo-tribe' is superseding 'subculture' as a heuristic device. The trend evidences an acknowledgement that post-war formations have become steadily disconnected from structural determinants (particularly class) and, especially in the late twentieth century, connected to elective consumption strategies.

Like earlier milieus, the post-rave technocultures under consideration are neo-tribal-like – especially as they achieve their fullest (sometimes only) expression in the festival, or, perhaps more accurately, the 'temporary autonomous zone'. Yet, the disruptive characteristics of decommodified dance event-spaces, especially those enabled by techno-anarchist sound systems (like Spiral Tribe and Ohms not Bombs), and the activist disposition of direct action techno festivals or *carnivals of protest* (like Reclaim the Streets and Earthdream2000), indicate that the Maffesolian approach requires renovation, or should at least be approached with caution. Emerging within the context of new, decentralized, social movements and coevolving with digital communications technology, these *technotribes* are networked in 'DiY culture', which McKay (1998) has described as 'a 1990s counterculture'– non-hierarchical in principle, attracting youth committed to voluntarism, ecological sustainability, social justice and human rights. Fashionably committed to pleasure *and* politics, such new formations are not disengaged from the political, but are future-directed, pursuing ideals consistent with an historical sensitivity and global sensibilities – as indicated by their reconciliatory gestures, direct action commitments and in their wider cultural output.

Neo-tribalism and Clubculture

Expounding the apparent re-enchantment of contemporary social life, for Maffesoli, post-modernity is characterized by the appearance of nebulous 'neo-tribes' or 'neo-communities' resisting the universal codes of morality imposed by the Prometheanism of the modern era. These protean aggregations are internally diverse, ephemeral nodes of identification, which, he argues, are distinctly disengaged from 'activist progressivism' (Maffesoli 1997: 27), returning to 'local ethics' – an 'empathetic sociality' (Maffesoli 1995: 11). Neo-tribes, it is claimed, are 'less disposed to master the world, nature and society than collectively to achieve societies founded above all on quality of life' (Maffesoli 1995: 62). Under recognizable icons, or 'empathetic images' (Maffesoli 1988: 150), evidencing a populist movement tending toward rediscovering 'mutual aid, conviviality, commensality [and] professional support' (Maffesoli 1995: 69), they are organized to fulfil the 'persistent and imperious need to be "*en reliance*", to be bound together' (Maffesoli 1997: 32). A Dionysian 'mass' of neo-tribes is said to constitute an 'underground centrality', which, we are informed, is the source of *puissance*, which is, by contrast with institutional power or *pouvoir*, the 'inherent energy and vital force of the people' (Maffesoli 1995: 1).

Enthusing over the '(re)birth of *homo aestheticus*', by which is meant the contemporary 're-ephiphanization' of the senses, of the body (Maffesoli 1997: 23), Maffesoli articulated the social and historical exigency of *puissance*, of collective non-rationality, revealed as 'passional logic', a kind of a sacred sensuality that 'has always animated and once again animates the social body . . . defract[ing] into a multiplicity of effects that inform daily life' (Maffesoli 1993: 1). 'Passional logic' is a theme most manifest in the 'orgiasm', a universal sociality which, 'contrary to a morality of "ought to be" . . . refers to an *ethical immoralism* which consolidates the symbolic link of all society' (Maffesoli 1993: 2). The Durkheimian 'logic' of such a condition is that it 'allows for the structuring or regeneration of community'. As Maffesoli has it, in 'the face of historic time dominated by production and parousia, there is a poetic and heroic time, a time of the amorous body, a second and hidden time around which are organized endurance and sociality' (Maffesoli 1993: 31). In this aloof 'unproductive life', there is a Bataillian desire for loss, for expenditure. The orgiastic reaches a licentious, contagious and unrestrainable climax in the *festal* – those moments of pure consumption occasioning transgressions of imposed morality (Maffesoli 1993: 92).

According to Maffesoli, in a 'de-individualized' society, sensory, consumer and spatial practices enable individuals to form allegiances with others. Under proliferating processes of identification in the post-war period, in the heat of shared interests, pleasures and tastes, and within affective locales, individual identities recede – if only temporarily. Furthermore, individuals flow between multiple signs and sites of belonging – an understanding approximating the 'post-modern personality', which Bauman (1996: 32) describes as restless, fickle and irresolute. In postmodernist cultural theory, post-war identities are complicated and fluid not unitary or fixed – a circumstance wherein traditional structural determinants (especially class, gender, religion) are transcended by 'de-traditionalizing' lifestyle tribes whose 'elective centres' (Cohen *et al*. 1987) occasion the embodied display of the persona. Maffesoli opposes the view that with burgeoning consumerism contemporary society experiences rampant individualism and/or massification. Neither is the case since social life is organized by a 'mass-tribe dialectic', which is said to be 'naturally inducing adherence and distance, attraction and repulsion' (Maffesoli 1995: 127). Society is both 'undifferentiated mass and highly diversified polarities' (Maffesoli 1995: 88). This is society's 'ambience', and networked social nuclei represent many possible sites of belonging for contemporary nomads.

Influencing post-structuralist interpretations of youth culture and leisure spaces, Maffesoli has been useful in responses to the lumbering modernist paradigm of youth 'subculture'. The rise of consumer culture and the proliferation of voluntary associations (especially those formed by and for youth), are circumstances which have seen a decline in the heuristic value of 'subculture' – conventionally conceptualized as class-based, oppositional and discrete. While neo-tribalism has been wielded as an appropriate trope to articulate diverse nodes of sociality, from the 'contact communities' of new urban spaces of consumption (Shields 1992) to the expressive lifestyles and collective identifications of marginal movements (particularly New Age Travellers in the UK, see Hetherington 1994, 1998), dance culture (or 'clubculture') has become a social field in receipt of the most liberal application of Maffesolian thought (cf. Halfacree and Kitchin 1996; Gore 1997; Malbon 1998, 1999; Gaillot 1999; Bennett 1999).

In their study of the popular music scene in Manchester and the ephemerality of post-rock social fragments, Halfacree and Kitchin (1996) had earlier hinted at the inadequacy of subculture as it had been applied in music studies. For Bennett (1999: 614), while 'subculture' imposes a 'hermeneutic seal around the relationship between musical and stylistic preference', neo-tribalism 'allows for the shifting nature' of such preferences, and the fluidity of youth cultural groups. Thus the persistence of 'subculture' as a discursive trope employed to circumscribe youth, music and style practices, is problematic for Bennett. In his study of the new urban dance music scene in Newcastle upon Tyne in north-east England, enthusiasts sample and mix diverse musical genres and visual styles (reflecting the digital compositional techniques employed by the music's producers). The polydimensional character of 'clubbing' – less a singular and monolithic activity, and more 'a series of fragmented, temporal experiences as [clubbers] move between different dance floors and engage with different crowds' (Bennett 1999: 611) – mirrors the non-rigid sociality of an era which has seen individuals appropriate and experiment with 'lifestyle' commodities as a means of articulating identity.[1] Clubbing is thus symptomatic of the eclecticism characterizing the consumption sensibilities of post-war 'style tribes'.

Drawing attention to the significance of corporeality and space in contemporary social theory, others have documented the sensate communality of the club or rave. According to Malbon (1999: 50), the club is a paramount site of identification for contemporary youth. Malbon discusses the social significance of music and dance in the articulations of identity *and* the development of a sense of belonging – an ethos – within the clubbing crowd. In a sensuous space where the 'stable identity of the individual is superseded by the much more fluid and ephemeral identif- ications of the persona' an 'emotional community', howsoever fleetingly, is generated (Malbon 1998: 279). Drawing upon Maffesoli's idea of the 'ethics of the present', Gaillot (1999: 23–4) celebrates the techno-rave community as a 'laboratory of the present', an essential mode of 'being together' that 'exists only in the actuality of dancing bodies, and is not based on any community of fact or appearance except the *fete* being shared at that moment'. Raves are 'the Dionysia of modern times'. Furthermore, with its 'ecstatic sharing made possible by machines' (Gaillot 1999: 33), the rave diverts technology 'from an instrument of isolation and reduction . . . into an instrument for bringing people closer together and for the free artistic political expression of their singularity' (Gaillot 1999: 19).

Maffesolian post-structuralism thus illuminates the fluid and 'passional' sociality of rave, providing a useful alternative to the subculture heuristic. But post-modernist accounts of youth culture have been indicted for neglecting, for example, that which Hollands (2002: 169) identifies as 'the stratified and hierarchical nature of leisure and lifestyle identities' which are developing among the young in a climate of growing corporate activity, state regulation and urban regeneration. So what are the limits in the applicability of the Maffesolian model? Martin (2002: 84) has indicated that neo-tribalism is not entirely suited to the explication of complex groups like New Age Travellers whose more recent members face immediate material deprivations and whose collectivity may be far from elective. What light might the perspective shed on a complex of youth formations herded under or adjacent to 'dance culture'?

The New Resistance and Counter-Tribalism

It appears that for some time into the 1990s, western youth culture was character- ized by hedonistic individualism or else a listless pessimism. In the former, leisure

---

1. The apparent 'hyper' quality to clubbing suggests that musical taste and visual image do not necessarily possess a homological relationship.

becomes religion and voracious consumerism is the panacea to a world of anxiety and insecurity. In the latter, 'GenX' 'slackers' submit *en masse* to cynicism, irony and modes of escape. Youth seemed to be caught between a rock of narcissism, and a hard place of 'disappearance'. While it is undoubtedly true that consumers readily submit to pleasure seeking and passivity in a period of increased uncertainty, these pursuits do not exhaust the life-strategies of contemporary youth.[2]

The late 1990s and the small hours of the twenty-first century saw a groundswell of proactive interventions undertaken by the politically dispossessed and agitated (including multitudes of young people) in the name of democracy, the environment, fair trade, debt cancellation and so forth. In what Naomi Klein (2000) has identified as a period of new resistance, in the struggle for 'the global commons', massive grassroots protests have been mounted against the global institutions of corporate capitalism. In a multitude of actions not disconnected from the mobilization of dispossessed indigenous farmers or exploited labourers in export processing zones, the period has seen student groups, labour rights activists and local environmental organizations unite to combat market fundamentalism. In this climate, diverse opponents have formed cells, blocs and alliances in their contestation of, for instance, trade liberalization, genetically modified food production and the proliferation of the nuclear industry. A sea of conscientious youth has participated in, for example, protests against the World Trade Organization in Seattle in November 1999 and the global May Day (or M1) protests. But perhaps of most significance was the massive global street party held on 18 June 1999 (coinciding with the G-8 meeting in Cologne, Germany). On that day, there were actions in seventy cities around the world. Groups, including Reclaim the Streets and the Peoples' Global Action (along with Bangladeshi female garment workers and Indian farmers), blockaded stock exchanges, superstores and big brand outlets, and occupied the offices of transnational headquarters and business districts. Signalling the 'crisis of legitimacy' of neo-liberal political agendas, J18 was the globalization of protest. As Klein comments, it was 'the coming out party for this new political player' (Klein 2000: 444).

Identified as a new multi-headed 'movement', a 'ragtag alliance', this global action against transnational capitalism possesses tactics and social units of organization that have been percolating for decades (indeed since the 1960s). The 1990s occasioned a groundswell of dissent in capitalist democracies out of which a range of activist micro-cultures emerged. These informal groups, such as new radical environmental movement organizations are reported in the UK and evident elsewhere to evince 'a new wave' of NVDA (or non-violent direct action). That is, groups like those united against genetically modified food such as the Earth

---

2. Although it must be pointed out that pleasure seeking, especially in unregulated zones, should not be dismissed as insignificant behaviour.

Liberation Front and the Genetics Engineering Network, anti road construction/ car-culture collectives like the UK Dongas Tribe (Plows 1995; McKay 1996), Road Alert!, Reclaim the Streets (Jordan 1998) and Critical Mass, and anticonsumerist groups (Purkis 2000), have run confrontational and disruptive campaigns, employing tactical repertoires possessing 'an ethos characterized by an intention to affect social and ecological conditions directly, even while . . . seek[ing] indirect influence through the mass media' (Doherty *et al.* 2000: 1).

With a variegated lineage traced through Earth First! affinity groups, antinuclear and peace movement groups, the Animal Liberation Front and other anarchist, traveller and student 'disorganizations', these 'new social movement' microcultures are based around informal networks, engage in a range of collective challenges and form alliances with related groups in a wider movement – as successfully transpired in the case of UK anti-roads protesting (McNeish 2000; Wall 1999) and the siege of the World Economic Forum at Melbourne's Crown Casino at S11 (11–13 September 2000). Following Melucci (1989), these activist neo-tribes demonstrate the growing significance of culture, information and identity. Their targets are less likely to be nation-states than the 'dominant cultural codes' legislated by the institutions of economic and cultural globalization (Doherty *et al.* 2000: 12). They formulate 'alternative cultural codes' and aesthetics, and forge expressive 'extended milieux' independent from state and corporate control. Thus, within the context of a 'global sociality' there has emerged a kind of planetary ethics of care grounded in affective identification (Jowers *et al.* 1999: 107). These microcultures appear in an era of advanced need fulfilment and deep introspection, hence their involvement in new spiritualities and the self-transformation movement. They often subscribe to the imputed philosophies and iconographies of indigenous cultures and traditional 'tribalism' – the replication of which may be regarded as the measure of an 'authentic' lifestyle (cf. Newton 1988; St John 1997) – and attract those who identify with an ethical-consumerism. And, excluded from or holding disdain for conventional channels of political participation, these counter-tribes seek to build or reconstruct community - proximate, autonomous and consensual.

Approximating that which has been identified as *DiY cultures*, these 'movement' nuclei are both expressive and conscientious, affectual and instrumental communities, their demeanour reflecting quests for authenticity, shared grievance and belonging combined with efforts to effect political outcomes. McKay (1998: 2) suggests DiY culture is 'a youth-centred and -directed cluster of interests and practices around green radicalism, direct action politics [and] new musical sounds and experiences'. DiY cultures attract youth committed to voluntarism, ecological sustainability, social justice and human rights. Significant for their cultural as much as their political activity, they are perhaps more accurately 'Do it *Ourselves*' cultures – networks of small, fluid *communities* of dissent (McKay 1998: 27).

Although group membership is commonly reported to be drawn from the middle class (albeit not-exclusively), possessing 'thick' solidarities and 'hot' loyalties (Turner 1999), these activist cultures manifest a new identity politics developing alongside or transcending more proscribed articulations based around class, ethnicity and gender (Hetherington 1998: 27).

One key characteristic differentiating DiY counter-tribes from pre-1960s and 1970s social movement vectors is that they are mobilized in response to complex anxieties and grievances resulting from real, though intangible and intractable, global threats associated with the nuclear, chemical, genetic engineering and other high-tech industries (for example, nuclear radiation and BSE – bovine spongiform encephalopathy). In an era of 'manufactured uncertainty' and mounting insecurity – said to have become pervasive features of that which Beck (1992) calls 'world risk society' – there is increasing awareness of the association between such 'mega-risks' and neo-liberal deregulationist policies. In a period where public confidence in expert decision-making practices has been undermined, 'solidarity from anxiety arises and becomes a political force' (Beck 1992: 49). Responding to mega-hazards and other grievances in local actions, DiY counter-tribes are not ideologically disengaged in the vein of Maffesolian neo-tribes. This is apparent in new tech-notribes, whose signs and practices cannot be reduced, in the lexicon of the Birmingham CCCS, to ineffectual 'rituals of resistance'. Not mere semiotic inversion or *bricolage*, or challenges to authority via endlessly looped stylistic homologies, the digitized dialogue, data streaming and other interventions of such nascent formations indicate a proactive sensibility to dangers posed by risks to health and the natural world.

DiY Technotribalism

The growth of modern mass communication technologies has given rise, part-icularly with the advent of computer-mediated communications (CMCs), to pervasive human-machine interfacing and the proliferation of cyber-enhanced (or even dependent) and networked micro-communities. As cyberculture has come to embody the constitution of a 'new order', 'through the transformation of the space of possibility for communicating, working and being' (Escobar 2000: 57), its technologies, while integral to capital's global reach, are being adopted by non-corporate and non-government social entities enhancing experience, participation and communication. New youth cultural formations have found contiguity with such Promethean advancements. Rapid developments in electronic media have shaped an aesthetically inventive youth culture, characteristically tolerant, non-sexist, ecological, global and detached from partisan politics. This new digitized environment provided the context for the emergence of technologically proficient counter-tribes, from alternative media collectives and community-access publishing outfits to sound systems, appropriating a range of increasingly accessible computer, audio and visual technologies. As Penley and Ross (1991: xv) point out, the repurposing of technology for countercultural ends has a lineage in early ham radio enthusiasts, personal computer hackers, independent radical desk-top publishers, audio and video scratchers, cable television, community radio stations, bulletin-board systems operators, and so forth. While the odds are perhaps still 'firmly stacked against the efforts of those committed to creating technological countercultures' (Penley and Ross 1991: xii), new technology has enhanced networking, educational and organizational capabilities, advanced tactics of dissent and globalized protest.

Amidst that which Castells (1996) has called the 'grass-rooting of the space of flows', CMC technologies have facilitated the emergence of DiY technotribes and strengthened the decentralized networking capabilities of existing organizational nodes as Pickerill (2001) suggests in her study of 'techno-environmentalism'. Of the 'techno-tribes' described by Terranova (2000) these new or enhanced nodes of resistance have perhaps more in common with 'New Edge' cyberpunks with their counter-cultural 'reality hacking' than 'Extropians' with their free-market libertarianism, though they probably do not share the evolutionary cyber-utopianism characteristic of both. Furthermore, electronic media, the Internet in particular, have facilitated 'translocal, associational forms of politics' (Redden 2001), enabling speedy cooperation between affinity groups for the purpose of mass resistance.

Here, I give specific attention to those technotribal nodes coevolving with a decentralized electronic music industry. Researchers have attended to the apparent 'democratized' status of techno music culture, accommodating local and global networks of sound composers, visual artists, music collectives and micro-labels, and largely sited beyond the reach of the transnational entertainment industry – despite efforts by the latter to assimilate it (Hesmondhalgh 1998; Gibson 2001). These post-rave technotribes are interconnected in an alternative technocultural network. Representing a possible site of belonging for technomads, each node, often possessing virtual presence (Gibson 1999), achieves its fullest (sometimes only) expression in the festal (in the real-time pleasurescape). As these youth formations are also configurations of 'DiY culture', they are fashionably committed to both pleasure *and* politics. Thus while they are 'passional' communities, evidencing the 'empathetic sociality' characteristic of Maffesolian neo-tribalism, they are not politically disengaged. Alongside the desire to disrupt the regulatory mechanisms of the state and counter corporate encroachment, these cultures harbour oppositional ideological agendas framed by risk-aware ecological sensibilities and non-colonialist attitudes. In the following I discuss two types of DiY technotribal events, the *party* and the *action*, both of which evidence youth cultural dissonance, and can be considered spaces of resistance.

Sound Systems and Party Politics

Sometimes referred to in Europe as a 'teknival', or in Australia, a 'doof', the free or by-donation (non-profit) dance party,[3] has its immediate background in the underground 'rave' tradition. Tactically resistant to commodification, such events rely upon voluntary contributions and are more likely than clubs to exude that which Gaillot (1999: 60) calls an 'horizontality of participation'.[4] They are often held by sound system collectives, which in the UK has included the DiY Collective, Exodus, the notorious Spiral Tribe, and more latterly Desert Storm and Bedlam. The sound system is a mobile DiY community, with roots in Jamaican dancehall and *émigré* reggae and hip-hop scenes. As a site of community performance, the sound system dance floor developed as 'a space of solidarity, survival and affirmation of communal sensibilities . . . a defensive enclave within a dominant white culture, a space in which the aesthetics, philosophies and pleasures of expressive Black cultures can be affirmed and celebrated' (Jones 1995: 8). In the UK, these 'collectively owned cultural and technological resources' (Jones 1995: 3), became infused with punk, traveller and from the late 1980s, techno-rave coordinates. The techno sound system saw intimate networks of sonic squatters hold discretely organized 'house' parties in disused warehouse spaces and at outdoor sites (cf. Rietveld 1998; Chan 1999; St John 2001a).

Many sound systems and party crews responsible for these events have responded to restrictive state regulatory processes, surveillance and encroaching commercialization corralling youth into domesticated leisure sites (clubs) – which Reynolds (1998: 424) has called 'pleasure prisons'. They have thus countered efforts to target and eliminate sites of transgressive youth practices, the most infamous being repressive measures under the UK Conservative government's 1994 Criminal Justice and Public Order Act, which, with the assistance of a series of heavy licensing laws, incriminated and 'almost decommissioned a lifestyle' (Dearling 1998: 1) – thereby fuelling direct action protests and overseeing something of a transition from entertainment to 'movement' (Jowers *et al.* 1999: 113; Hemment 1998). These unlicensed events, as evidenced by the early Blackburn warehouse parties, reconfigure disused industrial sites into transgressive sonorous spaces (Ingham *et al.* 1999). Backgrounded as such, these events have been widely reported to resemble a temporary autonomous zone (or TAZ) which Hakim Bey, in his highly influential anarcho-poetic tract (1991), described as the ultimate free

---

3. Free, minimal charge or by donation, such events are essentially non-profit – though sometimes community activist fundraisers.

4. Ostensibly non-hierarchical, nor representative of essential 'Truths' (for example, of the nation or religion), all participants are offered an equal share in the production of the art 'work', the event itself (Gaillot 1998: 62).

party architecture: an 'immediatist' enclave that, in its temporary duration, is beyond corporate media representation, commodification and state control.

The TAZ is an imaginal geography synonymous with the original acid house and free open-air raves. In these spaces, youth come to share a secret aesthetic, practising the 'forbidden' – transgressive embodiment, gender category rupturing, illicit substance use. Unlike the spectacularism attributed to subcultures like mod and punk, in rave, youth sought to 'disappear' (Rietveld 1993) from the gaze of the authorities and major media. In such sites where youth 'are leaving or "disappearing" themselves from the Grid of Alienation and seeking ways to restore human contact' (Bey 1993), the decentring or subversion of modern subjectivity is enabled. The *ekstasis* realized within such deterritorialized spaces has potentiated the rupturing of the possessive and Puritan codes of modern individualism. Influenced by Deleuze and Guattari's 'micropolitics of desire,' Hemment champions the 'incommensurable' and 'unassimilable' dance event as a sensuous intervention in the regulation of desire (1996: 26–7; see also Jordan 1995). As prelinguistic *jouissance*, the rave is also a refusal of the metaphysical priorities of the mind, enabling the disruption of phallocentric authority (Gilbert and Pearson 1999: 60–65, 87). In a further Foucauldian influenced position, Martin (1999: 95–6) argues that rave 'may prove to be one of the most dynamic political movements of recent years'. Techno-rave culture is ambiguous, decentralized and nomadic, and since it cannot be entirely known or controlled its inhabitants dwell outside total governmentality. While the transgressive character of the dance party evokes Maffesoli's 'second and hidden time' of the 'orgiasm', it is not strictly 'unproductive', as is the 'passional logic' of the festal, but is rather a site of becoming – potentiating 'narratives of dissensus' (Stanley 1995).

Political Partying: Reclaiming the Future

On the dance floor, it has been claimed, a 'politics of the moment' has come to replace a politics of representation. In dance cultural forms, '*being here now* was often given as the ultimate and only legitimate mode of political expression' (Gilbert and Pearson 1999: 172). While the act of 'disappearance' into the rave massive might approximate to little more than hedonistic individualism, the millenarian sensibility inscribed in its 'metaphysics of presence' (1999: 173) is valued by an expressive direct action politics. From the later half of the 1990s, in the UK and elsewhere, post-rave techno formations became implicated in modes of 'resistance' that, not necessarily synonymous with semiotic disruption, manifested a proactive and performative cultural politics. Facilitating *affect* and *meaning*, multimedia culture jamming has generated cultural works that – via sonic, visual and virtual manifestos reliant on an assemblage of new and pirated technologies (samplers, synths, MIDI, digital cameras, mobiles, laptops, CD ROMs) – have articulated alternative values and practices: a 'sound system for all'.[5] Raising spectacles designed to disrupt and alter social and political life, new formations and confrontational events demonstrate a highly reflexive technotribalism. By contrast to the near monolithic rave, where the demand for 'a shared present [conveys] . . . an imperative not to give in to the future' (Gaillot 1999: 17, 25), in such festal interventions technology is appropriated in order to reclaim the future (cf. St John 2001a).

Reclaim the Streets (RTS) is exemplary political partying. While South Downs Earth First! conducted the first roadblock in the Brighton 'Carmageddon' camp-aign in 1991 (Wall 1999), RTS did not evolve in its current 'carnival against capitalism' form until an action in London's Camden Town in 1995, which had followed mass road occupations mounted over the preceding years, especially against the M11 (Jordan 1998). Over the succeeding years, RTS actions, at once 'expressive symbolic acts and highly effective tactical techniques' (Szerszynski 1999: 215), have come to represent the contemporary face of popular public opposition to global capital. Street festivals wherein major city traffic arteries are occupied by coalitions of performers, 'avante gardeners', activists and ecstatic crowds dancing to the beat and rhythm of a sound system, these events have opposed repressive state legislation (Huq 1999: 22), challenged unsustainable transport/energy practices and drawn attention to the effects of a voracious car culture on local communities (cf. Luckman 2001). They are also a means by which privatized space – from which youth have been under constant threat of eviction – is reclaimed. Belonging to a lineage of folk and other musics involved in 'the struggle for a new culture' (Balliger 1995: 14), protest techno – that which Sydney's Pete Strong (also known as DJ Morphism) calls 'agit-house' – forms a prevalent sound track to these spontaneous communities of opposition.

Temporary liberation from the prevailing order, RTS and similar 'carnivals against capitalism' approximate the traditional carnival, often thought to represent a kind of institutionalized social 'safety valve'. Yet, direct action carnivals and 'ephemeral festivals of resistance' (Jordan 1998: 139) like RTS are, in the sense articulated by Szerszynski (1999), 'public rituals' or tactical 'performances' designed to achieve political agendas. The Situationist-style methods via which RTS activists 'reclaim' and reappropriate space, in a kind of mass public *detourne-ment* employing a range of theatrical and pragmatic tactics, exemplify Schechner's 'direct theatre': theatricalized political activity organized as 'a raw material for the universally displayed second theatre. TV news' (Schechner 1992: 104). Further-more, autonomous zones are where diverse alternative culture movement cells promote their agendas, amplify their message, disseminate literature, raise funds,

5. Ohms not Bombs sound system, http://www.omsnotbombs.org (accessed August 2002).

and recruit volunteers; these party-protests are diverse counter-spaces approximating to anarchist bazaars. And, as *fin-de-siècle* events indicate, such alternative cultural heterotopia hold significant alliance-building potential. Coinciding with G-8 leaders meeting in Birmingham, the global street party of 16 May 1998, which saw thirty RTS events mounted around the world, would see RTS take its place in a 'fledgling international grassroots movement' against transnational corporations (Klein 2000: 319).

With techno-activist youth collectives harnessing digital and cyber technologies in local campaigns to combat unethical industries and abuses of the rights of indigenous peoples, Australia has recently been a centre of RTS-like anarcho-corroborees. Earthdream2000[6] exemplified the progressive trajectory of contemporary youth formations, which in Australia, have demonstrated a growing awareness of the deep wounds of settler history upon the natural environment and Aboriginal inhabitants.[7] The direct action nomadic carnival attracted hundreds of people staging performances and mounting uranium mining actions in solidarity with Aboriginal people throughout southern and central Australia (cf. St John 2001b, 2001c, 2001d). Consisting of eco-activists, new spiritualists, electronic musicians, visual artists and circus performers, many of whom were affiliated with existing groups, Earthdream was a nomadic network of counter-tribes. Central to this mobile desert consortium were several techno sound systems including Ohms Not Bombs and Labrats, both formed to oppose the nuclear industry and support Aboriginal sovereignty. Originating in 1995 to protest French nuclear weapons testing in the Pacific, Sydney's Ohms has evolved into a mobile protest unit, their purpose built 'Peace Bus' a multi-media 'edutainment' complex (Strong 2001). Emerging from the successful 1998 Jabiluka uranium mine blockade, the Labrats consists of a clean energy sound-cinema system and a van operating on vegetable oil (Brown and Peckham 2001).[8]

In conjunction with other Earthdream contingents, in May 2000 these techno-tribes established a protest enclave on an intersection at the main entrance to the world's largest copper-uranium mine at Roxby Downs (Olympic Dam, operated by Western Mining Corporation [WMC]) 180 km to the south of Lake Eyre in South Australia. On day one of the camp, the Labrats van backed up on the main gate to the mine, its solar powered beats animating the carnival of protest fanning out ahead. Arabunna elder Kevin Buzzacott was at the helm exhorting WMC to cease the operation which represents a significant threat to natural and cultural heritage

6. Earthdream is an annual event, http://www.angelfire.com/mt/earthdream2000/ (accessed August 2002).

7. As is evidenced by 'feral' eco-tribes and other post-colonialist youth formations committed to the celebration and defence of natural and cultural heritage (St John 2000, 2001c).

8. Lab Rats, http://lab-rats.tripod.com (accessed August 2002).

values. That afternoon saw the inaugural Half Life Theatre Company stage an anti-uranium performance at the mine's gates. The pantomime, dramatizing corporate greed, land dispossession and radiation sickness under a hip-hop rhythm, was staged several times for protesters, miners, police and local school children (St John 2001b). Several 'camcordistas' and amateur film documentary makers captured events on film. DJ/producers played rhythms overlaid with audio snatches sampled from this and previous events.

Despite its diverse constituency, the Roxby protest enclave contextualized the generation of a group ethos, a kind of 'unicity'. But this 'ambience' was fuelled by a shared grievance: a common awareness of past injustices, present tragedies and pending horrors. Furthermore, demonstrating the potentials of new (and alternative) technologies in protest, this was a techno activist zone, a DiY multi-media event. It resembled a RTS event, which Szerszynski (1999: 221) argues is a significant site of 'performative' 'dialogue' with the wider community. As an event which aimed to 'draw in, involve and challenge the public observer', rather than merely occasion the 'emblematic performance of group membership', it draws further attention to the limitations within Maffesolian analysis, which does not anticipate the full social and political significance of contemporary tribalism.

Conclusion

The DiY technocultures and events described here demonstrate that while a 'passional logic' pertains, there are limitations to an unqualified Maffesolian approach. Accounts documenting networks of aesthetic and tragic micro-cultures present viable alternatives to subculture analysis, yet they are less than satisfactory when these are cultures of opposition. While contemporary consumer culture is excessive and festal, and where individuals are implicated in networks of identification (factors enhanced by digital and cyber technologies), post-structuralism tends to vacillate on the question of *being together* in opposition. What place does collective agency, the pragmatic effort to influence public opinion, have in 'postmodern sociality'? While the technocultural counter-tribes under consideration are not subculturalists, the suspect coordinates of an unqualified neo-tribalism have thus been identified. Are their members then 'post-subculturalists' in the manner implied by Muggleton (1997) who describes fluid subjectivities in a period of relative structural indeterminacy, amplified media saturation and multiple self-identifications? A definitive answer hardly seems appropriate. While such may indeed be the case for desubjectified nomads of the dance floor, the nodes of sociality and theatricality considered above consist of memberships responding to real threats and grievances, who employ a critical reason attributed to modernity. We would therefore at the very least lean towards the development of differential 'subcultural' modelling. This is not however, to suggest that new activist micro-cultures are always predominantly rationalist or strategic for, as we have seen, they are orgiastic and ideological, their intention a combination of party and protest, their rendezvous carnivals of dissent – often a cross pollination of the *festival* and direct *action*.

With a particular focus on the interfacing of technology and new youth form-ations, this chapter has revised popular tropes of youth as nihilistic or indifferent. While the technoculturalists and the post-rave posses explored here may be spectacular stylists, engaging in theatrical excess, their discourse, digitalized images, sounds and performances are data-streamed in the service of new activist causes. While the membership of the 'rave massive', at best, participate in a micro-politics of the present, technotribes are often critical of the past, dissatisfied with the present and involved in efforts to reclaim the future. Here is thus a productive cultural politics. Asserting control over an array of technologies and media, they are 'passional' communities variously establishing liberated space, reconciling with indigenous peoples, identifying with threatened nature, and so forth. Antag-onized by the commodification of life, as we have seen with sound systems and the TAZ, or motivated by ecological ethics and standards of social justice, as in Reclaim the Streets and Earthdream2000, post-rave technotribes evidence a strong will to venture beyond and define themselves against the 'parent culture'. With members possessing the surface appearance of style tourists, these technotribes may possess porous boundaries. Yet they also demonstrate a strong will to differ-ence, possessing a depth of meaning and purpose.

References

Balliger, R. (1995), 'The Sound of Resistance', in R. Sakolsky and F. Wei-Han Ho (eds), *Sounding Off: Music as Subversion/Resistance/Revolution*, New York: Autonomedia.

Bauman, Z. (1996), 'From Pilgrim to Tourist: or a Short History of Identity', in S. Hall and P. du Gay (eds) *Questions of Cultural Identity*, London: Sage.

Beck, U. (1986/1992), *Risk Society: Towards a New Modernity*, London: Sage.

Bennett, A. (1999), 'Subcultures or Neo-tribes? Rethinking the Relationship between Youth, Style and Musical Taste', *Sociology*, 33 (3): 599-617.

Bey, H. (1985/1991), *TAZ: The Temporary Autonomous Zone – Ontological Anarchy and Poetic Terrorism*, New York: Autonomedia.

Bey, H. (1993), 'Permanent TAZs', http://www.t0.or.at/hakimbey/paz.htm (accessed August 2002).

Brown, I. and Peckham, M. (2001), 'Tuning Technology to Ecology: Labrats Sola Powered Sound System', in G. St John (ed.), *FreeNRG: Notes From the Edge of the Dance Floor*, Melbourne: Common Ground.

Castells, M. (1996), *The Rise of the Network Society*, Malden MA: Blackwell.

Chan, S. (1999), 'Bubbling Acid: Sydney's Techno Underground', in R. White (ed.), *Australian Youth Subcultures: On the Margins and in the Mainstream*, Hobart: ACYS Publications.

Cohen, E., Ben-Yehuda, N. and Aviad, J. (1987), 'Recentering the World: the Quest for "Elective" Centres in a Secularized Universe', *Sociological Review*, 35 (2): 320–436.

Dearling, A. (ed.) (1998), *No Boundaries: New Travellers on the Road (Outside of England)*, Dorset: Enabler Publications.

Doherty, B., Paterson, M. and Seel, B. (eds) (2000), 'Direct Action in British Environmentalism', in B. Seel, M. Paterson and B. Doherty (eds), *Direct Action in British Environmentalism*, London: Routledge.

Escobar, A. (2000), 'Welcome to Cyberia: Notes on the Anthropology of Cyber-culture', in D. Bell and B. Kennedy (eds), *The Cybercultures Reader*, London: Routledge.

Gaillot, M. (1999), *Multiple Meaning: Techno – An Artistic and Political Laboratory of the Present*, Paris: Dis Voir.

Gibson, C. (1999), 'Subversive Sites: Rave Culture, Spatial Politics, and the Internet', *Area*, 31 (1): 19–33.

Gibson, C. (2001), 'Appropriating the Means of Production: Dance Music Industries and Contested Digital Space', in G. St John (ed.), *FreeNRG: Notes from the Edge of the Dance Floor*, Sydney: Pluto.

Gilbert, J. and Pearson, E. (1999), *Discographies: Dance Music, Culture and the Politics of Sound*, London: Routledge.

Gore, G. (1997), 'The Beat Goes on: Trance, Dance and Tribalism in Rave Culture', in H. Thomas (ed.), *Dance in the City*, London: Macmillan Press.

Halfacree, K. and Kitchin, R. '"Madchester Rave on": Placing the Fragments of Popular Music', *Arena*, 28 (1): 47–55.

Hemment, D. (1996), 'E is for Ekstasis', *New Formations*, 31: 23–38.

Hemment, D. (1998), 'Dangerous Dancing and Disco Riots: the Northern Warehouse Parties', in G. McKay (ed.), *DiY Culture: Party and Protest in Nineties Britain*, London: Verso.

Hesmondhalgh, D. (1998), 'The British Dance Music Industry: a Case Study of Independent Cultural Production', *British Journal of Sociology*, 49 (2): 234–51.

Hetherington, K. (1994), 'The Contemporary Significance of Schmalenbach's Concept of the Bund', *Sociological Review*, 42: 1–25.

Hetherington, K. (1998), *Expressions of Identity: Space, Performance, Politics*, London: Sage.

Hollands, R. (2002), 'Divisions in the Dark: Youth Cultures, Transitions and Segmented Consumption Spaces in the Night-Time Economy', *Journal of Youth Studies*, 5 (2): 153–71.

Huq. R. (1999), 'The Right to Rave: Opposition to the Criminal Justice and Public Order Act 1994', in T. Jordan (ed.), *Storming the Millennium: The New Politics of Change*, London: Lawrence & Wishart.

Ingham, J., Purvis, M. and Clarke, D. (1999), 'Hearing Places, Making Spaces: Sonorous Geographies, Ephemeral Rhythms, and the Blackburn Warehouse Parties', *Environment and Planning D: Society and Space*, 17: 23–305

Jones, S. (1995), 'Rocking the House: Sound System Cultures and the Politics of Space', *Journal of Popular Music Studies*, 7: 1–24.

Jordan, T. (1995), 'Collective Bodies: Raving and the Politics of Gilles Deleuze and Felix Guattari', *Body and Society*, 1 (1): 125–44.

Jordan, J. (1998), 'The Art of Necessity: the Subversive Imagination of Anti-Road Protest and Reclaim the Streets', in G. McKay (ed.), *DiY Culture: Party and Protest in Nineties Britain*, London: Verso.

Jowers, P., Durrschmidt, J., O'Docherty, R. and Purdue, D. (1999), 'Affective and Aesthetic Dimensions of Contemporary Social Movements in South West England', *Innovation*, 12 (1): 99–118.

Klein, N. (2000), *No Logo*, London: Flamingo.

Luckman, S. (2001), 'What are they Raving on About? Temporary Autonomous Zones and "Reclaim the Streets"', *Perfect Beat*, 5 (2): 49–68.

Malbon, B. (1998), 'Clubbing: Consumption, Identity and the Spatial Practices of every-night Life', in T. Skelton and G. Valentine (eds), *Cool Places: Geographies of Youth Cultures*, London: Routledge.

Malbon, B. (1999), *Clubbing: Dancing, Ecstasy and Vitality*, London: Routledge.

Maffesoli, M. (1988), '*Jeux de Masques*: Postmodern Tribalism', *Design Issues*, 4 (1–2): 141–51

Maffesoli, M. (1982/1993), *The Shadow of Dionysus: A Contribution to the Sociology of the Orgy*, Albany: State University of New York Press.

Maffesoli, M. (1988/1995), *The Time of the Tribes: the Decline of Individualism in Mass Society*, London: Sage.

Maffesoli, M. (1997), 'The Return of Dionysus', in P. Sulkunen, J. Holmwood, H. Radner and G. Schulze (eds), *Constructing the New Consumer Society*, London: Macmillan.

Martin, D. (1999), 'Power Play and Party Politics: the Significance of Raving', *Journal of Popular Culture*, 31 (4): 77–99.

Martin, G. (2002), 'Conceptualizing Cultural Politics in Subcultural and Social Movement Studies', *Social Movement Studies*, 1 (1): 73–88.

McKay, G. (1996), *Senseless Acts of Beauty: Cultures of Resistance since the Sixties*, London: Verso.

McKay, G. (1998), 'DiY Culture: Notes Toward an Intro', in G. McKay (ed.), *DiY Culture: Party and Protest in Nineties Britain*, London: Verso.

McNeish, W. (2000), 'The Vitality of Local Protest: Alarm UK and the British Anti-Roads Protest Movement', in B. Seel, M. Paterson and B. Doherty (eds), *Direct Action in British Environmentalism*, London: Routledge.

Melucci, A. (1989), *Nomads of the Present: Social Movements and Individual Needs in Contemporary Society*, London: Hutchinson Radius.

Muggleton, D. (1997), 'The Post-Subculturalist', in S. Redhead, D. Wynne and J. O'Connor (eds), *The Clubcultures Reader: Readings in Popular Cultural Studies*, Oxford: Blackwell.

Newton, J. (1988), 'Aborigines, Tribes and the Counterculture', *Social Analysis*, 23: 53–71.

Penley, C. and Ross, A (eds) (1991), *Technoculture*, Minneapolis MN: University of Minnesota Press.

Pickerill, J. (2001), 'Weaving a Green Web? Environmental Activists' use of Computer Mediated Communication in Britain', unpublished Ph.D. thesis, Department of Geography, University of Newcastle upon Tyne, http://www. jennypickerill.info/thesis.html (accessed August 2002).

Plows, A. (1995), 'Eco-Philosophy and Popular Protest: the Significance and Implications of the Ideology and Actions of the Donga Tribe', in C. Barker and M. Tyldesley (eds), *Alternative Futures and Popular Protest Conference Papers*, *Vol. 1*, Manchester: Manchester Metropolitan University Press.

Purkis, J. (2000), 'Modern Millenarians? Anticonsumerism, Anarchism and the New Urban Environmentalism', in B. Seel, M. Paterson and B. Doherty (eds), *Direct Action in British Environmentalism*, London: Routledge.

Redden, G. (2001), 'Networking Dissent: the Internet and the Anti-Globalization Movement', *Mots Pluriels*, 18, http://www.arts.uwa.edu.au/MotsPluriels/ MP1801gr.html (accessed August 2002).

Reynolds, S. (1998), *Energy Flash: A Journey Through Rave Music and Dance Culture*, London: Picador.

Rietveld, H. (1993), 'Living the Dream', in S, Redhead (ed.), *Rave Off: Politics and Deviance in Contemporary Youth Culture*, Aldershot: Avebury.

Rietveld, H. (1998), 'Repetitive Beats: Free Parties and the Politics of Contemporary DiY Dance Culture in Britain', in G. McKay (ed.), *DiY Culture: Party and Protest in Nineties Britain*, London: Verso.

Schechner, R. (1992), 'Invasions Friendly and Unfriendly: the Dramaturgy of Direct Theatre', in J. Reinelt and J. Roach (eds), *Critical Theory and Performance*, Ann Arbor MI: University of Michigan Press.

Shields, R. (1992), 'The Individual, Consumption Cultures and the Fate of Community', in R. Shields (ed.), *Lifestyle Shopping: The Subject of Consumption*, London: Routledge.

Stanley, C. (1995), 'Teenage Kicks: Urban Narratives of Dissent not Deviance', *Crime, Law and Social Change*, 23: 91–119.

St John, G. (1997), 'Going Feral: Authentica on the Edge of Australian Culture'. *The Australian Journal of Anthropology*, 8 (2): 167–98.

St John, G. (2000), 'Ferals: Terra-ism and Radical Ecologism in Australia', *Journal of Australian Studies*, 64: 208–16.

St John, G. (2001a), 'Doof! Australian Post-Rave Culture', in G. St John (ed.). *FreeNRG: Notes from the Edge of the Dance Floor*, Melbourne: Common Ground.

St John, G. (2001b), 'Techno Terra-ism: Feral Systems and Sound Futures', in G. St John (ed.), *FreeNRG: Notes from the Edge of the Dance Floor*, Melbourne: Common Ground.

St John, G. (2001c), 'Australian (Alter)natives: Cultural Drama and Indigeneity'. *Social Analysis: Journal of Cultural and Social Practice*, 45 (1): 122–40.

St John, G. (2001d), 'Earthdreaming for a Nuclear Free Future', *Arena Magazine*. 53: 41–4.

Strong, P. (2001), 'Doofstory: Sydney Park to the Desert', in G. St John (ed.). *FreeNRG: Notes from the Edge of the Dance Floor*, Melbourne: Common Ground.

Szerszynski, B. (1999), 'Performing Politics: the Dramatics of Environmental Protest', in L. Ray and A. Sayer (eds), *Culture and Economy After the Cultural Turn*, London: Sage.

Terranova, T. (2000), 'Post-Human Unbounded: Artificial Evolution and High-Tech Subcultures', in D. Bell and B. Kennedy (eds), *The Cybercultures Reader*, London: Routledge.

Turner, B. (1999), 'The Possibility of Primitiveness: Towards a Sociology of Body Marks in Cool Societies', *Body & Society*, 5 (2–3): 39–50.

Wall, D. (1999), *Earth First! and the Anti-Roads Movement: Radical Environmentalism and Comparative Social Movements*, London: Routledge.

6

Bridging the Micro-Macro Gap: Is There Such a Thing as a Post-subcultural Politics?[1]

Oliver Marchart

If we look back to the heroic years of cultural and subcultural studies what we will find is an increasing awareness of the fact that politics is deeply and inextricably inscribed into the field of culture. Following Gramsci, Foucault, DeCerteau and others, cultural and subcultural studies shifted the focus of social research towards what is sometimes called the 'micro-politics' of everyday life. The latent political nature of cultural practices and cultural identities came to be excavated during these years. Yet, by emphasizing cultural 'micro-politics', what had previously been considered ordinary politics (the political field, or 'macro-politics') was increasingly being pushed out of focus. As a consequence, macro-political questions seem to remain largely neglected today.[2] What in the following will be called the heroic version of cultural and subcultural studies, in the words of Lawrence Grossberg, 'too easily ignores the macropolitical success of hegemonic struggles in favour of abstract micropolitical struggle'; for such accounts of the popular, he argues, 'fail to address the actual context of relations, the articulations, between popular culture and systemic politics' (Grossberg 1997: 236). And he insists that 'popular discourse is not about culture, but about the struggles to articulate the relations between social and economic power, political forms of agency, and modes of discursive practices' (Grossberg 1997: 223). While many students of the

1. Some of the arguments of this chapter were presented at a section of the Third International Crossroads in Cultural Studies Conference, University of Birmingham, 24 June 2000. I would like to thank and acknowledge the coorganizer of the section, Shu-fen Lin, for the continuous discussion we had on this topic.

2. From the 'other side', that is from the point of view of 'macro-' political theory, only a few attempts so far have been made to enter a dialogue with cultural studies and subcultural studies. What is still lacking – with the exception of some attempts (for example, Street 1997; Finlayson and Martin 1997; Dean 2000) – is a theoretical exchange between cultural theory and political theory. Such a dialogue should not only consist of the exchange of more or less disconnected arguments but should alter the conceptual and theoretical framework of either field, thereby creating a new terrain of investigation.

field might subscribe to this view, the very *nature of the relation* between micro-politics and macro-politics, or, in other words, between the politics of culture and the politics of politics, remains ill defined and rather obscure. In what follows, I will argue that if one wants to be faithful to the initial *political* agenda of cultural and subcultural studies, and if one seeks to come to a clear account of the relation between micro- and macro-politics, it is imperative to redirect the focus once more towards macro-political questions.[3]

As it is impossible in one chapter to discuss in full length the genealogy of subcultural and cultural studies, I will restrict myself to a discussion of the category of the political and of the relation between micro- and macro-politics within the Gramscian and post-Gramscian frameworks. I hope to point out a way in which it will be feasible to (re-)introduce a *stronger notion* of the political into (post-)(sub)cultural studies by strengthening the conceptual and theoretical role of hegemony theory. To do so, we will have to revisit the moment in British Gramscianism during the late 1970s and early 1980s when, on the one hand, Birmingham cultural studies (stretching the 'micro'-aspects), and, on the other, hegemony theory as developed by Ernesto Laclau and Chantal Mouffe (stretching the 'macro'-aspect of politics), parted company. If today, as Angela McRobbie claims, 'the place and role of culture' . . . 'remains underdeveloped in Laclau's analysis' (1994: 51), then the place of macro-politics remains underdeveloped in most works in the field of cultural studies.[4] But, given the close theoretical relations within British

3. To call for a renewed engagement with macro-political questions might sound bewildering given the political self-understanding of cultural and subcultural studies. I would therefore like to emphasize that this call should in no way be confused with frequent accusations as to the decreasing political or practical engagement of cultural studies practitioners. I do not intend to accuse a whole (quasi-)discipline of losing its political verve. My call to once more engage with macro-political questions is restricted primarily to the *theoretical* plane. Yet to call for a shift towards macro-politics might sound bewildering for another reason, since all efforts of cultural and subcultural studies went into the deconstruction of the link between (sub)culture and the political, between the micro-and the macro-levels of politics. While this was an important effort to rehabilitate the realm of culture as political through and through, I hold that today we have to rethink where we want to put the emphasis in this operation, for the line between the micro and the macro seems to have become entirely blurred. However, we have to remember that to deconstruct a rigid binarism is not the same as to entirely conflate it. Today, our efforts should go into disentangling, rather than conflating, the micro and the macro.

4. There are only a couple of major works on questions of macro-politics such as Hall *et al.* (1978), Hall (1988) and Grossberg (1992). Is it not striking that in the 'Culture, Media and Identities' textbook series published by the Open University Press – perhaps the most elaborated presentation of cultural studies so far – macro-political issues were not included, or included, at best, only in the form of cultural *regulation* (see Thompson 1997)? This is all the more surprising as Stuart Hall (1997), in a key contribution to the *Regulation* volume, heavily relies on Ernesto Laclau. Where Laclau's own work is concerned there is not necessarily a disagreement with respect to the important role of culture in constructing a new hegemonic formation, but a difference in perspective: Laclau's focus is on politics, and culture is simply not part of his research agenda.

post-war Gramscianism between Laclau's early articles and Birmingham cultural studies under the directorship of Stuart Hall, a counter-reading of (sub)cultural studies through the eyes of Laclauian hegemony theory can easily be justified. Concepts like hegemony, articulation, populism or discourse are located within a space of shared theoretical and analytical concerns. It is safe to assume that Laclau's deconstruction of deterministic Marxism and his development – along Gramscian lines – of the concept of articulation (Slack 1996: 112–30), contributed enormously to the development of British cultural studies. It is by returning to this historical point of convergence of micro- and macro-theories of culture and politics that it will eventually be possible to re-engage with the following set of questions: what does it take for subcultures to be political? What criteria have to be met by micro-practices in order to 'go macro'? Do we need a new concept of 'organization'? Can there be a subcultural politics of pure particularism or does it take a dimension of universalism? And how do we have to tackle these problems in the times of *post*-subcultures? In short: is there or can there be a (post-)(sub)cultural politics?

After Subcultural Heroism

Today's position of decidedly *post*-subcultural studies must avoid the double-folded fallacy so characteristic of the heroic phase of cultural and subcultural studies. The first aspect of this fallacy consists in what one might call the 'incorporation myth'. By this I understand the common argument that presents the relation between subculture and mainstream in terms of the 'incorporation' of the former by the latter. Not only is 'incorporation' a myth because it underestimates the extent of multi-faceted collaboration between the seemingly small world of subculture and big business, but we will go even further by claiming that the very distinction between subculture and mainstream is not tenable anymore for both empirical and theoretical reasons. Secondly, it is imperative to take issue with the 'heroic' or romantic idea according to which the subordinate cultural groups act subversively or counter-hegemonically simply by virtue of their subordinate position. There is no intrinsic resistant or subversive quality to subcultures (which, by the way, is one of the reasons why it does not make sense to speak of 'cooptation' by the mainstream). Now, it would be difficult to present these two aspects of subcultural ideology - fear of incorporation and subcultural heroism – as distinct in nature. They are structured around a single, albeit absent, core: the exclusion or disavowal of the political.

This might be an irritating claim, for we came to know of cultural studies and subcultural studies as projects proud of their 'politicalness', as projects of *politicization* even, and I do not intend to deny the politicizing effects that cultural studies had on the humanities. However, if we have a closer look at the imaginary coordinates of the heroic ideology it will appear that all the seemingly political categories employed by this discourse on youth and pop culture – rebellion, subversion, dissidence and deviance, liberation, disturbance, and so forth – are based on rather simple and *non*-political binary oppositions. A vertical relation is posited between a subordinated term and a dominant term: subculture versus mainstream, underground versus 'overground', alternative labels versus major labels, individual production (for example, home-grown electronic music) versus music industries. These binary oppositions are definitely part of pop music's ideological self-description, but does that mean that they necessarily correspond to social reality?

Obviously, 'underground' in such a discourse is presented as authentic and innovative and is contrasted with a parasitic mainstream. This is also why the *movement* from the subordinate term 'underground' or 'subculture' to the dominant term 'mainstream' is often described as a process of *becoming mainstream* or *going overground*, to be opposed by any 'authentic' member of a given subculture. Common expressions like 'recuperation', 'cooptation', 'appropriation', 'incorporation', or, in more Deleuzian fashion, 'reterritorialization', are supposed to capture the overwhelming force of the dominant term, which has to be resisted at all costs (and the stronger the enemy the more heroic the resistance). On the other hand, a term like *sell out* is directed against those members of the subordinate group who dare to change sides, thereby acting like 'traitors' to the cause of subcultural resistance. In all cases the 'heroic' term is the subordinated one, and it remains heroic as long as it *resists* any movement towards the dominant term.

It goes without saying that the heroic view of subculture is a rather simple one (and today, in the post-heroic phase of subcultural studies, we are witnessing the breakdown of those heroic fantasies). But is it a *political* one? I submit that while the heroic ideology of subculture plays with the inventory of political terms like 'resistance', 'subversion', and so forth, in most cases there is no politics in subcultural 'politics'. To substantiate this claim as to the lack of politics in subcultural politics and to allow for a better understanding of the functioning of the heroic phase of subcultural studies, we should return, for a moment, to the *locus classicus* of the heroic phase, Dick Hebdige's *Subculture: The Meaning of Style* (originally published in 1979), which is, of course, one of the cornerstones of what came to be called the 'resistance through style' or 'resistance through rituals' paradigm of 1970s subcultural studies. In Hebdige's work, one will encounter the assumption that from the point of view of the media mainstream, subcultures represent noise, disturbance and blockage of the system of representation; and the tendency is strong to ascribe a subversive and resistant power to such noise. What in his view 'style' and 'expressive forms' of subcultures express is the fundamental tension between those in power and those in subordinated positions. This does not always amount to a naïve idealization of deviant youth cultures, as Hebdige sees very clearly that, to some extent, they stand on a common ideological ground with the dominant culture: they speak a language commonly available at that time. Punk, for instance, expressed the widely publicized mood of crisis in the late 1970s, the 'gloomy, apocalyptic ambience' with massive unemployment and riots like that of the Notting Hill Carnival. Yet, 1970s cultural studies often resorts to a view of ideology and a model of hegemony according to which the hegemonic block, in order to remain consistent, has to absorb supposedly *pre-given* cultures of resistance: 'a credible image of social cohesion can only be maintained through the appropriation and redefinition of cultures of resistance (e.g. working-class youth cultures)' (Hebdige 1987: 85). Here, Hebdige comes close to construing subcultures as some sort of substance – *noise* from the viewpoint of the dominant system, and that *precedes* any cooptation by the latter. For the same reason he takes subcultures to be the source of original innovations: innovations that 'freeze' as soon as they enter the commodification process. As a consequence of this hidden economism, he arrives at the quasi-mythical model of an eternal cycle of incorporation: 'The cycle leading from opposition to defusion, from resistance to incorporation encloses each successive subculture' (Hebdige 1987: 100). This myth of an unavoidable movement from the 'authentic' self-made or street-style subculture to the 'synthetic' appropriation by the image and fashion industries is precisely that: a myth. It is the subcultural myth of temptation, treason and heroic resistance against commod-ification.

Post-heroic research in subcultures has shown, on the other hand, that it is more than questionable to present as schematic a model as the 'cycle of incorporation'. Steve Redhead, for instance, could demonstrate that in the case of Acid House and the 1988 'Summer of Love', early media reports did not in the least detect anything new or irritating, no signs of subcultural 'noise': 'The tale was that Acid House was nothing new; it was merely another, much lauded, link in the subcultural chain, replaying and reworking the 1950s, 1960s, or 1970s - the "Golden Age" of youth culture and youth subcultures' (Redhead 1990: 1). At that point, the 'style' of the ravers was not understood as being subversive, irritating or 'resistant'; rather it was taken to be 'a style without substance', as the *Sunday Times* put it. It was only in October 1988 that the phase of more-or-less disinterested reports came to an end, and the apocalyptic dimensions of Acid House came to be construed by the media: now newspapers headlined with 'Acid House Horror', 'Ban this Killer Music', 'Girl 21 Drops Dead at Disco', and 'Evil of Ecstasy'.[5] Redhead concludes *against* Hebdige that one has to give up the notorious explanations of subcultural theory in as far as they presuppose a 'depth model' (Redhead 1993: 23): cultural studies

---

5. It is noteworthy that today, fourteen years later, the media still report on the dangers of ecstasy – which, among other things, attests to the fact that the category of 'news value' is largely a fiction.

and sociological theories of deviance always presupposed a 'real', authentic subculture *behind* its representation in the media; and the latter were accused of distorting the real picture of subculture: 'Previous theorists of post-war pop and deviance had tended to look beneath, or behind, the surfaces of the shimmering mediascape in order to discover the "real" subculture, apparently always distorted by the manufactured press and television image' (Redhead 1990: 2). Redhead takes issue with this depth model arguing that punk, to take only the most prominent example, should not be understood as pure street-culture nor should one think of it as merely another art-school fake; rather, it constitutes a hybrid mixture between synthetic manufacturing and 'authenticity'. If we accept this observation as valid, then we can infer two things: *empirically* it is impossible to detect a clear line between the authentic and the synthetic, and *theoretically* such a distinction would be unfounded in the first place because it presupposes a depth-model according to which one part of social reality is more 'real' or more 'authentic' than another part.

From 'Indirect' to Direct Action: Antagonism

It should by now be clear in what sense the incorporation myth of 'going Big Business' stands in the way of any meaningful theorization of the process of 'going macro-political'. As long as the main goal is to resist economic cooptation by defending micro-political practices *eo ipso*, the question of forging a passage towards the macro-political will simply not be on the agenda. In other words, as long as subcultural practices are considered always already political (simply by virtue of resisting cooptation) there is no further need to take the second step into the macro-political. The always already-structure of the argument allows heroic theorists to define micro-politics as an oblique, non-self-conscious, indirect form of counter-hegemonial disagreement. This is why Hebdige can claim that 'the challenge to hegemony which subcultures represent is not issued directly by them rather it is expressed obliquely, in style' (Hebdige 1987: 17). Yet, such form of 'oblique' challenge can be called political only in a very qualified sense. At best it could be called conspiratorial as opposed to confrontational (which would be, as we will see, the macro-political form of resistance). How and why should this form of '*in*direct action' ever turn into 'direct action'?

If something is astonishing in Hebdige's *Subculture* book, then it is precisely the author's aversion to direct action, which is expressed by his eagerness to distinguish subcultures from 'counterculture' as defined in a footnote. By counterculture, Hebdige, following Clarke *et al.* (1976), refers to 'the amalgam of "alternative" middle-class youth cultures – the hippies, the flower children, the yippies – which grew out of the 60s, and came to prominence during the period 1967-70' (Hebdige 1987: 148). In contrast to subcultures, countercultures oppose the dominant culture in an explicitly political and ideological way, that is, by political action and the elaboration of alternative institutions such as Underground Press, communes, cooperatives, and so forth. Hebdige concludes the passage with the observation: 'whereas opposition in subculture is, as we have seen, displaced into symbolic forms of resistance, the revolt of the middle-class youth tends to be more articulate, more confident, more directly expressed' (Hebdige 1987: 148). Now, one need not employ a particularly sophisticated deconstructive reading strategy in order to realize that this passage – the only one conceptually making the link to macro-politics - is situated at the *margins* of the book: in a footnote. Still it is this footnote on which the whole macro-political aspiration of *Subculture* silently hinges. Or, to put it differently, in the symptomatic reading I propose, *the political* in the form of counterculture is 'buried' in this footnote where counterculture serves as sub-culture's political mirror-image which, as it were, keeps *haunting* subcultural theory.[6] The 'implicit' politicization that, more often than not, is only read into a given subculture by the subcultural theorist, is contrasted in this passage with the image of an 'explicit', that is, more articulate, confident and direct politicization close to the structure and strategy of political movements. And yet these macro-political forms of youth-cultural action are discarded as middle class and relegated into a footnote.

So the main ambition of the heroic phase of subcultural studies – and also of what came to be known as 'cultural populism' (McGuigan 1992) – was to blur the line between the cultural and the political, between subcultural resistance 'at a level beneath the consciousness of the individual members of a spectacular subculture' (Hebdige 1987: 195) and 'self-conscious' countercultural action, that is to say, between the micro- and the macro-aspects of politics. And it certainly was neces-sary at that time to direct our attention towards the *latent* political aspects of popular culture. Yet even at the high point of heroic subcultural studies it made no sense to ignore completely the line between micro and macro and the moment when the 'culturally' latent becomes 'politically' explicit. Of course, one secretly knew and one had to account for the fact – be it only in a footnote – that there will

6. More than a decade after Hebdige, Steve Redhead (1990: 75) sees different reasons to question such view: 'Such standard ways of reading the relations between subcultures, youth culture, pop and deviance in particular social formations dissolved in the 1980s as the fixed identities and meanings of youth styles gave way to supposed fluidity of positions, poses and desires and a much-hailed (in post-modernist circles) transitory, fleeting adherence to lifestyles – for some theorists, the sign of post-modernity'. While it is certainly true that the youth-cultural picture has become more complex and confusing, I would refrain from understanding Hebdige's remarks as only a historical account of 1960s counterculture. Rather, the latter plays the role of a distant relative who pays an unexpected visit reminding the self-enclosed subcultural family of the outside world. It is as if Kafka knocked at the door of the club reminding the 'in-crowd': 'In the struggle between yourself and the world, second the world.'

always remain a difference between, say, supposedly 'active' audience reception and political action proper, between subcultural rituals – as flawlessly described, from a Bourdieuian perspective, in Thornton (1995) – and countercultural politics. Yet there was no way of accounting for the *logic of the passage* from culture to politics as long as one was caught in the heroic myths of subcultural studies. Thus, one stopped at an analysis, which is of course necessary but not sufficient, of sedimented micro-political common sense (Gramsci's *senso comune*) instead of studying the political moment of the latter's *reactivation*. What is needed today is an analysis of the passage between culture and macro-politics, that is, an analysis of the process of 'becoming macro'; because it is via this process that popular common sense is re-coded politically (as progressive, conservative, reactionary, resistant, or revolutionary).[7]

At this point it is advisable to bring in hegemony theory, for what it offers is not only an explanation of macro-political structures but, first and foremost, a theory of the *passage* from the micro-political to the macro-political, that is to say, on the moment of political reactivation when subcultures turn into politicized counter-cultures (or when, to name the other important field of 'heroic' micro-political research, 'active audiences' become *macro*-politically active and start functioning as citizens). This moment, the moment when *the political* in the strict sense enters the scene, can be found in the conversion of what Laclau and Mouffe call 'relations of subordination' (which are socio-cultural) into 'relations of oppression' (which are political in the strict sense):

> We shall understand by a *relation of subordination* that in which an agent is subjected to the decisions of another - an employee with respect to an employer, for example, or in certain forms of family organization the woman with respect to the man, and so on. We shall call *relations of oppression*, in contrast, those relations of subordination which have transformed themselves into sites of antagonisms. (Laclau and Mouffe 1985: 153–4)

It is important to understand that the representation of relations of subordination within popular culture – for example, stereotypes of women in subordinated gender positions in TV programs – can only be studied as an indicator of *latent* antagonization, respectively *sedimented* antagonisms. While they do have political roots, it would not be correct to describe such relations as antagonistic in the strict sense because

---

7. One way of framing this movement is through a theory of populism, which I cannot, for reasons of space, develop in this chapter. For a somewhat more detailed account of, on the one hand, the relation between culture (or the popular) and politics (or the 'people'), and, on the other hand, of the even more fundamental relation or difference between politics and the political, see Marchart (2002b).

a relation of subordination establishes, simply, a set of differential positions between social agents, and we already know that a system of differences which constructs each social identity as *positivity* not only cannot be antagonistic, but would bring about the ideal conditions for the elimination of all antagonisms - we would be faced with a sutured social space, from which every equivalence would be excluded. (Laclau and Mouffe 1985: 154)

In other words, a social system which could be described as a 'sutured', closed and self-contained system of differences would not be able to establish any antagonistic, that is, macro-political relation in which differences will be united against a common enemy into a chain of equivalence.[8] Under these conditions – without any politics proper – one actually would encounter the 'pure' social or cultural: sedimented forms of traditions, rites, stereotypes, clichés in a purely repetitive and differential form. It is worth quoting Laclau and Mouffe at length on this point:

> It is only to the extent that the positive differential character of the subordinated subject position is subverted that the antagonism can emerge. 'Serf', 'slave', and so on, do not designate in themselves antagonistic positions; it is only in terms of a different discursive formation, such as 'the rights inherent to every human being', that the differential positivity of these categories can be subverted and the subordination constructed as oppression. This means that there is no relation of oppression without the presence of a discursive 'exterior' from which the discourse of subordination can be interrupted. (Laclau and Mouffe 1985: 154)

Let us take the example of racist constructions of cultural identity. Nothing in these racist representations automatically triggers a civic rights movement, nothing automatically leads to the politicization of sedimented micro-frontiers within popular culture into a political antagonism. What has to be assumed is an additional category if we want to account for the moment of reactivation where the sedimented racist practices suddenly come to be perceived as relations of oppression one has to confront. The role of such an additional category which comes 'from outside' can be played, for instance, by human rights discourse, which might turn out to be the universalizing means to effectively establish a chain of equivalence around certain topics (certain relations of subordination). But in a more radical sense it is *the antagonism itself* that comes from the outside, because it is not itself an element of a differential system of subordination but, rather, the event by which

---

8. This is why antagonism is defined by Laclau and Mouffe as an *equivalential* relation: a series of differential positions is united into an equivalential chain against the 'entity' that denies it. Yet this inimical 'entity' is something purely negative, it is, one could say, the principle of negativity, because if it constituted one more difference it would immediately enter the chain of differences and could not anymore serve as the latter's constitutive outside.

this very system is restructured into an equivalential chain. It is through this struggle – the event of the political breaking into the field of the socio-cultural – that cultural relations of subordination are retroactively revealed as political relations of oppression. So if we are prepared to follow Laclau and Mouffe, we have to conclude that the passage from relations of subordination to relations of oppression is a passage from culture (the field of micro-politics) to politics (the field of macro-politics) 'mediated' by the emergence of a third term: *the political* in the form of antagonism. Insofar as the political can emerge in any social and cultural area – that is, insofar as *all* relations of subordination can potentially be turned into relations of oppression – it must be distinguished from the political system in the narrow sense. Hence, from the viewpoint of hegemony theory, there is a constitutive difference between the political (as the moment or event of antagonism) and the field of politics as a social subsystem – a difference that cultural studies does not account for.[9]

The distance between Laclau and Mouffe's hegemony theory and cultural and subcultural studies can be measured precisely with the yardstick of this difference. By focusing on micro-politics and by leaving to political scientists and theorists the study of the moment of politicization, cultural studies became, to a large degree, the study of political frontiers in their *sedimented form* and not in their *reactivated form*. This point is sometimes conceded by cultural studies practitioners – for instance, in the recognition by John Fiske that Laclau's 'concern is primarily with the radical and the macropolitical, whereas I believe popular culture to be most effective in the progressive and the micropolitical' (Fiske 1991: 159). In a manner similar to heroic subcultural studies, Fiske assumes that one must not expect the links between popular culture and politics, between the tactic and the strategic, 'to be direct or immediate – rather, we must expect them to be diffuse, deferred, and not necessarily entailed at all' (Fiske 1991:165). While this might be correct from the viewpoint of a student of micro-political forms of resistance, and while Fiske agrees that the 'forging of productive links between the resistant tactics of the everyday and action at the strategic level is one of the most important and neglected tasks of the left' (Fiske 1991: 162), it does not really answer how the popular becomes linked to macro-politics, how indirect forms of action turn into direct forms. What is missing is a clear determination of the nature of the link between the 'micropolitics of everyday life and the macropolitics of organized action' (Fiske 1991: 161).

So far we have presented the concept of antagonism as an answer to this question. However, this answer is not yet entirely satisfactory. Not because, presented as a logic of difference and equivalence, it was too abstract, but simply

9. One can suspect that cultural studies' negligence regarding the difference between politics and the political – which is of categorical and not only gradual nature – has to do with cultural studies' allegiance to the discipline of sociology rather than political theory.

because antagonism, as we said, comes from the outside as an event in the radical sense, that is to say, as a disturbance and dislocation of sedimented socio-cultural patterns. This outside, though, is only an outside when we look at it from the sphere of culture. From the perspective of politics, on the other hand, an antagonistic chain of equivalence is something which in most cases has to be constructed and organized, for example in the form of an alliance between differential positions. A newly emerging political force and project does not come from nowhere. In politics, more than anywhere else, the principle counts: *ex nihilo nihil fit*. A 'collective will', as Gramsci would have it, *has to be organized*. It is from this point of view that we now, in the last part of this chapter, have to once more reflect on the nature of the line between the micro- and the macro-political. Does this line, we have to ask, belong to the side of micro-politics of everyday life or do we have to think of it as part of macro-politics? In other words, is the link between the micro- and the macro-sphere to be forged by micro-political tactics or is it to be forged by macro-political strategy? Without denying the political importance of culture, from the perspective of hegemony theory it seems obvious where the emphasis must lie: if we do not believe in the idea of the revolutionary spontaneity of the masses, then we have to assume that the link between the micro-political and the macro-political is primarily to be established *macro-politically*.

The Missing Link: A Modern Prince?

Our claim that the link between micro-politics and macro-politics can only be constructed from a macro-political standpoint might become less controversial if we consider for a moment Gramsci's own conception of 'politics'. It is true that in Gramsci's work his conception of (macro-)politics remains somewhat elusive, perhaps precisely because his main theoretical achievement lies in the expansion of our conception of politics due to which the cultural has been granted new political dignity. Borrowing the famous feminist slogan 'the personal is political', we can say, and cultural studies effectively says it, that, after Gramsci, 'the cultural is political'. The field of culture turned into the field of micro-politics. However, this 'standard view' of Gramsci misses an important aspect of his conception of politics which, as a rule, remains neglected by most cultural studies accounts of hegemony. This ignorance is even more curious as Gramsci's whole political project (as a cofounder of Italy's communist party) hinges upon that very aspect.

The point is simply that any counter-hegemony, any new political will, has to be incorporated and organized by what Gramsci calls – following Machiavelli – the 'modern Prince'. By this he understands nothing other than the political party-form: the form of a party that takes up the task of founding a new social order by way of constructing a popular – that is, collective – will. Gramsci himself explains the function of the modern Prince as follows: 'The modern Prince must be and cannot but be the proclaimer and organizer of an intellectual and moral reform, which also means creating the terrain for a subsequent development of the national-popular collective will towards the realisation of a superior, total form of modern civilisation' (Gramsci 1971: 132–3). So he explicitly speaks about *two* tasks of the modern Prince that turn out to be two aspects of the same operation: the party's task is both moral and intellectual reform and the construction of a collective will. One does not fully understand the Gramscian notion of hegemony as long as one restricts hegemony to micro-political questions of culture rather than taking into account the macro-political function of cultural *re-organization* ('intellectual and moral reform') and the construction of what today we would call a political project (the 'collective will'). Nowadays, of course, the form of the party is not the only one available, there are all kinds of social movements and political actors, but what is important is the fact that in order to organize, synthesize and give a direction to otherwise entirely dispersed micro-political struggles, there must be *some* form-ational agent, some institutional nodal-point on the macro-political level.

Let us now, on the basis of what has been said so far, sum up in a few words four necessary preconditions for the passage from the sphere of micro-politics to the sphere of macro-politics. What has to be given for this passage to occur is: (1) a situation of explicit antagonization; (2) the emergence of a collectivity; (3) the function of organization, and (4) a movement towards universalization.

The emergence of antagonism (the moment of the political in the radical sense) was identified earlier as the key category indicating the moment in which sedi-mented socio-cultural practices are reactivated and in which, all of a sudden, their political roots and the fact that 'things can be changed' becomes apparent. Let us therefore move to the second precondition: the emergence of a collectivity, which can in fact be derived from the logic of antagonism. A political collectivity is nothing that could be found in form of a pre-given entity in 'social reality' because it is the very outcome of the logic of equivalence. Only in as far as antagonization occurs, and the differential positions in social space become structured along the line of an equivalential chain, can we speak about collectivity. Of course, this does not entail the disappearance of all internal differentiations (no antagonization is ever total) but collectivity emerges only *with respect* to the constitutive outside that negates the differentiality of social positions, thus constituting an inside. Hence, there is no politics which is not concerned with the problem of inclusion/exclusion and with the question of 'where to draw the line' (Marchart 2002a: 69). The same argument also explains why every politics is collective and why, contrary to the liberal view, there is no such thing as a politics of the individual. Not because, as Lenin said, 'there is no politics without the masses' (by which he actually under-stood class politics), but because there is no politics within a pure field of differences, that is, without some degree of antagonization.

When we move to the third condition, the function of organization, we can again rely on Gramsci. It should be evident that every collectivity, if it is to be stable, must be organized in some way. The role of the organizer is played in Gramsci by the famous 'organic intellectual'. This category is supposed to capture the organizing activity of those individuals who organize a given hegemony and articulate the elements of a given historic block or counter-hegemonic movement. What is frequently forgotten is that, for Gramsci, *the movement itself* (as the modern Prince) is nothing but a *collective* organic intellectual. Again we should not be fooled by a certain individualism: it is the collectivity itself that acts as the organizer. Individuals without connection to a larger political project would not be organizing anything except their own project (which would be indistinguishable from what in liberal-capitalist societies is called a 'career'). The result would again be something like a 'political pointilism' of monadic struggles without any real effects. What is important here to recognize is that when Gramsci talks about the 'organizer' of a 'collective will' he cannot be accused of voluntarism.[10] The modern Prince of the party – although for Gramsci it has to have some mass basis, some sort of institutional structure and some form of 'democratically centralized' leadership – must not be confused with the voluntarist or sociological idea of a social actor who is the sole source of his/her own actions, for Gramsci explicitly says that the Prince 'is at one and the same time the organizer and the active, operative expression' (Gramsci 1971: 133) of the collective will. Therein Gramsci anticipates the anti-essentialist stance of later versions of hegemony theory according to which it is not a pre-given social identity that acts as the source of organization and articulation but it is the *function of articulation* that establishes social identities in the first place. For this reason Laclau is eager to emphasize that 'the "intellectual" is not for Gramsci a segregated social group but that which establishes the organic unity of a set of activities, which, left to their own resources, would remain fragmented and dispersed' (Laclau 1990: 195). Thus, rather than speaking about the 'function of the intellectual', Laclau prefers speaking about the 'intellectual function'.

We might now see more clearly what is required for micro-political practices to assume macro-political effectivity and for subcultures to turn into countercultures. What 'cultural populism', as in the case of Fiske, is not prepared to confront is the problem of how a 'collective will' can be forged out of all these disconnected everyday practices of supposed resistance. As such, they only constitute an array of diverse 'tactics' in which they might even counteract or cancel out each other. By themselves (for example, without any organizing function) these tactics will never add up to a broader strategy: *ex nihilo nihil fit*; nor do the disconnected

10. This is less clear, however, in the case of Sorel (who serves as one of Gramsci's sources of inspiration) and his notion of the general strike.

practitioners of these 'subversive' tactics form a collective, because social space cannot be antagonized from *within* the cultural alone, that is, on the basis of a sphere of pure differences. The same must be said, *mutatis mutandis*, for subcultures. As long as subcultures remain on the level of 'symbolic resistance' or 'resistance through rituals' they remain within the sphere of micro-politics. Only when these rituals enter an antagonistic chain of equivalence do they become *politicized*.

This brings us to the fourth minimal condition: a movement of universalization. By universalization one must understand the movement through which a given particular demand is linked up to a larger set of demands, thus constituting a more universal 'project' or movement. As long as subcultures close themselves up into the nutshell of their own particularism – and is this not one of the main characteristics of most subcultures? – they will not be able to universalize their demands (if they have any). Subcultures, to again borrow a Gramscian concept, remain in the 'economic-corporate' phase and do not seek to enter the hegemonic phase of politics which would require some sort of universalization. But, as Roger Simon sums up, 'a class becomes hegemonic in the extent to which it transcends its corporate phase and succeeds in combining the interests of other classes and social forces with its won interests' (Simon 1991: 33). Leaving aside the remnants of classism for a moment, it is clear that every social actor, if it wants to become a (counter-)hegemonic force, has to become 'the universal representative of the main social forces which make up the nation' (Simon 1991: 33). Let us rephrase the argument from our point of interest: a subculture *goes* macro, that is to say, turns political in the extent to which it transcends its own particularistic interests and links up with other social forces beyond the subcultural sphere thereby universalizing its own demands. Or, to employ an Arendtian metaphor, a subculture becomes political in the extent to which it leaves the darkness of the Club and steps into the light of the public realm.

References

Clarke, J., Hall, S., Jefferson, T. and Roberts, B. (1976), 'Subcultures, Cultures and Class', in S. Hall, and T. Jefferson (eds), *Resistance Through Rituals: Youth Subcultures in Post-War Britain*, London: Hutchinson.

Dean, J. (ed.) (2000), *Cultural studies and Political Theory*, Ithaca NY and London: Cornell University Press.

Finlayson, A. and Martin, J. (1997), 'Political Studies and Cultural Studies', *Politics*, 17 (3): 183–9.

Fiske, J. (1991), *Understanding Popular Culture*, London and New York: Routledge.

Gramsci, A. (1971), *Selections from the Prison Notebooks*, (edited by Q. Hoare and G. Nowell Smith), New York: International Publishers.

Grossberg, L. (1992), *We Gotta get out of this Place: Popular Conservatism and Postmodern Culture*, New York and London: Routledge.

Grossberg, L. (1997), 'Replacing Popular Culture', in S. Redhead, D. Wynne and J. O'Connor (eds), *The Clubcultures Reader: Readings in Popular Cultural Studies*, Oxford: Blackwell.

Hall, S., Critcher, C., Jefferson, T., Clarke, J. and Roberts, B. (1978), *Policing the Crisis: Mugging, the State, and Law and Order*, London: Macmillan.

Hall, S. (1988), *The Hard Road to Renewal: Thatcherism and the Crisis of the Left*, London and New York: Verso.

Hall, S. (1997), 'The Centrality of Culture: Notes on the Cultural Revolutions of Our Time', in K. Thompson (ed.), *Media and Cultural Regulation*, London: Sage.

Hebdige, D. (1987), *Subculture: The Meaning of Style*, London and New York: Routledge.

Laclau, E. (1990), *New Reflections on the Revolution of Our Time*, London and New York: Verso.

Laclau, E. and Mouffe, C. (1985), *Hegemony and Socialist Strategy: Towards a Radical Democratic Politics*, London and New York: Verso.

Marchart, O. (2002a), 'On Drawing a Line: Politics and the Significatory Logic of Inclusion/Exclusion,' *Soziale Systeme*, 8 (1): 69–87.

Marchart, O. (2002b), '*Austrifying* Europe: Ultra-Right Populism and the New Culture of Resistance', *Cultural Studies*, 16 (6): 809–19.

McGuigan, J. (1992), *Cultural Populism*, London and New York: Routledge.

McRobbie, A. (1994), *Postmodernism and Popular Culture*, London and New York: Routledge.

Redhead, S. (1990), *The End-of-the-Century Party: Youth and Pop Towards 2000*, Manchester and New York: Manchester University Press.

Redhead, S. (ed.) (1993), *Rave Off: Politics and Deviance in Contemporary Youth Culture*, Aldershot: Avebury.

Simon, R. (1991), *Gramsci's Political Thought*, London: Lawrence & Wishart.

Slack, J. D. (1996), 'The Theory and Method of Articulation in Cultural Studies,' in S. Hall, D. Morley and K.-H. Chen (eds), *Stuart Hall: Critical Dialogues in cultural studies*, London and New York: Routledge.

Street, J. (1997), *Politics and Popular Culture*, Cambridge: Polity.

Thompson, K. (ed.) (1997), *Media and Cultural Regulation*, London: Sage.

Thornton, S. (1995), *Club Cultures: Music, Media and Subcultural Capital*, Cambridge: Polity.

Part III
Urban Tribes

7

Unlearning to Raver: Techno-Party as the Contact Zone in Trans-Local Formations
Toshiya Ueno

'Techno is akin to a kind of enchantment in a disenchanted world' (Gaillot 1998: 27).
'Techno is communism applied to the emotions' (Saunders 1996).
'Not tribal war, but tribal dancing!' (From a flyer on Psy-trance party)

In the first half of this chapter, I engage with an overview of recent (post-) subcultural theories and their implications for the open-air techno-party or festival scene. Then, in the second half, through an ethnographic and interpretative discussion, I examine some aspects of the open-air rave scene in Japan. The latter half is closely related to the theoretical discussion traced in the first.

Rethinking Resistance: Performative Politics in Techno-Tribal Formations

Throughout the past decade, numerous researchers in cultural studies, especially those belonging to the so-called 'post-CCCS generation', have interpreted and analysed the open-air techno-party scene (also known by the generic term 'rave'). Most of these researchers have problematized the applicability of the major concepts of the CCCS – moral panic, homology, magical solution to social contradictions and so forth – to an analysis of the techno scene. They argue that, because such notions were originally developed to analyse rock and other popular (sub)-cultures, they have turned out to be inappropriate for recent (post-)subcultural theory.

There are three main reasons for this view. First, it is argued that rave or techno-party culture is not a working-class based phenomenon or an alternative expression of class struggle. Second, it can therefore no longer be conceptualized as a symbolic 'resistance through rituals'. Third, this culture is not political in itself; it might even be interpreted as apolitical and amoral, and can be summarized as 'the celebration of a great void' (Rietveld 1998: 266). As Maria Pini (1997: 118) has said, rave's 'politics is not one concerned with "changing the world", but rather with the constitution of a particular mind/body/spirit/technology assemblage which makes for alternative experiences of the self.'

It is interesting that those researching the techno-party scene frequently use the term 'tribes' (or 'neo-tribalism') as a crucial sociological concept. At the same time, the crowds in different dance music genres also like to use the terms 'tribes' and 'tribal', which can easily be found on the flyers for these scenes. Conversely, the writers considering 'tribal belongings and formations' within sub/counter/ popular culture are often interested and involved in the techno-party scene. It can be said therefore that the study of contemporary youth culture, or 'post-subcultural studies', implies a sort of 'Urban Tribal Studies' (Ueno and Perasovic 2001). I myself define 'urban tribes' as the small or subsocial groups based on urban (youth) subculture, which consist of shared choices of styles, tastes, fashions, behaviours and rituals, and so forth (Ueno 1997).[1] Although there are some criticisms of the use of 'tribe' as a replacement for the concept of 'subculture', the shift in terminology has been useful in drawing attention to the aforementioned limitations of the CCCS analysis.[2] In fact, it would be possible to engage in a comprehensive, critical review of CCCS concepts and schema on youth culture, but as the most typical and representative debate, I will examine here criticisms of their notion of 'resistance' that have been raised in recent (post-)subcultural studies.

In her influential work on club culture, Sarah Thornton moves away from the 'traditional' CCCS model of resistance. As she says, 'this book is not about dominant ideologies and subversive ideologies, but about subcultural ideologies' (1995: 9–10). Her intention is not to 'de-politicize popular cultures' but to focus on a more complex politics of the popular.

> A shift away from the search for 'resistance' actually gives fuller representation to the complex and rarely straightforward politics of contemporary culture. The distinctions examined through multiple methods in this book demonstrate the rich creativities and originalities of youth culture as well as their entanglement in micro-politics of domination

---

1. In this context, it is noteworthy that a best-selling novel entitled *The Season of The Sun* was published in Japan in 1955. The story of hedonistic, dissident and urban subcultural youth, it caused a sensation at the time with many young people all over Japan imitating the gestures, behaviours and styles of the youth in the novel. The dominant culture, mobilized by mainstream media, termed such youth 'the Sun Tribe' (Taiyo-Zoku). After this event, the Japanese dominant or mainstream culture have always used the term 'tribe' (Zoku) to define unknown youth subcultures: for example, motor speed tribe (Bouso-Zoku), Crystal tribe (Japanese yuppies, Crystal-Zoku), Otaku-Zoku (media mania or nud). It is therefore possible to analyse the Japanese subcultural scenes in each era by addressing them as various types of tribes (Ueno and Mouri 2002).

2. Hodkinson (2002: 19, 23) provides both a review and critique of this shift in terminology in recent subcultural studies.

and subordination. However, this economy of the 'hip' and happening is but one dynamic in a huge array of popular distinctions. (Thornton 1995: 168)

In another ethnographic study of clubbing, Ben Malbon raises the alternative notion of 'playful vital activity' – 'a sense of individual and collective euphoria, induced through the playful practices that constitute dancing' (Malbon 1999: 164). Here, in contrast to a treatment of the scene via a CCCS 'ritual as resistance' approach, clubbing is regarded as a celebration of togetherness or merely an escape-attempt from everyday life. But Malbon still retains some crucial ideas of resistance in his interpretation of the clubbing scene, because even the experience of losing and finding the self during a rave can sometimes be interpreted as 'resistance'. Hence, although 'this is not a resistance to a parent or "dominant" culture . . . the playful vitality experienced through clubbing is no less significant to the lives of those who experience it than, for example, the so-called "resistance" experienced and expressed by "youth cultures" and student movements in the late 1960s' (Malbon 1999: 164, 181).[3]

So rather than merely abandon the notion of resistance, I suppose, it is possible to 'overhaul' it. This does not consist of insisting on any classic, leftist idea of subversion, but is more concerned with an elaboration of an open-ended 'alternative' (in the sense of changing one's own native) culture and society. Angela McRobbie has already contended that resistance in subculture might be 'downsized' from the macro-political level to the 'the more mundane, micrological level of everyday practices and choices' (McRobbie 1994: 162). What I intend here by 'overhauling' is exactly about this shift, whereby resistance is not merely reduced and restricted to political insurrection or revolution but defined in a way through which culture can be actualized and empowered. Because this can always emerge from even relatively modest compromise and negotiation, the notion of resistance can be deconstructed, rather than simply discarded.

Resistance as proposed here is not a passive or reactive movement against a power-bloc; rather, it is a constitutive element within power relations; it can be plural, diverse and polymorphous in its contradictory character; it can take various shapes through its tactically extended versions, especially on the subcultural scene. Resistance in the form of negotiation and communication, for instance, enables the critical relativization of one's own position by addressing the position of the other in different cultures and scenes, or even imagining the other within the self in formations of various subcultural tribes. When the tribe of psychedelic trance-techno imagines or contacts the other position in, for example, the hip-hop tribe, such a relativization of identity could emerge. In that perspective, the notion of resistance can still be meaningful, even productive, and a significant

3. But see the critique of this position by Taylor (2001: 179).

communicative mode for all (sub)cultures that articulates and translates between the macro and micro levels of society. Therefore, it is equally possible to propose to 'up-size' the micro-phenomena within everyday life (or the local) to the macro-political system (or the global).

This notion of 'resistance though relativization' can be understood by referring to Zygmunt Bauman's discussion of the conception of 'the stranger' (Bauman 1995: 190, 1997: 33). Although tribalism is usually understood as a logic of intolerance to the 'other', this interest with solidarity and alliance amongst tribes (or neo-tribalism), Bauman contends, also has the potential to give rise to a resistance against intolerance through a negation of the 'other'. Bauman argues that the basis of society – constructing a sense of togetherness or collectivity – lies in constructing differences, for instance, in inventing the stranger and the 'Other'. Here, the Other is a by-product or leftover of social spacing. Because self-consciousness is always constructed in relation to the existence of the Other, this relation consists of a social spacing where conflicts and negotiations between the self and the Other are deployed. Sometimes, the excluded moment in this spacing is projected and transferred onto the specific other, such as the examples of 'Jews' that Bauman gives in his work. Thus, the stranger-ness (or the otherness) of the Other and the security of social spacing are closely related (Bauman 1995: 189).

The post-modern era and its condition are based on both mutual cohabitation and antagonism amongst different small groups or 'tribes'. If there was exclusively antagonism, a resurgence of violence and discrimination would be inevitable. But, if the stranger who has different cultures could be recognized as just the other or another 'self', then, at least, the possibility of violence and discrimination could be avoided. In that sense, the seeds of conflicts and antagonism amongst different tribes can paradoxically provide the condition for tolerance in the extreme case. The positive and emancipatory emphasis placed on the term 'tribes' within sub-cultures definitely but unconsciously echoes such an understanding. Certainly, Bauman's argument on post-modern tribalism might look pessimistic, but one should not neglect his nuanced understanding of this ambivalence in the notion of tribes and tribalism. Otherwise, one may easily miss the reason why he used the term ' Tribal Moralities' for one of the chapters in his (1995) book.

Generally, critical discussions about techno-party culture are described though, or concerned with establishing, sets of dichotomies such as: chaos and order, unity and difference, the unarticulated and the articulated, the pre-linguistic and linguistic, the non-discursive experience and discursive language. Maria Pini (1997), for instance, focuses on the loss of the self in unification with a wider body or the natural wholeness and totality of the world and universe, through the experience of rave. Ben Malbon (1999: 108–17), in seeking to explain the 'affect' of ecstasy, trance, euphoria, empathy and altered states of mind during the clubbing scene, adopts the Freudian concept of 'the oceanic experience'. Gilbert and Pearson

(1999: 61–7), through reference to the texts of Barthes and Kristeva, extend this conceptual linkage to post-structural descriptions of 'the semiotic', 'jouissance', and 'signifiance' as pre-linguistic forms of ecstatic experience. In a more stark way, Simon Reynolds (1997: 106) defines the rave or open-air party as expressing jouissance and a return to 'pre-pubescent childhood or pre-Oedipal infancy.'

The comparison of the open-air party with a carnival, or a searching for the 'sacred site' in an anthropological sense, also prevails in recent (sub)cultural studies worldwide (Gore 1997: 62; Gaillot 1998: 50). Here 'DJ-ing is evangelism' (Bennett 2000: 89), where DJs can spin the discs and play the music tracks through 'reading' the vibration on the dance floor during the techno-party and considering the weather and atmosphere of the party site.[4] In attempting to explain this (anti-) structure of 'affect' or feeling of ecstasy on a collective and social level amongst a techno-party crowd, and the many attempts of a subversive and mocking type against the usual conventions and regulations of the moral and legal order, a number of writers have adopted from the works of both Mikhail Bakhtin and Victor Turner concepts such as 'carnival', 'communitas', 'anti-structure', 'liminality', 'marginality' and 'outsiderhood' (the strangers) (Hetherington 1998: 97, 107, 113; 2000: 55, 64; Malbon 1999: 156; Taylor 2001: 185).

Victor Turner makes a distinction between the marginal man who is posited in an ambiguous state, and the liminoid who lives from one state to another through the use of rituals. Both positions have been applied to the description of the open-air party culture; for the travel and moving which enables the shifting and mutation of identity is defined through 'communitas', as anti-structure. Of course, in so far as the model of communitas actualizes the symbolic transgression and the experience of ecstacy, trance and togetherness, it can also be defined as a different form of empowerment and 'resistance'. But this perspective might be misleading. By placing the disorderly, the festive and the marginal experience on one hand, and the structural, the legal order and the central on the other, this theoretical polarization has itself been repeated ever since the initial attempts at theorizing the 1960s counterculture.

Instead, the dialectical opposition drawn from Turner's argument, between the centre and the marginal and the orderly and the disorderly, could support the empowering of the central ordering itself. In other words, the chaos and disorder of the marginal can actualize the central order through mutual interfacing. Even though ecstatic trance dancing seems to lack the articulated structure of ordinary language, it has its own different (non-discursive) logic and articulations. What is crucial here, then, is the simultaneous and transversal emergence and coexistence of the articulated, empirical living world and the unordinary, seemingly unarticulated universe. Even the seemingly unarticulated and chaotic can constitute the

---

4. In this way the function and role of the DJ can be compared to those of a Shaman.

plane of everyday life by auto-articulation in each moment. For instance, a techno-party as festival can be an apparatus through which to forget and escape one's daily difficulties and troubles; but at the same time, through organizing or joining some aspects of a party, one can bring back many experiences, skills and behaviours into the 'usual and normal' experiences of everyday life.

Then, how can the alter-native politics or 'overhauled' version of resistance be seen in the techno-party scene? Because of its lack of an ostensive, verbal message, techno dance music, unlike rock and pop-music, seems not to be concerned with any external politics or the political in general. In such a field and horizon, dance (or dancing) is seemingly very crucial. Generally, dance seems to resist discourse (Gilbert and Pearson 1999: 6), but it contains 'significance' even in its non-discursive process. As I have already mentioned above, techno-dance is considered to be a 'vital activity' (Malbon 1999) or a 'merging with a transcendent bigger body and nature' (Pini 1997) and so on. But, it is also possible to grasp dancing as an unconventional version of 'resistance'. Through this understanding, dance turns out to be a matrix for politics in a radical sense, in other words, a proto-politics (Miklitsch 1998). And this is because techno-dance is always driven by mimesis and mutual mimicry as an unconscious '(un)learning' process by which to constitute the social-body and body-politics.

There have been various sociological or philosophical theories that regard mimesis as a basis for the construction of society. Unlike in conventional and traditional sociology, however, the mimesis embodied in dance music is not endowed with any specific, original model to be imitated. What should be considered here is the cultural and political (in a broader sense) space opened up by the mimesis without a model. For instance, one can wonder how and why it is possible to see almost completely the same type of dancing in the psy-trance party scene, regardless of whether the party might be held at Goa, London, Tokyo or Taipei, etc. It is unlikely that the techno-party crowd 'learn' and imitate the way of dancing from particular individuals. There is no 'original' in the mimesis on the dance floor. Nevertheless, there are always common and similar steps and behaviours in each dance music genre.

Of course, there is an authentic or classic dance culture based on well-programmed direction and choreography, but there are myriads of techno-dance cultures as entertainment in contemporary culture – and dance as entertainment does not generally have a clear and articulated choreography. Techno-dance consists of a series of gestures and behaviours that are, in each moment, experienced, experimental, repetitive, mimetic and performative. This 'unlearned' dance, which is transmitted, propagated and imitated in an unnoticed way, through 'entraining' rhythms and beats from one body to another, is dependent on the mimesis without a model. If any model as a representative type or style can be discovered, it would always have emerged retroactively.

In this context, the recent debate on performativity in studies of gender and sexuality is helpful and significant. According to Judith Butler, identity has the 'citational' nature, by which the terms of agency like gender or sexuality are constructed and produced retroactively, not through any origin but as an effect of performativity. In order to articulate the 'imitative structure of gender itself' (Butler 1990: 137), she argues that performativity has its basis in the repetition of certain rituals or customs. Through the citation and invocation of invisible codes or conventions, this performative acting out makes possible the belonging to and positionality of identity (of gender, sexuality and various subcultural tribes). Performativity, she says, 'consists in a reiteration of norms which precede, constrain, and exceed the perfomer' (Butler 1993: 234). The same is definitely true for techno dancing, in which the original itself is always already a copy open to an infinite reiteration of gestures.

Thus, the mimesis in a techno-party is, first and foremost, a performative gesture and activity. It can be found running through the conjunction and production of partial similarities of gestures and figures of the body, without an awareness of what is the ultimate or ideal model for dancing. To constitute the social(ity), mimesis seemingly requires at least two conditions: first, repetitive rhythms and beats crossing over between and integrating the subject and the environment, and second, the performative embodiment (Thrift 1997: 139–47). As far as dance can afford and enable these different modes of communication and sociality, as represented by such terms as 'affective alliance' or 'tribal solidarity', it contains a sort of hesitation, reluctance and resistance to conventional or 'normal' communication and social relationships in everyday life.

If a performative resistance or politics exists within the party scene, it is not only about developing an alternative community or public sphere but also (perhaps more) about presenting a vector towards the condition of 'the belonging without identity'. Certainly, any scene can produce and transform its own space, site, place, zone and territory, but it is not immediately related with any 'real' politics. Rather, the issue here is concerned with the spatial logic of identity and its positionality through subcultural experience and practices. By tracing the argument of Giorgio Agamben, Lawrence Grossberg succinctly formulates the (coming) community that is mediated neither by any specific belonging nor by the simple absence of it, but by 'belonging itself' (Grossberg 1996: 104). A certain mode of crowd provides a community and solidarity not anchored on identity or identification, hence, 'the belonging without identity'.[5]

Here, Grossberg tries to identify a radical sense of politics and transformative practice that articulates between the common and the singular, the collective and

5. The example raised by Agamben in his explanation is somewhat extreme, for he is referring to the crowd and event at Tiananmen Square, China.

the individual. Placed in the context of a techno-party event, the affect and feeling of belonging as 'resistance' seem to be very important, but surely the crowd there would neither be preoccupied with either a party political or national sense of belonging, nor with raising any specific, concrete model of an alternative society. They simply set out the condition and possibility of it by bringing about 'the belonging as such', never qualified by a fixed or determinate belonging 'to something'. In other words, pure belonging does not have any specific attachment 'to which'. It is defined as a zero degree of appurtenance, participation, joining, engagement and commitment. Grossberg, via Agamben, would consider such an event to be 'the exteriority, the exposure, of the singularity of belonging' (Grossberg 1996: 104).

There is no common identity or fixed character that defines the crowd in the techno-party scene besides the fact that they are together or have togetherness on the dance floor and also in the organization of the party. Certainly, in any sub-cultural scene, crowds can be identified as belonging to particular tribes, such as techno, trance, Drum 'n' Bass, reggae, hip-hop and so on. But the 'object' of belonging can also be constantly shifting. There is therefore no absolute or universal belonging, but many overlaps and interconnections between these different tribes. The subcultural tribes intersect, contact and conflict with each other in 'archipelagos' and constellations weaved by and around themselves. It points toward something more than a mere eclecticism or cynicism as a post-modern cultural condition. In this context, the particular belonging to specific tribes is no longer crucial. What is at stake here is pure belonging, regardless of, deprived of, belonging 'to which'. It enables and empowers the 'affective alliance' or 'tribal solidarity' in each subcultural scene and crowd, even though these are temporary, mobile and volatile.

The Techno-Party as the Contact Zone: A Japanese Case Study

The recent debate in anthropology on 'post-modern' ethnographic practice is particularly helpful for interpreting and analysing the techno-party scene. In the introduction to a representative work, James Clifford confirms the general position of the book's authors that 'the poetic and the political are inseparable' (Clifford 1986: 2). More frankly, Tyler says that 'postmodern ethnography attempts to recreate textually this spiral of poetic and ritual performance' (Tyler 1986: 126). Of course, this should not be read simply as a statement that ethnography could be no more than fiction, an expressive voice and poetic writing. But it is also true that ethnography can adopt a performative and expressive approach in a certain context.

From this post-modern perspective, ethnographic writing and description are always bound up with the political and social subject position held by the researcher in the field. It also matters how agents other than the ethnographer are positioned in relation to the object of research. Within ethnographic accounts all involved parties must be questioned on their positioning to both the object of research and the wider network of social relations in which they join. In this way, one can never listen to 'a legitimated, autonomous analytic voice' within the field (Marcus 1986: 184).

As an example, Marcus focuses on a 'sleight-of-hand' within Paul Willis's legendary (1981) work on youth culture, *Learning to Labour*, by raising the interpretative and epistemological questions: does the ethnographer discover the insight, analysis and interpretation articulated from an observation of the field and informants, or does he/she induce these insights by affecting the informants in a mutual communicative and interactive speech act as 'rapport'? Willis sidestepped this issue by proclaiming the position of ethnographer as 'midwife', and on a more practical level by making a distinction between ethnography and structural analysis. But either way, the insight drawn from ethnography (in Willis's work, it was a 'critical theory of capitalism') must not be a mere construction and invention by the ethnographer through engagement in the field via their subject position as researcher. Rather, the issue here is 'a mutual dialogical production of a discourse, of a story of sorts . . . it rejects the ideology of "observer-observed"' (Tyler 1986: 126). In the arguments of Willis, the cultural poetics as an interplay of different voices and positioned utterances or gestures should therefore be traced through and identified.

In current anthropology, this is a burning issue. With regard to the application of ethnographic method to contemporary subcultures, where the observer and the observed are often cooperative and where these two roles may even coexist in the same person, cultural poetics as performative ethnography is especially important. Within ethnographic practice and writing, researchers and observers of youth subcultures always pay attention to the shifts and mutations of their own subject position. This self-reflection on changes in thought and consciousness during the fieldwork experience is why ethnography can sometimes assume an autobiographical character. But it does not mean we can neglect scientific procedures or merely literalize such experiences rhetorically.

Thus, in post-subcultural studies, the ethnographic and cultural poetics engages itself with a sort of literary or performative production (poiesis)[6] by the researcher-as-subject, as a tactical mode of expressive ethnography. There is no external position for the researcher or meta-level of knowledge in subcultural ethnography.

6. Poiesis in the Greek language means producing or manufacturing, and is etymologically linked to the term 'poetics'. Generally, this term is used in philosophical discourse but is sometimes also seen in cultural studies.

This tactic, of entering into the enthusiasm and trance-like feeling in each scene and elaborating theory and language from within, can be called a 'trance-critique'. It is enabled only by the gesture of shuttling rapidly between the transcendent theoretical terms and the 'affect' within the scene.

As one such attempt, I present a case study of the open-air techno-party scene in Japan. There is much difficulty, worldwide, in staging an open-air party. The UK Criminal Justice and Public Order Act 1994 is just one representative example of regulations enforced against the open-air party. There are several reasons why raves are controlled, or even banned: the inconvenience deriving from the noise produced by the sound system, the perceived danger of recreational drugs or illegal substances, and the strange character of the associated tribal lifestyles and appearances. To stage a party without permission runs the risk of intervention by the police and other agencies. Fortunately, at this moment, there is no regulation such as the CJA in Japan but, of course, the police and local authorities may exert controls. This volatile 'temporary autonomy' and fragile 'Indian summer' of the party scene are a result of communications and negotiation between techno-party tribes and 'ordinary' (native) people in the local regions. In Japan, one can say that the negotiation and communication with the local society is a kind of replacement for a license for holding the party.

Recently, the open-air party scene in Japan has exhibited two different, main tendencies. One is towards a commercialized, entertainment-oriented event that constantly accepts huge number of crowds of between 8,000–10,000 people. This type of party tends to feature famous international DJs and musicians. Some Japanese pop has appropriated quasi-techno sound idioms to help increase the number of fans and, thus, the party crowd. Even though it is true that 'newcomers' to this scene (the so-called new generation 'Gal-Trance') can sometimes change the vibration and atmosphere of the party, the relatively established 'core' tribal members do not have any explicit opposition to them. The other tendency is more oriented towards the underground, despite relatively large-scale crowds of 2,000–6,000 or more people. The party organizers in this scene are not so much concerned with international artists and DJs as with site-specific relationships and communications with local and domestic cultures. This type of party wishes to retain the feel and vibration of a quasi-illegal, unauthorized event.

It is possible to appropriate the term 'contact zone' for an analysis of rave and the open-air party scene. In order to articulate the encounter between urban techno-tribes and the local, 'native' people at the party site, the notion of 'the contact zone', as raised by Mary Louise Pratt (1992) and revised by James Clifford (1997), is a relevant, heuristic device. The contact zone is defined as 'the space of colonial encounters, the space in which people geographically and historically separated come into contact with each other and establish ongoing relations, usually involving conditions of coercion, radical inequality, and intractable conflict' (Clifford

1997: 192).[7] As Clifford says, 'contact zones are constituted through reciprocal movements of people, not just of objects, messages, commodities and money' (Clifford 1997: 195). For instance, where local people prepare domestic food dishes in their shops or cafe at a party, the urban techno-tribe can enter into the contact between the local, native culture and the urban, underground culture. When some older people collaborate with techno musicians or DJs by playing traditional drums during a party, connections between the urban and the local (which are no longer dependent on the relation between the centre and the marginal) could arise.

Usually, it is relatively depopulated places that are able to host a party. There are many such sites around Tokyo. The local government and authorities in those areas have difficulty raising enough taxes because of the small population, especially after the economic recession. Party events enable money to be made for the local countryside, in that people can expect the promotion of local industries and domestic cultures. Although it is generally the case that the party culture is represented as an object and target of 'moral panic' in the mass media and a sort of intruder into 'everyday life', the techno-party culture in the Japanese scene could be accepted into the local environment, given the difficult economic conditions.

It is usual to have negotiations and communications with relatively older, senior local people in order to organize a party but recently, in most locations, younger generations are appearing as a local negotiating partner. If these locals wanted to emphasize the alternative status and 'meaning' of the party, rather than merely use it as a way of making money and doing good business, then the party organizers would be interested in the singularity of the location and widen the sensibility of the event to see the encounter with local people and culture as the purpose of the party. Needless to say, the problems that local areas experience are also related to those in the megalopolis and even to global issues. Nowadays, whatever is the problem – such as environment, education, transportation, population, migration and so on – the local is always already inextricably tied up with the global. Thus, the term the 'trans-local' is rendered meaningful (Gilroy 1997: 32; 2001).

Encountering the local culture and its conditions through the organization of a party does not imply turning one's back on the global situation. The period taken for the preparation of a party is not so short (usually, it is more than two weeks), and is shared by both the party tribes (the urban) and the local people (the native). Between both of the groups, a 'rapport' in the anthropological sense – based on living in a concentrated space, sharing cultural customs and establishing

7. This kind of contact is a historical, social and political construction, even though it might appear 'natural'. Clifford (1997) attempts to posit the museum as a contact zone. When tribal rituals and native customs are conserved and recorded in this institution, what is taking place is a repetition of (trans)cultural contact between the self and 'other', and also the 'salvage' of cultural gestures and rituals which are otherwise lost, or remain invisible, in contemporary urban life.

meaningful interactions – can emerge, though which the city and the domestic (or the global and the local) can be recombined and reconnected. Thus, the position undertaken by party organizers and DJs becomes closer to that of fieldworker, ethnographer and anthropologist. Through organizing the party, they experience new and different relationships and encounters with local, domestic sites and cultures.

In such a trans-local context, one can find different ways of encountering cultural resources, rituals, folklores, traditions and myths compared to conventional procedures. Sometimes, it happens that the party site found with difficulty in the countryside is a significant, sacred place for particular myths and traditions, often overlaid with conservative and reactionary meanings. For example, Izanami and Izanagi (the God and Goddess in the myth of the origin of Shintoism) buried the placenta of Amaterasu at the top of the mountain Ena, in the Gifu prefecture. Very nearby, on a site where a party is often held, there is a Shinto shrine to the three of them. In one of the most extreme cases, in the Yamanashi prefecture, the party space and its parking lot were also the site of a commemorative tree planting by the Emperor family.

Generally, these coincidences occurred quite by accident, unlike the case of the new-age oriented party at Stonehenge, UK. Yet, just as in the case of Stonehenge, where the party becomes a contested space of cultural politics for local residents and urban techno-tribes, the use of 'controversial' sites in Japan can also be seen as an oppositional moment against established ideas and conceptions of place. In certain circumstances, the open-air party could provide a matrix for, and a mixture of, political, economic, cultural, spiritual and spatial practices through performative and expressive identities in collective formations. In this way, the techno party tribe can re-encounter the native, local cultures.

Raising this kind of ideological opposition to dominant conceptions of place may sometimes be in vain as there can certainly be some tribes who merely wish to combine Shintoism or a reactionary belief in the ideology of the Emperor system with new-age thought and culture. Most organizers and tribes, however, have respected the original contact with myths and cultures in the countryside, appreciating the meaning of such landscapes and nature. As one of my informants who was both a party organizer and DJ said, 'even if the location for the party was the special site for the celebration of planting trees by the Emperor, then, regardless of its dominant ideological implications, we can use that site tactically with ironical pleasure and ideas.'

Of course, such a discourse is highly problematic and risky as it is often difficult to maintain a critical distance from right-wing ideology. But at the same time, in some cases, it could set out a position that escapes nationalistic ideology or implicitly neutralizes it. At least one could say that having a party at such sites would be an occasion to enter the arena of local political and economic issues, to think about the appropriation or recuperation of paganistic and syncretic belief systems within the local regions. It allows us to re-encounter history, tradition, and even the colonial and imperial past.

Certainly, one can point out that a party held at the Shinto shrine is politically incorrect; for Shintoism as the 'national myth' is definitely a historically constructed cultural-ideological apparatus, and the Shinto shrine is a site of conservative and reactionary ideology. But such a leftist political discourse may not permeate the 'unconscious' sensibility of party tribes or the more widespread crowd. The leftists and 'liberal' intellectuals are not particularly aware of how strong the aversion to leftist discourse is amongst the younger generations. However, as some critical historians of religious thought such as Hiroko Yamamoto (1998) have clearly described, the syncretism in Shintoism has passed through a complicated process since medieval times. Shintoism as (counter or sub) culture, before being appropriated by nationalistic ideology, contained various paganistic ideas and mythical rituals. Thus, to use such a shrine for an open-air party does not necessarily carry 'reactionary' meanings.

For the past few years there have been concert events and some techno parties held at the Meiji shrine in central Tokyo, and some radical, or at least 'liberal', artists and musicians such as Ryuichi Sakamoto have joined in those events. But it is impossible to ignore that some organizers have forced the crowds and these participants to bow to each of the entrance gates of the shrine. It is important to criticize such events and their dominant ideological implications. As already mentioned earlier, however, the mainstream of Japanese 'leftist' discourse is not sufficient for this task, so a more tactical detour is demanded.

In his interesting essay, 'On Amenouzume', Japanese philosopher, Shunsuke Tsurumi considers the mythical figure of a goddess, Amenouzume, in Kojiki (Tsurumi 1991). In the story, Amaterasu, the sun-goddess and central figure in the Japanese Shinto myth, confined herself to a cave because of her anger and hatred against the violence and scatological deeds committed by her brother God, Susanowo, and the world became completely dark because of the absence of Amaterasu. Amenouzume, the goddess of trance and humour, invoked by other Gods to call back Amaterasu and bring back the light, tried to get her out from the cave (Amanoiwato) by performing a trance-dance and doing a form of 'strip-tease'. Tsurumi called Amenouzume the first stripper in Japan and he compared her behaviour with Bakhtin's remarks on carnival (Tsurumi 1991: 75, 134, 141). In another version, she appeared as a singular character that could freely communicate with the not-yet-domesticated strangers in the archaic and mythical regime in Japan. In her figure and gestures, Tsurumi wishes to discover the tactics of the humouristic escape-attempt from being subsumed by the state's power. Amenouzume, through her emancipative or humouristic ability and by trance-dancing, would destroy the rigid ways of living and communicating. Her affective gestures and anti-logical ways are considered to be 'far away from a vertical form of logic' (to use Tsurumi's expression). Tsurumi's interpretative attempt is a bit forced. However, it is highly tactical one in so far as it would extract a model of symbolic resistance from the canon of ideology of the Emperor system. As such, Tsurumi's interpretation overlaps with his vision to articulate 'the direction towards Truth within a ideological trap', in his influential works on political conversion.

Probably, the techno-party tribe could follow Tsurumi's way of living through subtle and flexible activity. In other words, if various thoughts and intentions can escape being incorporated and appropriated by the new-age right-wing thinkers or the Shinto-mysticism oriented political ecology, then it would be worth elaborating and cutting 'n' mixing those cultural moments within texts, as well as in the sphere of everyday life that includes the open-air party.[8] The party as the 'contact zone' can also have other possibilities and developments. Some veteran organizers are trying to establish the party as a gathering of different tribes and generations. They are thinking about collaborations amongst various groups and workshops (social movement against the war, or environmental issues) and media activities (from free or pirate FM radio to Internet streaming). The open-air party can become a sort of node or entrance to different activities and 'tribes' in a global as well as local context. In this way it can surely become the en-trance (a gate of entering the unknown field with pleasure) to various movements and activities.

If a party exhibits a singular alternative communicative mode, it is not based on education in a one-sided direction but pedagogy in a mutual and interactive procedure. There is no politics of representation by ' intellectuals'. In other words, it is a practice of unlearning and the unlearned. I use this term in the sense of 'unlearning' what one learned as a privilege (Spivak 1988: 295). Sometimes, even subcultures threaten to be caught in quasi-elitism as a sort of self-centred tribalism. However, one tribe always presupposes the (co) existence of the other tribe so as to avoid conflicts or fatal antagonism amongst different tribal formations.

Unlearning with the other does not just mean having sympathy with the other or even speaking and acting on behalf of the other. Rather, at issue here is encountering the other in the self, the heterogeneous other (the stranger or the alien) as a different tribe in one's own tribe. The same is true for the relationship and communication between urban tribes and local (native) people. As Spivak says in her influential paper:

8. There is another direction. It is possible to see the party as a kind of exhibition. One can even interpret the party itself as the 'museum without walls', a term formulated by Andre Malraux and appropriated by Hetherington (2000: 137) on party culture. Decorations, flyers and images can all be seen and exhibited as installations. It is also possible to make visible the overlaps and differences between 'tribal' cultures and the hyper-techno cultures.

To render thought or the thinking subject transparent or invisible seems, by contrast, to hide the relentless recognition of the Other by assimilation. It is in the interest of such cautions that Derrida does not invoke 'letting the other(s) speak for himself' but rather invokes an 'appeal' to or 'call' to the 'quite-other' (*tout-autre* as opposed to a self-consolidating other), of 'rendering *delirious* that interior voice that is the voice of the other in us'. (Spivak 1988: 294; original emphasis)

Actually, rave and raving means 'speaking or shouting in delirium'. So, the open-air rave party as the contact zone can be a site and medium for 'rendering delirious' the other within.

References

Bauman, Z. (1995), *Life in Fragments: Essays in Postmodern Morality*, Oxford: Blackwell.

Bauman, Z. (1997), *Postmodernity and Its Discontents*, Cambridge: Polity.

Bennett, A. (2000), *Popular Music and Youth Culture: Music, Identity and Place*, Basingstoke: Macmillan.

Butler, J. (1990), *Gender Trouble: Feminism and the Subversion of Identity*, London: Routledge.

Butler, J. (1993), *Bodies that Matter: On the Discursive Limits of 'Sex'*, London: Routledge.

Clifford, J. (1986), 'Introduction: Partial Truths', in J. Clifford and G. E. Marcus (eds), *Writing Culture: The Poetics and Politics of Ethnography*, Berkeley CA: University of California Press.

Clifford, J. (1997), *Routes: Travel and Translation in the Late Twentieth Century*, Cambridge MA: Harvard University Press.

Gaillot, M. (1998), *Multiple Meaning Techno: An Artistic and Political Laboratory of the Present*, Paris: Dis Voir Edition.

Gilbert, J. and Pearson, E. (1999), *Discographies: Dance Music and the Politics of Sound*, London: Routledge.

Gilroy, P. (1997), 'Exer(or)cising Power: Black Bodies in the Black Public Sphere', in H. Thomas (ed.), *Dance in the City*, London: Macmillan.

Gilroy, P. (2001), *Between Camps: Race, Identity and Nationalism at the End of Colour Line*, London: Allen Lane.

Gore, G. (1997), 'The Beat Goes On: Trance, Dance and Tribalism in Rave Culture', in H. Thomas (ed.), *Dance in the City*, London: Macmillan.

Grossberg, L. (1996), 'Identity and Cultural Studies: Is That All There Is?' in S. Hall and P. du Gay (ed.), *Questions of Cultural Identity*, London: Sage.

Hetherington, K. (1998), *Expressions of Identity: Space, Performance, Politics*, London: Sage.

Hetherington, K. (2000), *New Age Travellers: Vanloads of Uproarious Humanity*, London: Cassell.

Hodkinson, P. (2002), *Goth: Identity, Style and Subculture*, Oxford: Berg.

Malbon, B. (1999), *Clubbing: Dancing, Ecstasy and Vitality*, London: Routledge.

Marcus, G. E. (1986), 'Contemporary Problems of Ethnography in the Modern World System', in J. Clifford and G. E. Marcus (eds), *Writing Culture: The Poetics and Politics of Ethnography*, Berkeley CA: University of California Press.

McRobbie, A. (1994), 'Shut up and Dance: Youth Culture and Changing Modes of Femininity', in A. McRobbie, *Postmodernism and Popular Culture*, London: Routledge

Miklitsch, R. (1998), *From Hegel to Madonna – Towards a General Economy of Commodity Fetishism*, Albany NY: State University of New York Press.

Pini, M. (1997), 'Cyborg, Nomads and Raving Feminine', in H. Thomas (ed.), *Dance in the City*, London: Macmillan.

Pratt, M. L. (1992), *Imperial Eyes: Travel Writing and Transculturation*, London: Verso

Reynolds, S. (1997), 'Rave Culture: Living Dream or Living Death?', in S. Redhead, D. Wynne and J. O'Connor (eds), *The Clubcultures Reader: Readings in Popular Cultural Studies*, Oxford: Blackwell.

Rietveld, H. (1998), 'Repetitive Beats: Free Parties and the Politics of Contemporary DiY Dance Culture in Britain', in G. McKay (ed.), *DiY Culture: Party & Protest in Nineties Britain*, London: Verso.

Saunders, N. (1996), *Ecstasy: Dance, Trance and Transformation*, Oakland CA: Quick Trading.

Spivak, G. C. (1988), 'Can the Subaltan Speak?' in C. Nelson and L. Grossberg (eds), *Marxism and the Interpretation of Culture*, Urbana and Chicago IL: University of Illinois Press.

Tsurumi, S. (1991), *The Story of Amenouzume (Amenouzume Kou)*, Tokyo: Heibonsha.

Taylor, D. T. (2001), *Strange Sounds, Music, Technology and Culture*, London: Routledge.

Tyler, S. A. (1986), 'Post-Modern Ethnography: From Document of the Occult to Occult Document', in J. Clifford and G. Marcus (eds), *Writing Culture: The Poetics and Politics of Ethnography*, Berkeley CA: University of California Press.

Thornton, S. (1995), *Club Cultures: Music, Media and Subcultural Capital*, Cambridge: Polity.

Thrift N. (1997), 'The Still Point: Resistance, Expressive Embodiment and Dance', in S. Pile and M. Keith (eds), *Geographies of Resistance*, London: Routledge.

Ueno, T. (1997), 'Techno-Orientalism and Media Tribalism: On Japanese Animation and Rave Culture', *Third Text*, 47: 95-106.

Ueno, T. and Perasovic, B. (2001), 'Urban Tribes and their Territories', in T. Ueno and G. Lovink (eds), *Electronic Street Cultures*, Ossaka: Inter Medium Institut.

Ueno, T. and Mouri, Y. (2002), *The Practice of Cultural Studies* (*Zissen Kaluchural Sutadiizu*), Tokyo: Chikuma-Shobo.

Willis, P. E. (1981), *Learning to Labour: How Working Class Kids get Working Class Jobs*, New York: Columbia University Press.

Yamamoto, H. (1998), *Medieval Myths* (*Chusei Shinwa*), Tokyo: Iwanami.

–8–

Constructing 'Neo-Tribal' Identities through Dress: Modern Primitives and Body Modifications

Theresa M. Winge

While conducting ethnographic research during the late 1990s in Minneapolis and St. Paul, Minnesota with different subcultures (for example, goths, neo-punks, and Modern Primitives), I found myself increasingly focusing on the latter of these groups. According to Vale and Juno (1989) the Modern Primitive subculture has been growing in numbers since the late 1960s, while Kleese (1999) places its origin in California during the 1970s. Today, various assemblages of this subculture can be found in larger urban areas across the US and parts of Europe. Modern Primitive members are most often identifiable by their body modifications, such as black-work (all black) tattoos, brands, keloids (raised areas of skin, created by rubbing substances into fresh incisions in the flesh) and septum piercings.

Fakir Musafar,[1] a self-proclaimed Modern Primitive and body artist, is considered the 'father of the Modern Primitive movement', and the foremost authority on the subculture (Musafar 1996: 325). He is also well known in both the subcultural and mass media for his participation in extreme body modification rituals (as seen in the 1985 documentary film by Mark and Dan Jury, *Dances Sacred and Profane*), his body modification schools (such as Body Piercing and Branding Intensive Workshops), and his body modification publications (such as *Body Play and Modern Primitive Quarterly*). Musafar has been credited with originally giving the Modern Primitives their name (Camphausen 1997: 114).

While the name Modern Primitive may appear to be an oxymoron, it is actually quite descriptive of this subculture's ideology. Musafar chose 'Modern' because it indicates the contemporary urban setting within which members of this subculture

---

1. Musafar's real name is not known; he took this name from a *Ripley's Believe It or Not* article. More details can be found at *Fakir Musafar's Home Page, Bodyplay Magazine and Piercing School*, http://www.bodyplay.com/ (accessed October 2002). The original Fakir Musafar was a nineteenth-century Sufi, who wandered around for eighteen years with daggers and heavy metal objects inserted into and hanging from his skin (Vale and Juno, 1989: 8–9). For more details on the Surfis religion see Ling (1970: 2713–16).

exist (Vale and Juno 1989). And while the term 'Primitive' is often used in an ethnocentric way to refer to cultures that are non-Western and therefore not 'civilized', Musafar chose 'Primitive' because it means 'first' or 'primal'; also because it represents the cultures that influenced and inspired this subculture (Musafar 1996; Vale and Juno 1989).

Coming from the orientation of studying dress and design, I was fascinated not only by the Modern Primitives' spiritual endeavours regarding body modification rituals, but also by the resulting body modifications. Moreover, as I shared specific examples of my research with others, their reactions to the Modern Primitives' body modifications provided me with eye-opening demonstrations of the power that dress has as a form of non-verbal communication (Eicher and Roach-Higgins 1992). Academics with an anthropological background often suggested that I read various anthropological texts (where I inevitably found a similar ritual that resulted in a similar body modification), and regaled me with stories of their time in the field researching various ethnic groups, where they themselves had seen similar body modifications. Other academics tended to react with apprehension; I was even questioned as to why I was interested in groups of people who would 'mutilate their bodies' in this way. A third reaction came from people outside of academia, which I found most compelling, and yet seemed to relate on some level to the anthropological reactions. On more than one occasion, I heard these people comment how the Modern Primitive body modification looked like something 'tribal' or 'primitive.' Regardless of the specific reaction, most people made assumptions about the way this subculture must live and exist, without knowing anything about them, based solely on the non-verbal communication of their body modifications.

According to Modern Primitive literature, such as that by Polhemus and Randall (1996), Gatewood (2001), and Vale and Juno (1989), Modern Primitives expect such reactions. As my research has shown, the ideology and symbolism of the Modern Primitives draws upon and emulates those ethnic groups they have ident-ified as 'primitive tribes', and is reflected, most notably, in their body modifications. In this chapter, I employ a symbolic interactionist perspective to demonstrate that, although Modern Primitives have managed their appearance to communicate a 'tribal' identity,[2] the texts, symbols and imagery used in this process can have negative consequences for the perception of this identity by both insiders and outsiders to the subculture. Despite the word 'tribe' having long fallen from favour

---

2. Kleese (1999: 23) notes that some Modern Primitives self-identify as tribal. This may be equally true of many individuals who have tattoos and piercings based on non-Western cultures. A photograph of a woman with arm and wristband tattoos and piercings in both her nipples appears in Polhemus and Randall (1996: 36) accompanied by the caption, 'I look tribal, I feel tribal, I am tribal'.

with most academics (Royal Anthropological Institute of Great Britain and Ireland 1951), both this and the term 'primitive' still carry ethnocentric and stereotypical associations. I argue, however, that Modern Primitives are not attempting to replicate a traditional, 'authentic' primitive tribalism, and conclude by suggesting that this subculture would therefore be better conceptualized as 'neo-tribal'.

Body Modifications and Rituals

Since the terminology and subsequent meanings for dressing the physical body vary greatly across cultures, it becomes necessary to establish a useful, unified, and clearly defined classification. Accordingly, Eicher and Roach-Higgins (1992) have replaced the term 'dress' with a more scientific definition – as 'an assemblage of body modifications and body supplements displayed by a person' (Eicher, Evenson and Lutz 2000: 4). Subsequently, the term 'body modification' is a higher form of abstraction and classification of dress, or a means of dressing the physical body. Specifically, body modification has been defined as a general 'term for a variety of techniques aimed at changing one or more parts of the body from the natural state into a consciously designed state' (Camphausen 1997: 110). Many people from Western society perceive body modifications as radical changes or transform- ations of the physical body. However, a body modification is also any transformation of the hair, skin, nails, muscular system, skeletal system, teeth, eyes, or breath (Eicher *et al.* 2000). Therefore, hairstyles, diet, bodybuilding, manicures, pedicures, orthodontic work, piercing, scarification, and surgery (for aesthetic reasons) are body modifications (see also Featherstone 1999: 1).

The accessibility of popular mass media photographs and articles such as those in *National Geographic* and *Time Magazine,* and anthropological texts such as *Marks of Civilization: Artistic Transformation of the Human Body* (Rubin 1988) and *Black Elk Speaks: Being the Life Story of a Holy Man of the Oglala Sioux* (Neihardt 1932/1979) – have provided Modern Primitives with ample information about non-Western ethnic groups, once referred to as 'tribes' (Kleese 1999; Vale and Juno 1989: 3–4). Influenced by these sources, the Modern Primitives aim to create an idealized realm and identity similar to those of 'primitive tribes'. This idealized realm is based on a romanticized version of a past culture, such as that of the North American Indians prior to European influences. Vale and Juno further identify it as a space that exists in a 'shadowy zone between the physical and the psychic', where 'insight and freedom may be reclaimed' (1989: 4).

In essence, the Modern Primitives' idealized realm is an escape that provides a space for freedom and self-expression, where life is less hectic and complicated than their modern existences. Eubanks (1996) interprets this as a discontent with a rapidly changing, image-saturated culture.

Modern Primitives are not expressing a desire to return to 'authentic primitive culture', but are acting on a desire to reform their own culture. They argue that all our conceptions of the world are colonized by the virus of images created by the media. They follow this rationale to argue that 'truly unique, first-person experience' and 'one's basic "identity"' have collapsed in the face of these images, in the face of this simulacrum society. (Eubanks 1996: 75)

This late-modern era, it is argued, creates a profound 'ontological insecurity' where people become increasingly reflexive about their identity (Giddens 1991). One consequence of this is a growing concern to engage in identity management through 'body projects' (Featherstone 1999: 5; Kleese 1999: 19). As Vale and Juno (1989: 3) put it, Modern Primitives are living in a world that is ever-changing and have a sense of being powerless; thus, these individuals are modifying that which they do have control over – their physical bodies.

To this end, the Modern Primitives explore these desired realms with their own bodies, via body modifications. Modern Primitives' body modifications are often referred to as 'tribal' and 'primitive' because they are similar to those of the idealized examples of body modifications created by non-Western ethnic groups (Gatewood 2001; Vale and Juno 1989). Some examples of Modern Primitive body modifications that contribute to their 'tribal' identity are, for example, septum piercings (similar to those worn in Papua New Guinea), elongated earlobes (similar to those of some North American Indians), scarification designs (similar to those of the Tiv in Africa) and blackwork tattoos (similar to those of Borneo).

Technology, both ancient and modern, has an important role in the acquisition of body modifications, especially for the Modern Primitive subculture. In recent years, body artists have attended schools and secured licenses to demonstrate that they possess not only the artistic ability to modify bodies but the technical expertise as well. The ancient technology that is used ranges from charcoal and herbs, which can be safely rubbed into an open cut to create a raised scar in a desired design, to sharpened bones used for tattoos. One such example was the topic of an article in *Savage Tattoo*, which described how Modern Primitives are creating 'primitive' tattoos by applying them with ink and bone needles, similar to those found on a recently discovered mummy (Siggers and Rowanchilde 1998: 9–11).[3]

Examples of modern technology that Modern Primitives use would include multiple needle tattoo guns, metal hollow piercing needles, and brands. However, the most modern technology being used for Modern Primitive body modifications

---

3. Ötzi is the mummy of a Stone Age hunter that was found frozen in Ötztal Alps, in 1991, nicknamed Ötzi because of the area where he was found. This mummy had numerous tattoos that scientists have speculated were used for medicinal and spiritual reasons (Tanaka 1996; Siggers and Rowanchilde 1998).

was that invented by Steve Haworth,[4] a Modern Primitive who creates medical instruments to implant 3D Teflon shapes into individuals wishing to modify their appearance. He has successfully implanted horns in the performance artist, Enigma, and a metal spike mohawk in a young man's scalp, among others (Mercury 2000: 65).

In addition to the body modifications that contribute to the 'tribal' identity of the Modern Primitive, there is also, for some, a body modification ritual or ceremony. Victor Turner defines ritual as a predetermined set of behaviours (performance) for a life-affecting event, which references an ideology of supernatural beings, powers, or energies (1982: 79). In most cases, these rituals are intended to resemble those read about in anthropological texts. Most notably, Musafar has participated in numerous body modification rituals inspired by such texts. These rituals include the Kavandi-bearing ceremony,[5] where spears of Siva pierced his skin, the Hindu Ball Dance,[6] where he wore forty-eight weighted balls that hung from hooks in his skin, and the Sun Dance,[7] where he himself hung from hooks inserted into his chest piercings (Kleese 1999; Vale and Juno 1989).

Eric Gans (2000: 163) has stated that, for the Modern Primitive subculture, the information presented on the skin with a body modification is the narrative for the ritualized experience of receiving them. Likewise, Musafar has claimed that body modification rituals are often rites of passage for Modern Primitives, and that the remaining body modification is a record of that experience.[8] His own experiences with body modification rituals have brought him to new levels of spiritual transcendence (Musafar 1996: 325–34).

4. Steve Haworth owns HTC Body Adornments in Phoenix, Arizona. He has been documented in over twenty-seven documentary films, featured in many magazine and newspaper articles, and television shows.

5. The Kavandi-bearing ceremony, where participants wear Spears of Siva that pierced the skin, is performed in India in early February as part of a festival. It is considered a way for the average person to gain spiritual enlightenment through physical pain (Vale and Juno 1989: 34).

6. The Hindu Ball Dance is practiced by an Indian holy man, the Sadhu, who stitches heavy fruits to his body. As the fruit dies and shrivels, it is removed and strung on to a chain that is then worn between the new hanging fruit (Vale and Juno 1989: 18).

7. The Sun Dance of the North American Plains Indians was an eight-day spiritual ritual intended to represent the hazards of a warrior's life, specifically being captured, tortured, and the escape (Beck, Francisco and Walters 1995: 23–4).

8. On the fourth day of the Sun Dance, the incisions or surface piercings were made in the dancers' backs or chests, and pieces of wood or metal fashioned into hooks were connected to leather straps and inserted through the surface piercings, under the chest or back muscles. The straps were tied to the Sacred Pole, located in the center of the ceremonial site, and the dancers were hoisted into the air, forcing the captured warriors to gaze into the sun. This was the pinnacle of the ritual, and was called the Gazing-at-the-Sun (Beck, Francisco and Walters 1995: 23–4). The scars served as reminders of the participation in the Sun Dance and the subsequent spiritual transformation.

Symbolic Interaction Theory

There is a strong tradition in the US of using a symbolic interactionist framework to explain how dress is a meaningful form of communication (for example, Blumer 1969; Stone 1981; Kaiser 1990; Kaiser, Nagasawa and Hutton 1991). Symbolic interaction theory was originally developed in the academic fields of social psychology and sociology, and has a comprehensive set of premises by which to define the relationship between the individual self and society. It is based on three basic assumptions: firstly, that communication occurs through the creation of shared symbols and meanings; secondly, that identity is constructed through negotiated interactions and communications with others; thirdly, that society is constantly created by the ongoing coordinated and understood interactions and communications between individuals (Cooley 1902; Mead 1934; Blumer 1986).

Although once confined to scholarly texts, the sources and inspirations for body modifications have spread into many areas of popular culture, including television documentaries, fashion magazines and advertising (Kleese 1999: 34). This 'colonization' of the public domain increases the likelihood that both insiders and outsiders to the subculture share references to the symbols and meanings that are communicated in Modern Primitive body modifications, and which facilitate the construction of the Modern Primitive 'tribal' identity. Yet, such shared information also provides more opportunities for exploitation and misinformation about these cultures. From a symbolic interactionist perspective, successful communication is not guaranteed but depends on how clearly a message is sent and how accurately those receiving it identify, interpret and negotiate the intended symbolic meanings. There is, in other words, always the potential for a disjunction between what Kaiser (1990) terms 'appearance management' (the construction of appearances to communicate a particular identity) and 'appearance perception' (the manner in which these appearances are interpreted by significant others).

What cannot be overlooked in the case of the Modern Primitives is that the terms 'primitive' and 'tribal', which the subculture aligns itself with, are associated with ethnocentric and racist stereotypes that are not beneficial in the necessary symbolic interaction for the communicative process of identity construction. Viewed though the historical context of a colonial legacy, 'in the self-construction of the "West", the "primitive" has functioned as the homogenized notion of the racialized "other"' (Kleese 1999: 24). The term 'other' is understood here in the same way as used by Edward Said when discussing the colonial European study of Oriental cultures. The 'other' may be determined to be a kind of cultural projection of concepts – often negative and stereotypical - about a culture or people different from one's own culture. Moreover, the 'other' is typically subjugated by and has less power than those that are making the projections (Said 1978). Hence, those external to the subculture – the lay person, various cultural and media commentators and some academic researchers – are likely to be guided in their attempts at 'appearance perception' by the 'primitive' symbolism, and its assoc-iated negative connotations, of the Modern Primitives. The result tends towards the stereotyping and categorizing of Modern Primitives as the homogenized tribal 'other', my own examples of which I related earlier in the chapter.

The fact that body modifications have the potential to be perceived in a way that perpetuates racial and ethnocentric generalizations about the exotic 'other' might seem to reveal more about the receiver of these symbols than the sender. Yet, importantly, if the 'West' constructs its own identity via racist and ethnocentric representations of traditional tribal lifestyles and appearances, then the Modern Primitive subculture itself, as well as the sources that it draws upon, cannot simplistically be located externally to this Occidental framework of perception. In this way, 'Modern Primitivism allies itself with a tradition which played a signif-icant role in the justification of colonial rule and subordination . . . this describes the limitations of a self-declared radical movement, whose associates perceive of themselves as radical opponents of Western modernity. They remain captured in some of the highly problematic discursive assumptions shaping this modernity' (Kleese 1999: 18). As we have already noted, anthropological texts play an important role in the construction of Modern Primitive body modifications and related rituals, and it is around the subculture's uncritical use of such texts that the above debate on the reproduction of racialized stereotyping takes place.

The Uses and Abuses of Anthropological Texts

In the last century, anthropological texts, especially ethnographies, have brought forth an enormous amount of information to general readers worldwide about non-Western cultures. According to Marcus and Fischer (1986: 7–17), the critical function of cultural anthropology and its subsequent ethnographic texts is to examine our unconscious assumptions about our own (Western) culture that become inscribed within such texts. Our task is therefore to read anthropological texts critically to uncover the ideological assumptions and power relationships through which they operate. A major issue here is the inherent bias in their present-ation of cultural ideals and exotic ideas about the 'other'. James Clifford (1986: 7) has noted that the legitimacy and accuracy of ethnographic texts have been quest-ioned since they first were written. Whether on the inside or outside of a culture, the ethnographer has bias that is impossible to overcome: 'ethnographic truths are thus inherently *partial* – committed and incomplete' (original emphasis).

Since ethnographers inevitably write from a place that is removed from the culture under study, they therefore risk the very creation of this exotic 'other'. Marianna Torgovnick (1990) has, for example, discussed how such inaccurate, romanticized, racist, and sexist anthropological texts have contributed to the unrealistic concept of 'primitive tribes' in Western society and formed the basis for some groups' fascination with them. It is both the personal collection of such old anthropological material by some Modern Primitives and its uncritical repro- duction in *Body Play and Modern Primitive Quarterly* that forms the basis of Kleese's critique:

> The ambivalences of colonial discourses are particularly obvious in the practices of early ethnographic photography. This photography was part of the project of colonial sciences to construct a generalized notion of 'otherness', to categorize, evaluate, control the colonized 'others' in order to secure their governability . . . This functioned as a further subjugation of the racialized others, silenced and exposed to the 'colonial gaze', the objectifying view of the spectator. (Kleese 1999: 26)

As with many written texts about a people, anthropological works also tend to suggest the culture being discussed is frozen in time and this can help explain why Modern Primitives have an unrealistic and romanticized view of these cultures and their rituals as timeless and unchanging. Virginia Eubanks discusses how, in its establishing of a link (via a 'primal urge' for body modification) to a simpler 'authentic' primitive culture – 'one that pre-dates a perceived cultural violation by Western progress' (1996: 77) – Modern Primitive philosophy does not recognize the historical, geographical or cultural specificity of the symbols of their body modifications and related practices (1996: 74). What is therefore created, she argues, is a universalized, essentialized and homogenized representation of a traditional tribal 'body' that, in providing the sources of inspiration for contemporary sub- cultural practices, only serves to reinforce such dichotomies as 'modern/primitive', 'culture/nature', 'White/non-White' upon which the Western hegemony of 'self/ other' rests.

Both Eubanks and Kleese are accurate in their assessment that Modern Primitives have a romanticized perception of the ethnic groups they have identified as 'primitive tribes'. Yet, by focusing on a textual critique of ethnographic material, both authors avoid any analysis of the actual material practice of 'appearance management' by the Modern Primitives themselves. I am therefore less concerned in this chapter with the construction of idealized representations of primitive tribes than I am with how contemporary subcultures actively appropriate the use of such symbols in the material construction of their dress codes. As Kleese (1999: 30) him- self admits, the Modern Primitives employ these sources in a way that is neither uniform nor faithful to the original contexts; rather, their use is both 'eclectic' and 'instrumental'. In fact, I would argue that it is precisely by 'dehistoricizing . . . [non-European] . . . practices and rituals, appropriating and commodifying them, and applying them, completely out of context' (Eubanks 1996: 74–5) that

Modern Primitives are able to engage in '*bricolage*' – 'the re-ordering and re-contextualisation of objects *to communicate fresh meanings*' (Clarke 1976: 177; my emphasis).[9]

This selective symbolic negotiation also leads us away from the ideological reinforcement of such binary oppositions as modern/primitive, Western/ethnic, urban/tribal, and towards their physical dissolution as embodied in the material appearances and practices of the Modern Primitives. Unable to escape modernity yet marginalized within it, the subculture uses 'primitive' symbols yet reinterprets them within a Western framework. The result is neither an 'authentic' recreation of a non-Western tribe, nor a homogenized, racialized representation as objectified from source material, but a hybrid ensemble, one that in its marriage of modernity and tradition can be regarded as a truly post-modern phenomenon (Mizrach n.d.).

A 'Neo-Tribal' Identity

During the past several years, a number of journalists, academics and cultural commentators (such as Polhemus 1994: 128–9; 1996: 37–51; Polhemus and Randall 1996: 8) have latched on to the term 'tribe' and applied it, arguably indiscriminately, to many subcultural groups in the US and Europe, especially those whose members have 'customized' their bodies in various ways. Yet, as noted above, Modern Primitives are not attempting to achieve, though their rituals or resulting body modifications, an identical recreation of a non-Western ethnic 'tribe'. Although a body modification practitioner may establish much of the set of behaviours during a ritual, subcultural members can personalize the ritual to reflect their individual beliefs, and can do so through the choice of body modification, the culture(s) drawn-upon, the personal elements included (such as music, candles, and cultural artifacts) and the meaning attached to any or all of these. As Sweetman (1999: 70) argues, 'tattooing and piercing can be seen as postmodern practices in their eclectic appropriation of techniques and imagery from a global scrapbook of design sources and procedures'. Through this practice of *bricolage*, Modern Primitive subculture members 'own' their body modification rituals by creating unique and contemporary versions of traditional 'tribal' rituals.

A good example of this process is that of Thomas Potter,[10] a Modern Primitive from Neenah, Wisconsin, who used the expertise of a professional licensed tattoo artist and her technology, in Minneapolis, Minnesota, for his contemporary body

---

9. Torgovnick (1995), for example, argues that Modern Primitives produce different forms of modification to those in traditional societies. The resulting constructions are viewed as post-modern in their eclecticism.

10. Personal information. The name is a pseudonym.

modification rituals. His tattoos were based on several past cultures. The braid tattoo on the top of his scalp was inspired by Viking (Scandinavian) braid artworks, the knotwork on the back of his scalp was inspired by ancient Dark Age Celtic and Saxon designs, and the spiral design on his throat was inspired by the Picts' artwork. The ritual for each of his tattoos was dictated by the procedures that the tattoo artist followed, but Potter made it his 'own' with the personal meanings behind each tattoo (for example, the spiral was a protection tattoo, the knotwork was a celebration of his wedding, and the braid was a homage to his heritage). What this example highlights is the way that 'tribal' sources are selectively appropriated as part of an ongoing social process that, as Kaiser *et al.* (1991) would argue, fosters 'ambivalence' in the resulting stylistic ensemble. The extent to which this effect undercuts the tendency towards homogeneity in appearance perception by those external to the subculture rather depends upon the perceiver's relationship to (and, hence, interpretation of and negotiation with) the basis of shared symbols and meanings for the Modern Primitive body modifications. Yet, in terms of appearance management, what is constructed has at least the potential to be 'symbolically ambiguous' (Kaiser *et al.* 1991: 167).

As the above example indicates, the Modern Primitives embrace both the 'modern' and the 'primitive' dimensions of existence, selectively discarding that which do not find applicable to their identity. Some Modern Primitives have piercings made with modern technology (such as metal hollow needles), along with keloids created with ancient technology (for example, incisions made with a sharpened knife and charcoal). Clearly, as Bryan Turner (1999) has commented, communicating a 'tribal' identity in this way involves very different meanings and functions from those evident in many non-Western traditional cultures with their ascribed identities, fixed loyalties and collective solidarities. In such 'pre-literate' societies, body marks were 'obligatory' statements of culturally predetermined rites of passage, marking a tribal member's successful journey though stages of the life-cycle; a function that is largely obsolete in late-modern, industrial societies with their heightened individualism and voluntary membership of various 'life-style' groupings.

Lou Taylor (2002: 12) has similarly argued that while dress and body adorn-ment has typically functioned in small-scale societies as a traditional marker of ethnic identity, it is 'misleading' to equate the so-called 'tribal' markings of contemporary subcultures with those 'specific cultural practices and values used to identify ethnic differentiations' in traditional communities. Following the example of Daniel Wojcik in his book *Punk and Neo-tribal Body Art* (1995), Taylor condones the use of 'neo-tribal' as a more accurate label for those urban subcultures that connote ideas of 'tribes'. Such a concept is intended to capture new (late- or post-modern) forms of association that are characterized by more fluid, individualized and expressive forms of identity than those found in traditional, small-scale or pre-literate 'tribal societies.[11] As Bryan Turner remarks on the type of group affiliations constructed through contemporary body modifications:

> It is useful to think about these playful marks as illustrations of the neo-tribalism which is described in Michel Maffesoli's *The Time of the Tribes* (1996) . . . Tattoos and body piercing are no longer functional, but indicate the social construction of traditional patterns of sociability in the modern world. Tattoos operate in a field or Dionysian desire and consumer pleasure, but consumerism has not produced its own (authentic) mythology or consumer theology, and therefore tattoos have no cosmic foundation from which meaning could be derived. (Turner 1999: 41)

This is not to argue that contemporary body modifications and rituals are meaningless; rather, that they signify in post-modern terms – their hybridized meanings produced through the relocation of traditional symbols in a late-modern, urban context.

While the Modern Primitives' rejection of modern society frequently ensures they are linked to the revival of 'primitivism' and 'tribalism', this perception therefore rests upon the particular definitions of the terms on offer here. Indeed, evidence suggests that the more 'traditional' connotations of 'tribe' are rejected by contemporary subcultures as inadequate to their 'own definitions of the situation'. Maureen Mercury (2000: 5), for instance, in discussing the Modern Primitive movement, states 'this is not a return to a primitive tribal behavior. We are not those people. We are too diverse a population and geographically isolated to belong to a tribe, and very few Westerners would consider themselves "primitive"'. Modern Primitives claim that body modifications are explorations of spirituality and attempts to gain a higher consciousness (Mercury 2000; Califa 1994). Yet the Modern Primitive lifestyle suggests they are content in their modern, urban, Western culture, while they romantically pay homage to ethnic non-Western groups they have deemed 'primitive tribes'.

References

Beck, P., Francisco, N. and Walters, A. (eds) (1995), *The Sacred: Ways of Knowledge, Sources of Life,* Tsaile AZ: Navajo Community College Press.
Blumer, H. (1969), 'Fashion: From Class Differentiation to Collective Selection', *Sociological Quarterly,* 10: 275–91.

11. These post-modern neo-tribes are different also to the 'tribal' solidarities of modern, Western, tattooing and associated subcultures based around firm class identifications and collective loyalties, such as the skinheads (see Sweetman 1999).

Blumer, H. (1986), *The Symbolic Interactionism: Perspective and Method*, Los Angeles CA: University of California Press.

Califa, P. (1994), 'Modern Primitives, Latex Shamans, and Ritual S/M', in *Public Sex: The Culture of Radical Sex*, Pittsburgh PA: Cleis Press.

Camphausen, R. C. (1997), *Return to the Tribal: A Celebration of Body Adornment*, Rochester VT: Park Street Press.

Clarke, J. (1976), 'Style', in S. Hall and T. Jefferson (eds), *Resistance Through Rituals: Youth Subcultures in Post-War Britain*, London: Hutchinson.

Clifford, J. (1986), 'Introduction: Partial Truths', in J. Clifford and G. Marcus (eds), *Writing Culture: The Poetics and Politics of Ethnography*. Berkeley CA: University of California Press.

Cooley, C.H. (1902), *The Looking Glass*, New York NY: Charles Scribner's Sons.

Eicher, J.B. and Roach-Higgins, M. E. (1992), 'Definitions and Classification of Dress: Implications for Analysis of Gender Roles', in R. Barnes and J. B. Eicher (eds), *Dress and Gender: Making and Meaning*, Oxford: Berg.

Eicher, J.B., Evenson, S. and Lutz, H. (2000), *The Visible Self: A Global Perspective on Dress*, New York NY: Fairchild Publishing.

Eubanks, V. (1996), 'Zones of Dither: Writing the Postmodern Body', *Body & Society*, 2 (3): 73–88.

Featherstone, M. (1999), 'Body Modification: An Introduction', *Body & Society*, 5 (2–3): 1–13.

Gans, E. (2000), 'The Body Sacrificial', in T. Sierbers (ed.), *The Body Aesthetic: From Fine Art to Body Modification*, Ann Arbor MI: University of Michigan Press.

Gatewood, C. (2001), *Primitives: Tribal Body Art and the Left-Hand Path*, San Francisco CA: Last Gasp.

Giddens, A. (1991), *Modernity and Self Identity*, Cambridge: Polity.

Kaiser, S. (1990), *The Social Psychology of Clothing: Symbolic Appearances in Context*, 2 edn, New York: Macmillan.

Kaiser, S., Nagasawa, R. H. and Hutton, S. S. (1991), 'Fashion, Postmodernity and Personal Appearance: A Symbolic Interactionist Formulation', *Symbolic Interaction*, 14 (2): 165–85.

Kleese, C. (1999), '"Modern Primitivism": Non-Mainstream Body Modification and Racialized Representation', *Body & Society*, 5 (2–3): 15–38.

Ling, M. (1970), 'Sufis', in R. Cavendish (ed.), *Man, Myth and Magic: An Illustrated Encyclopedia of the Supernatural*, New York NY: Marshall Cavendish Corporation.

Maffesoli, M. (1996), *The Time of the Tribes: The Decline of Individualism in Mass Society*, London: Sage.

Marcus, G. and Fischer, M. (1986), *Anthropology as Cultural Critique: An Experimental Moment in the Human Sciences*, Chicago IL: University of Chicago Press.

Mead, G.H. (1934), *Mind, Self and Society*, Chicago IL: University of Chicago Press.

Mercury, M. (2000), *Pagan Fleshworks: The Alchemy of Body Modification*, Rochester VM: Park Street Press.

Mizrach, S. (n.d.), 'Modern Primitives: The Accelerating Collision of Past and Future in the Postmodern Era', *Public Domain Inc, Performations*, 6, http://www.pd.org/topos/perforations/perf6/modern-primitives.html (accessed November 2002).

Musafar, F. (1996), 'Body Play: State of Grace or Sickness?' in A.R. Favazza, MD. (ed.), *Bodies Under Siege: Self-Mutilation and Body Modification in Culture and Psychiatry*, Baltimore MD: John Hopkins University Press.

Neihardt, J. (1932/1979), *Black Elk Speaks: Being the Life Story of a Holy Man of the Oglala Sioux,* Lincoln NE: University of Nebraska Press.

Polhemus, T. (1994), *Streetstyle*, London: Thames & Hudson.

Polhemus, T. (1996), *Style Surfing: What to Wear in the 3rd Millennnium*, London: Thames & Hudson.

Polhemus, T. and Randall, H. (1996), *The Customized Body*, New York: Serpents Tail.

Royal Anthropological Institute of Great Britain and Ireland. (1951), *Notes and Queries on Anthropology,* 6 edn, London: Routledge and Kegan Paul.

Rubin, A. (ed.) (1988), *Marks of Civilization: Artistic Transformation of the Human Body*, Los Angeles CA: Museum of Cultural History, University of California Press.

Said, E. (1978), *Orientalism*, New York NY: Random House.

Siggers, J. and Rowanchilde, R. (1998), 'How the Iceman was Tattooed', in J. Miller (ed.), *In the Flesh*, Hoboken NJ: Casey Exton.

Stone, G. P. (1981), 'Appearance and the Self: a Slightly Revised Version', in G. P. Stone and H. Farberman (eds), *Social Psychology through Symbolic Interaction*, 2 edn, New York: John Wiley & Sons.

Sweetman, P. (1999), 'Anchoring the (Postmodern) Self?: Body Modification, Fashion and Identity', *Body & Society*, 5 (2–3): 51–76.

Tanaka, S. (1996), *Discovering the Iceman: What was it Like to Find a 5,300-year-old Mummy?* Toronto: Madison Press.

Taylor, L. (2002), *The Study of Dress History*, Manchester and New York: Manchester University Press.

Torgovnick, M. (1990), *Gone Primitive: Savage Intellects, Modern Lives*, Chicago IL and London: University of Chicago Press.

Torgovnick, M. (1995), 'Piercings', in R. de la Campa, E. A. Kaplan and M. Sprinker (eds), *Late Imperial Culture*, London and New York: Verso.

Turner, V. (1982), *From Ritual to Theatre: The Human Seriousness of Play*, New York: PAJ Publications.

Turner, B. (1999), 'The Possibility of Primitiveness: Towards a Sociology of Body Marks in Cool Societies', *Body & Society*, 5 (2–3): 39–50.

Vale, V. and Juno, A. (eds) (1989), *Re/Search #12: Modern Primitives. An Investigation of Contemporary Adornment & Ritual*, San Francisco CA: Re/Search Publications.

Wojcik, D. (1995), *Punk and Neo-Tribal Body Art*, Jackson MS: University Press of Mississippi.

–9–

Between Criminal and Political Deviance: A Sociological Analysis of the New York Chapter of the Almighty Latin King and Queen Nation
Louis Kontos

> Our goal is to safeguard and ensure the cultural existence of our Latino people and that of our ancestors.
>
> (Latin King Bible, n.d.)

In the academic literature gangs are typically thought to have a culture of deviance that serves to justify a range of aberrant and anti-social acts, but little else in the way of culture. And yet many gangs are themselves cultures, replete with folklore, ideology and symbolic systems of communication. The gang 'Almighty Latin King and Queen Nation' falls under this category. It first appeared in Chicago circa 1940s when several existing Latino gangs consolidated under its banner. Founding members wrote a set of principles and later developed a constitution, lessons, and a manifesto. This literature, referred to as the *Latin King Bible*, has grown steadily over the years and now includes artwork and poetry. The New York Chapter, like every state chapter of Latin Kings, has its own constitution.[1] The *Latin King Bible* outlines a commitment, in principle, to both organized crime and political activism as methods of collective advancement.

According to this literature, the Kings embody the ideals of their cultural heritage, which they trace to the 'Inca Empire', including an ethos of cooperation and sharing, and a commitment to collective independence. The Latino community in the US, by contrast, is said to be plagued by disparate evils that maintain its complicity, including internalized stereotypes, tokenism, physical addictions, television, false needs and beliefs, the welfare system, and a lack of intra-group cooperation and solidarity. In order to empower 'Latinos who are oppressed', according to this literature, it is necessary to build networks and institutions through similar means as the 'white man' – including legitimate business, organized crime and political participation.

---

1. It should be added that there are several versions of these texts in circulation, and that the distinction between original and supplemental material is only clear in a few 'lessons' where the date and place of origin are identified.

We expect by the year 2000 that all our members will have mastered our teachings and set new higher goals into the 21ˢᵗ century for the A.L.K.N. [Almighty Latin King Nation – this name was changed at some point in New York to the name Almighty Latin King and Queen Nation.] Our goal is to have a network of computerized state of the art communication centers in each of our centralized locations across the country and abroad by the year 2000. Our goal is to safeguard and ensure the cultural existence of our Latin people and that of our ancestors. (Latin King Bible n.d)

The New York chapter began in Collins Correctional Facility reportedly by a single individual, Luis Felipe, a.k.a. King Blood. King Blood had joined the Kings in Chicago after leaving Cuba in 1980. In Collins he wrote a set of principles to inaugurate a separate chapter of the organization in New York. Later he would write a separate constitution for the new organization and several lessons to be added to its official literature, together with occasional commentaries (labelled 'manifests') that were distributed to members. This writing repeats the central themes of the *Latin King Bible* in a form that is more polemical as well as personal. King Blood claims that 'the government' has intensified its efforts against dissident groups, and that he himself has been targeted for trying to 'upraise' Latino youth and give the Latino community 'a voice'. He is not claiming that his crimes are political in nature but instead that they are 'mistakes' that have allowed the government to take him off the streets and thereby neutralize the threat he represents, namely of 'revolution' – notwithstanding the fact that King Blood's notion of revolution is decidedly apolitical.

A reporter asked me during interview if I was trying to create a revolution. I told him no, the revolution has been already created in 1986 at Collins. Yes, a revolution of the mind, a revolution of knowledge, a revolution of Latin of pride, a revolution of self confidence, a revolution of I'm me, a revolution of freedom, a revolution of harmony, a revolution of self-understanding and refusing to come back to darkness (ignorance) because we have already see the light through our crowns, a revolution of love between us, the 3ʳᵈ world of warriors (King Blood, Manifest, n.d.).

Under King Blood's leadership the Kings developed a reputation as one of New York's first 'national' gangs, and amongst its most violent (Corbiscello 1997). (King Blood himself is now in prison serving a 'life' sentence for ordering a string of murders from Rikers Island while waiting trial on other charges.)

During King Blood's various terms in prison, successive interim leaders left a legacy of brutality and corruption. In 1996, when it became clear that he would be spending the rest of his life in prison without the possibility of parole, he appointed Antonio Fernandez, a.k.a. King Tone, permanent leader (see Brotherton and Barrios – forthcoming). Tone was a former leader of a local tribe and had developed the reputation of a true believer and the credentials of a reformer. By his account, he was 'crowned' (i.e. became a member) in Rikers Island in 1992 while serving time for drug dealing, and decided to turn his life around there and then upon finding something in which he could believe, namely: Kingism. This is what members call their way of life and system of beliefs.

Under Tone's direction numerous revisions were made to the *Latin King Bible*, including striking out the term 'obedience' from the New York Constitution and references to 'violations' (beatings) throughout. In addition, 'structural' changes were implemented. Among them, the procedure for exit was formalized. Exiting members were now required to sign notarized documents, called 'Golden Gates' (in which they absolve the organization of responsibility for any future misdeeds). Ordinary members gained voting rights on such matters as the promotion and demotion of other members, and gained (at least formally) the right to publicly contest the decisions of leaders. 'Universal' meetings (for the whole group) were now held regularly each month, and 'culture' classes were held weekly in each 'tribe' – in which designated members would 'teach' lessons from the 'Bible' together with other texts dealing with Latino culture, US history and assorted other topics. Ideological resistance and conflict emerged throughout these changes, particularly between old and new members – the former in general being more concerned with preserving the cultural identity of the group and less with activism. These dynamics are examined below.

Literature Review

Rather than treating gangs as complex organizations, researchers tend to focus on crime and mayhem and to explain these aspects by reference to individual pathologies as well as 'situational' and 'structural' factors. This tendency is underscored through an increased reliance on police statistics (Curry and Decker 2003). In addition, in tandem with other sociological fields (Kontos 2001), gang research increasingly involves the use of literary techniques that simulate a scientific mode of discourse; for instance, a passive voice, colourless language and the trope of irony. The result is that the complexity of gangs is undercut and members' decisions and actions come to appear predetermined and inadvertent in relation to seemingly transparent interests. Thus, typically missing from sociological explanations of gangs is any recognition of the diversity of interests and ideologies that exists within them, and the role of this diversity in producing and transforming 'gang culture'.

It is worth noting that the first sociological studies of gangs, namely those of the Chicago School, treated them as cultural phenomena by focusing on their ways of life as the most sociologically significant thing about them. Moreover, in this body of work, most notably the studies of Frederick Thrasher (1927/1963), gang culture is conceived of as relatively fluid and as a dimension of social action rather than a cause, as later subcultural studies (such as Cohen 1955; Miller 1958) would have it. The Chicago-area gangs that Thrasher studied adopted cultural norms and values from larger, ethnic cultures, while members appeared to develop distinctly American attitudes and desires. In this regard, gang culture appears as a vehicle for Americanization. In Thrasher's language, it is a 'natural' response to social forces and conditions. But not merely so. Rather, the 'gang boys' he describes maintain elaborate codes and imaginative representations that mediate their relations with one another and the outside world. This is what makes the gang a symbolic community (see Hunter 1974).

Moreover, the extent to which expectations are clearly defined depends on the type of gang. For instance, the Cholo gangs that James Diego Vigil (1988) refers to as 'established' are quasi-institutional in nature, in that they have a life beyond the current generation of members, and they have explicit and elaborate rules regarding membership. To join a group like this is to make a qualitatively different kind of commitment than that which is entailed in joining a street-corner group. In addition, the resources available to established gangs makes it possible for them to make long-term plans that serve to alter their relation to other groups and the outside world generally. For instance, as Sudhir Venkatesh (1996) points out, gangs that call themselves 'organizations' and 'nations' have often sought out a certain degree of social legitimacy, which entails added demands on the conduct of members. In all cases, however, researchers 'discover' the same demands, including codes of secrecy and sacrifice for the well being of their organization. Yet it must also be understood that not all such demands translate into real expectations, and different expectations can emerge in response to external events and from internal dynamics. Thus, it is necessary for social researchers to move beyond what members say about their values and beliefs and discover their contextual embeddedness, and therefore the expectations that maintain or subvert particular values and beliefs.

For instance, it can be shown that there is normally a significant investment among gang members in the attitude of 'machismo'. This routine discovery is given an interesting turn (because some historical context is added) in the work of Ruth Horowitz (1983) and Joan Moore (1991), where it is shown to have been associated with positive characteristics in traditional Latin American societies, including the willingness to defend the community from outside forces. According to these authors, attitudes that once served a positive function become problematic when they are separated from the needs of the community; which is to say, when attempts to protect the community do not occasion them, but instead they serve to undermine such attempts.

One problem with this and other imputations of value systems, however, is a lack of recognition of the ways in which their expression is mediated by structured expectations. William Sanders (1994) identifies this problem in his attempt to explain the rise of lethal violence of gangs on the west coast in the 1980s. His argument underlines a basic social-psychological fact, namely that values and ideologies do not necessarily lead to any given behaviour. Rather, values like 'machismo', 'honour', and 'respect' become a source of violence in situations where the alternatives to it are deemed impractical because they are perceived to result in a loss of face and therefore the esteem of other members. Sanders presents gang violence itself as a contextually embedded phenomenon, in that violent retribution is expected – for instance, in response to acts that represent violent retribution. In addition, performative displays of identity are said to normally entail 'character contests' that lead to violence in the world of gangs, which is described as a closed world. Sanders does not find situations, conversely, where gang members are given (or give each other) a way out of escalating character contests, or where the interpretation of modal norms supports non-action – for instance, where honour dictates not fighting with someone for whatever reason.

Others have highlighted the fact that 'mass culture' is more insipid and pervasive than during the times that Thrasher was writing about. This would mean that notions of 'honour' and 'respect', which are associated with traditional societies, must now be ignored or reconciled to the norm of competition and the value of individual status and achievement. This is the view of Martin Sanchez Jankowski (1991), who points out that excessive ('defiant') individualism supports the most unseemly aspects of the underground economy where alliances are fleeting because everyone is out for himself, and where competitors are simply taken out in any way possible. He does not, in turn, find many signs of cooperation or community in the gangs he studied. Felix Padilla (1992), by contrast, argues that gang members typically have conflicting motives and are also usually manipulated by powerful people in the organization. Thus, it appears that the majority join for camaraderie and protection, and that they also believe that they will be able to make money as they see others do, but instead they find themselves working for those others while absorbing most of the risk. Such descriptions serve to illustrate the complexity of modern gangs. However, in the process, they replace subtlety with irony, thus inviting the reader to look 'beneath the surface' at processes that escape the attention and understanding of members, and that researchers have identified as 'social facts' that they – already – know much about. Alternatively, it is possible to discover the self-understanding of members and the ways in which it is related to action in practical social contexts, and further to engage this self-understanding critically in order to determine its epistemic validity and sociological implications.

My observations of the Latin Kings are based on ethnographic research conducted over a three-year period, 1998–2000. During this time, I attended meetings at the invitation of leaders, and I observed members in casual and official gatherings, as well as during protests, speak-outs, and demonstrations. Between four to six hours weekly were spent with members. Over eighty members were interviewed; twenty were recorded. (None were remunerated.) Recorded interviews were semi-structured while the rest were informal; most lasted between one and a half and two hours. My first encounters were with high-ranking members who acted as gatekeepers, providing access to members and situations. In the course of doing interviews and observing members in disparate settings, significant differences emerged within and between factions in New York City and Long Island, which are illustrated below. The names of members, gangs and settings are fictitious or distorted in ways that ensure that identities are protected.

Politicization of the Kings

By the summer of 1998, when I began my research, the Nation, as members refer to it, had become a regular participant in political rallies, demonstrations, and speak-outs throughout New York City. Representatives were giving interviews to the media – mainstream as well as alternative. And the group had garnered the support of other groups that were revered in the community, including the National Congress for Puerto Rican Rights, and Mothers Against Police Brutality. It also had the support of local clergy. During my study most of the universal meetings were held at St. Mary's in Harlem, Father Luis Barrios' church.[2] For those who were further removed from the Kings, but also seemingly willing to give them a chance to prove themselves, the central issue was whether their motives could be trusted rather than what they were actually doing. And opinions about motive hinged largely on the credibility of a single individual with a problematic background, namely, King Tone. The *New York Times* simultaneously captured and exacerbated this dilemma in its headline 'Man of Vision or of Violence? Where Gang Leader Talks Peace, Police See Just Talk' (Bearak 1997: 1). The Kings were in fact not saying that they had decided to be non-violent, but instead that they were trying to effect political change around specific issues, to which they are also trying to lay claim. The primary issue for the Kings – police brutality – resonated widely in the community but was given little attention by the mainstream media and the political establishment of New York.[3] The Kings took up the issue by holding demonstrations outside of city hall, and by sending hundreds of members to rallies held by Mothers Against Police Brutality, amongst other groups. The Kings' participation was widely seen as a primary reason for the success of Mothers, particularly by Iris Baez, the founder and leader of the organization. By her

2. Father Barrios ultimately lost this church for his political activities, which included speaking out on behalf of the Kings. See Barrios (1998), Barrios (forthcoming).

3. In fact, the escalation of reported cases of police abuse and brutality, coupled with the lack of official response, has made nonsense of talk of 'police accountability'. See Kontos (2000).

account, in addition to participating in rallies by the hundreds, 'they did security and they went to court every day' (*ABC Nightline*, 8 April 1997).

As the Kings were developing a public, political persona, they were also attracting a different kind of member from that which had been typical up to that point. That is to say, after 1995, the Kings began to attract members with little or no criminal background, with stable jobs or college careers, and therefore whose 'decision' to join took place against a broader range of options. Yet most positions of authority were distributed among the old guard. At the same time, codes of conduct, particularly those pertaining to inter-group association, were becoming blurred and the contradiction between criminal and political deviance was becoming explicit and difficult to reconcile.

The Old Guard

I count among the old-guard those existing members who were given positions of authority prior to the change of leadership in 1996. These individuals were by definition advocates of change because they had survived a massive purge (rumoured at between 500 and 1000 members). Therefore, their advocacy provided a necessary bridge between contradictory representations and expectations. Indeed, the Kings were claiming, in their own vernacular, to have evolved into a stronger organization with less negativity' rather than having simply tried to make peace with rivals or undergone some kind of spiritual awakening or moral cleansing, as they had been consistently caricatured as doing by the mainstream media and even by some researchers (see, for example, Corbiscello 1997). The complexity of this phenomenon is captured in the following remark by Willie Morales, a Boston YMCA director and former member of the X-Men:

> I saw them at a public speakout in New York City a year and half ago. It was a pretty positive event. I saw it as legit from the get-go . . . I admired them. They're not saying, 'we are former Latin Kings'. They are saying, 'we are Latin Kings'. They're not trying to hide their past. I think their past makes them more credible with young people. (quoted in Rodriquez, 1999: B1)

However, as the old-timers were both powerful and influential – because their time with organization meant that they had paid sufficient 'dues' – any equivocation on their part caused a stir among the membership and cast a shadow of doubt over the possibility of trying to transform a gang into a social movement (to put it in simplified terms). Below, the circumstances of three high-ranking members are examined.

The first, 'King Old-Timer', has been with the organization for twelve years and has played a key role in establishing the independence of the first Long Island tribe. The problem now, he says, is that 'almost anyone can join', and therefore it is impossible to trust anybody. He points out that when he made his decision to join it was understood to be a life-long commitment without the possibility of exit, and that talking to outsiders about the organization (violating the code of secrecy) was punishable by death. His story is typical of the old guard, that is, of being lost in 'negativity' before joining the Kings and subsequently turning his life around. By his account, prior to joining, he sold drugs for two years with a partner who was then, unbeknownst to him, a Latin King. The rest of the account is as follows.

One day he asked the respondent to attend a meeting. There he met a member whose brother was a high-ranking member in Attica prison and who needed money. After coming through with the money he was 'crowned' by the inmate, and the crowning was made official in a ceremony after the inmate was released from prison.[4] I asked him why he joined.

> *King Old Timer:* I focused on it for about a year before becoming a King. I became a King, 14 November 1992.
> *LK:* How is it that you remember that exactly?
> *King Old Timer:* That's like our birthday, our born-again day.
> *LK:* Do you celebrate that?
> *King Old Timer:* Yeah I do, with the brothers. We have two birthdays, the Nation birthday and our age birthday. New Kings, I don't think they acknowledge when they are crowned. But to us it means a lot.

(Interview, 12 May 1999).

In my observations, new members were just as likely to remember the exact date they were 'crowned' and to use the language of 'rebirth' to describe their newly found sense of community and sense of purpose in the organization. However, they stood out in other ways, including the fact that they were generally better able to fit into other, conventional settings and groups, thereby being (or at least appearing to be) less committed to the organization. Those members are far removed from the prison-gang days, and while most of them have been through at least one correctional facility, they have generally not done hard time. Four out of five new members who were interviewed fell into this category, whereas only one in ten of the old guard who were interviewed did so. This meant, accordingly, that they had not been properly 'tested'.

4. This crowning was later revoked upon the objection of King Tone, who was then without any rank, on the grounds that it had not been subjected to a vote. The member, who is now an old-timer, went through the process of being approved by the extant membership, and eventually rose to a high rank as a member of the Supreme Council of the Latin Kings.

One of the closest allies of King Tone was King Skibee, who carried the distinction of having been crowned in prison by King Blood himself. In a short article entitled 'What is the Sacrifice of a True Royal King?'[5] he claimed that his membership has involved him in plenty of trouble with parole officers and cost him the right to see his daughter from a previous marriage. It is also nearly costing him his current marriage as he is constantly busy with the Nation. But he has no regrets, he adds. 'No matter under any circumstances in my righteous beliefs, or any obstacles, will I betray the crown of the Almighty Latin King and Queen Nation. Not even if my destiny is to do life.' King Skibee embodied the spirit of the Latin Kings together with all their contradictions, and thus was able to provide continuity between the different worlds that they simultaneously inhabited. He was the public face of the Kings regardless of what the organization was doing. His tattoos have been featured in several local hip-hop magazines. In a *PrimeTime Live* (14 January 1998) documentary on the Kings, he is shown publicly denouncing a member accused of rape. At a rally in front of city hall – protesting against the killing of Amadou Diallo, upon whom four police officers fired forty-one times after, they claimed, mistaking his wallet for a gun – King Skibee was given the last word by the *Village Voice,* which quoted him 'let[ting] out a long whistle. "Giuliani done started some shit"' (Trebay 1999).

More common than either supporters or detractors among the old guard were those members who were constantly struggling to surmount personal problems that compromised their effectiveness and made them constantly vulnerable to leadership contests. A version of this can be seen in the case of 'King Old-School', whom I met in the summer of 1999 during a meeting of a local tribe in Suffolk County, Long Island. He had been demoted earlier from a leadership position to a regular member, and had been given a probationary status. He voiced opposition during the meeting by saying 'I want us to be closer together. I have much love for all of you. And even though you put me on "Five Alive," I'm still a King. I have much love for you guys and I'm still a King whatever happens.'[6] In response to King Old-School's attempt to redeem himself for his crime – a heroin addiction relapse – he was further admonished. A few days later I was able to interview him.

5. This article can be found in the October 1998 issue of the Kings' monthly newsletter, *El Grito* (literally: *The Shout*).

6. 'Five Alive': a term used in the group slogan 'Five Alive, Six Must Die'. 'Five', in this context, refers to the five-point crown with which the gangs in the People Nation coalition represent their affiliation, versus gangs that belong to the side of the Folk Nation, whose members 'represent' with a six-point crown. In this context the phrase refers to probationary status, as if one were initially trying to join the Latin Kings and thereby asked to proclaim allegiances.

LK:	What do you mean Old-School?
King Old-School:	I got years under my belt. Putting up with police [laughs]. Most of the guys in [this town] only have months . . . [One ranking member of the local tribe] has a year. Only . . . [three members] were there when I joined. Most of the guys from back then are in jail now.
LK:	Anything else?
King Old School:	Yeah, I been tested. I been to jail. I been there for the brothers. When I had my house [prior to parents' separation] everybody, almost everybody, either stayed there or lived there at one time or another . . .
LK:	Why did you join the Kings?
King Old-School:	I had just separated from my wife . . . I guess I was looking for a family.
LK:	What does the organization give to you now?
King Old-School:	It has given a lot. It has given me self-esteem. It has made me, like, optimistic. It's made me believe in something, you know, be part of something. Most every brother is going to tell you that. There's a lot of love, man. You know how we are, we hang out together, we get into trouble together, we go through problems together. You know? We're a family. That's what I love about it. That's the main thing about being a King.

(Interview, 18 June 1999).

During the time of my interview, King Old-School was still trying to kick his drug habit by going to a rehabilitation centre. A few months ago I discovered that he did not succeed – that is, he was arrested on a drug charge and provided damaging information about group members in exchange for reduced punishment.[7] While this type of 'betrayal' is commonplace for the organization, it is felt deeply on Long Island – a more tightly knit and insular faction.

Cultural Spread and Contrasts

It is widely recognized among researchers that the spread of gangs is cultural rather than structural in nature (Maxson 1998; Hagedorn 1988). The Kings were no exception. That is to say, while they shared a common culture, and while they were formally bound to the same rules and regulations and a centralized chain of command, they maintained a distinct identity and they were autonomous in most respects. Both cultural and structural autonomy were facilitated through a system

7. Another part of the deal was that he would make a public statement, without having to expose his identity; however, the news show in which he was featured did little to disguise his appearance and voice and he was easily recognizable to even the remotest acquaintance.

of governance comprised of interlocking 'crown structures', with five 'crowns' for each tribe, governing its day-to-day affairs.[8] But the relationship amongst tribes was ambiguous, because those in Long Island were more insular than their urban counterpart. It was, in fact, only after the reforms described above were implemented, that a majority of them began showing up as a group to monthly 'universal' meetings. By contrast, only a fraction (fewer than one in ten) showed up to the rallies and demonstrations. Everyone claimed to agree with these 'in principle', yet they were time-consuming, given distances of thirty to sixty miles to the city depending on the location of the particular tribe, and they revolved around issues that did not affect members personally. In addition, Long Island members proved to be more politically apathetic and troubled by publicity than their urban counterparts, even though they had less to live down and were no more committed, rather less in fact, to the 'old ways' of the organization.

There were three popular versions of how the first tribe of Latin Kings appeared on the island. In the first version, King Marco was made regional leader by King Blood while serving time with him in Collins Correctional Facility. According to this version, Marco initially recruited from his own circle of family and friends. In the second version, it was not until a few years later that Long Island Kings established a separate identity, that is, only after several dozen members who were 'crowned' in prison returned home to Long Island. In this version, a high ranking member, King Fats, who was living in Long Island and reporting to Brooklyn, obtained permission to establish a separate tribe in Long Island. According to that version, less than a dozen members were living there at that time, and it was expected that recruits would be drawn from the neighbourhoods and local detention facilities. In a third version, a few dozen members were living in Long Island and reporting to various tribes in the boroughs of New York City – although it was generally agreed that the bulk of members were reporting to Brooklyn prior to the development of a separate tribe on the island. At the same time, Long Island tribes maintained a stronger connection to Brooklyn than other tribes in New York City, as a result of original connections of friendship and family, even though Queens is closer.

Each version of the founding of the first Long Island tribe corresponded to members' personal allegiances to the individuals who claimed the status of founders. This made it impossible to resolve the question of origins – whether the first Long Island tribe began in 1986 by King Marco, or 1992 by King Fats. Whatever the case may be, the Kings are recognized as being among the first national organizations to appear on Long Island (Domash 1998). These types developed against the backdrop of waves of deindustrialization, when many of the older 'crews' and

---

8. Five crowns also constitute the central leadership, together with a Supreme Council, and, after King Tone became leader, a Supreme Team was added to effect transition.

'posses' began to consolidate and new organizations began to appear that took their names from west-coast and mid-west gangs, and recreated their rivalries. But none besides the Latin Kings could be considered very organized. At the same time, despite their level, organization, size, and name recognition, they were practically invisible.

The Long Island Kings never managed to accomplish what Phil Cohen (1972) says about youth subcultures, namely that they 'win space'. While they maintained a distinct style of dress, symbols, rituals, argot and the rest, their activities as a group were truncated in private space and the corners of society that no one cared about – including parks at night, abandoned buildings and warehouses on the outskirts of town (again, only at night). Indeed, during the course of research, the Long Island Kings were constantly looking for safe areas to meet and hang out, and none that became available could be maintained for any extended period of time. It was significant in this regard that the Long Island Kings managed to meet with a great deal of frequency anyway; even more so than their urban counterparts. Whereas New York City tribes met once a week, Long Island tribal meetings were typically held bi-weekly.

Although the Kings in New York City regularly complained about being hassled by the police when they were out together in small numbers without causing trouble, that was about the extent of their problem with public space. Even their meetings, both tribal and universal (always held in New York City) were usually problem-free – notwithstanding the constant presence of police surveillance that was supposed to be hidden, but was usually visible. Neighbourhood parks provided easy access and relative safety. And, most importantly, they had access to Church buildings. Besides Father Barrios, Father Eddie Lopez of Tremont United Methodist Church in the Bronx maintained an open-door policy for the Kings. And Father Gordon Duggins employed as many as 100 of them at any given time on various sites and, on occasion, allowed the group to meet in large numbers. On Long Island, by contrast, a single youth pastor had made some misguided overtures toward the Kings in the summer of 1998. Although the Church could provide safety from the police and rival groups, members expressed fears that they would be subjected to indoctrination, and agreed only reluctantly to its use after receiving assurances to the contrary. In exchange for 'space', promises were made to take care of the facilities and also participate in 'youth' classes once a week. It appeared, however, that the Church and members each had a different conception of the youth class. For the latter, it meant an opportunity to talk with 'brothers' in a protective setting about issues that mattered to them. 'This is great because here we get a chance to rap' was the way one enthusiastic member put it to me. For the Church, by contrast, it appeared to mean that religious doctrine had to be tailored to problematic youth in order to bring them into the fold. The relationship between the Kings and the Church was to dissolve in this instance for yet another reason, namely, the opposition of the congregation. The clergy translated this opposition into the demand that individual members could go by themselves, not in large numbers or as identifiable 'members'. This seemingly well-meaning but contradictory stance was immediately responded to as an unforgivable breach.

Whereas the Kings in the city could lay claim on a variety of forms of public space, the Long Island faction of the Kings was constantly on the defensive. Whereas the urban faction was developing a public, political persona, the suburban tribes were busy trying to maintain the viability of their organization away from public scrutiny. They were treated with a mixture of indifference and hostility by most of the locals, notwithstanding the fact that they recruited exclusively from local neighbourhoods (and the same population from the prisons). In New York City, Latin Kings could join protest rallies and public demonstrations of all kinds on a regular basis, assuming only the desire to do so. This was simply not the case in Long Island. Therefore, Long Island members who were especially politically conscious and motivated spent a lot of time in the city – as did members who were looking for fast money or street life.

Conclusion

The Latin Kings caught the attention of the New York public in the late 1980s when they were experiencing phenomenal growth and developing a reputation for extreme violence. They became the subject of public controversy a decade later when they began to reinvent themselves as a political organization. However, it was neither their grievances nor their tactics that made them controversial, as these were consistent with the 'tactical repertoire' of the activist base of the community rather than being new or different. Instead there was a question about their sincerity, and at every opportunity doubts were cast on their motives by the NYPD and other detractors, all of whom claimed that the Kings were actually staging an elaborate propaganda campaign for nefarious reasons. The objective of this chapter has not been to resolve the issue of motive, but instead to illustrate the dynamics of particular sociological phenomena. In that way it also serves to underline the fact that, regardless of motive, actions have meaning and consequence.

References

Barrios, L. (2003), 'The Almighty Latin King and Queen Nation and the Spirituality of Resistance: Religiosity, Agency, and Liberation in the Making of a Street Organization', in L. Kontos, D. C. Brotherton and L. Barrios (eds), *Gangs and Society: Alternative Perspectives*, New York: Columbia University Press.

Barrios, L. (1998), '"Santa Maria" as a Liberating Zone: A Community Church in Search of Restorative Justice', *Humanity and Society*, 22 (1): 55–78.

Bearak, B. (1997), 'Man of Vision or of Violence? Where Gang Leader Talks Peace, Police See Just Talk', *New York Times*, Section B (20 November): 1.

Brotherton, D. C. and Barrios, L. (forthcoming), *Between Black and Gold: The Street Politics of the Almighty Latin King and Queen Nation*, New York: Columbia University Press.

Cohen, A. K. (1955), *Delinquent Boys: The Culture of the Gang*, Glencoe IL: Free Press.

Cohen, P. (1972), *Subcultural Conflict and Working Class Community*, Working Papers in Cultural Studies 2, CCCS, University of Birmingham.

Corbiscello, G. V. (1997), 'The Almighty Latin King and Queen Nation of New York and Environs', *Journal of Gang Research*, 4 (2): 59–74.

Curry, G. D. and Decker, S. H. (2003), *Confronting Gangs: Crime and Community*, 2 edn, Los Angeles CA: Roxbury Publishing Co.

Domash, S. F. (1998), 'Our Gangs: Wars, and Warriors, Go Local', *New York Times*, Section 14 (22 November): 1 and 16.

Hagedorn, J. (1988), *People and Folks; Gangs, Crime and the Underclass in a Rustbelt City*, Chicago IL: Lakeview Press.

Horowitz, R. (1983), *Honor and the American Dream*, New Brunswick NJ: Rutgers University Press.

Hunter, A. (1974), *Symbolic Communities: The Persistence and Change of Chicago's Local Communities*, Chicago IL: University of Chicago Press.

Jankowski, M. S. (1991), *Islands in the Street: Gangs and American Urban Society*, Berkeley and Los Angeles CA: University of California Press.

Kontos, L. (2000), 'Review of "Turnaround: How America's Top Cop Reversed the Crime Epidemic" by William Bratton', *Humanity and Society*, 24 (4): 421–5.

Kontos, L. (2001), 'Differentiation and Complexity in the Functionalist Corpus: Rethinking the Metaphor of System', *The American Sociologist*, 32 (1): 100–6.

Maxson, C. L. (1998), 'Gang Members on the Move', *Juvenile Justice Bulletin* (October): 1-11, US Department of Justice, Office of Justice Programs, Office of Juvenile Justice and Delinquency Prevention.

Miller, W. B. (1958), 'Lower Class Culture as a Generating Milieu of Gang Delinquency', *Journal of Social Issues*, 14: 5-19.

Moore, J. (1991), *Going Down in the Barrio: Homeboys and Homegirls in Change*, Philadelphia PA: Temple University Press.

Padilla, F. (1992), *The Gang as an American Enterprise*, New Brunswick NJ: Rutgers University Press.

Rodriguez, C. (1999), 'NYC Gang Offers Local Youth a New Message. Latino Elders, Police Doubtful of Group's Motives', *Boston Globe*, Metro Section, (23 April): B1.

Sanders, W. G. (1994), *Gangbangs and Drive-bys: Grounded Culture and Juvenile Gang Violence*, New York: Aldine de Gruyter.

Trebay, G. (1999), 'Disobedience Training: Mayor Taunts City and a Coalition Forms', *Village Voice*, 24–30 March.

Thrasher, F. (1927/1963), *The Gang: A Study of 1313 Gangs in Chicago*, Chicago IL: University of Chicago Press.

Venkatesh, S. A. (1996), 'The Gang and the Community', in C. R. Huff (ed.), *Gangs in America*, Thousand Oaks CA: Sage.

Vigil, J. D. (1988), *Barrio Gangs: Street Life and Identity in Southern California*, Austin TX: University of Texas Press.

Part IV
'Race', Ethnicity and Hybridity

–10–

Radical Hybridity: Latinas/os as the Paradigmatic Transnational Post-subculture

Angharad N. Valdivia

One of the vexing issues facing scholars of popular culture is that we cannot tell when a subculture is indeed an emerging culture without the aid of hindsight. However, as the post-subculture, local substream and global mainstream theoretical move indicates (Weinzierl 2001), contemporary conditions compel us to move beyond this culture/subculture binary divide to a position wherein there is more flexibility to acknowledge and account for fluidity, hybridity, and collaboration and/or cooptation between the substream and the commercialized mainstream. This current conceptualization of local substreams and global mainstreams (LSGM) brings subcultural theory and research into the new millennium where empirical and theoretical currents exhort us to expand our framework of analysis.

Latina/os in the US provide an opportunity for an empirical case study to illuminate the LSGM model.[1] They are the population who can trace part or most of their background, ancestors, and/or heritage to Latin American countries and they compose a growing part of the US population, both in absolute and proportional terms. Already poised to outnumber the previously more numerous US minority of African-Americans, both popular culture and legal discourse have had

1. Deciding who is a Latina/o and what counts as 'Latinidad', the culture produced by Latina/os and the practices of being Latina/o, has proven to be a nearly impossible task. The fact is that it is untenable to classify Latina/os by race, ethnicity, class, religion, language, food, dance and musical proclivities – to name but a few of the vectors of difference that often delineate the margins between one cultural group and another. Latina/os come from a variety of territorial origins. Many come from Latin America but many others predate the arrival of Anglo populations to the North American continent. Many speak Spanish, but many have adopted a hybrid language. This whole area of scholarship is made more complex by the radical hybridity of Latina/o populations both in the US and throughout the world (Gómez-Peña 2000; Kraidy 1999, 2002; Moreiras 1998). As Lipsitz (1999a) reminds us, a turn to Latina/o studies forces us to explore the radical hybridity that composes every population, especially in the US. In terms of the emerging interdiscipline of US Latina/o Studies (Darder and Torres 1998; Flores 1993, 2000; garcia, Leger and Valdivia, forthcoming), this research project urges us to look at ethnic hybridity in the US, beyond the still dominant Black-and-White formulation and beyond the bi-coastal geographic tendencies.

to account for this growing segment of the population. US Latina/os also challenge previously dominant cultural conceptions of subcultures as they exhibit large and radical degrees of three of the components of the LSGM model, namely, fluidity, hybridity, and collaboration and/or cooptation between the substream and the commercialized mainstream.

Whereas the commercial arena has certainly acknowledged the presence and the marketing benefits of Latina/os and Latinidad (Cepeda 2001; Dávila 2001), there are also many Latina/os and those practising Latinidad who exist at the margins, not necessarily greatly partaking of mainstream hypercommercialized products. It is difficult to make generalizations about Latina/os and Latinidad, but it is useful to study this local substream through the construction of community formation via a form of expressive culture, namely salsa. Using salsa as a metaphor for Latinidad we can explore the construction of borders within the Latina/o community itself; for as Lugo (2000), Stoler (2000), and Oboler (1995) among many others have noted, there is a large gap in our knowledge of this topic within research into cultural groups.

My argument in this chapter is that post-subcultural formations are not necessarily related to a specific social class; they can be more than ethnically mixed – they can, in fact, be ethnically hybrid; they are not necessarily confined to youth but rather are multi-generational. I show that imported hierarchies of nationality, ethnicity and gender do not disappear in new, local settings. Rather they are renegotiated and often replanted, re-established and re-enforced. Global mainstreams flow through these local substreams in not altogether revolutionary or emancipatory ways. At the level of community formation, the local substream creates an alternative space, but often it replicates certain global power differentials. Or, as Moreiras (1998) suggests, even the immigrant imaginary is subject to the homogenization of difference. Thus the cooptation functions not so much at the level of the subcultural stream *vis-à-vis* commercialized mainstream, but rather in relation to global discourses of difference.

The research on which this chapter is based began in the spring of 1995 and is ongoing. It is a study of a Midwestern, US community referred to as Cornsoya. Lying somewhere between two major US cities, Cornsoya is the location for one of the major 'Big Ten' universities, a consortium of institutions of higher education which reside on land grant locations and exchange resources as well as battle with each other in collegiate sports, most notably US football and basketball. This community ranges from 100,000 people during the university terms to about 65,000 people when the university is on break, a classic university small town. Surrounded by more than 100 miles of corn and soya fields, on which are employed large numbers of seasonal, mostly Latina/o labour, the community has a range of both permanent and temporary residents, from highly paid professionals to the immigrant and mostly poverty-ridden agricultural and fast-food workers.

This is the somewhat predictable human mix in this Midwestern town.[2] I explore the hybridity of this group in an effort to understand the indigenous formation of boundaries and belonging (Brah and Coombes 2000). Participant observation and ethnographic inquiry were employed in a number of settings including dance instruction, band rehearsals, salsa parties, and dance nights at local bars. Extensive interviews (the majority of which were conducted in 2000) were also undertaken with different members of this community, ranging from immigrant field workers and local residents to graduate students, faculty, and university administrators in the local university. Through this combination of methodologies (Abu-Lughod 1991; Denzin 1997), I investigate the conscious process of identity formation that goes on in a community with little or no history of Latina/o populations.

Latin Music and Dance

There is a nearly irresistible tendency to associate Latin and now Latina/o populations with dance[3] and conversely to associate dance with Latina/os. If movies are any reliable indicators[4] an easy way to code a festive tone, at the very least, or a sensual-leading-into-sexual moment, in a more intense deployment of Latin signification, is to background the scene with Latin music, whether it be bossa nova, cha cha cha, samba, tango, or salsa. Latin music has come to signify not just Latina/o populations but also festivity, sensuality and sexuality.

Until recently the majority of essays and books about Latin music of all sorts (such as Best 1995; Manuel 1995; Rohler 1990) and about salsa (for example, Boggs 1992; Calvo Ospina 1995) focused on the music, its roots, its influences, its popularity and its changing characteristics, but not on the dance itself (Bergman 1985; Leymarie 1985; Calvo Ospina 1995). While more recent scholarship has begun exploring the dance as compared to the music (Delgado and Muñoz 1997; garcia 1997; Lipsitz 1999b), Desmond (1997) urges us to approach the study of

2. Where possible I will give the ethnicity, profession or student status and residency status of the participants in this community as it is important to show the broad diversity of origins, as well as occupations, of those who are active in the formation of a community of expressive culture.

3. This identity marker of Latina/o proposes, among other components, a pan-Latina/o and pan-ethnic diverse identity whose boundaries are still quite unclear. For example, some exclude Brazilian origin populations despite that country's immense contribution to musical and dance trends, whereas others include people of Spanish origin, such as Antonio Banderas and Penelope Cruz.

4. For example, in the film *The Battle of Algiers*, the colonial French teenagers in a soon-to-be-bombed discotheque are dancing to some cha-cha-cha, and I have interviewed people from places as diverse as Ghana and Turkey who associate dancing music with Latin music. I choose *The Battle of Algiers* as an example precisely because, although not a Hollywood film, it is still subject to particularly US proclivities.

music and the study of dance together. This is all the more important, she suggests, given that dance is a much 'bracketed-off' form of expressive culture. At least in the US, dance 'mark[s] clearly the continuing rhetorical association of bodily expressivity with non-dominant groups' (Desmond 1997: 35) and is often linked to African-American and Latina/o populations. Desmond thus challenges us to unmask the supposed transparency of dance expressivity and its essentialist links to particular populations.

While there are many possible Latin dances to study, such as cumbia, merengue, tango, samba, quebradita, vallenato, etc., the focus of my study is on salsa, partly because one of its origins can be traced to the US. Thus, Calvo Ospina (1995) and Boggs (1992) explicitly trace the roots back to Cuba but the active creation to New York City.[5] Although there is considerable disagreement as to the roots of salsa, there is nonetheless a nod to the possibility that salsa is a music and dance created by Latina/o populations living in the US as a result of an active, resistant and dynamic combination and extension of previous musical and dance forms in a minority and hostile cultural situation. The presence of Latina/os throughout the US means that, of course, one should expect to find salsa in New York and Miami. However, perhaps unexpectedly to many, one can also find salsa in many other places such as Detroit, Chicago, Champaign, Saint Louis, Seattle, New Orleans, San Diego, Austin, and San Antonio. In these and many other locations one can find some or all of the following: salsa bars, salsa nights, salsa lessons and/or Latin nights where salsa is a popular form of dance and music. This is the 'noctural map' (García Canclini 1995) of salsa.

The creation of both the music and the dance is linked to previous cultural forms available in popular culture, albeit the popular culture of an ethnic group, appealing to both Latina/o and non Latina/o populations. However, as we know from the study of a broad range of cultural forms, it is difficult to police the national boundaries of cultural expression (Benítez-Rojo 1992; Flores 1993, 2000; Rodríguez 1997; Shohat 1998; Shohat and Stam 1994). So salsa as a form of cultural expressivity spreads transnationally throughout the Americas but particularly in the Spanish/Hispanic Caribbean nexus – Cuba, Puerto Rico, Cali in Caribbean Colombia, Veracruz in Caribbean Mexico, Venezuela, Miami, and New York, both of the latter being sites of much Caribbean migration. This is all to be expected, the proximitous spread of a cultural form. However, and undoubtedly building on the historically grounded coding of Latin music as dance music, salsa also spreads much more broadly both throughout the rest of the Americas, though not with as much intensity as in the previously mentioned areas, and through the world. This has to do with both the spread of the musical form and with the diasporic population of Latina/os.

5. The book by Calvo Ospina (1995) is also a testament to the global spread of salsa and of salseros, as it was originally published in Dutch, in Antwerp.

The Salsa Story

Within this isolated yet unexpectedly heterogeneous context of Cornsoya, many groups and individuals host parties in their homes or in some type of hall. It was in one such occasion that Rodrigo, a Colombian computer science student, decided to teach a couple of girls at a party to dance salsa. Rodrigo decided to begin hosting lessons in his living room, but even these small, word-of-mouth occasions proved to be challenging to handle inside a student's quarter. Another local resident, Scott, an Anglo young man and former violin university student who was born and raised in this community, happened to be walking home, drunk, after another party when he came upon one of Rodrigo's lessons/parties (inevitably all of these lessons would turn into a festive occasion) and could not walk by without stopping. Scott was hooked and returned for more, week after week. From Suriname, Margarita had travelled to Louisiana to pursue graduate computer studies. While there she organized an international, Latin American student group that would also celebrate with dances. When she moved to this community, she gravitated to the Rodrigo group and, by the time Scott's drunken trip home took him by way of the lesson, she was there, as Rodrigo's girlfriend, to help Scott learn to dance. These are some of the principals in this Midwestern story of community formation through cultural expressivity. I mention them, not to single out these individuals, but to show the arbitrariness of the forces that came together to begin a thriving salsa community in the middle of corn fields and thus to underscore the potential for creativity and community formation in even the most unlikely of places.

As Rodrigo was not the only person who could salsa, regular parties with other Colombian, Latina/os, Spanish and so forth students and local residents began to spring up. Rodrigo had to obtain an assistant, a fellow Colombian, to help him teach the classes and had to secure a larger place, which he did through the School of Music, to teach an ever growing number of people who wanted to take the classes. At this time the university Latina/o cultural centre and the university dance club, both official university groups, began to offer salsa and, to a lesser extent, merengue lessons to the community at large. The former were taught by a Peruvian community resident; the latter by Anglo students at the university. Simultaneously Chloe, a Chinese-Canadian graduate student in ethnomusicology, began her own salsa band. This galvanized many and served notice to the larger community as well as to local bars that there was both desire and an audience for this type of music. All of this coalesced into the creation of a salsa community with several main players, different levels of 'authenticity' of groups and players, and different locations for the learning and performance of salsa, the music and the dance.

This would be a modernist tale of progress were it not for the fact that a university community has a shifting and unstable population and that, since many of the salseros of note – Rodrigo, Margarita, and Chloe – were students, there were bound to be breaks and socio-geographic mobility. Nearly simultaneously, Rodrigo left to study computer science abroad and Chloe went to Cali, Colombia, to conduct her ethnographic research on the salsa scene there. The lessons had to be taught by someone else. The band folded, albeit temporarily. Yet this was not a moment of death, but one of expansion and change. Margarita took over the lessons and sought help from her Colombian friend, Helena. They approached dance instruction in a very different manner than had Rodrigo. They made out instruction plans, dissected salsa moves, and enlisted a drummer to incessantly beat the *clave*[6] to those rhythm-impaired souls taking the classes.

Margarita and Helena were very punctual in their approach to instruction, and, in addition to plastering community boards with announcements, began to develop an email listserve through which they would notify class takers – at least those who were online – of location changes, parties, radio shows, and so forth. The inclusionary and exclusionary potential of this electronic device would become more explicit as the salsa scene developed (an example of which we discuss later in this chapter). They also enlisted Scott, who by this time resided in a perfectly suited large, wooden-floored loft, and had traded in his Birkenstocks for dancing shoes to host the parties. Furthermore, they established a dress code for these parties so they would be even more like salsa dancing in the big cities. Parties drew hundreds of people so that Margarita and Scott had to sit at the door and turn people away.

Within one term of Margarita and Helena's dedicated approach, the number of students showing up for the beginner class jumped from roughly between twenty to thirty in the early Rodrigo days to over 150! The class had to be divided into two, and Margarita co-taught one of these with Scott who had, by then, become a highly proficient dancer. Helena co-taught with Kevin, a Filipino medical student. Both classes had an ethnically diverse teaching couple, one of them without a Latina/o component. To aid and augment this process, Margarita began to pursue other venues. She approached the local community radio station for air time, which would only grant her a half-hour weekly show of 'world music.' She also began to approach local bars and dance halls for the opportunity to DJ a regular salsa night. She successfully gained access to one bar only to be summarily replaced by a male DJ. She then moved to another bar and later to a large dance hall that had the best and largest dance floor in town. Margarita, with the help of Helena and Manuel, a Cuban medical student, became the salsa impresario in this community.

At this time Eliseo, an undergraduate Mexican-American music education student, began to form his own band. Putting together a combination of local musicians and students proved to be quite a challenge in this isolated university

6. The *clave* is the basic 2-3 beat of salsa. It is what distinguishes salsa from merengue or cha cha cha or from other forms of music and dance.

community. To begin with, nearly all salsa musicians are self-trained, as the university does not offer anything in the way of salsa music instruction (a subtle method of policing the boundaries of 'acceptable' music). This made it very difficult to find a vocalist, for nearly all Spanish-speaking singers had no vocal training and none of the local vocalist students had any training in salsa singing. An initial effort at importing band members from Chicago, two-and-a-half hours away, proved economically unfeasible, and Eliseo had to try to find people locally. This band eventually found the perfect female lead vocalist but only at the farewell performance of the band, shortly before its founder and many of its members were about to graduate and move out of town. The vocalist dilemma applied to instrumentalists as well, especially to the pianist. In fact, once a good pianist was found he ended up playing for both Eliseo's band and the new version of Chloe's band, which by all accounts was much better than the original. Thus, for a while this community actually had two competing home-grown salsa bands.

The return of Chloe and Rodrigo to the community coincided with Margarita's, and later Helena's, departure, the former to Holland and the latter to Colombia. Chloe assiduously set about re-forming the band, and enlisted Manuel, the DJ and drum player previously employed by Margarita and Helena to beat the *clave* during lessons. Upon Margarita's departure Manuel took over DJ duties, although he had already began to host a radio show, which he later cancelled because of its ungodly hour of 2.00–4.00 a.m. and the resulting low audience. Other enlisted members included a university professor and a university cultural centre director. Both bands were composed of a heterogeneous group of students, faculty and local residents. Chloe/Manuel's band, however, was able to enlist a steadier line-up of attractive and charismatic Puerto Rican female singers. This band was also able to get gigs as far as Chicago and in the surrounding communities. Manuel proved to be as consummate at business as he was a drum player and salsa dancer.

Many members of the now fully developed and growing salsa community noted that neither band was headed by a 'real' salsero. Chloe's indeterminate Chinese-Canadian features, coupled with her attire, hair style and make up, could have easily 'passed' as Latina, yet to many of those interviewed she remained, until her departure, a 'Latina wannabe'. Eliseo, a Mexican American trumpeter and an excellent dancer himself, was questioned because he was Mexican, and Mexico is not seen as a source of salsa or of dancing music, especially by the other Latina/os and Latin Americans of the community. Sofía, a Mexican-American member of Chloe's band who could dance, play, and sing salsa, was always treated as inauthentic in every setting: in the salsa community people reacted to her salsa skills with the comment 'but you are Mexican!' In the Mexican-American community friends often asked her 'why do you salsa if you are Mexican?' The fact was that she hailed from Veracruz, a Caribbean outpost in Mexico where her uncles and relatives were all very involved in the local salsa scene.

Such 'authenticity' measures[7] in the Anglo musician community revolved much more around musical competence. Thus Eliseo was highly appreciated for his musical sense, both as band director as occasional DJ, as well as his 'suave' dancing style. Sofía was considered an 'impeccable' musician. Chloe's chords were considered simplistic and repetitive. In short, the community had grown to such a size and level of specialization that its members had began to police their own borders and to differentiate each other. In constructing a community at the margins, this subculture of a global stream policed identity in a Nietszchean manner (Nietszche 1967), defining itself in opposition to an 'other' (McCarthy 1998). Yet, whereas the community had formed partly in response to being policed by and out of the mainstream, it was by now developing its own set of inclusions and exclusions. There was now both margins and a mainstream, insiders and outsiders, *within* the salsa scene.

Group Differentials

From the outset, certain characteristics of the founders influenced the way salsa was seen as authentically 'belonging' to particular groups, or combinations of groups, in this particular community. Within this construction of authenticity, certain national origins were granted more legitimacy than others. Rodrigo's initial and now legendary status – he left the community when he finished his degrees – coded salsa dancing as something Colombians did extremely well. In fact, Colombians fulfil significant criteria of authenticity for a number of other reasons. The New Year's Salsa Festival in Cali, Colombia, which hosts and has hosted most of the world's major salsa bands and singers, holds the imagination of many, including many in this community. Not only did one prominent member, Chloe, write her entire dissertation about salsa in Cali, but many of the people, Colombian or not, have travelled to Cali in a sort of salsa pilgrimage. The combination of Colombian teachers, Cali, and musical style all influenced the high status of authenticity of Colombians within this community. This meant that Colombians who could not dance salsa were, and continue to be, seen as an anomaly. At least one such male student stopped attending salsa nights because of the incessant incredulity of others when they found out he, a Colombian, could not salsa. In this community, being Colombian equalled being a salsero.

After the Columbians, two other nationalities claiming a direct and authentic connection to salsa were Cubans and Puerto Ricans, whether recent immigrants, temporary students, or second or third generation citizens of the US. Not only did

---

7. For a definition and discussion of authenticity as it relates to the construction of inter- and intra-subcultural boundaries, see Muggleton (2000) and Linder (2001).

people not question the authentic credentials of this second grouping, but they also attributed to them particular characteristics about dancing. For example, 'Cubans are *caballeros*', and 'Puerto Ricans look away when they dance with you.' There is really no overwhelming agreement as to the attributes, but their dancing was complex and authentic enough to deserve differentiation. Moreover, very good dancers were often assumed to be either Cuban or Puerto Rican though they actually came from any number of places.

Somewhat lagging behind the Colombians, Cubans, and Puerto Ricans were a polyglot mix of other nationalities. These people somehow acquired salsa skills, sometimes in local lessons or sometimes in other communities, but seldom in their land of origin. By and large this third group learned to salsa in the US, although many of them were attracted to the music and the dance in their country of origin. This group included many of the other Latina/os and Latin Americans.[8] Whereas Rodrigo claimed to have learned salsa 'in the womb' and Rodolfo, a Venezuelan graduate student, learned it at home dancing with his mother, this third group had to seek some type of formal or informal instruction. As an Argentinean sociology student tells it, 'When I moved to Texas I found I was no longer Argentinean but Latina. Then I found that to be really Latina I had to dance salsa. So I took lessons from a Chilean teacher who had gone through the same process a few years earlier.' This third group also included a Chilean dancer whom everyone thought was Puerto Rican, precisely because she danced so well.

A fourth group was a little more heterogeneous and, arguably, the most dedicated to salsa as they consciously sought to refashion their identity within this Latina/o coded community. This group included an Anglo art student who learned to salsa while travelling through Mexico; a Turkish molecular biology doctoral student who taught classes with Scott and was sometimes confused as a Latina because she was small, with dark, curly hair, and was an excellent dancer; a Moroccan woman with 'Latina' features and superior dancing skills; an assortment of Spanish students, many of whom learned to dance salsa in Spain, and others who took classes in this community; and French, Indian, and Russian – to name a few of the many nationalities – students and community residents who had gravitated to the salsa scene as a place of belonging and where they could dance or watch others dance. Some of these people told me they could not separate social from dancing occasions. As one Vietnamese graduate student said, 'In White parties people

---

8. Beyond the Latin Americans who learned to dance salsa, this third group included Black diaspora peoples, whether African-American, Caribbean, South American, or European, for example Afro-Portuguese. By virtue of skin colour, many in the salsa community assigned these participants relatively high legitimate status despite their wide variety of origins and salsa competencies. Insiders to this group were those considered Latin and/or of colour enough to be included as such, partly because they would be the same ones coded as outsiders within the mainstream of US popular culture.

drink, smoke and talk, but whenever you get people of colour there is also dance.' This heterogeneous third group was composed of people accepted as salseros, albeit not the 'truly authentic' ones.

The fifth group, possibly the most numerous of all, was a heterogeneous combination of Mexicans and Mexican-Americans. There were many common-alities among them, yet also strong identity differences between them. Many of the Mexican-Americans were first generation, working-class college students, both undergraduate and graduate. The Mexicans, however, were composed of three distinct groups; some of them came from upper or upper middle classes in Mexico and attended the university; some students came from the suburbs of the nearest major metropolitan area; finally the bulk of this group was composed of seasonal agricultural and low-wage migrant workers, many documented and a few undoc-umented. In Mexico, as is the case with most Latin American countries (see Lugo, forthcoming), skin colour roughly maps out over class. This resulted in the Mexican university students being lighter, by and large, than the workers. Of course, members of the community who spoke Spanish could differentiate among these three Mexican/American groups by their different language competencies and accents. Yet, among those who could or cared to perceive differences among the members of this group, there was also a tendency to homogenize this group into one undif-ferentiated category in relation to the other groups. In sum, there was a barely subterranean anti-Mexicanness among many other Latina/os and Latin Americans in this community. This hostility was lost on non-Latina/os and non-Latin Americans, as well as on many Mexicans and Mexican-Americans.

Prejudice, however, can have material ramifications both on the dance floor as well as in access to the dance floor. Thus when Manuel attempted to play some Mexican ranchera music at a Sunday salsa night at one of the most popular and crowded bars, some prominent salseros, including many of the ones foregrounded in this study, loudly proclaimed 'This is not music!' or 'This is against my religion' and conspicuously walked out of the bar till either merengue or salsa was played. Interviews with other salseros suggested that non-Mexican Latina/os and Latin Americans shared a prevailing anti-Mexican perspective in general that in the salsa community translated into the view that Mexico has contributed neither music nor dance to 'Latin' culture. This resulted in a number of exclusionary patterns. At the very least some of the reservation towards Eliseo's band and to Sofía was due to their Mexican-Americanness. Some members of the community who learned to dance from Eliseo were chided by more 'authentic' participants of the first two groups for learning from a Mexican-American. This was all beyond the perception and awareness of many of those in groups four through to six.

It was also evident that measures than other than verbal policing developed to minimize Mexican and Mexican-American participation. After the local dance hall cancelled salsa nights because of smoking in the dance floor and outdoor 'disturbances,' some significantly blamed the Mexicans and Mexican-Americans for lacking the manners to participate in this social space. This was all the easier to sustain given the general class difference (and, therefore, access to decision-making) within the salsa community between, on one hand, the bulk of Latina/os and Latin Americans not of Mexican descent, who were either students or middle-class members of the community, and on the other, the majority of the Mexicans who were either farm or fast-food workers. A plan was worked out to reopen the dance hall but with a revised dress code – as if the dress code itself could take care of class differences, which in a cosmetic way it did. However, this decision was also accompanied by stopping the posting of notices about salsa nights and classes in local Mexican grocery stores and Mexican food restaurants so as 'to not attract that undesirable group'. This had the effect of reducing the participation of working-class Mexicans, as few of them are online. Of the few who managed to find out about the dances and show up, some were turned away at the door because of violation of the dress code.[9]

Finally, we must note the formation of an ever-growing sixth group, of mostly Anglos, in the process of learning to dance, or more fundamentally, learning to tell the difference between merengue and salsa and to recognize the beat within each of these musics. Some of them, mostly gringos, doggedly participated in this scene, and, as Margarita noted, 'sadly cannot get the beat'. Most numerous amongst this group of beat-impaired souls were Anglo students like George, who got dragged into his first class by a friend who wanted to 'pick up chicks'. When his friend left, George stayed, continuing to take salsa lessons, always struggling with the beat, and always marked as an outsider, albeit a well-liked one. Other participants, such as Scott, had taken part in this community since its very inception. Thus while he became a consummate dancer, dated and hung out with the best female dancers, many of them of high legitimate status, he was never quite considered an insider. Comments such as, 'He sure dances well, for a gringo!' could often be heard as he danced.

Conclusion

All of the participants in this dance scene sought an alternative place for music, dance, community, and cultural affinity to that of the mainstream. Whether Latina/os

9. Of course hegemony is never complete, and several Mexican salseros became part of the in-group. One of them became the DJ in the most popular salsa night and another, who entered the community as a recent farm worker immigrant, was even placed in local salsa competitions. By 2002 Mexican cumbia had become a regular staple in salsa nights. However it is important to note that there is this undercurrent of discrimination, which is invisible to the non Latina/o or Latin American members of the community.

and Latin Americans sought to reconstruct a dance hall/party feel in contrad-istinction to the hard-rock, beer-hall predominance in a university town, or whether all sorts of other people, from all over the country and the world, gravitated toward a more porous space of ethnicity, music, and dance, all of the participants in this salsa scene actively moved and contributed to the salsa scene in Cornsoya. These participants were reacting to mainstream popular culture tendencies by creating a hybrid local substream while drawing on global population and cultural networks to police the boundaries within and around this new community (Lindner 2001). In the process they created an alternative space for leisure and desire.

Within this burgeoning heterogeneous and dynamic community in Cornsoya, composed of hybrid individuals and groups who found themselves in close prox-imity to others from a varied set of origins for a diverse set of reasons, there were no easy demarcations between insider and outsider status. In a sense everyone was simultaneously an insider, in the salsa community by choice, and an outsider, to the mainstream music and dance community, both by choice and design. Thus, the borders that demarcate 'authenticity' were extremely difficult to police, though that did not stop people from trying. Because of the particular, and partly random, origins of this salsa community, Colombians achieved hyper-authentic status. Yet, it would be difficult for most in the wider community – that is, beyond the salseros – to tell the difference between a Colombian and a Turk. In fact, as discussed above, it was often difficult for members of the salsa community themselves to determine the origin, and thus the authenticity, of many of the participants in the salsa scene. Studies of heterogeneous communities, such as this one, force us to acknowledge the danger of essentializing ethnicity as well as the difficulty of draw-ing boundaries around ethnic populations and ethnic cultural forms, particularly with such a hybrid ethnicity as Latinidad. Yet, as the process of the construction of boundaries has shown, this was not a community without internal prejudice.

We must therefore be cautious not to romanticize its cultural creativity beyond critical inquiry. As this study suggests, this community exhibits, indeed creates, exclusionary tendencies along lines of ethnicity, class, gender and national origin which should cause us to pause, both in terms of homogenizing ethnic groups such as Latina/os (among ourselves, it turns out, we are not without prejudice) and of romanticizing the unity and conviviality at the margins. Latina/os discriminate against other Latina/os. Some Latina/os internalize essentialist notions that Latina/os, for example, are natural dancers. Nearly everyone in the community, including Latina/is and non Latina/os, immediately assumed that African diaspora partic-ipants also had an innate dancing ability. This automatic inclusion was achieved through uncritical acceptance of narratives of racial difference. Some women achieved high authenticity status both through performing Latinidad in appearance and achieving dance skills while others crossed that 'trying too hard' invisible line (see Muggleton 2000: Ch. 5) and were labelled 'wannabes.'

Finally, we cannot assume that ethnicity and its forms of cultural expression function as puddles of oil in a pool of water as in a classic diaspora paradigm. Salsa is a metaphor for Latinidad but not only Latina/os salsa. In the salsa halls of this community, new identities were being constructed and relationships between and among ethnic groups flourished. Differential migratory patterns influenced the power of individual and group players. Yet migration, both of people and cultural form, itself enabled this new space for the performance of identity. In this way, the global affects the local so that the salsa scene included both diasporic and local groups and individuals (Wilson and Dissanayake 1996), while salsa, rather than any particular ethnicity, functioned as the loose ingredient that drew people together locally in this amorphous community. Salsa is thus a way for Latinidad to police its borders as well as, in the more traditional sense, for Anglo mainstream communities to engage in a desire of the 'other'. Or, in a more enduring sense, a way for the larger global community to include a pleasurable and internally conflictual form of expressive culture in its mix of dynamic and hybrid local and global identities.

References

Abu-Lughod, L. (1991),'Writing against Culture', in R. Fox (ed.), *Recapturing Anthropology: Working in the Present*, Santa Fe NM: School of American Research Press.

Benítez-Rojo, A. (1992), *The Repeating Island: The Caribbean and the Postmodern Perspective*, Durham NC: Duke University Press.

Bergman, B. (1985), *Hot Sauces: Latin and Caribbean Pop*, New York: Quill.

Best, C. (ed.) (1995), *Barbadian Popular Music and the Politics of Caribbean Culture*, New York: Alterations Consultants Inc.

Boggs, V. W. (1992), *Salsiology: Afro-Cuban Music and the Evolution of Salsa in New York City*, New York: Greenwood Press.

Brah, A. and Coombes, A. E. (eds) (2000), *Hybridity and its Discontents: Politics, Science, Culture*, London: Routledge.

Calvo Ospina, H. (1995), *Salsa: Havana Heat, Bronx Beat*, New York: Monthly Review Press.

Cepeda, M. E. (2001), '"Columbus Effect(s)": Chronology and Crossover in the Latin(o) Music "Boom"', *Discourse*, 23 (1): 63–81.

Darder, A. and Torres, R. D. (eds) (1998), *The Latino Studies Reader: Culture, Economy & Society*, London: Blackwell.

Dávila, A. (2001), *Latinos Inc.: The Marketing and Making of a People*, Berkeley CA: University of California Press.

Delgado, C. F. and Muñoz, J. E. (eds) (1997), *Everynight Life: Culture and Dance in Latin/o America*, Durham NC: Duke University Press.

Denzin, N. K. (1997), *Interpretive Ethnography: Ethnographic Practices for the 21st Century*, Thousand Oaks, CA: Sage.

Desmond, J. C. (ed.) (1997), *Meaning in Motion: New Cultural Studies of Dance*, Durham NC: Duke University Press.

Flores. J. (1993), *Divided Borders: Essays on Puerto Rican Identity*, Houston TX: Arte Público Press.

Flores, J. (2000), *From Bomba to Hip-Hop: Puerto Rican Culture and Latino Identity*, New York: Columbia.

García Canclini, N. (1995), *Hybrid Cultures: Strategies for Entering and Leaving Modernity*, Minneapolis MN: University of Minnesota Press.

Garcia, M. (1997), '"Memories of El Monte": Intercultural Dance Halls in Post-World War II Greater Los Angeles', in J. Austin and M. Nevin Willard (eds), *Generations of Youth: Youth Cultures and History in Twentieth-Century America*, New York: New York University Press.

Garcia, M., Leger, M. C. and Valdivia, A. N. (forthcoming), *Geographies of Latinidad: Mapping Latina/o Studies into the Twenty-First Century*, Durham NC: Duke University Press.

Gómez Peña, G. (2000), *Dangerous Border Crossers: The Artist Talks Back*, New York: Routledge.

Kraidy, M. M. (1999), 'The Global, the Local, and the Hybrid: A Native Ethnography of Glocalization', *Critical Studies in Mass Communication*, 16 (4): 456–76.

Kraidy, M. M. (2002), 'Hybridity in Cultural Globalization', *Communication Theory*, 12 (3): 316–39.

Leymarie, I. (1985), 'Salsa and Latin Jazz', in B. Bergman (ed.), *Hot Sauces: Latin and Caribbean Pop*, New York: Quill.

Lindner, R. (2001), 'The Construction of Authenticity: The Case of Subcultures', in J. Liep (ed.), *Locating Cultural Creativity*, London: Pluto Press.

Lipsitz, G. (1999a), Remarks made at 'Territories and Boundaries: Interdisciplinary Perspectives on Theory, Methodology, and Curriculum in Latina/o Studies', Centre for Advanced Study, University of Illinois, Champaign-Urbana, 24 March.

Lipsitz, G. (1999b), '"Home is where the Hatred is": Work, Music, and the Transnational Economy', in H. Naficy (ed.), *Home, Exile, Homeland: Film, Media and the Politics of Place*, New York: Routledge.

Lugo, A. (2000), 'Theorizing Border Inspections', *Cultural Dynamics*, 12 (3): 353–73.

Lugo, A. (forthcoming). 'Border Inspections: The Case of the El Paso-Juarez Area', in M. Garcia, M. Leger, and A. Valdivia (eds), *Geographies of Latinidad: Latina/o Studies into the Twenty-First Century*, Durham NC: Duke University Press.

Manuel, P. (1995), *Caribbean Currents: Caribbean Music from Rumba to Reggae*, Philadelphia PA: Temple University Press.

McCarthy, C. (1998), *The Uses of Culture: Education and the Limit of Ethnic Affiliation*, New York: Routledge.

Muggleton, D. (2000), *Inside Subculture. The Postmodern Meaning of Style*, Oxford: Berg.

Moreiras, A. (1998), 'Global Fragments: A Second Latinoamericanism', in F. Jameson and M. Miyoshi (eds), *The Cultures of Globalization*, Durham NC: Duke University Press.

Nietzsche, F. (1967), *On the Genealogy of Morals* (translated by W. Kaufman), New York: Vintage.

Oboler, S. (1995), *Ethnic Labels, Latino lives: Identity and the Politics of (Re)presentation in the United States*. Minneapolis MN: University of Minnesota Press.

Rodríguez, C. E. (1997), *Latin Looks: Images of Latinas and Latinos in the US Media*, Boulder CO: Westview Press.

Rohler, G. (1990), *Calypso and Society in Pre-Independence Trinidad*, Port of Spain, Trinidad: Gordon Rohler.

Shohat, E. (1998), *Talking Visions: Multicultural Feminism in a Transnational Age*, New York: MIT Press.

Shohat, E. and Stam, B. (1994), *Unthinking Eurocentrism: Multiculturalism and the Media*, New York: Routledge.

Stoler, L. A. (2000), 'Sexual Affronts and Racial Frontiers: European Identities and the Cultural Politics of Exclusion in Colonial Southeast Asia', in A. Brah and A. E. Coombes (eds), *Hybridity and its Discontents: Politics, Science, Culture*. London: Routledge.

Weinzierl, R. (2001), 'Subcultural Protest in Times of the Pop Entrepreneur', www.eipcp.net/diskurs/d06/text/weinzierl_en.html (accessed October 2002).

Wilson, R. and Dissanayake, W. (eds) (1996), *Global/Local: Cultural Production and the Transnational Imaginary*, Durham NC: Duke University Press.

–11–

'Race' and Class in the 'Post-subcultural' Economy

Martina Böse

The study of multi-culture and the study of youth got routinely allocated to separate subdisciplines for whom the issues of racism and anti-racism were an embarrassment. The racism of white working class youth was not, for example always at the top of the subculturalists agenda while the existence of a youthful and utopian, anti-racist counter-power was something that disrupted the tidy symmetry of some moralistic analyses of racial politics, particularly those in which the relationship between race and class was left unthought.

(Gilroy 1993)

Where is the 'Black' in (Post-)subcultural Theory?[1]

During the last twenty years the number of subcultural styles has multiplied, 'old' styles have been re-invented, and moral panics have emerged over other youth-related causes. Changed also have been the interpretations of subcultures and of their meanings by the 'general public', by cultural theorists, and not least by the researched subculturalists themselves. New academic courses and degrees have been developed to incorporate the study of subcultures and, more generally, popular culture into the academic curriculum, thus also institutionalizing the inter-disciplinary field of cultural studies (see Wolff 1999). Finally, and most recently, the increasing dissolution of old oppositions between 'culture' and 'politics', and 'culture' and 'economics', has opened up new questions about the changed meanings and roles of 'culture' in analyses of the political economy (du Gay and Pryke 2002).

This paper offers an engagement with some of the more recent criticisms of what has been called 'the CCCS approach' (see Muggleton 2000) to the study of subcultures, and to a lesser extent a contribution to the mainstreaming of a subcultural knowledge base. I will be approaching the subject matter from a sociological perspective and will explore issues around symbolic interactions as well as social structures, but will also be drawing on theory developed in fields outside the

1. This subheading is a paraphrase of the title of Stuart Hall's (1992) paper.

narrow confines of traditional sociological texts. The focus of my analysis will be on the position of 'race' and class in a revised analysis of subcultures. The empirical data on which this paper is grounded consist of forty-five semi-structured interviews that I conducted between January 1999 and January 2001 as part of my ethnographic research with a variety of so-called 'cultural practitioners' (DJs, club promoters and venue managers, music producers, flyer designers and media workers), based in Manchester, England. Two thirds of my interviewees are of Afro-Caribbean descent.[2]

Black youths[3] – likewise, most notably, women – did not, however, feature prominently in early subcultural studies. The principal context in which Blackness was mentioned was the role of Afro-Caribbean music for predominantly, if not exclusively, White subcultures (see Hebdige 1987) such as the mods, who 'constructed a style based partly on their perception of Black "cool"' (Gilroy and Lawrence 1988). Unlike other subcultures, the mods were described as more sympathetic (or at least indifferent) to Afro-Caribbean youth. Yet, according to Gilroy and Lawrence, 'what sociologists and subcultural theorists tended to miss out was the extent to which this romantic imagery was underpinned by racist common sense'. The image of Black people tended to be that of 'by nature happy-go-lucky, colourful, rhythmic and amoral' (Gilroy and Lawrence 1988: 131).

Another context familiar from the early days of subcultural research that has since tended to be associated with Black youth is that of 'moral panics' – the process by which the deviant behaviour of young people is exaggerated and stigmatized by the mass media. The term originated from radical sociology in the early 1970s before entering the realm of politics – Stuart Hall's *Policing the Crisis* (Hall *et al.* 1978) providing an important theory of moral panic (McRobbie 1994). Since Cohen's (1972) famous use of the term in the context of media representations of mods and rockers in the 1960s, which crafted them into threatening 'folk devils', it has been suggested that his arguments could also be applied to subsequent processes of stigmatization and stereotyping of youth subcultures (Osgerby 1998).

A critique of the victimization of youth that is intrinsic to most interpretations of moral panics, is offered by Sarah Thornton (1996). She argues, contrary to analyses such as Cohen's, that negative news coverage is often a goal of youth cultural pursuits and that moral panic should therefore be understood as a 'culmination and fulfilment of youth cultural agendas' (Thornton 1996: 129) and as 'a form of hype orchestrated by the culture industries that target the market' (Thornton 1996: 136). While this interpretation highlights an important element of youth

2. Most of the interviewees are in their twenties and early thirties.
3. Adopting the terminology used by my informants I will use the term 'Black people' to refer to people of Afro-Caribbean descent and 'Asian' for people of South Asian descent.

cultures, it risks overlooking another crucial aspect, namely the racializing tendency of moral panics. Gilroy and Lawrence (1988) have drawn attention to the fact that moral panics about the activities of mainly White, working-class male youths did not accidentally arise just at the time when Black cultural forms were being incorporated into White subcultures. Thus, Black music and Black-influenced White music and artists were demonized.

Some of the more recent work on subcultures has addressed questions of ethnicity, while a number of studies embedded in the post-colonial 'niche' of cultural studies have located Afro-Caribbean and South Asian youth more centre-stage and, in particular, 'outside the narrow parameters of "racism studies"' (see Huq 2001). Yet, as I will argue in this contribution, twenty years after Gilroy and Lawrence's analysis was first published, racist common sense is still being repro-duced within the popular cultural economy.

'Black Style' and Prejudice

Recent critiques of CCCS interpretations of subcultures have tended to problem-atize the emphasis placed on style as a symbolic response to social exclusion. David Muggleton (1997, 2000), in taking an explicitly post-modern stance, claims that style is losing its potential for resistance. Drawing on Jameson and Baudrillard for the development of his ideal-type of the 'post-subculturalist', Muggleton suggests that 'stylistic heterogeneity has been pushed to its utmost limits as the outward appearance of rebellion becomes merely another mode of fashion', 'post-punk stylistic revivals are examples of pastiche' and hence 'merely "simulacra", representing nothing more than our "pop images" and "cultural stereotypes" about the past' (Muggleton 1997: 195). In fact, post-modern theory goes even further and 'denies that there exists any province of the social to which subcultural styles can be a cultural response.' (Muggleton 2000: 46) This latter contention shall be challenged in the course of this paper where I will explore alternatives to the contested view of subcultural 'originality' and 'authenticity' as an attempted solution to real social contradictions, while remaining open to the possibility of a relation between subcultural style and social contexts.

A central claim in Muggleton's approach is that 'post-subculturalists no longer have any sense of subcultural "authenticity", where inception is rooted in particular sociotemporal contexts and tied to underlying structural relations' (Muggleton 2000: 47). Opposed to the 1970s, the 1980s and 1990s have been described as post-modern 'decades of subcultural fragmentation and proliferation, with a glut of revivals, hybrids and transformations, and the coexistence of myriad styles at any one point in time' where individualistic subculturalists 'move quickly and freely from one style to another as they wish', a practice referred to as 'style surfing'. It might well be that a 'high degree of sartorial mobility is the source of playfulness and pleasure' (Muggleton 1997: 198) for some, but it seems that this pleasure is reserved for privileged sections of dominant cultural groups. Rupert Weinzierl's conception of a 'hybrid mainstream formation which can hardly be demarcated from subcultural scenes' (Weinzierl 2001) also seems not to take account of such social stratifications. However, as has been emphasized by Floya Anthias, only those who occupy 'a space of "new stability and self-assurance" (can tell) the stories that we tell ourselves, that we are all becoming global, hybrid and diasporic' (Anthias 2001: 619). In a similar vein, Rey Chow suggests that 'the enormous seductiveness of the postmodern hybridite's discourse lies . . . in its invitation to join the power of global capitalism by flattening out past injustices'.[4] As John Hutnyk paraphrases rather cynically: 'Forget colonial violence, white supremacy and systematic exploitation and oppression: hybridity saves' (Hutnyk 2000: 116).

A discussion of the wider problematics of hybridity discourses would go beyond the scope of this paper but can be reviewed in a growing body of texts (for example, Hutnyk 2001; Brah and Coombes 2000). Instead, I will concentrate here on an illustration of the critical implications of a strictly post-modern interpretation of style, drawing on Hutnyk's analysis of the culture industry as well as specific examples from my empirical research. It is the global resources of a cultural industry that has enabled (sub)cultural symbols and practices – from old, school trainers to body piercings, from bindis to tattoos – to spread increasingly quickly across the world. Even though the specific locality where subcultural styles are expressed and cultures 'lived out' is considered as significant to an individual's cultural practices (Bennett 2000), the mobility of styles is hardly contested. Yet disagreement emerges at the level of its interpretation. On the one hand, the politics of authenticity have themselves been questioned by the questions: 'Who is real? Who is a replicant? Who cares? Enjoy' (Polhemus 1997: 151). On the other hand, it can easily be argued that some people do actually care, because the processes of defusion and diffusion that lead at the same time to dispersal and diversity (Muggleton 2000) do not impinge upon everybody in the same way. Using the example of the World Music industry, Hutnyk reminds us of:

> Paul Simon's refusal to grant Fun^da^mental clearance for a song sample from 'The sound of Silence . . . this from Mr World Music himself, happily trading on recycled sounds and borrowings from afar. It is not the borrowing that is offensive here, but the differential operation in the mix: hybridity never threatens Mr. Simon's identity or security as it supposedly does for 'non-traditional', devalued, marginal, cross-cultural beings (it is always cross-cultural for some, and entrepreneuerial for others). (Hutnyk 2000: 117–18)

4. Chow (1998 quoted in Hutnyk 2000: 115)

Subcultural symbols are thus open to being perceived and used in different ways by different groups represented in different societies in different locations, depending on their position in the exchange of cultural goods – as a producer, trader or consumer. A further element demanding consideration in this context is the material effect of those interpretations held by respective onlookers who are often involved in spatial surveillance and exclusion practices. These regularly include people who happen to hang on to notions of *meaning*-laden symbols, albeit declared outdated by some. My argument is not leading towards a denial or rejection of the notion of post-modern modes of consumption. It does suggest, however, a need to move beyond simplistic and superficial post-modern concept-ualizations of consumption, including the ambiguous concepts of 'hybridity' and 'diversity'. The 'diversity of culture' has been discredited by Hutnyk as 'the happy narrative that hides the structural socioeconomic disjunctions of the world' (Hutnyk 2000: 124), while he has described 'hybridity-talk' as serving 'as a cloaking device, not of cultural authenticity (for what is that if not a strategic construct?) but of political, social and economic differentials' (Hutnyk 2000: 117).

The differentials of which Hutnyk reminds us here, were partly taken into account in the early theorizations of subcultures. This acknowledgement of socio-economic and socio-political contexts is worth preserving from 'classical' subcultural theory, in combination with the consideration that young people might be 'playing' with their looks in ways that are not entirely unrelated to the social settings they live in outside of their night out. Even if the players in the 'post-modern pleasure-dome' were indeed beyond interpretation and identity politics expressed through style, how can we account for the regular interpretations of outfits or styles by the regulating agencies in licensed night life which often impinge on personal style politics? Typical examples of such symbolic interactions are the gatekeeping practices of clubs (see Thornton 1996; Malbon 1999), where the interpretation by the door security of a displayed style regularly leads to the wearer's admission or exclusion from the venue.

Thus, even if Rastafarian dreadlocks are 'preempted by runaway fashion models and rock (not necessarily reggae) musicians', as noted by Kaiser *et al.* (1991 quoted in Muggleton 2000: 43), they are still likely to prompt stereotypes of 'a reggae- and pot-head' in the minds of police officers on the look out for 'trouble-makers', when sported by a Black youth. The significant role of the semiotic baggage of style is addressed in the following quotation from an interview with a female Afro-Caribbean cultural practitioner in Manchester, who has dreadlocks.

> *B:* I honestly and truly think they, I truly believe that my hair in a way hinders me in
> my work.
> *M:* Really?

B: Yes. It does. You know it's their uhm stereotype of what a woman with locks is. Because they think they believe this is a certain kind of life, like.

M: like smoking weed or . . .

B: Yeah that's what they think. That's what they think. You know rather than, just say: 'oh, a rounded woman', you know. And 'you're an individual and you do this and you do that' – so yes! And then you say, I suppose also as well it can be seen as being quite religious in that like in the 1970s when everybody had an Afro and it was a big Black Power-movement . . . and yes, it was! It was, because you were making a statement. You ARE.

Later in the same interview, the woman speaks about an experiment she employed at the start of teaching a racism-awareness-course to members of the Metropolitan Police Force.

B: I said to the police: 'I walked in here now and you tell me what your very first thing when you saw me was. Just forget about all the stuff that your superiors been telling you. The very first thing that you think about'. And what did they think about? They think about weed. Of course! They look at my hair and then think: 'yeah yeah yeah. Is she on dope?' Because you can't help it!

Against the backdrop of incidents of stereotyping or selective policing based on style, the choice of a specific hair or dress style suggests more than a post-modern liking for eclecticism and irony. Stuart Hall has described style as a distinct feature of 'Black popular culture'. This '*style* – which mainstream cultural critics often believe to be the mere husk, the wrapping, the sugar coating on the pill – has become *itself* the subject of what is going on' (Hall 1992: 27; original emphasis). And Kobena Mercer has pointed to the importance of Afro and Dreadlocks hairstyles in their historical contexts as 'marking a liberating rupture, or "epistemological break" with the dominance of white-bias' (Mercer 1987: 421). However, the subsequent de-politicization of these diasporic styles and their incorporatation into mainstream fashions within the dominant culture, which Mercer also discussed, complicates any clear-cut interpretations of 'Black style'. While Mercer's further analysis focused on the different logics of Black stylization and its (counter-) appropriations, I want to draw attention to another aspect of style: namely its potential subjection to a politicized interpretation by others, independent of the individual's personal style politics and agenda. As long as the proclaimed 'breakdown in the signifying chain' (Jameson 1991) does not lead to a dissolution of stereotypes based on physical appearances and in particular racist stereotypes, we need to find other analytical tools to describe this significant section of empirical life. In the meantime, those agents in society who are equipped with a definitional power over 'suspicious subjects', from CCTV operators and police officers to security staff at the doors of a club, will ensure that the 'construction of complex appearances through the self-conscious act of stylistic bricolage' (Muggleton 1997: 191) will – for some people more than others – regularly include a consideration and resentment of stereotypes that are ascribed and stabilized by others.

The depicted restriction of the 'free flow' of signifiers through the persistence of 'modern' interpretations of (possibly post-modern) style, does not, however, preclude the possibility of playful post-subculturalist responses. Of course, any Black youth can also switch from wearing dreadlocks to a clubbing-style peroxide-blond, and some do. Yet the meanings attached to such a decision by the individual, and those read into it by the onlooker, often suggest a higher degree of complexity than that implied by the notion of 'style surfing'. When an Afro-Caribbean shop manager and interviewee views his dreadlocks as 'the ultimate expression of Blackness' and an invitation for other Black people to come into his shop, then this enunciation points, beyond the possible use of an 'ethnic marker' as a marketing strategy, to the construction of meaning; firstly, by and for the speaker himself and, secondly, for other – especially Black – people. It starkly contradicts a post-modern interpretation of style as 'no longer articulated around the modernist structuring relations of class, gender, ethnicity or even the age span of "youth"' (Muggleton 1997: 199), and rather reminds us of our earlier remarks on Hall's discussion of style in Black popular culture (Hall 1992). The particular example of the dreadlocks also recalls Mercer's assertion that 'hair functions as a key ethnic signifier . . . Through aesthetic stylization each Black hairstyle seeks to revalorize the ethnic signifier' (Mercer 1987: 199, 421). The subsequent description of the style as a 'totally natural fit' by the same interviewee, indicates a meaning of a different nature than a mere playful indulgence with signs. It is closer to the incorporation of a visual style into a 'personal system of identity politics' that Andy Bennett (2000: 78) describes. Even though we might not necessarily read 'ideological commitment' into this position towards style, it hints to the multifold variety of personal style politics. A neglect of these various 'in-between' constellations would also risk over-looking the constraints imposed by persistent 'modernist' social structures and exclusions that are embodied in the 'wrong' responses to (post-modern) style.

Beyond the self-related meaning, the interviewee expects the same meaning of the dreadlocks to be readable by other recipients, in particular by other Black people. More precisely, he suggests that his 'ultimately' Black hairstyle will make Black people feel more welcome in the space he is working in. In other words, he expects a reaction to the displayed symbol that is dependent on a shared under-standing. This interpretation by the interviewee sustains an argument for an analysis of subcultural style in its socio-political context. As such, style is seen as producing reactions, as well as itself being a reaction (see Gelder 1997), which in the referred case is also to the socio-spatial context. The aforementioned shop is situated in a formerly run-down city centre area that has been subjected to urban regeneration. While it is popular with young White people 'in the know'[5] because of the local (sub)cultural infrastructure, it is avoided by many Black people due to a lack of a sense of 'belonging' that results primarily from exclusion practices in the local cultural industries. 'Ethnicity' can thus be considered as one of several structuring factors in the use of the area.

Still Winning Space!

The use of space and the symbolic 'marking out' of space through style, as briefly addressed in the previous section, is another theme familiar from subcultural theory. Marking the 'spatial turn' in the social sciences, the connection between youth, style and space has increasingly been theorized in the more recent literature on youth cultures. Andy Bennett, for example, refers to music and style as the principal sites of young people's 'struggle to win and mark out urban spaces'. The 'local' is further understood as a 'space that is crossed by a variety of different *collective* sensibilities each of which imposes a different set of expectations and cultural needs upon that space' (Bennett 2000: 66; my emphasis). Interestingly, Bennett disagrees with the view that the 'new urban narratives' that young people construct through the appropriation and reworking of urban spaces involve the formation of a subcultural identity. He finds young people, however, responding in very specific ways to 'particular local circumstances in which they find themselves, each response being underpinned by a common set of knowledge in different ways and to different ends' (Bennett 2000: 67). These 'new urban narratives' enable their creators to 'view the local in particular ways', and furthermore to 'apply their own solutions to the particular problems or shortcomings that they identify with their surroundings and the policies and practices that shape these surroundings' (Bennett 2000: 66).

A particular problem shared by young Black and Asian men (and, to a lesser extent, women) in Manchester, is the experience of exclusion from popular cultural venues in the city. The risk of being stopped by the police in the street, or not getting beyond the doors of a club, tends to be considerably higher for these groups than for White youth. These instances of selective policing and racial exclusion have to be viewed in their socio-historical context in Britain. After a long history of associating 'race' and youth with violence and crime, Black youth was increasingly demonized and constructed as 'threatening inner city youths' in Thatcherite Britain. Since the so-called 'riots' in UK cities in the 1980s, youth unemployment and 'race' were identified as the prime elements of uprisings (McRobbie 1994; Gilroy 1981; Gilroy and Lawrence 1988).

---

5. I am referring here to Thornton's (1996) understanding of 'subcultural capital'.

The persistence of such prejudice in the leisure spaces of the contemporary city too has led local Black youth in Manchester to devise various strategies of 'collective problem-solving'. One example is the organization of coach-trips to clubs in other cities, because the local night time economy does not provide for all 'taste cultures'[6] given the equation of Black music[7] with 'trouble-makers'. The following extract from an interview with a club promoter illustrates how spatial exclusion is implemented and how it is perceived by some young Black and Asian locals.

S: People say 'let's get out of town' because people basically don't promote their stuff down there. You know what I mean? ... They're getting like trouble on the door: pressure on the door. Like bouncers or whatever won't let them in. Ignorant! Bouncers! Don't know anything you know. And basically all what they're doing is: they're perpetrating the stereotype! So I know there's just a lot of crap that, and I mean you're still getting that kind of racism at the fucking door and shit.

The '"all-dressed-up-and-nowhere-to-go" experience of Saturday evening' that Clarke *et al.* (1976) named as symptomatic of the 'symbolically displaced "resolutions"' of subcultural styles, is a surprisingly contemporary experience for many Black youths today. However, the exclusion practices in today's night-time economy are often based on 'old-fashioned' racisms. They are not limited to the realm of cultural consumption, but are also at work in the field of cultural production. Despite the growing academic interest in various aspects of the 'production of culture' or the 'culture, cultural or creative industries', issues of marginalization and exclusion have so far remained rather under-explored.[8]

Consonant with Huq's reminder of the implications of an interventionist weighted subject such as cultural studies 'for real people in real struggles' (Huq 2001), I would suggest that a heightened sensitivity towards aspects of exclusion would be well placed on every research agenda that looks into 'lived (sub)cultures' today. In engaging with culture in a specific (mostly) urban context it is vital to go beyond the theorizing of 'cultural clusters' and 'cultural quarters' and explicitly investigate relationships of power in the industries that make culture work.

6. Thornton employs the term 'taste cultures' to describe 'club crowds' whose shared tastes are not limited to music, but include also the 'consumption of common media and most importantly, their preference for people with similar tastes themselves.' (Thornton 1996: 3)

7. While soul and rhythm-and-blues nights have traditionally been labelled as 'Black nights', UK garage nights have gained this label more recently in the local clubbing landscape in Manchester.

8. See Negus (2002), McRobbie (2001) for positive exceptions to this trend.

'Sociality' – Or Still Social Class?

A common critique of the CCCS-related work on subcultures is focused, on the one hand, on the interpretation of class, more precisely on the working class as a structuring force, an inescapable source and reference point of subcultures, and on the other, the interpretation of subcultures as a symptom of, and a resolution to, a working-class in decline. Beyond the critical reviews of 'the CCCS approach', discussions of 'class' appear to have become a 'no-go area' in many more recent analyses of young people's expressions of (post-)subcultural sociality. Where 'class' still does find acknowledgement as a 'structuring' element is, for example, in the previously mentioned context of access to clubbing venues, where 'structures of exclusion and stratification found elsewhere' tend to be duplicated (Thornton 1996; Malbon 1999). However, once inside the space of subcultural consumption, it is suggested that in the course of a 'usually transitory feeling of social identific-ation', 'notions that are central to our personal biographies – our understandings of our own and other's gender, ethnicity, social class – can become temporarily eclipsed by what it is that we share with those with whom we are co-present' (Malbon 1999: 50). Thornton writes about the 'fantasy of classlessness', on which the assertion of subcultural distinction in part relies, and the supposed demo-cratization of youth culture through 'acid-house-cum-rave' (Thornton 1996). It is, indeed, the 'ecstasy-influenced "friendliness" of the clubbing years' (McRobbie 2001) that many of my informants in Manchester have described as 'opening up social spaces' usually precluded by differences in social class or ethnicity as well as age. So where does this leave the position of class in a theory of (sub)cultures today?

One of Muggleton's hypotheses is that post-modern subculturalists do not typically regard themselves in collective terms. His informants, as well as the young people Polhemus (1997) writes about, refrain from labelling themselves. Few of them are prepared to say: 'I'm a Raver', 'I'm a Cyber-Punk', and so forth. My own interviewees also tended not to label themselves in subcultural terms but many did actually consider themselves as being affiliated to one rather than another 'scene', usually defined in terms of a musical style. Based on the interpretation of my empirical data, I would therefore refrain from reading the refusal of self-labelling as evidence for the lack of one or more meaningful collective entities.

Social class was a recurring theme throughout various contexts in my inter-viewees' accounts of the clubbing scene in contemporary Manchester, one context being the composition of the popular cultural infrastructure in the city. The lack of a significantly sized Afro-Caribbean middle-class was often named as one of the reasons why Black people did not have a more significant presence in the cultural economy of the city, as venue owners or managers, as music producers or promoters. The lack of a local Black radio station was likewise interpreted as a 'class problem'.

In arguing for the impact of a lack of educational and financial resources and, hence, 'why class matters' for an entrance into the industry, many cultural practitioners drew comparisons with the socio-economic composition of the 'Black community' in London or many cities in the United States, where a 'Black culture industry' exists.

Another context in which class was often mentioned was the fragmentation of specific (music) scenes into different subsections. The following interview extract illustrates the respective perceptions of such structuring factors in Manchester's popular cultural 'scene-scape'.

> I suppose the ecstasy scene is kind of like, it's like the hip-hop scene here as well, you know what I mean. And there are two distinct hip-hop scenes here. There is a Black hip-hop scene and there is a White surfer hip-hop scene. It's a class thing as well as - as much as colour it's a class thing. And just happens to be that in Manchester most of the, most of the, the class that most Black people are in, is in the underclass! And those who aren't don't really seem to go out!

The term 'underclass'[9] was used frequently by my Afro-Caribbean informants to describe the condition of 'the Black community' in Manchester. According to this position it is because of the social class background of many local Black youths that only a minority tend to frequent the nightclubs in the city centre. Beside the threat of being 'hassled by the police', these young people simply 'can't deal with all the middle-class students hanging about'.[10] In most cases the speakers who employed the derogatory and politically highly charged term 'underclass' positioned themselves as members of this class. It is here that affiliations along class lines that cut across ethnic boundaries were emphasized most explicitly, as illustrated in the following extract from an interview with a self-proclaimed member of the 'underclass':

> The amount of Asians that were saying: 'oh yeah, we're ethnic minorities'. And I thought: well yeah, you might be an ethnic minority, but you're NOT a deprived or disadvantaged community. Because quite big chunks of the Asian community are middle class! You know I feel a lot more of alliance to a guy in Salford, a White guy in . . .[11]

9. In the sociological literature the term 'underclass' is very controversial. The debate over the so-called 'Black underclass' caused a considerable backlash for youth researchers operating from a radical perspective in the US in the 1980s. In this debate the defining elements were usually unemployment, teenage pregnancy, a lack of socio-economic mobility more generally and the existence of a 'survival culture'. Opponents consider the notion of a 'Black underclass' as a victim-blaming thesis in disguise (Griffin 1993).

10. Quotations from personal interviews.

11. Here the interviewee names several working-class areas in Manchester.

I got a hell of a lot more in common with them. Because, you know, yeah when I was growing up, I had cockroaches in the room, you know, I am sorry to say what you do with the cockroaches you learn how to kill them and they're buggers to kill. You know what I mean.

The speaker in this quotation used to work as a DJ in local youth centres and, later, also in regular clubs in Manchester. In our conversation he argued very persuasively, in line with a rich body of literature on the socio-political significance of different forms of Black music, how hip-hop informed his class identity when growing up.

Gilroy (1993) suggested that youth cultures can be viewed as 'an embattled feature of plural societies in which groups that may be culturally different in terms of religion, language, history and traditions or which may have an interest in having themselves perceived to be so, are ranked in relationships of domination and subordination' (Gilroy 1993). Against the backdrop of today's celebration of 'fusion culture' and 'DIY biographies', where 'Blackness' and 'working-class' are mainly reduced to their signifying value, Gilroy's perspective might seem outdated to some. A hybridity-embracing industry further contributes to the de-politicization of cultural artefacts. As Hutnyk has put it so poetically in the context of the 'Asian turn' in contemporary dance music: 'Shorn of political roots, toned down and sweetly packaged as exotic magical mystery tourist fare, these transnational flavours do not burn the tender tongues of middle-class liberalism' (Hutnyk 2000: 116).

To conclude, we are left with a number of indications that the characteristic concerns of the early work on subcultures – power relations linked to 'race' and class, social segregation and exclusion – are still central to our understanding of the (life)styles and cultural choices and practices of young people today. Without confirming the contested thesis that (sub)cultural styles should be understood primarily as a reaction to shared material conditions of existence, I want to argue for a reconsideration of these material conditions of existence in the analysis of youth and young people's participation in, as well as their contribution to, the cultural landscape of a specific location. Since the conceptualization of subcultures by CCCS scholars in the 1970s, not only have the styles changed but so too have the cultural industries and the symbolic and economic position allocated to 'urban cultures'. While the sites of popular cultural production and consumption are thus becoming increasingly integrated into the marketing strategies of cities, and new alliances are being formed between 'cultural intermediaries' and city governing agencies, it might again be time to look beyond conspicuous styles and study *absences*.

References

Anthias, F. (2001), 'New Hybridities, Old Concepts: the Limits of "Culture"', *Ethnic and Racial Studies*, 24 (4) (July): 619–41.

Bennett, A. (2000), *Popular Music and Youth Culture: Music, Identity and Place*, London: Macmillan.

Brah, A. and Coombes, A. E. (eds), (2000), *Hybridity and its Discontents: Politics, Science, Culture*, London: Routledge.

Chow, R (1998), *Ethics after Idealism: Theory-Culture-Ethnicity-Reading*, Bloomington IN: Indiana University Press.

Clarke, J., Hall, S., Jefferson, T. and Roberts, B. (1976), 'Subcultures, Cultures and Class: a Theoretical Overwiew', in S. Hall and T. Jefferson (eds), *Resistance Through Rituals*, London: Hutchingson.

Cohen, S. (1972), *Folk Devils and Moral Panics: The Creation of the Mods and Rockers*, London: MacGibbon and Kee.

Gay, P. du and Pryke, M. (eds), (2002), *Cultural Economy*, London: Sage.

Gelder, K. (1997), 'Introduction to Part 7', in K. Gelder and S. Thornton (eds), *The Subcultures Reader*, London: Routledge.

Gelder, K. and Thornton, S. (eds), (1997), *The Subcultures Reader*, London: Routledge.

Gilroy, P. (1981), 'You Can't Fool the Youths: Race and Class Formations in the 1980s', *Race and Class*, 23 (2–3): 207–22.

Gilroy, P. (1993), *'Between Afro-Centrism and Euro-Centrism: Youth Culture and the Problem of Hybridity'*, *Youth*, 1 (2), http://www.alli.fi/nyri/young/1993-2/y932gilr.htm (accessed August 2002).

Gilroy, P. and Lawrence, E. (1988), 'Two-Tone Britain: White and Black Youth and the Politics of Anti-Racism', in H. S. Bains and P. Cohen (eds), *Multi-Racist Britain*, London: Macmillan.

Griffin, C. (1993), *Representations of Youth: The Study of Youth and Adolescence in Britain and America*, Cambridge: Polity.

Hall, S., Critcher, C., Jefferson, T., Clarke, J. and Roberts, B. (1978), *Policing the Crisis: Mugging, the State, and Law and Order*, London: Hutchingson.

Hall, S. (1992), 'What is this "Black" in Black Popular Culture?' in G. Dent (ed.), *Black Popular Culture. A Project by Michele Wallace: Dia Centre for the Arts, Discussions in Contemporary Culture, Number 8*, Seattle WA: Bay Press.

Hebdige, D. (1987), *Cut 'n' Mix: Culture, Identity and Caribbean Music*, London: Comedia and Methuen.

Huq, R. (2001), 'CultureShock', http://culturemachine.tees.ac.uk/Reviews/rev7.htm (accessed August 2002).

Hutnyk, J. (2000), *Critique of Exotica: Music, Politics and the Culture Industry*, London: Pluto Press.

Jameson, F. (1991), *Postmodernism, or the Cultural Logic of Late Capitalism*, London: Verso.

Kaiser, S., Nagasawa, R. H. and Hutton, S. S. (1991), 'Fashion, Postmodernity and Personal Appearance: A Symbolic Interactionist Formulation', *Symbolic Interaction*, 14 (2): 165–85.

Malbon, B. (1999), *Clubbing: Dancing, Ecstasy, Vitality*, London: Routledge.

McRobbie, A. (1994), 'Folk Devils Fight Back', *New Left Review*, 203: 107–16.

McRobbie, A. (2001), 'Clubs to Companies: Notes on the Decline of Political Culture in Speeded Up Creative Worlds', www.nelp.de/beitraege/02_farbeit/mcrobbie_e.doc (accessed August 2002).

Mercer, K. (1997), 'Black Hairstyle Politics', in K. Gelder and S. Thornton (eds), *The Subcultures Reader*, London: Routledge.

Muggleton, D. (1997), 'The Post-Subculturalist', in S. Redhead, D. Wynne and J. O'Connor (eds), *The Clubcultures Reader: Readings in Popular Cultural Studies*, Oxford: Blackwell.

Muggleton, D. (2000), *Inside Subculture. The Postmodern Meaning of Style*, Oxford: Berg.

Negus, K. (2002), 'Identities and Industries: the Cultural Formation of Aesthetic Economies', in P. du Gay and M. Pryke (eds), *Cultural Economy*, London: Sage.

Osgerby, B. (1998), 'The Good, the Bad and the Ugly: Postwar Media Representations of Youth', in A. Briggs, and P. Cobley (eds), *The Media: An Introduction*, Harlow: Longman.

Polhemus, T. (1997), 'In the Supermarket of Style', in S. Redhead, D. Wynne and J. O'Connor (eds), *The Clubcultures Reader. Readings in Popular Cultural Studies*, Oxford: Blackwell.

Thornton, S. (1996), *Club Cultures: Music, Media and Subcultural Capital*, Hanover NH: Wesleyan University Press.

Wolff, J. (1999), 'Cultural Studies and the Sociology of Culture', *Invisible Culture*, 1, The Worlding of Cultural Studies, http://www.rochester.edu/in_visible_culture/issue1/wolff/wolff.html (accessed August 2002).

Weinzierl, R. (2001), 'Subcultural Protest in Times of the Pop-Entrepreneur', http://www.eipcp.net/diskurs/d06/text/weinzierl_de.html (accessed August 2002).

−12−

Diaspora Experience, Music and Hybrid Cultures of Young Migrants in Vienna
Roman Horak

This chapter is primarily based on the study 'Musical Behaviour of Second Generation Children of Migrant Workers in Vienna',[1] but also on the fieldwork which
was an essential part of the ethnography courses I have held at the Department of
Political Science, University of Vienna, between 1996 and 2001. The object of the
chapter is a preliminary analysis of the ethnographic material obtained from both
the courses and the aforementioned study. In the introduction I will give a brief
overview on the history of migration and the situation of young migrants in
Vienna. In the first section I will then deal with the reception of music as the
tension between hip-hop and 'folk music'; in the second and concluding part, I will
discuss dance and body awareness in the context of a hybrid mixing of styles.

Introduction

Vienna has a long tradition as a 'multicultural' city. There has been a strong
tradition of migration since the nineteenth century, with migrants coming particularly from the eastern parts of the Habsburg Empire. At the turn of the twentieth
century the number of people who were not born in Vienna but had migrated to the
city was up to 60 per cent: about 410,000 of them coming from Bohemia and

1. The main object of this study was to identify the importance of music in the lives of young
people in families from Turkey and the former Yugoslavia who were either born in Vienna or came
to Vienna at a very early age. This first, exploratory study was not intended to present, as it were, an
'all-inclusive' general view; instead its purpose was to describe those special problem areas involving
music in the everyday and leisure activities of young second-generation migrants. We therefore chose
a number of open ethnographic techniques consisting of individual and group interviews with young
Turks, Roma, Croats, Serbs, and others in four secondary schools and four municipal youth centres
located in Viennese districts with a high migrant population. In addition to the author, the following
colleagues worked on his research project: Noraldine Bailer, Mehmet Emir, Vlasta Ratkovic, and
Alfred Smudits. The project was conducted in the first half of the 1990s at the University of Music
and the Performing Arts (Vienna) and was sponsored by the Austrian Federal Ministry of Education
and the Arts.

Moravia, 300,000 coming from Czech-speaking regions, 43,000 coming from Slovakia, 11,000 from the Croat-language regions of the Hungarian part of the monarchy, and about 90,000 from other parts of Hungary (John and Lichtblau 1990: passim). There were also Italians, Greeks, Turks, and Jews from various parts of the Empire, so it can be stated that the 'authochthonus population' by that time was just a minority in Vienna. In reference to this situation the term 'melting pot' is now retrospectively being used by urban historians to characterize the 'multi-cultural' features of *fin-de-siècle* Vienna (cf. John and Lichtblau 1990). This, however, should not lead us to celebrating Vienna as a peaceful multi-cultural city, when in fact there were many racisms, particularly antisemitism – a tradition that is still very strong within Austrian society.

Since 1945 more than 2.5 million people have come to Austria as migrants, refugees or migrant workers (cf. Fassmann and Münz 1990); about 750,000 of them have settled here, which makes 9 per cent of the total population (SOS Menschenrechte 2002). During the 1960s and 1970s, in the years of economic boom, people from Yugoslavia, and later Turkey, were lured to Austria in order to fuel the needs of the economy. Special regulations – above all the so-called principle of rotation – were installed to bring workers to the country and to hire and fire them, so to have them replaced by new ones later. This rather inhuman strategy did not work at all, with the majority of those migrant workers having now lived more than a decade in Austria. Thus, despite racist conceptions of a culturally and ethnically 'pure' country, such a situation is actually changing the concept of 'being Austrian' again.

With the collapse of the Eastern bloc in 1989 the number of migrants coming to Austria again increased dramatically. The situation is particularly striking in Vienna. In 1992, according to official sources, between 16 and 20 per cent of the Viennese population were not in the possession of the Austrian citizenship (cf. Perchinig 1995: 114), and recent figures (in 2000 – 18.1 per cent) present the same image (SOS Menschenrechte 2002). In 1998 the percentage of migrants among the population in Vienna was higher than in most other European capitals (Vienna: 17.5 per cent, Berlin: 13 per cent, Paris: 13 per cent); only London (20 per cent) had a bigger proportion of migrants (SOS Menschenrechte 2002).

But it is not just the number of migrants that has grown: a change in the age structure can also be detected. Whereas in 1971, 5 per cent of the then foreign workers were in the age group fifteen to nineteen years, throughout the 1970s and 1980s the number decreased. But in 1989 the figure had increased again to 5.1 per cent, while only two years later, in 1991, it had gone up to 9.5 per cent. In 1993, 11 per cent of the migrants were in the age group ten to eighteen years (cf. Perchnig 1995: 118). Or to put it differently: one in five youths aged ten to eighteen years old belonged to the migrant population in Vienna. If one also includes the age group nineteen to twenty-nine, the picture presented is even more striking. About

38 per cent of the whole migrant population were aged between ten and twenty-nine years.

In the mid-1990s the number of young people in Vienna not having Austrian citizenship was about 120,000, the majority coming from the former Yugoslavia (about 37,000) and Turkey (26,000) (SOS Menschenrechte 2002). This, however, is not a precise figure and gives only an impression of what we are actually talking about. For example, children whose parents came from the former Yugoslavia and have taken on Austrian citizenship may statistically not be part of the migrant group; yet in fact most of them still experience the same racist hostility that other migrants (with no Austrian passport) are exposed to – a situation that has worsened with the election of the new right-wing government in 2000.

This is the background to what will be discussed on the following pages. So the chapter is about organizing one's everyday life as a member of a migrant group (sometimes even community) in a racist society; it is about the stresses and strains that come from the day-to-day experience of living between (at least) two cultures and simultaneously within them. And it is, finally and above all, about the very cultural processes in which they are engaged to find some sort of new and hybrid identity.

Different Musics: Between Hip-Hop and 'Folk Music'

Going out of one's way to stress the importance of music in adolescents' lives must seem (as Bennett 1995, 2000 might have said) like carrying coals to Newcastle. Young people listen to music, and indeed the omnipresence of music seems to constitute a guiding influence in their lives. These and similar thoughts are based primarily on the growing consumption of recorded popular music. Blanket statements such as this, however, are inaccurate because there is no longer a precise term for this broad area. From since the end of Punk, during the late 1970s, 'dominant' styles of popular music have, or so it seems, ceased to exist. The current scene seems to be determined by what has been called a post-modern mixing – David Muggleton (2000) talks about 'post-modern subcultures' – and by the simultaneous 'validity' of a wide range of trends. heavy- and death-metal, indie, rave, dance, and hip-hop (in its chart form), and so forth, all coexist and form something like a common pool.

It has been argued that the end of a leading style means a decline in the importance of popular (rock) music in youth culture. Steve Redhead (1990: 8) has contended that rock music 'is no longer simply "youth music"; music that became associated with the post-war construction of notions like the teenager, generation gap, youth culture and youth subculture is now assisting in the imminent destruction of these categories'. Lawrence Grossberg (1997), however, in his discussion of the 'rock formation' has reminded us to focus on the different contextual effectivities of popular music. This discussion considerably influenced our project, because we were, after all, interested in finding out how young foreign migrants in Vienna organize their musical preferences and which kind of music plays what role in their life. We proceeded on the assumption that Anglo-American popular music plays a substantial role, but that (in one way or another) it has a different effect on them than on young, indigenous Austrians.

In order to elucidate the importance of music in the everyday lives of adolescent migrants I have used the following structural model to discuss how they organize their everyday lives in the context of the tension resulting from the meeting of three cultures.[2] First, there is the parent culture – the dominant folkways and interpretative patterns of the country from which the parents and (some of) the young migrants originally came to Austria. Second, there is the culture of the host country with its sometimes strange norms that must be adopted (at least outwardly), but that can also be understood as an opportunity to escape the narrowness of the traditional parent culture. Third, there is the highly varied world of Anglo-American media culture: America as the image of freedom, as the symbol of 'boundless opportunities'.

In the course of our interviews a number of different levels emerged from the general interpretative framework with respect to the importance of music. The first is defined by the relationship between Anglo-American popular music and the 'folk music'[3] of the traditional parent culture; the second is marked by the attitude of different age groups to popular music, while the third is their relationship to the music (mostly the pop music) of Austria, the 'host country'. In the remainder of this chapter we focus on the first of these levels.

> I handle it like this. The music I listen to depends on the kind of people I'm with. I can listen to every kind of music. When I'm with people who listen to operettas, I also listen to operettas, though I don't like to. Let's say I listen to Yugoslav folk music at home and disco-music when I'm in a disco . . . It all depends on what I happen to like at the moment. For instance, I like some modern folk music. I think everyone follows his own taste (Julo, Roma male, 16 years).

These rather hesitant answers indicate several basic aspects of music consumption by adolescent migrants. Initially, there is the importance to them of the music of the country they come from. In a nutshell: they do not reject this music out of hand, but they have no strong ties to it.

2. It must be stated here that this model is, of course, simplifying and only a rather provisional attempt to make differences visible. In real life there are no neatly separated cultures.

3. This again is a tricky term. 'Folk music' was referred to as either some more traditional kind of roots music or some sort of mainstream – Turkish, Croat and so on – folk pop by the young people we interviewed.

Another interesting aspect present in the above interview passage is how different music is assigned to different spheres of life. At home they also listen to folk music, while with their peers they listen to dance floor, pop, etc.

> At home I only listen to Turkish music. I like European music very much but only when I go to the disco. But more Turkish, you know, Arab, 'Özgün music,' or some Turkish pop, too. (Murat, Turkish male, 17 years)

> When my parents aren't home I listen to my own music, I mean rap or Roxette or something else. And when they're at home I listen to folk music because I like folk music a lot, too. We listen to it together. (Dragica, Croat female, 17 years)

The difference between music reception 'when I'm with my friends' (as one of our interviewees put it) and at home, reflects the living in two worlds and between two worlds – one could refer here to Homi Bhabha's term 'third space' (see Rutherford 1990) – which young foreign migrants experience in this country. On the one hand, they have ties to the tradition of their traditional parent culture (no matter how hybrid it may be), while on the other they are required and willing to meet the demands of the host country's cultural standards. One of these standards of everyday youth culture is a certain basic expertise in Anglo-American pop music. There is a positive aspect to this facility in that it provides topics of conversation about various DJs, bands, singers, and so forth, as well as the opportunity for differentiation once given musical styles are received as 'one's own'. Most of all this applies to rap and hip-hop, the musical culture of the socially deprived Blacks in the American ghettos, which our interviewees especially favoured.[4]

This conflict situation also expresses itself through spatial differentiation. To return again to the expression used by one of the young people we interviewed, 'when I'm with my friends' is where the norms and orientation patterns of Americanized everyday culture apply. In their parents' apartment the norms of the old country (which more often than not they only know as tourists) hold. This could be understood as attempt to (re)invent/ re(create) some sense of 'home', or 'Heimat', to use the German word (cf. Morley and Robins 1995).

Of course there are also disagreements with parents over music. The young migrants, who are required to make their way in a (sometimes) strange world while struggling to get away from their 'roots' *and* inventing them anew, encounter a lack of understanding when it comes to organizing their leisure time. In this area – even parents with weaker ties to the culture they grew up in seem to believe this – those norms should apply that cannot be realized in the everyday world of work and

---

4. I understand rap and hop-hop as moments of one formation: the interviewees themselves seemed to make no distinction between the two terms.

school. It should therefore come as no surprise that conflicts can arise over music consumption.

The young people interviewed are quite articulate about these conflicts. On the one hand, they describe the antagonism as a 'generation problem': their parents are too old, they don't understand new music. In this way they are no different to their Austrian peers. But, on the other – and this is the difference – they are accused of no longer being 'real Turks', of betraying their 'own culture' as it were, because they listen to Anglo-American music (as either Turkish-Austrians or Croat-Austrians and so forth they are doubly foreign in the eyes of their parents). Yet their attitude to this kind of music is not straightforward, as the following interview excerpts show.

> Even English music [i.e., music with English lyrics] gets boring after a while. You have to listen to Turkish music, too, now and again. Or else you'll forget your language as well. (Mehmet, Turkish male, 16 years)

> After a while I get bored. At school there's pop and all that, and almost all of it is in English. I don't understand much. You can't say you understand everything they sing. Nobody does, or almost nobody. And if I'm at home or . . . if I want to listen to something I want to understand it. It's better when you understand it. Somehow you can think better. (Asli, Turkish female, 17 years)

Music also tells a lot about language and ties to the traditional parent culture. Listening to songs whose words you understand, but also listening to them in order not to lose contact with a 'mother tongue' you may seldom speak, is of crucial importance to many young foreign migrants even if they wish to remain in Austria and see themselves as 'Austrians'.

> What I saw and heard from my parents is still my culture, a little bit. I don' remember anything about Turkey because I was very young when I came here . . . Music, films, food, are all I have left. (Mehmet, Turkish male, 16 years)

Dance and Body Awareness: Routed Identities[5]

Paul Willis has pointed out that pop music's strongest sensual aura is found in music that can be danced to, where its direct sexual arousal causes intensified self-esteem and body awareness (Willis 1990). We can generalize from these thoughts

5. Gilroy (1993a) sees the Black Atlantic as a modernist countercultural space not organized by African roots but by a 'routed' set of vectors and exchanges. Gilroy aims to erode the monolithic notion of roots and tradition by emphasizing the 'restless' and 'recombinant' qualities of Afrodiasporic culture

on the importance of dance for (Black and White) youth in England, for dance as an expression of body awareness was also of crucial importance for the young migrants we interviewed. It is no accident that they especially like 'music you can dance to.' As I mentioned earlier, rap/hip-hop was their favourite kind of music

> Even if you don't understand it [the English lyrics], it just sounds good . . . It's the so-called beat that moves people when they dance. If you want to understand it you'll do anything for it. If you don't want to understand it, then you don't understand it. (Murat, Turkish male, 17 years)

The 'beat' *moves* people. This is an excellent, suggestive way of putting it. Whereas in conventional dance more or less experienced couples have to thoughtfully pattern their movements to the rhythmic patterns of the waltz, samba, and so forth, the beat is a driving force that simply moves those who dance according to its impulse.

What the young people want is direct expression, even in those cases in which they have to practice certain movements. We were struck in our fieldwork by the large number of male youths who ventured onto the dance floor. One might describe this seemingly casual presentation of self through dance as 'mating behaviour.' I do not mean 'dance' in the sense of spending an extended period of time on the dance floor. The culture of motion of the young migrants under study (mostly of Turkish origin) is a show consisting of a constant effort to try to look relaxed. They exchange a few words with a friend, they dance a little, and, of course, they constantly watch (potential) rivals out of the corner of their eye.

Body awareness expressed through dance is only one aspect in the repertoire of the male presentation of self. It is an integral part of the element of direct masculine expression (almost always with erotic undertones) that manifests itself in fighting. The young migrants also employ a considerable amount of violent rhetoric in their struggle for a male role. It was common in our interviews for potential subjects to lose interest once we began to talk about music. They wanted to talk about 'fighting,' 'brawls,' or 'gangs.' We ought not to take this too literally, though we should also not dismiss those utterings as mere showing off. The borderline between imagination and reality is blurred and fluid, and the boundaries between dancing and fighting are fluid as well. Much as it may upset or even outrage trained dancers, for adolescents both forms are important aspects of experiencing their bodies (experiencing the boundaries and oppositions between closeness/distance, outside/inside, above/below, and so forth).

But let us come to our central subject of dance, diaspora and hybridity. Dancing as a youth-culture activity in the narrow sense affects girls and boys of the most diverse ethnic and cultural backgrounds, yet in whatever different ways. In this context a central question concerns dance styles. Do young migrants create new styles or do they simply adopt those that popular culture presents to them via the media? This, in turn, raises the far more basic question of the origin, transfer, and transformation of youth-cultural styles.

In the wake of the CCCS, youth culture research has emphasized (a number of its critics would say overemphasized) the creative processes by which young people create new styles from various (to a certain extent historic) styles or stylistic elements. This has been done by using the concept of 'bricolage' borrowed from Lévi-Strauss. As John Clarke has put it, 'the generation of subcultural styles, then, involves differential selection from within the matrix of the existent. What happens is not the creation of objects and meanings from nothing, but rather the *trans-formation and rearrangement* of what is given (and "borrowed") into a pattern which carries a new meaning, its *translation* into a new context, and its *adaption*' (Clarke 1976: 178; original emphasis). Whatever one thinks of the possible (modern) limitations of the CCCS work on youth culture, for our purposes it seemed quite helpful to use this definition. We were interested in knowing whether there are tendencies in the interviews we conducted with young migrants that point either to blind acceptance of Anglo-American styles or at attempts to create autonomous styles. Questions about dance threw some interesting light on the topic.

> I don't dance, but I can say something about it anyway. It changes like what you wear. There's a style, a few know how to do it, then a few more learn it, and when everybody's learned it they change it again. It always changes with the music. It used to be the Jacksons. The Yugoslavs always used to dance to that. Now it's rap. And everybody dances rap. (Kemal, Turkish male, 18 years)

The above interview passage shows that there is a stylistic transfer, a 'diffusion,' of certain dances. Yet we ought not to overlook what was said about 'what you wear'. There is a complex inner connection between listening to a certain kind of music and wearing a certain outfit, which, in turn, demands a certain dance style. We must, however, not view this connection as static, as its essence consists of constant change. Most of all, we are interested in the style of dance. Our interview subject also describes the process of acquisition. 'A few know how to do it, then a few more learn it', he says, 'and when everybody's learned it they change it again'. Let us stay on this level for a moment. Learning through imitation does not obviously indicate productive creation; indeed, the fact that he mentions the Jacksons, a 1970s Soul/Disco band which included a young Michael Jackson, eventual megastar of the 1980s, might lead us to believe that we are basically dealing with simple imitation.

During our field work in youth centres we observed young Turks imitate Michael Jackson. Every step, indeed every movement looked as if it had been calculated to be as much like their model as possible. Yet the replication was not exact. We could leave it at that and attribute the difference with respect to the original to the simple fact that although imitation is imitation, M. Rimeh, born in Anatolia and raised in the Erdberg section of Vienna, is not Michael Jackson. Yet the point is that so long as (and especially when) imitation is not performed by a professional, but is the playful presentation of self in youth cultures, it always contains an element of creativity. Precisely because the young people are not Michael Jackson, they always express something about their own cultural background, regardless of how fragmented this background might be. Their threefold definition (parent culture, culture of the host country, and Anglo-American media and popular culture) colours this expression. They both copy and add something, which is what we have termed, 'the difference with respect to the original': something new comes into being. But what is added and what comes into being?

> Everything gets combined. If, let's say, you dance to rap music, you do it like an Oriental dance . . . The dance they have now is a combination with belly dance. I mean it's almost like belly dance. They way you move, etc. No one would have danced like that a few years ago. If we had danced like that last year they would have laughed at us (Bülent, Turkish male, 16 years).

What we notice here and what was confirmed by the 'group dances' we observed in the youth centres is one of the most interesting results of our study: the combination of Western and Eastern dance and movement patterns, acted out to the soundtrack of Black Anglo-American popular music. What we witness here is in fact the creation of an autonomous style as a symbolic activity that, on the one hand, returns to the roots of the eastern culture while, on the other, productively uses the dance possibilities of Black American popular culture. It is no accident that they fall back on hip-hop culture. The young Turks especially (and to a lesser extent the Croats, Serbs, Bosnians and so forth) are well aware of what this music stands for, even if they understand very little of the radical lyrics.

The result is, I think, a particular construction of Blackness that cannot be simply equated with the one that young non-migrant Austrians find attractive.[6] Against the background of ethnic and social discrimination, the adoption of Black youth cultural styles and forms of expression and their incorporation in a new hybrid culture can be read as a struggle for identity via difference (cf. Gilroy 1993b). To me, this points to an understanding of identity as discontinuous points of identification (cf. Hall 1990). While identifying themselves with 'Blackness' through Black popular culture, the minority ethnic youths, firstly, emancipate

---

6. Cf. Simon Jones (1988) on the different ways of how 'Black music' can become effective in different ethnic backgrounds.

themselves from the (traditional) parent culture without actually leaving it, hence the oriental dancing; and, secondly, oppose the racism they experience by – symbolically – stressing their minority status.

In his paper on German rap culture Andrew Bennett has argued that the radical nature of hip-hop comes less from its origins than from its uses (cf. Bennett 1995: 4, 2000: Chapter 6). However, what we discuss here goes beyond a simple transfer of rap into a non-Black culture, it is not just about a re-reading of rap in a different (political, social, cultural) setting. The very ways in which the 'consumption' of hip-hop takes place point to the fact that there is not just 'one' Europe, but that there is a historical rupture between the West (with its long tradition of Modernity) and the East.[7] The practice of oriental dancing to rap and hip-hop music by young Turks and other young migrants in 1990s Vienna symbolically undermines not only fixed ideas of Blackness, but also the concept of Europe as the West that is predominant within Austrian society. It indicates that besides the general dualism of the West and the Rest there is also a division of the West and the Rest *within* the West (Hall 1992).

References

Bennett, A. (1995), *Hip Hop am Main: The Localisation of Rap Music and Hip Hop Culture*, unpublished paper, Department of Sociology, University of Durham.

Bennett, A. (2000), *Popular Music and Youth Culture: Music, Identity and Place*, Basingstoke: Macmillan.

Clarke, J. (1976), 'Style', in S. Hall and T. Jefferson (eds), *Resistance Through Rituals: Youth Subcultures in Post-War Britain*, London: Hutchinson

Fassmann, H. and Münz, R. (1990), *Einwanderungsland Österreich? Gastarbeiter-Flüchtlinge-Immigranten*, Vienna: Austrian Academy of Sciences.

Gilroy, P. (1993a), *The Black Atlantic: Modernity and Double Consciousness*, London and New York: Verso

Gilroy, P. (1993b), *Small Acts: Thoughts on the Politics of Black Cultures*, London: Serpents Tail.

Grossberg, L. (1997), *Dancing in Spite of Myself: Essays on Popular Culture*, London and Durham NC: Duke University Press.

Hall, S. (1990), 'Cultural Identity and Diaspora', in J. Rutherford (ed.), *Identity: Community, Culture, Difference*, London: Lawrence & Wishart.

Hall, S. (1992), 'The West and the Rest: Discourse and Power', in S. Hall and B. Gieben (eds), *Formations of Modernity*, Cambridge, Polity Press in association with the Open University.

7. Edward Said's (1995) notion of 'orientalism' touches this issue.

John, M. and Lichtblau, A. (1990), *Schmelztiegel Wien: Einst und Jetzt*, Vienna: Böhlau.

Jones, S. (1988), *Black Culture, White Youth*, London: Macmillan.

Maffesoli, M. (1995), *The Time of the Tribes: The Decline of Individualism in Mass Society*, London: Sage.

Morley, D and Robins, K. (1995), *Spaces of Identity: Global Media, Electronic Landscapes and Cultural Boundaries*, London and New York. Routledge.

Muggleton, D. (2000), *Inside Subculture: The Postmodern Meaning of Style*, Oxford and New York: Berg.

Perchinig, B. (1995), 'Ausländer in Wien - die Zweite Generation', in N. Bailer and R. Horak (eds), *Jugendkultur: Annäherungen*, Vienna: Wiener Universitäts-verlag.

Redhead, S. (1990), *The End-of-the-Century Party: Youth and Pop Towards 2000*, Manchester: Manchester University Press.

Rutherford, J. (1990), 'The Third Space: Interview with Homi Bhabha', in J. Rutherford, (ed.), *Identity: Community, Culture, Difference*, London: Lawrence & Wishart.

Said, E. (1995), *Orientalism*, London: Penguin.

SOS Menschenrechte (2002), http://www.sos.at/ (accessed 30 July 2002).

Willis, P. (1990), *Common Culture*, Milton Keynes: Open University Press.

Part V
Music and Post-subcultural Politics

-13-

Global Youth Cultures in Localized Spaces: The Case of the UK New Asian Dance Music and French Rap
Rupa Huq

Music is the cultural form best able to cross borders – sounds carry across fences and walls and oceans, across classes, races and nations.

(Frith 1996: 269)

As someone with an interest in ethnicity and pop music beginning doctoral research into youth culture in the 1990s, the omens looked bleak for me. Although pop had long been seen as pivotal to youth culture, media commentary in the UK and US had begun to argue that a *dearth* of original pop music, due to retrograde tendencies and increased competition from other youth leisure markets, threatened the *death* of youth culture.[1] Yet, by the end of my research, change was discernible. The year 1998 saw Anglo-Asian pop group Cornershop reach number one in the UK singles charts with the loosely Indian-themed 'Brimful of Asha'. On the other side of the Channel, meanwhile, rappers of immigrant origins were taking France by storm, as in the huge 1999 Summer hit 'Tomber La Chemise' by mixed-race Toulousian collective Zebda. This chapter considers the new Asian dance music (NADM) of the UK, and French rap music, and how they reflect (trans)national European identities. It draws on research conducted in London, Manchester and Strasbourg and reaches some conclusions about the changing nature of early twenty-first century musically centred youth cultures, while illuminating some of the ideas raised by post-colonial theory.

The twentieth century saw music move from a folk-form loosely based on the oral repositories of story telling to an industrialized, commodified product of mass

---

1. Examples include Caroline Sullivan's claim that 'The current crop of pop idols is the most pallid, personality-free and conservative ever' (*Guardian*, 21 November 1990) and Simon Reynolds's assertion that 'backward-looking rock is in danger of devouring itself' (*Guardian*, 11 November 1990). Also see 'Why pop music ain't what it used to be' by Charlotte Raven (*Guardian*, 6 March 2001), which commented that her generation were 'sounding like our mothers when we say that pop records all sound the same.'

culture. Nowhere was this more pronounced than in the US. Indeed, in keeping with conventional wisdom, Grossberg (1992: 201) has stated that 'Rock music is about growing up in the US', a remark perhaps evidenced by the need for such labels as Britpop, a style of 1990s UK guitar-based music. Yet some of the most vibrant sites of youth musical culture have emerged from the immigration of former colonized peoples to European nation states such as France and the UK, which form the main backdrop to this chapter. Although the term 'post-colonial' is a term not used in France (Hargreaves and McKinney 1997), the NADM and French rap are both products of 'post-colonial' circumstances of production if we take this descriptor to apply to the period after 1945, which has seen the formal independence of former colonies.

Comparing different phenomena across two different countries is not always straightforward. To begin with, basic conceptual differences exist and before moving on, I want to flag up three key examples. Firstly, French rap is commonly held to be a music of the *banlieue*; yet while this is translated as 'suburb' in most French-English dictionaries, the connotations of the *banlieue* as a dangerous zone (Cathus 1994) are quite different from associations commonly held of Anglo-Saxon suburbia representing safety.[2] Due to post-war French urban planning, *banlieue* neighbourhoods are physically located on the peripheries of large urban settlements. Secondly, the UK's non-White population is considered as 'ethnic minorities', the composition of which entails 'ethnic monitoring' on official forms such as the Census. In France, meanwhile, a country with a stronger tradition of citizenship (Couturier 1983; Silverman 1996), people belong to one of the mutually exclusive categories of 'Français' (French) or 'immigrés' (immigrants). Thus youth with parents from the former French colonies of north and west Africa technically hold French nationality although their identifications are often more complex than this. Thirdly, French and UK immigrants hail from different parts of the globe. Hence the peculiarly UK definition of the word 'Asian' used in this chapter refers largely to the Indian 'subcontinent'. French terminology, too, has developed to describe its immigrants. The word 'beur', used in self-appellation, describes second-generation youth of the Mahgrebian countries of Tunisia, Morocco and Algeria. Striking similarities also exist between French and English discourse on youth. At the same time as commentators were decrying supposedly directionless 1990s' youth as 'generation X' and 'slackers' in the UK and US, the term 'generation bof' from an idiomatic expression to convey indifference was common currency amongst journalists in France. Yet the emergence of vibrant youth cultural scenes such as rap in France and NADM contradicts such facile stereotyping.

2. The word *banlieue* means literally 'suburb'. Yet many British commentators, such as Hargreaves and McKinney (1997) and Thoday (1995), leave it untranslated as it has negative, ghetto-type associations that the word 'suburb' lacks.

Defining the New Asian Dance Music and French Rap

Importantly, both musics that I am going to deal with are umbrella terms covering a range of stylistic subgenres. In the UK, the term 'The New Asian Dance Music' (Sharma, Sharma and Hutnyk 1996) spans both the DJ-centred 'Asian Underground' club scene and live music acts of the more traditionally rooted *bhangra* scene (Banerji and Bauman 1990). Whilst there is a wealth of sonic difference between, say the militant Muslim rap of Fundamental and *bhangra*-star Punjabi MC's *dhol* (drum) driven rhythms, both combine Western pop styles with Indian influences. At the height of NADM media coverage, mainstream pop performers such as Madonna and Boy George drew on Indian fashion and musical stylings. The scene's principal personnel, however, were, and continue to be, second-generation British born youth with parents who migrated from India, Pakistan and Bangladesh. Similarly, rap in France reflects its post-colonial present with youth originating from former French colonies at its centre. It has the same significance for second-generation French-Arab 'beurs' (a term described below) and African youth as the NADM has for young Britons of the Indian-subcontinent diaspora. Along with breakdance and graffiti, rap is a component of a wider French hip-hop culture. Although it is little known outside the French-speaking world, French language rap has made France the second worldwide market for rap after the US.

French rap can be subdivided into the 1983–90 underground scene in Parisian *banlieue* districts and the years following 1990, which have been characterized by its move to a fully fledged overground youth culture (Lapassade 1996). This second phase can be further bifurcated into 'hardcore' and 'cool' rap, tendencies represented by the combative, radical message music of NTM and Ministère AMER[3] in the first category and more consensual MC Solaar in the second (Bazin 1995: 214). However, such demarcations are somewhat simplistic, as binaries always are. Outfits such as the Marseilles mixed race band IAM are somewhere between the 'cool' and 'hard' camps and others have crossed boundaries. NTM were long seen as a 'hardcore' act although their most recent album has seen something of a shift in style with more peace-seeking lyrics than their earlier offerings, demonstrating the dynamism of French rap.

The youth cultural-commercial incorporation cycle, whereby youth cultures start off with an élite before moving to the general public following official, mass media and market exposure (see Hebdige 1979: 92–9) can be seen in both French rap and NADM. Sometimes these three converge. Rap is at the forefront of campaigns to export French music worldwide as seen in its promotion by the part-French industry, part-French government financed French Music Bureau. In terms

3. NTM stands for 'Nique Ta Mère' – fuck your mother – an adoption of the US 'motherfucker' formula; AMER connotes 'Action, Musique Et Rap' and is an acronym spelling bitter.

of official recognition, it took until 1996 for the appropriately named Alliance Ethnik (sic) to become the first French rappers to be named best group at France's Victoires de la Musique awards. A similar honour was bestowed on Talvin Singh who won the UK Mercury Music Prize in 1999 for his new Asian dance album 'OK'. The backing from major record labels has been key in explaining why these forms of music have risen to prominence. Asian underground's precursor, 1980s' *bhangra* music, is seen to have not made the same breakthrough as 1990s' Asian British youth music due to most of its consumption being via cheaply and illegally copied cassettes in specialist shops outside the official sales charts (Banerji and Bauman 1990).

Nonetheless what the multinationals give can just as easily be taken away. Whilst the major label signings of NADM acts Bally Sagoo and Talvin Singh (to Sony and Island) attracted attention (Sharma *et al.* 1996), both were subsequently dropped after just two albums apiece had failed to sell in the quantities anticipated. This suggests that large labels look primarily at the short-termism of profit margins and are not prepared to nurture talent through the development of musical careers. French rap has to an even greater extent crossed over into the mainstream recording business. Many leading acts are signed to large labels. MC Solaar is currently on Warner Brothers having previously been a Polydor artist, NTM are on Sony and IAM on Delabel/Virgin. This has happened in the space of a decade beginning from the 1990 compilation 'Rapattitude' issued on Virgin records which has been seen as marking the beginning of French rap's commercial recognition.

Indeed French rap has probably enjoyed a greater crossover than NADM. Despite the Mercury prize listing of Nitin Sawhney and the group Asian Dub Foundation (ADF) and the winning of the award by Talvin Singh, all remain somewhat niche artists in the UK. However, we have seen two-way cultural flows in both musics. In France ADF's album 'RAFI' sold 20,000 copies on the independent French label Delabel before they signed a major deal with London Records, and several new Asian dance acts have toured France. French rap has a wider constituency than just French ghetto youth - it sells massively amongst the French White middle-class, without which it could never attain the sales figures that it does. In addition to this it boasts export sales worldwide, particularly in Francophone Switzerland, Belgium and Canada. Virgin UK have issued two compilations of French rap for non-French audiences 'Le Flow' and 'Le Flow 2' and by 2001, a decade after his discovery in France, MC Solaar was recipient of fulsome praise in the UK press. Both musics also reach a post-youth public – the category of thirty-something 'middle youth'. Both rap in France and NADM face the paradox of juggling credibility with mass acceptance. This highlights a tension. Practitioners want to obtain mainstream success without a loss of any 'cool' cachet.

As well a greater commercial accessibility, it is a commonplace assumption to attribute a growing confidence amongst second-generation youth as a reason for the spread of these diasporic musics. This confidence is seemingly buttressed by a growing visibility of youth of second-generation ethnic origins in the mainstream media reflecting the changing perceptions of minorities in the popular imagination from 'immigrants' to 'settled population'. Yet we should not read this as implying a lack of confidence within the first generation, as this denies earlier waves of political activity by minorities in Britain and France. Examples exist in the industrial action at the Grunwick film processing plant led by exploited Asian women workers or the anti-fascist action by the Southall Youth Movement in the UK in the 1970s. In France the 1983 *marche des beurs* was a large-scale march demanding political rights for a generation, some of whom have subsequently entered positions of power – for example Tokia Saïfi, the first beur to the French Cabinet as minister of sustainable development under Prime Minister Jean-Pierre Raffarin in 2002.

The Politics of Dancing: Integration vs. Multiculturalism

If we compare French and British national policies of accommodating ethnic difference, the NADM and French rap have crucially evolved from different circumstances of production. Although both nations have significant minority populations as a result of their former colonial interests, the UK prides itself on following a broad ethic of 'multi-culturalism', which has the tolerance of ethnic difference as its cornerstone. Yet in France 'intégration' is practised whereby minorities assimilate into mainstream French society taking on 'French' characteristics and eventually, following a long enough period of stay, French nationality. There is, of course, some overlap in the practice of these two approaches, although both can be critiqued. Integration, if practised in its strictest form, suppresses differences. The integration-allied notion of secularism in the French classroom made the headlines with a number of test cases concerning the Islamic headscarf and its legality in schools (Brulard 1997; Gaspard and Khorokasvar 1995). In UK non-denominational schools the celebration of all religious ceremonies – the Muslim Eid and Hindu Diwali and Jewish Hannukah as well as Christmas – has become normal in recent years. However, the idea of 'tolerance' itself can be seen as a rather patronizing notion implying that minorities and their differences are there to be 'put up with' but only on limited terms – as long as they do not get too powerful and have any real influence in society; this in keeping with the way that UK nationals have traditionally been conceived of as *subjects* of the crown and not citizens. The post-1997 Labour government has introduced state funding for 'faith schools' where pupils of certain religions are educated apart from others; a policy that has been criticized as leading to an inevitable ghettoization of minorities.

Coming up with watertight definitions of national identities in France or the UK is deeply problematic (Perry 1997; Storry and Childs 1997). National stereotypes

(Oakland 1998; Rosello, 1998) should theoretically dissolve as we move towards a more internationally oriented popular culture under the aegis of European harmonization and globalizing tendencies in both communications and world security (Kaschuba 1993). Yet this has not stopped the articulation of these in recent years including the Thatcher/Major evocation of traditional 'Victorian values' and 'back to basics'. Corresponding pronouncements from right-wing politicians in France from FN leader Jean-Marie Le Pen to President Jacques Chirac reached a fever pitch in the 2002 presidential election where the theme of *l'insecurité* became the over-riding electoral issue. The subtext in both cases of yearning for 'the good old days' valorizes pre-twentieth-century immigration times rather than facing up to the multi-ethnic nature of contemporary Britain and France. The same period, however, has seen a growing Western fascination with 'world' (largely non-Western) music, a fascination that demonstrates a desire to return to simpler, more innocent times that have not been corrupted by Western capitalism. Barrett (1996: 241) comments 'It is not surprising that world music has flourished in recent years, given the advance of Green politics, New Age-ism, multiculturalism and other counter-measures'. As Kellner (1995: 40) observes, in an age of galloping free markets 'difference sells', becoming a competitive advantage. Accordingly, following the launch of 'Cool Britannia' by Tony Blair's government, aimed at projecting a tolerant, open, multi-cultural national image, Talvin Singh was invited to play at the Labour Party conference. Regardless of recent attempts to manufacture national cultural identity, NADM and French rap are both characteristic of the nations that they hail from underlining that national identity is not static but forever shifting. They are redefining Britishness, Frenchness and Europeaness.

French rap has notably been coopted by both the French left and right for political purposes. The week-long 'Université du Hip Hop' festival of Summer 1996 organized by Été Jeune, the Ville de Strasbourg (local council) youth arts and cultural service serves as an example of the use of rap via progressive municipal involvement in youth cultural activities. However, the local state sponsorship of concerts plus graffiti and DJing workshops during the event aroused some suspicion for countervailing the dispossessed/protest aspect of hip hop (Cross 1993; Rose 1994; Toop 1995; Vulbeau 1992). French academic theories of rap, whilst noting its connections with immigrant youth culture, nonetheless see it as part and parcel of integration (Lapassade, 1996: 13).

Still, the actions of Strasbourg's benevolent socialist local government contrast sharply with those of Front National (FN) regimes.[4] The most notable example of

---

4. Various prohibitive extreme-right local government decisions on youth culture were reported in the media around the same time as this decision. The Chateauvallon theatre in Toulon, known for imaginative multi-cultural programming, was closed down soon after the FN accession to power, as

these is the sentencing of rap group NTM to six months prison and a 50,000 FF fine for the ancient and little-used or known offence of 'outrages par paroles' – offensive (anti-police) remarks. These were made by NTM at a festival in FN run Toulon, in the South of France during the summer of 1995. The NTM affair made a public example of two individuals whose immigrant origins were ceaselessly stressed ('Kool Shen' Bruno Lopez is of Portuguese stock and 'Joey Star' Didier Morville Antallaise is Caribbean). The widely attacked decision was later partially overturned by the national justice department.[5] The rallying of anti-racist pressure groups to NTM's defence has not been the only time when rap and anti-racist politics have been yoked together. Just as anti-racist organizations, student unions, pressure groups and trade unions were amongst those who demonstrated in support of NTM against the censure, similar alliances were mobilized against racist immigration policy, and against Le Pen, in the period between the first and second rounds of the French Presidential elections in 2002.

Political awareness is important to various NADM acts. Just as Apache Indian was much written about for his multicultural message (see, for example, Gilroy 1993; Lipsitz 1994; Polhemus 1994; Taylor 1997), Fundamental and Asian Dub Foundation have been beloved by left wing academics (see, for example, Sharma *et al.* 1996; Hutnyk 2000) for their political activism. Growing out of a London community music project, ADF have also played at numerous anti-racist events and notably campaigned, via the single 'Free Satpal Ram', for the release of a young Asian waiter jailed for self-defence following a racist attack. When witnessed live (at London's, Shepherd's Bush Empire on 3 February 1998), other radical performance statements were made supporting the women's pressure group the Southall Black Sisters and past struggles such as the Amritsar massacre. DJ John Pandit, the band's 'political strategist', initially in ADF's career maintained a day job as a youth worker for a civil rights advice and support group in Tower Hamlets, east London. Their album, with the deeply unfashionable title 'Community Music', took its name from their locally run public-sector financed youth music-making project in east London. Marseilles rappers IAM also share the same 're-investing in the community' ethos, having established recording studios for local youth in

---

was the Sous-Marin alternative music café in Vitrolles (bordering Toulon) on the pretext of drugs and noise. The four FN-run municipalities also have a reputation for withdrawing books on ethnic populations from their libraries and renaming streets after right-wing luminaries.

5. The affair, which raised questions of morality, far-right cultural policy, youth in the *banlieues* and the sanctity of artistic creation, was much debated: FN leader Jean-Marie Le Pen went on record as stating: 'Rap, tag [graffiti] sont des modes pasagères des excroisances pathogènes' – rap and tag are passing fads of pathogenic outbursts (*Le Monde* 23–24 June 1996). *Le Monde* (16 November 1996), left leaning daily *Libération* (16 November 1996) and the weekly *Télérama* (27 November 1996) all ran editorials attacking the decision.

their home town. Not all NADM is political, however. Talvin Singh sees himself essentially as musician and not a vehicle for post-colonial vengeance: 'I don't really want to be political all the time. I don't fit into that and I don't want to. I wanna enjoy things which I like whether they have an Asian value or not . . . rather than going "you fucked us up. I'm gonna fuck you up". Fuck *who* up? Are these people any part of that? Let's move our shit on.'[6]

Are the NADM and French rap about Black identity assertion? Lapassade (1996: 52–65) notes 'noirceur' (Blackness) as critical to rap in general. However, a number of White practitioners have been active in French rap, for example MC Solaar's producer Jimmy Jay, Kool Shen (Bruno Lopez) of NTM and IAM's Akenaton. Furthermore, there is an increasing body of 'homegrown' rap in European countries that one might normally imagine as White-faced, with growing academic histories to match, for example Switzerland (Goldstein 1992), Germany (Bennett 2000, Cheesman 1998, Soysal 1998, 2001) and Italy (Wright 2000). Interestingly, whilst previous research has found that Asians dislike applying the term 'Black' to themselves (Baumann 1996), it has been shown more recently (Ghelani 2001) that by adopting urban Black stylistic codes such as American hip-hop derived fashion and language through media imagery in what they claim is an ironic way, British Asian youth are 'reconfiguring what it means to be Asian'. Gilroy (1993) likewise asserts that British Asian styles owe much to Black American 'borrowing'. However, some of the traits cited – for example, the call and response of African music and reggae dancehall – apply as equally to traditional subcontinental styles. Meanwhile, in France, the phrase 'black, blanc, beur' – a multi-cultural update of the *tricolore*'s (the French flag's) bleu, blanc, rouge colours – was much used by commentators to describe the multi-ethnic 1998 soccer World Cup winning team, neatly underlining the contribution made by immigration to modern France. These diverse examples illustrate how it is highly simplistic to automatically assume that these musics are flying the flag for Black identity.

Conclusion: The Global Implications of the New Asian Dance Music and French Rap in the New Europe

The post-colonial era has meant a serious re-thinking for both the UK and France with the realization that they are no longer the seemingly unassailable imperial powers that they once were. Although the decolonialization of former empires is a political imperative, ostensibly relating more to questions of governance and statecraft than youth culture and pop music, the socio-cultural effects of this

---

6. Personal interview, *The Vibe Bar,* 1 October 1998.

movement have been profound, particularly when taken along with the forces of globalization by which interdependency becomes an increasing necessity in a post-war new world order. As Morely and Robins (1995: 108) remark, 'globalization as it dissolves the barriers of distance makes the encounter of colonial centre and colonialized periphery immediate and intense.' To some extent these hybridized musical forms underline a new internationalism in youth culture and a move away from the old 'American dream'. This can also be seen in rave's contemporaneous multiple sources in Frankfurt techno, Belgian newbeat, the Ibiza sound, Balaeric beats, Goa trance, Chicago house and so forth. French rap is commonly understood to be 'street' music, but it has not simply evolved from the same street or boulevard or rue as its US equivalent. It is incontestably French in the same way that NADM is inherently British. Situating NADM and Francophone rap is not straightforward. In terms of classifying them in record store sections, as multi-faceted European musical forms they cannot, for example, be easily categorized as world music – the rise of which replicates colonial relations in a guilt-ridden search for authenticity in an inauthentic world.

The France and Britain inhabited by French rap and British new Asian dance are not mono-cultural and fixed entities but multi-cultural and dynamic. With ethnic minority youth at their centre, they contradict received, retarded notions of national identity rooted in Whiteness. Equivalent hybridized, diasporic musics can be seen in numerous countries (Mitchell 2001). All are cultures of diversity in a world characterized by a diversity of cultures. Predictably all the studies of French rap (Bazin 1995; Cachin 1996; Cannon 1997; Lapassade 1996) copiously acknowledge and reference large quantities of US rap; a compliment unsurprisingly not returned in US endeavours (Cross 1993; Rose 1994; Toop 1995). The emergence of these two musical styles at a time when many fear the onset of 'globalization',[7] so often a synonym for 'Americanization', seems to suggest an opposite decentring of the West. Both are crucial strands that are woven together with counterparts from elsewhere to make up the cultural fabric of the new Europe and, indeed, the new world order. Indeed, in a further twist, music from second-generation British Asians is now being exported back to the Indian subcontinent. Both France and the UK are home to various widely exported migrant popular cultural forms combining both humour and music, including *banlieue* films such as *La Haine* and *100%*

---

7. As Mike Featherstone writes:

This term refers to the sense of global compression in which the world is increasingly regarded as 'one place' and it becomes more difficult for nation states to opt out of, or avoid, the consequences if being drawn together into a progressively tighter figuration through the increasing volume and rapidity of the flows of money, goods, people, technology and images. (Featherstone 1995: 81)

Arabica, or stand-up comedy with figures such as French comic Smaïn and the UK 'Goodness Gracious Me' team, stars of BBC television.

Both the musically expressive youth cultures of NADM and French rap starkly highlight the inadequacies of the influential 1970s British CCCS youth subcultural theory; notably the necessarily problematizing analyses of second-generation ethnic minority youth cultures as caught 'between two cultures' (Anwar 1976; Watson 1977). Rather than stuck between two stools, it is more useful to see these styles as reflecting a duality or multiplicity of cultural points of identification for youth who are products of post-colonial diasporic flows, in keeping with Gilroy's (1993) concept of 'double consciousness'.[8] The two musical forms that have been discussed similarly confound old CCCS class-centred theories. As Rojek (1995: 55) has pointed out, 'the conditions of post-Fordist society have simply engendered new cultural forms and practices and revealed hybrid constellations and identities which the battery of concepts forged under classical Marxism is incapable of capturing'. Unlike the CCCS paradigm of fixed pre-determined lifecycles and cultures rooted in the territorialized physical space of street corners, NADM and French rap operate in undeniably globalized conditions where ideas, music, technology and people can circulate on a scale unseen before. The use of trans-national imagery in sometimes very localized settings again illustrates how the socio-spatial map has been dramatically reconfigured in recent times. As Morley and Robins (1995: 116) put it, 'globalization is like putting together a jigsaw puzzle: it is a matter of inserting a multiplicity of identities into the overall picture of a new global system'. In this new world order, boundaries are more fluid than before.

Although, in its commercialized form, it may have initially been 'born in the USA', contemporary popular music exists literally everywhere, just as traditional vernacular song has for centuries. As Mitchell (2001) asserts in his collected volume on non-US rap, 'For a sense of innovation, surprise and musical substance . . . it is becoming increasingly necessary to look outside the USA to countries such as France, England, Italy, and Japan, where strong local currents of hip-hop indigenization have taken place.' Whilst studies of English rock and pop are not new, English-language literature has only relatively recently begun to trace traject-ories in the 'parallel universes' of the non-English-speaking world, and highlighted the rich diversity of multicultural, post-colonial, youth cultures alive in the new Europe (see Förnas, Lindberg and Sernhade 1995; Gudmundsson 1993; Pilkington 1994). The growing number of academic accounts addressing British Asian youth (Alexander 2000; Bhatti 1999; Baumann 1996; Gillespie 1995; Sharma *et al.*

8. New times demand new neologisms. Kaur and Kalra (1996), for example, have come up with the term 'Br Asian' to define the British Asian who inhabits both of these cultures as opposed to being caught between them, as earlier works dictated (see Anwar 1976; Watson 1977).

1996) are also much welcome after a long period of silence on this subject. One hopes that further studies of such transnational phenomena elsewhere follow, thus counteracting youth studies' long-standing limited focus of analysis within discrete homogenous national units. Much of the existing academic work on popular music has emerged from the US. However, the adoption and adaptation of various prima-facie US musical styles by youth in various countries, and the growth of new musically based youth cultures, is challenging the once assumed American hegemony in youth culture. At a time when the flows of people, ideas and music are circulating on a scale unseen before, we should re-think traditional dichotomies and binaries of 'them' versus 'us', 'Europe' versus 'US' and 'East' versus 'West', and instead work towards a new conceptualization of 'globalization' that substitutes a one-way flattening process of Americanization for a more inclusive definition. Monocultural studies will arguably become more and more difficult to undertake given that we now inhabit a distinctly 'post-colonial', as well as ageing, world.

At the start of the twenty-first century, that minority youth can actively instigate youth musical culture is beyond doubt. Furthermore, quite apart from their important functions in potentially enfranchising marginalized youth and highlighting the repositioning of nation states within the new Europe of the new world order, both the new Asian dance music and French rap make jolly good listening and are warmly recommended as the perfect twin soundtracks for a new century.

References

Anwar, M. (1976), *Between Two Cultures*, London: Community Relations Council.

Alexander, C. (2000), *The Asian Gang: Ethnicity, Identity, Masculinity*, Oxford: Berg.

Banerji, S. and Baumann, G. (1990), 'Bhangra 1984-8: Fusion and Professionalisation in a Genre of South Asian Dance Music', in P. Oliver (ed.), *Black Music in Britain: Essays on the Afro-Asian Contribution to Popular Music*, Milton Keynes: Open University Press.

Barrett, J. (1996) 'World Music, Nation and Postcolonialism', *Cultural Studies*, 10 (2): 237-247

Baumann, G. (1996), *Contesting Culture: Discourses of Identity in Multi-Ethnic London*, Cambridge: Cambridge University Press.

Bazin, H. (1995), *La Culture Hip Hop*, Paris: Desclee de Brouwer.

Bennett, A. (2000), *Popular Music and Youth Culture: Music, Identity and Place*, Basingstoke: Macmillan.

Bhatti, G. (1999), *Asian Children at Home and at School*, London: Routledge.

Brulard, I. (1997), 'Laïcité and Islam', in S. Perry (ed.), *Aspects of Contemporary France*, London: Routledge.

Brake, M. (1980), *The Sociology of Youth Cultures and Youth Subcultures*, London: Routledge.

Cachin, O. (1996), *L'Offensive Rap*, Paris: Galliamard.

Cannon, S. (1997), 'Paname City Rapping: B-Boys in the *Banlieues* and Beyond', in A. Hargreaves and M. McKinney (eds), *Post Colonial Cultures in France*, London: Routledge.

Cathus, O. (1994), 'La Vibration de la Rue' in J. Barreyere and A. Vulbeau (eds), *La Jeunesse et la Rue*, Paris: EPI/DDB Éditions.

Cheesman, T. (1998), 'Polyglot Pop Politics: Hip Hop in Germany', *Debatte*, 6 (2): 191–214.

Couturier, B. (1983), *Une Scène-Jeunesse: Cultures-Jeunes, état des Lieux*, Paris: Éditions Autrement.

Cross, B. (1993), *It's Not About A Salary: Rap, Race and Resistance in Los Angeles*, London: Verso.

Featherstone, M. (1995), *Undoing Culture: Globalization, Postmodernism and Identity*, London: Sage.

Fornas, J., Lindberg, U. and Sernhede, O. (1995), *In Garageland: Rock, Youth and Modernity*, London: Routledge.

Frith, S. (1996), *Performing Rites: On the Value of Popular Music*, Oxford: Oxford University Press.

Gaspard, F. and Khoroskavar, F. (1995), *La Foulard et la République*, Paris: La Découverte.

Ghelani, T. (2001), *Asian Young People's use of African American Commodified Cultures*, Paper presented at 'Beyond Hip-Hop: Youth Cultures and Global-ization' ESRC Interdisciplinary Youth Studies Seminar, Sheffield University, 26 November.

Gillespie, M. (1995), *Television, Ethnicity and Cultural Change*, London: Routledge.

Gilroy, P. (1993), *The Black Atlantic: Modernity and Double Consciouness*, London: Verso.

Goldstein, J. (1992), *Let's Move, Let's Spray, Let's Tag*, Geneva: Éditions IES.

Grossberg. L. (1992), *We Gotta Get Out of this Place: Popular Conservatism and Postmodern Culture,* London: Routledge.

Gudmundsson, G. (1993), 'Rock Music as a Synthesis of International Trends and National Cultural Inheritance', *Young: The Nordic Journal of Youth Research*, 1 (2): 48–63

Hall, S. and Jefferson, T. (eds) (1976), *Resistance through Rituals: Youth Sub-cultures in Post-War Britain*, London: Hutchinson.

Hargreaves, A. and McKinney, M. (eds) (1997), *Post Colonial Cultures in France*, London: Routledge.

Hebdige, D. (1979), *Subculture: The Meaning of Style*, London: Methuen.

Hutnyk, J. (2000), *Critique of Exotica: Music, Politics and the Cultural Industry*, London: Pluto.

Kaschuba, B. (1993), 'Everyday Culture', in M. Shelley and M. Winck (eds), *Aspects of European Cultural Diversity*, London and Milton Keynes: Open University/Routledge.

Kaur, R. and Kalra, V. (1996), 'New Paths for South Asian Identity and Musical Creativity', in S. Sharma, A. Sharma and J. Hutnyk (eds), *Disorienting Rhythms: The Politics of the New Asian Dance Music*, London: Zed.

Kellner, D. (1995), *Media Culture: Cultural Studies, Identity and Politics*, London: Routledge.

Lapassade, G. (1996), *Le Rap ou La Fureur de Dire*, Paris: Loris Talmart.

Lipsitz, G. (1994), *Dangerous Crossroads: Popular Music, Postmodernism and the Poetics of Place*, London: Verso.

Mitchell, T. (2001), *Global Rap: Rap and Hip Hop Outside the USA*, Hanover NH: Weslyan University Press.

Morley, D. and Robins, K. (1995), *Spaces of Identity: Global Media, Electronic Landscapes and Cultural Boundaries*, London: Routledge.

Oakland, J. (1998), *British Civilization: An Introduction*, London: Routledge.

Perry, S. (ed.) (1997), *Aspects of Contemporary France*, London: Routledge.

Pilkington, H. (1994), *Russia's Youth and its Culture: A Nation's Constructors and Constructed*, London: Routledge.

Polhemus, T. (1994), *Streetstyle*, London: Thames & Hudson.

Rojek, C. (1995), *Decentring Leisure: Rethinking Leisure Theory*, London: Sage.

Rose, T. (1994), *Black Noise: Rap Music and Black Culture in Contemporary America*, Hanover NH: Weslyan University Press.

Rosello, M. (1998), *Declining the Stereotype: Representation and Ethnicity in Contemporary France*, New England: Dartmouth University Press.

Sharma, S., Sharma, A. and Hutnyk, J. (eds) (1996), *Disorienting Rhythms: The Politics of the New Asian Dance Music*, London: Zed.

Silverman, M. (1996), 'The Revenge of Civil Society: State, Nation and Society in France', in D. Cesarini and M. Fulbrook (eds), *Citizenship, Nationality and Migration in Europe*, London: Routledge.

Soysal, L. (1998), 'Diversity of Experience, Experience of Diversity: Turkish Migrant Youth Culture in Berlin', *Cultural Dynamics*, 13 (1): 5–28.

Soysal, L. (2001), *Hip-Hop, Globalization and Migrant Youth Culture*, Paper presented at 'Beyond Hip-Hop: Youth Cultures and Globalization' ESRC Interdisciplinary Youth Studies seminar, Sheffield University, 26 November.

Storry, M. and Childs, P. (eds) (1997), *British Cultural Identities*, London: Routledge.

Taylor, T. (1997), *Global Pop*, London and New York: Routledge.

Thoday, P. (1995), *Le Franglais*, London: Althone.

Toop, D. (1995), *Ocean of Sound: Aether Talk, Ambient Sound and Imaginary Worlds*, London: Serpents Tail.

Vulbeau, A. (1992), *Du Tag Au Tag*, Paris: Descleé du Brouwer.

Watson, J. (ed.) (1977), *Between Two Cultures: Migrants and Minorities in Britain*, Oxford: Blackwell.

Wright, S. (2000), '"A Love Born of Hate": Autonomist Rap in Italy', *Theory, Culture and Society*, 17 (3): 117–35.

–14–

Heavy Metal and Subcultural Theory: A Paradigmatic Case of Neglect?

Andy R. Brown

This chapter examines the subcultural status of heavy metal. Heavy metal is perhaps unique in that its thirty-year history – as the object of tribal loyalty and youth cultural activity – unravels on both sides of the subculture that was seen to be the last word in cultural theorizing: punk. David Muggleton (2000: 2) has remarked that on reading Dick Hebdige's account of punk, in *Subculture: the Meaning of Style* (1979), he could find no reflection there of his own experiences as a punk. As a fan of heavy metal, (before I embraced 'prog rock', jazz-fusion and then punk),[1] I do not even have the satisfaction of claiming this, because the account of heavy metal in subcultural theory is, at best, marginal; at worst, simply 'invisible'. What follows is an attempt to investigate this 'invisibility' but also to explain it.[2]

My argument is that heavy metal, although it ought to have qualified for subcultural status, did not. Firstly, because it did not show up on subcultural radar and, secondly, when it did, it was rejected as 'inauthentic' on political grounds. This is because I view subcultural theory as a theoretical-political framework for categorizing 'radical' cultural activity. The problem with this framework is that it depends upon a rather fabricated idea of *commodity stylization* as a necessarily restrictive class *practice*. Thus, while all working-class youth suffer structural oppression, only a minority are able to articulate 'resistance' through a creative and class-affirming 'subversion' of leisure consumption. This assumes, among other

---

1. This transition from one subcultural style to another was not just signified by a change of clothing but by changes in my record collection. This involved a reordering and categorizing of what was 'cool' or just 'acceptable' and what wasn't. In this respect, the impact of punk was to severely limit my collection: it was a 'ground zero' operation. My 'prog' and metal records were now an embarrassment and I sold them to one of my mates who was still into metal and therefore a bit of a 'dinosaur'. Now, of course, all these records sit happily together.

2. This ought to involve uncovering 'the subjective meanings, values and motives of those involved' (Muggleton 2000: 5). But given the thirty-year gap, nothing short of a time machine would be effective in achieving this!

things, that youth have an oppressive relationship to the cultural commodity 'market', just as they do to the other institutions of 'social control'. At the same time we are asked to believe that the 'youth culture industry' is parasitic on subcultural stylization, in wanting to exploit it, once the process of 'moral panic' has passed to an 'incorporation' phase. This exploitation involves selling radical stylization as 'novel' style to the rest of working-class youth, but emptied of its class-articulated meanings. Thus the model posits a 'heroic', because unequal, struggle between radical 'appropriation' as style, against a recuperative act of 'dislocation' of class-made meanings that become the source of attraction to non-radical youths. The reason this division inheres is because in order to distinguish radical consumer stylization from just any stylization, the class colouring must be 'pure' and uncontaminated by the media, the market or the (non-radical) majority of the working-class itself.

Importantly, Sarah Thornton (1995: 119) has argued that this model rests on a radical fantasy of a 'media-free space', prior to exposure, prior to incorporation. But it equally involves a fantasy of a 'market-free' space, won through subcultural struggle against incorporation into the 'mainstream'. It is my argument that youth commodity stylization is much more widespread than subcultural theory makes it out to be, and that there are as many subcultural styles as there are markets to distinguish them. What matter are the criteria we bring to the definition of subcultural markets themselves, because membership is not necessarily defined by class but through subcultural identification with the practice of stylization. It follows that the class character of such stylization is much messier and less pure than subcultural theory would like. It also has more to do with the existence and demise of subcultural markets than with subcultures understood as the autonomous practices of minority radical stylists within an otherwise undifferentiated mass of the working-class.

Subcultural markets are not, as Angela McRobbie (1994: 136–7) argues, a post-punk phenomenon, but a condition of the popular expansion of post-war style-culture itself. One subcultural example that makes this clear is heavy metal, although I am sure there are plenty of others. The commodity stylization of heavy metal culture revolves around a collective investment in a 'fantastic' masculinity, made possible by the existence of a dedicated market of records, concerts and other activities. The development of this market allows this culture to develop and to complexify, to become subject to internal modification and to external change. Like accounts of class subcultures, the style of heavy metal culture is rooted in contradictions of class, gender and ethnicity, which are mediated through its style of expression and which are the source of its attraction. While heavy metal music cannot resolve these contradictions, it can stage an imaginative encounter with them that is both pleasurable and meaningful (cf. Walser 1993).

Heavy Metal: A Subculture without any 'Style'

Despite emerging in the period 1969–70, as a distinctive musical style that was able to recruit a substantial working-class and lower-middle-class following, heavy metal was ignored, dismissed or marginalized by Birmingham CCCS subcultural theorists and in the newly emergent youth and popular music studies. Receiving not a single reference in the pioneering CCCS work (Hall and Jefferson 1976) or those that sought to revise it (Mungham and Pearson 1976; Brake 1980; 1985: 72–80), heavy metal's working-class and student popularity was belatedly acknowledged in a bemused footnote to Hebdige's celebrated (1979) work. Here, 'heavy metal rockers' (Hebdige 1979: 84) are identified as one of a range of 'youth cultural options' open to ordinary youth, who are *not* subcultural stylists. The appended note is presumably to explain this option to the uninformed reader. Thus,

> Heavy metal is, as the name suggests, a heavily amplified, basic form of rock which relies on the constant repetition of standard guitar riffs. Aficionados can be distinguished by their long hair, denim and 'idiot' dancing (again, the name says it all). Heavy metal has fans amongst the student population, but it also has a large working class following. It seems to represent a curious blend of hippy aesthetics and football terrace machismo. (Hebdige 1979: 155, n.12)

This 'reading' from Hebdige, the self-styled semiotician *par excellence*, is curiously flat and one-dimensional. This is presumably because heavy metal can simply be read 'on its surface'. It does not represent a 'crime against the natural order', like punk's coded and oblique 'white noise', but a rather dull elaboration of past elements, of rock and hippiedom. Hebdige clearly views the behaviour of the followers of heavy metal as 'comical' ('idiot dancing') and yet this public behaviour, which he incorrectly identifies (actually *headbanging*), could quite plausibly qualify as an element in, and evidence of, a subcultural homology. What the phenomenon lacks, of course, is a tightly knit sense of stylistic innovators who are coded 'working class'. The surprising alliance between 'scruffy students' and the working-class is attributed to a reactionary *alliance* of the counterculture and 'machismo', rather than a *cross-class bricolage*. In the Hall and Jefferson (1976) classic CCCS text, football terrace machismo is romanticized, even admired, as a 'defence of space' (for example, Clarke 1976b); yet in this context it is simply 'machismo'. The confused class composition of the heavy metal audience, its obvious lack of style and its self-evident consumer origins mean that it does not express a 'ritual of resistance' but rather of conformity to 'traditional' values of working-class masculinity, which the consumer style of heavy metal exploits.

Here, in capsule form, we have the 'problem' of the subcultural status of heavy metal and it is, I shall argue, a problem *not* of heavy metal but of subcultural theory. Heavy metal is simply invisible to the radar of subcultural theory, despite the fact that it was, throughout the period of formation of the CCCS approach, a popular cultural form that attracted the spending and leisure focus of a large quantity of male (and some female) working-class and lower middle-class adolescents. Indeed, it could be argued, in terms of the CCCS model, that the emergent stylistic ensemble of heavy metal youth culture announced a similarly striking unity of group cohesion and identity to those groups – the teds, mods, skins and punks – that formed the empirical focus of Birmingham subcultural theory. Such a subcultural recognition might have allowed a clearer understanding of the stylistic transition that led from the mid-1960s 'rockers' or motorbike gangs, via the 'hippie' counterculture (two styles distinctly *contrasted* within Willis's 1978 study), to the post-rocker, *sans*-motorbike 'greasers' or 'grebos' because these 'greasers' began to exhibit the stylistic elements that Deena Weinstein (2000: 100) identifies as 'hippie-biker' or 'outlaw-biker-gang', from which heavy metal style is derived.

'Headbanging': The Panic that Wasn't

It is Cashmore (1984) who is the first to extend Hebdige's dismissal. Cashmore's approach is notable because it makes explicit the features that ought to have qualified heavy metal as a subcultural 'style of resistance', yet perversely fails such criteria. Like Hebdige, Cashmore identifies its emergence amidst 'punk versus Ted skirmishes' in the late 1970s – 'a mass following of youth, their denim clothes covered in studs and appliqué, their hair long and wild so as to swing freely when they shook their heads in time with the music – what they called 'head-banging' (Cashmore 1984: 37).

> This head-banging was the source of the only genuine moment of panic about heavy metal when a youth died after inflicting on himself brain damage through continually jerking his head at a concert in the Midlands town of Wolverhampton. But heavy metal generally failed to arouse the kind of hysteria or panic associated with most youth subcultures. This said, the heavy metal kids didn't actually do much of note: they went to concerts, very big outdoor concerts, and they gave the appearance of being threatening without actually being threatening. That's all. It would be unfair to call heavy metal conservative: inert would be more accurate. (Cashmore 1984: 37)

What Cashmore is actually describing is the 'New Wave of British Heavy Metal', a term coined by *Sounds* music journalist, Geoff Barton, to capture the aggressive resurgence of heavy metal bands in the wake of punk (Barton 1979, 1990; Brown 2001). Taking the 'grass roots', DIY aesthetic, speed and aggression of punk, a whole new wave of heavy metal influenced bands began to emerge in the 1979–80 period. Cashmore views this revival, like Hebdige's account of the teds, as a form of youthful, working-class conservatism. Yet his account is unable to 'explain' the coherence of the style or its practices. For clearly this group has a definite identity, argot and ritual. They are also clearly working-class 'white kids' but Cashmore is unable to 'locate' them within a class 'contradiction'. The one familiar element, the moral panic potential of 'headbanging', fails to provoke sustained media coverage. For Cashmore, this is symptomatic of the political 'inertness' of the movement, which is vaguely threatening, but ultimately socially introverted, because it is based around consumption.

The 'Problem' of Heavy Metal

It is my argument that the case of heavy metal can reveal how it was possible for subcultural theory to get it wrong. In other words, the 'problem' of heavy metal is actually a problem of the compatibility of the emergent features of the youth culture with the conceptual framework the CCCS developed to explain the striking synchrony or 'homology' of elements of style to the class 'messages' that sub-cultures carried. This ought to be a methodological issue, of how empirical features are gathered and ordered in the construction of a theoretically adequate explanation (cf. Muggleton 2000: 20) but, in fact, the problem with Birmingham subcultural theory is an over-bearing *political* 'theoreticism', which is compelled to identify subcultures as 'authentic' expressions of working-class 'resistance'. As Steve Redhead (1990: 25) puts it, '"Authentic" subcultures were produced by subcultural theories, not the other way around.' What I want to add to this is that particular elements in the theoretical mix of subcultural theory have particular outcomes in terms of the account of subculture. Drawing on aspects of the growing critiques of the CCCS (Gelder and Thornton 1997), I want to illustrate how the case of heavy metal offers a paradigmatic critique of the theoretical procedure of subcultural theory in recognizing and categorizing subcultures.

Firstly, the CCCS take their subcultural categories from media coverage and then trace them back to an original 'moment' of authentic stylistic creation. Although such an approach wishes to separate 'authentic' subcultures from their sensationalized exposure in macro media, it is only after the fact of this exposure that subcultures can be recognized as distinct (Thornton 1995: 119). Significantly, there is no account of the role of the media or cultural industries until after 'pure' subcultures become subject to moral panic coverage and commercial diffusion/ defusion as 'consumer style'. The 'problem' with heavy metal is that it was not subject to specific moral panic until 1980–1, ten years after its first emergence. This means it is 'invisible' to subcultural recognition. It also means that it literally doesn't exist in the 'tightly-knit' form that subcultural theory would recognize as 'authentic'.

Second, subcultural theory presents an account of post-war subcultures as entirely working-class in origin, in terms of their locations of emergence (almost exclusively London) and their membership. They do recognize the 'counterculture' as a middle-class phenomenon, which articulates the 'focal concerns' of this class. But the 'hippies' are not 'subcultural' in the way that working-class groups are. Rather the 'counterculture' is composed of students, ex-students and 'drop outs' from the class system, it is therefore a quite diffuse 'milieu' (Clarke *et al.* 1976). The problem of heavy metal here is that, although it is possible to trace its working-class emergence in the UK midlands and the north in terms of early bands and followers,[3] it also has middle-class fans that, as we have seen, are identified as 'scruffy students'.

Third, unlike heavy metal, none of the post-war subcultures are identified with the emergence of particular music scenes. The mod music scene, for example, is seen to emerge after the mods and to involve a commercialization of their 'original' style (Clarke 1976a: 187). The exception here should have been punk, but Hebdige (1979) overemphasizes its style politics at the expense of its existence as a music phenomenon (Laing 1985), while failing to locate its origins in the middle-class/ art school/ student 'milieu' (Frith and Horne 1989). The other 'possible contender' for a subculture with a music origin is 'glamrock', which Ian Taylor and Dave Wall (1976) argue is instrumental in the demise of the skinheads. However, if this thesis is accepted 'it breaks the pattern of post-war youth culture in Britain' (Mungham and Pearson 1976: 7). This is because Glamrock is a commercialization of the counterculture in a 'hardrock' style, calculated to appeal to the working class (Taylor and Wall 1976: 106). It is therefore a 'prefabricated' subculture that has no 'authentic' roots in working-class experience. What is striking about this debate is that the 'hardrock' style of Glam music is not contextualized within a musical genealogy (see Cagle 1995: Chapter 6), which would have to include heavy metal, as well as garage-punk. Also, that the problem of the emergence of heavy metal is a dry rehearsal of these kinds of arguments, five years earlier.

This inadequate periodization of musical styles also disables Hebdige's account of post-war rock, as part of his wider claim that all subcultural styles rehearse a

3. Emerging in the period 1969–70, bands such as Black Sabbath, Judas Priest (Birmingham, West Midlands) and Budgie (Cardiff, South Wales), to note only the most well known, were clearly working-class in origin, as were their followers. This pattern of emergence from formerly heavily industrialized conurbations also holds good for heavy metal's second wave, the so called New Wave of British Heavy Metal, composed of bands such as Def Leppard (Sheffield), Saxon (Barnsley) and Venom (Newcastle). There is also a clear north/south pattern to the development of the genre. Although some bands formed in and around London, notably Led Zeppelin, Deep Purple and Iron Maiden, the stronghold of support for metal lay in the Midlands and the north (indeed, Plant and Bonham were West Bromwich born and played in the Birmingham band, Band of Joy, prior to cofounding Led Zeppelin).

'phantom history' of Black/White relations in terms of a reaction/accommodation to the 'black immigrant presence' (Hebdige 1979: 44–5). As Gary Clark argues, because Hebdige 'examines only selected areas of articulation as opposed to the mass appropriation of black music [he wrongly] suggests that black and white links were absent during the early seventies' (1990: 88–9). The most significant 'Black-White' articulation occurring in this period is, of course, that of heavy metal, in the riff style and lyrics of Black urban blues, meeting the psychedelia of the late 1960s (Walser 1993: 9). The contradictions involved in this cultural syncretism are just as significant, in terms of racism and 'White' ethnicity, as Hebdige's account of the music of the teds and skins.

Radical Consumer Stylization: The Importance of Records

This point takes us to the heart of the problem: the inadequate treatment of popular music within subcultural analysis. There are broadly two reasons for this. Firstly, the 'ideology' of classless youth, contested by subcultural theory, identified the notion of a 'youth generation' as 'rooted in the new consciousness carried by progressive rock music' (Murdock and McCron 1976: 22). Subcultural theory was therefore keen to show that the 'counterculture' had an almost exclusively middle-class membership and that the musical tastes of the middle- and working-classes were separate and divergent. As Murdock and McCron put it, 'far from dissolving class differences and creating a homogeneous generational culture, the bifurcating cultures of pop and rock became one of the main means through which these divisions were extended into the sphere of leisure' (1976: 23).

But the cost of this position is that the issue of music is consistently downplayed within subcultural theory. This produces a contradictory account of the relationship of subcultural style to musical preferences, in term of group 'homologies' and expressive style. In the main theoretical exposition of the concept of homology in *Resistance Through Rituals,* John Clarke claims that the 'neatest description' of the relation between object and group is George Melly's characterization of rock 'n' roll as '"screw and smash" music for the Teds' (Clarke 1976a: 179). In fact, all the examples Clarke gives are musical ones. Yet, as Cagle (1995: 39) puts it, although CCCS theorists 'view music as integral to the homology of the subculture, very little is said about how and why the music plays a significant role in the identity making process of the subculture'. This is because records are conceived of by the CCCS as 'objects' and materials, ripe for appropriation by the group in the 'genesis of style' (Clarke 1976a: 183). As such they pre-exist their subcultural adoption as one of many circulating commodities whose 'meanings' are inscribed by the dominant culture in ways that reflect the 'preferred' meanings of the economically dominant class. Here the absence of a theorization of media and the culture industries leads to confusion between these institutions and those of 'formal' social control.

This is because subcultural theorists conceive the relationship between working-class subcultures and the leisure industry as a structurally oppressive one. Thus, subcultural stylization is an act of resistance that involves collective action, part of which is action against the tyranny of the commodity: 'neither money nor the market could fully dictate what groups used these things to *say* or *signify* about themselves' (Clarke *et al.* 1976: 55). The notion of 'resistance' turns on a notion of a passive/active relationship to the youth leisure market. Subcultural groups 'use' and 'appropriate' materials and commodities rather than 'consume' them. The idea of consumption here is that of passivity, inaction and conformity to social role and position. Thus, 'far from being the ideal passive consumer of capitalist society, consuming the commodity in the form in which it is presented, the mods raised the possibility of an active relation to the commodity' (Clarke and Jefferson 1976: 153). The claim for the radical and subversive nature of subcultures involves a conception of active 'appropriation', 'transformation and rearrangement' of particular objects (the act of *bricolage*) which are, or can be made to be, 'homologous' with the group's 'focal concerns'. That is, a 'fit' is accomplished between the structural context of the class sub-group and the objects 'in which they can see their central values held and reflected' (Clarke *et al.* 1976: 56).

Hebdige (1979: Chapter 8) notably departs from the idea of homology in punk style, and thereby from the 'tightly organized' relationship between objects and class meanings but, as Paul Willis maintains, both 'homology' and 'signifying practice' 'imply a subversion of the received and commercially fixed meanings of cultural items in favour of a subculturally specific meaning' (Willis 1982: 91). The problem, as Hebdige recognizes, is the polysemic nature of commodities, their instability of meaning, which he argues punk takes to its terminus, by signifying chaos 'at every level' (Hebdige 1979: 113). Despite the fact that Hebdige carries this analogy over to his account of the music of punk, what he misses is that punk records were not commodities inscribed with commercially fixed meanings. Here, subcultural theory cannot allow for the idea that commodities can already have meanings that are 'expressive' and 'homologous' with stylists. Yet this idea is nonetheless suggested throughout the *Resistance Through Rituals* text. Clarke, for example argues that, 'It is the objective potential of the cultural form (in this case, music) and its fit with the subjective orientation of the group which facilitates the appropriation of the form by the latter, leading (sometimes) to a sort of stylistic fusion between object and group' (1976a: 179). It is surely significant here that it is music that is often given as a 'good' example.

These inconsistencies lead me to question the *relative* potential for meaning of the 'found' items employed within a subcultural practice of *stylization*. The meanings, latent or otherwise, in a record are much greater than those residing in a safety pin or a pair of work boots. Records are not simply commodities in this way but already 'art-culture' objects that circulate within genre markets. What is therefore being suppressed in CCCS accounts of working-class subcultural styliz-ation is the development of subcultural markets that are dependent upon and reactive to subcultural stylists themselves. In other words, we are asked to believe that cultural commodities have no meaningful connection to youth groups until their meaningfulness is recognized as integral to a particular class identity. The discussion of diffusion/defusion is also significant here. As Clarke (1976a: 188) argues, the eventual commercialization of a style means that it is 'dislocated from the context and group which generated it'. But there is absolutely no reason why the moment of creativity must come before the style becomes more widespread; surely it is the very breakthrough of the style that marks it as significant? By working back from this 'moment' subcultural theory avoids the most important issue: why it was that this style 'took off', was widely meaningful, and so forth.

Willis and the Emergent Stylization of Heavy Metal Culture

As we have seen, it is crucial to subcultural theory that music consumption has a class pattern that corresponds to the contrasting structural location of working-class and middle-class groups. We have also noted that, although music is readily invoked as expressive of group homologies, the radical stylization of subcultural groups is authenticated by the novel meanings their active use makes possible and this is diffused when such meanings become identified with the style as com-mercially 'novel'. It is therefore very significant in Willis's (1978) study that he abandons the absolute separation of commodity consumption and stylistic use in his account of the subcultural relation of the hippies to 'their' music consumption. The reason he does so is because the music of the hippies escapes the logic of commodification by the music corporations. This is because 'rock' artists had artistic control of their product, did not produce music simply for profit, and were themselves derived from the community their music addressed.

> The hippy case contrasts with that of the motor-bike boys who could only select from what was provided, the hippies, or people very much like them, *could* exert a powerful influence on their music . . . the crucial characteristic of 'progressive' pop during the . . . late 1960s was that the performers, not the controllers, were able to decide on the artistic content of the music. Now these performers very often came from some version of the hippy culture. The music, therefore, came to reflect and develop more and more closely the concerns of this cultural group. (Willis 1978: 164–5)

Willis' argument, then, is that despite the status of 'progressive' records as com-modities, the condition of the market's expansion was that creative control remained with the artists rather then those who financed it. Thus, the particular stylization of consumption of the hippies exerts a demand for a particular kind of cultural product that is determinant of the success of the market. This is therefore an art-culture market, despite the fact that the records 'make a lot of money'. But this relationship to consumption is not possible for the working-class bike boys because they do not have this kind of control over what they consume.

The significance of this for identifying heavy metal as an unacknowledged subcultural stylization that 'produced' its own distinctive market should now be clear. But there is further 'hidden' significance to Willis's study, in that the musical characteristics identified by the hippies as epitomising the 'progressive' culture that was integral to their class identity – such as the development of distortion techniques, a disregard for the temporal confines of the song form, and so on – are identified as those of formative heavy metal bands, such as Led Zeppelin. And, in terms of the 'messy' class location and consumption of heavy metal, as I have argued it, there is a further irony. As Muggleton comments, 'Reading *Profane Culture*, it seems beyond the bounds of possibility that some bikers may have become suedeheads, or that certain hippies could have transformed themselves into glam rockers or punks, so imprisoned are individuals by group homologies' (Muggleton 2000: 26). It is my argument that the emergence of heavy metal, as a distinctive market 'expression' of subcultural stylization, depends upon exactly this sort of thing occurring. That is, some members of both these opposed and contrasting groups went on to become, after 1969, heavy metal or progressive rock fans or more likely both, and that this tendency is clearly evident in the Willis study. For example, Willis's claim that the rockers' music constitutes a 'physical' homology between the motorbike and musical timbre, points to a moment in the formation of heavy metal culture (1976: 63).[4] Or as Andy Bennett puts it,

> The fan base for heavy metal and progressive rock was essentially the same audience, largely comprising hippies and bikers. Indeed, by [the late] sixties [the] 'rocker' version of motorbike culture, with its attachment to fifties rock 'n' roll, had all but disappeared and been replaced by a new type of biker whose endorsement of the hippie lifestyle was unmistakable. (Bennett 2000: 184)

This is also confirmed by Deena Weinstein's account of the emergence of the heavy metal subculture as a 'hippie-biker' hybrid youth culture which began to appear in late 1960s as psychedelic music was getting harder. Weinstein's argument is that, with the collapse of the 1960s youth culture,

---

4. The biker anthem, 'Born to be Wild' by Steppenwolf (1968), contains many of the formative elements of heavy metal cultural stylization, not least the line 'heavy metal thunder'. The motorbike has remained a dominant 'iconic' signifier of heavy metal, despite the fact that most fans do not own bikes.

both the blue collar and longhairs and the psychedelic bands were left stranded. Eventually they found each other with the help of the music industry and the result was the heavy metal subculture [. . .] The important thing to note here is that the subculture was not a fabrication of the popular-culture industry, but existed, in germ, before heavy metal music as a distinctive genre erupted (Weinstein 2000: 101).

Conclusion: From Woodstock to Cockrock: Popular Music Studies and Heavy Metal

Given the elements of syncretism emergent within Willis's (1978) account of the hippies and the motor-bike boys, elements that later find their expression in the formation of heavy metal culture, we would expect approaches to youth, based on musical preference, to be more sympathetic to such developments. But this is not the case. In fact such approaches largely reproduce the negative characterization of heavy metal, but do so by contrasting its negative divergence from the radical stylization of the middle-class 'counterculture'. The key feature of this argument is the relative autonomy of middle-class 'hippie culture' to articulate a progressive social vision through 'rock' music. As Frith (1983: 213) puts it, 'rock had become an art form which bound a community'. Rock ideology expressed the sentiments and spirit of what was, in effect, a new 'deviant' middle-class: but in a 'universal' language.

The significance of this, and its connection to subcultural theory, is that the 'hippies' were the one subcultural style, outside of the working class, recognized as a potentially *radical* subcultural milieu. This was because the hippies were able to articulate their critique of capitalism, whereas for other subcultures such a critique was 'coded' and in need of deciphering. It is against this class framework that the negative impact of heavy metal is decisively codified. This is because the commercial success of heavy metal as a mass music, sold to adolescent, working-class or lower-middle-class males, is seen to signal the demise of the 1960s 'counterculture'. Its emergence, at the close of the 1960s, becomes critically identified with the commercial *reappropriation* of the 'authentic' rock community and the rock 'artist' by the music business. Frith argues,

as the decade developed it became increasingly difficult to make sense of heavy metal as student music. Bands like Black Sabbath, Uriah Heep, and Deep Purple had their own armies of scruffy working-class fans, and the dismissive response of *Rolling Stone* to hard rock as a genre (and to all its exponents except its original 1960s founders) was symptomatic. The huge popularity of Grand Funk Railroad, in 1970–71, symbolized the arrival of a rock culture of working-class fans who didn't even read *Rolling Stone*; and the rise of Kiss later in the decade was an even clearer indication of how rock could be integrated into the traditional marketing modes of teenage *pop*. The result was a music that had no significance for 'the intelligent' rock fan at all. (Frith 1983: 214–15)

Here, the 'problem' of heavy metal is that it devalues rock music – the voice of a wider, inclusive community, articulated (through critical journalism) and supported (through consumption and participation) by a 'new', radical middle-class – by transforming it into a 'loud populism', sold to working-class males. Such a view is based on the assumption that a popular cultural form must fail the criteria of artistry when tied to the logic of the market, and is also central to the account of subcultural stylization as minority radical practice. Therefore the cross-class *bricolage*, represented by the development of heavy metal, must represent a devaluation of rock culture, because its majority audience is working class. The market standardization of heavy metal allows it to be 'sold', like earlier forms of pop, as an industrialized genre. As Taylor and Wall argue, the 'inequality of access to the middle-class culture of liberation has been resolved at the expense of that culture' (Taylor and Wall 1976: 112). The elements of heavy metal, borrowed from rock, become 'empty' forms of stylization, such as 'guitar virtuosity'.

The result of this process is that working-class males, by adopting the music and trappings of the counterculture, reinvent it as a celebration of 'wild masculinity' and commodified 'machismo'. This is clearly brought out in an account offered by Chambers (1985: 123) where heavy metal is described as 'closely tied to the immediate emotions of loud music, beer and communal maleness'. This view, of how heavy metal culture allows a collective celebration of lower class masculinity, is itself derived from the seminal account, by Frith and McRobbie (1978/1990), of heavy metal as 'cockrock'. McRobbie, along with Frith, was one of the earliest theorists to dismiss heavy metal because its public consumption, by male youths, rested on the passive consumption of sexist mass culture. Thus, the 'sexual liberation' promised by the counter culture is transformed into a sexist machismo that finds a ready audience of working-class males.

Despite the fact that heavy metal is denied subcultural status, the centrality of masculinity to the commodity stylization of heavy metal is the feature that significantly connects it to other post-war working-class styles. But the characterization of this masculine stylization as a traditional machismo or as a commodification of sexism is inadequate. Indeed, the point is not that it is a masculinized style, but that such masculinization is dependent upon consumption. Hence, the problem for subcultural theory is that the stylization of masculinity in heavy metal does not articulate a 'defence' of class, but rather seeks to 'escape' or transcend class through a sci-fi /gothic/ heroic/ tragic dramatization, made possible by consumption stylization itself, and which the subcultural 'market' of heavy metal makes possible.

References

Barton, G. (1979), 'The New Wave of British Heavy Metal, part 1', *Sounds*, 19 May.

Barton, G. (1990), Liner notes to *New Wave of British Heavy Metal: '79 Revisited*, Compact Disc, Vertigo: 846 322-2.

Bennett, A. (2000), *Popular Music and Youth Culture*, Basingstoke and London: Macmillan.

Brake, M. (1980), *The Sociology of Youth Cultures and Youth Subcultures*, London: Routledge & Kegan Paul.

Brake, M. (1985), *Comparative Youth Culture: The Sociology of Youth Cultures and Youth Subcultures in America, Britain and Canada*, London: Routledge & Kegan Paul.

Brown, A. R. (2001), 'Punk and Metal: Antithesis, Synthesis or Prosthetic?' Paper presented at No Future?: Punk 2001, University of Wolverhampton and Lighthouse, UK, 21–23 September.

Cagle, Van M. (1995), *Reconstructing Pop/Subculture: Art, Rock, and Andy Warhol*, London: Sage.

Cashmore, E. (1984), *No Future*, London: Heinemann.

Chambers, I. (1985), *Urban Rhythms: Pop Music and Urban Culture*, London: Macmillan.

Clarke, J. (1976a), 'Style', in S. Hall, and T. Jefferson (eds), *Resistance Through Rituals: Youth Subcultures in Post-War Britain*, London: Hutchinson.

Clarke, J. (1976b), 'The Skinheads and the Magical Recovery of Community', in S. Hall, and T. Jefferson (eds), *Resistance Through Rituals: Youth Subcultures in Post-War Britain*, London: Hutchinson.

Clarke, J. and Jefferson, T. (1976), 'Working Class Youth Cultures', in G. Mungham and G. Pearson (eds), *Working Class Youth Culture*, London: Routledge & Kegan Paul.

Clarke, J., Hall, S., Jefferson, T. and Roberts, B. (1976), 'Subcultures, Cultures and Class', in S. Hall, and T. Jefferson (eds), *Resistance Through Rituals: Youth Subcultures in Post-War Britain*, London: Hutchinson.

Clarke, G. (1990/1981), 'Defending Ski-Jumpers: A Critique of Theories of Youth Subcultures', in S. Frith and A. Goodwin (eds), *On Record: Rock, Pop and the Written Word*, London: Routledge.

Frith, S. (1983), *Sound Effects: Youth, Leisure and the Politics of Rock 'n' Roll*, London: Constable.

Frith, S. and Horne, H. (1989), *Art into Pop*, London: Methuen.

Frith, S. and McRobbie, A. (1978/1990), 'Rock and Sexuality' in S. Frith and A. Goodwin (eds), *On Record: Rock, Pop and the Written Word*, London: Routledge.

Gelder, K and Thornton, S. (eds) (1997), *The Subcultures Reader*, London: Routledge.

Hall, S. and Jefferson, T. (eds) (1976), *Resistance Through Rituals: Youth Subcultures in Post-War Britain*, London: Hutchinson.

Hebdige, D. (1979), *Subculture: The Meaning of Style*, London: Methuen.

Laing, D. (1985), *One Chord Wonders: Power and Meaning in Punk Rock*, Milton Keynes: Open University Press.

McRobbie, A. (1994), *Postmodernism and Popular Culture*, London: Routledge.

Muggleton, D. (2000), *Inside Subculture: The Postmodern Meaning of Style*, Oxford: Berg.

Mungham, G. and Pearson, G. (eds) (1976), *Working Class Youth Culture*, London: Routledge & Kegan Paul.

Murdock, G. and McCron, R. (1976), 'Youth and Class: the Career of Confusion', in G. Mungham and G. Pearson (eds), *Working Class Youth Culture,* London: Routledge and Kegan Paul.

Redhead, S. (1990), *The End-of-the-Century-Party: Youth and Pop Towards 2000*, Manchester: Manchester University Press.

Taylor, I. and Wall, I. (1976), 'Beyond the Skinheads: Comments on the Emergence and Significance of the Glamrock Cult', in G. Mungham and G. Pearson (eds), *Working Class Youth Culture*, London: Routledge & Kegan Paul.

Thornton, S. (1995), *Club Cultures: Music, Media and Subcultural Capital*, Cambridge: Polity.

Walser, R. (1993), *Running With the Devil: Power, Gender and Madness in Heavy Metal Music*, Hanover NH: Wesleyan University Press.

Weinstein, D. (1991/2000), *Heavy Metal: The Music and its Culture*, Chicago IL: De Capo Press.

Willis, P. (1978), *Profane Culture*, London: Routledge & Kegan Paul.

Willis, P. (1982), 'Male School Counterculture', Open University, U203 Popular Culture, Block 7, *The State and Popular Culture*, Unit 30, Milton Keynes: Open University Press.

–15–

The Death and Life of Punk, the Last Subculture[1]

Dylan Clark

Punk is dead. Long live punk.

(graffito in use since 1970s)

Punk had to die so that it could live.

With the death of punk, classical subcultures died. What had, by the 1970s, emerged as 'subcultures' were understood to be groups of youths who practised a wide array of social dissent through shared behavioural, musical, and costume orientations.[2] Such groups were remarkably capable vehicles for social change, and were involved in dramatically reshaping social norms in many parts of the world. These 'classical' subcultures obtained their potency partly through an ability to shock and dismay, to disobey prescribed confines of class, gender, and ethnicity. But things changed. People gradually became acclimatized to such subcultural transgressions to the point that, in many places, they have become an *expected* part of the social landscape. The image of rebellion has become one of the most dominant narratives of the corporate capitalist landscape: the 'bad boy' has been reconfigured as a prototypical *consumer*. And so it was a new culture in the 1970s, the punk subculture, which emerged to fight even the normalization of subculture itself, with brilliant new forms of social critique and style. But even punk was

1. Many sentences and ideas in this chapter first appeared in Clark (2000), and were presented at the unforgettable 'No-Future: Punk 2001' conference, University of Wolverhampton, and Lighthouse, England, 21–23 September 2001.

2. Although subculture has far broader meanings, it has come to signify the twentieth-century category for youth groups who possess some sort of marked style and shared affiliations. Whereas sociologists use the term to describe an infinitely wider array of groups – sport fishermen, West Texas Baptists, or toy train hobbyists – 'subculture' is more popularly used to characterize groups of young people. From the flappers of the 1920s to the Chicano cholos of the 1970s, 'subculture' is above all a container that attempts to hold various groups of young people whose affect, clothing, music, and norms, deviate from a mythological centre. That these subcultures are often 'White' in their ethnic composition is regularly unmarked in academic discussions, despite its enormous import. I should add that my research focuses on the US, though people from many nations may recognize similar trends.

caught, caged, and placed in the subcultural zoo, on display for all to see. Torn from its societal jungle and safely taunted by viewers behind barcodes, punk, the last subculture, was dead.

The classical subculture 'died' when it became the object of social inspection and nostalgia, and when it became so amenable to commodification. Marketers long ago awakened to the fact that subcultures are expedient vehicles for selling music, cars, clothing, cosmetics, and everything else under the sun. But this truism is not lost on many subcultural youth themselves, and they will be the first to grumble that there is nothing new under the subcultural sun.

In this climate, constrained by the discourse of subculture, deviation from the norm ain't what it used to be. Deviation from the norm seems, well, normal. It is allegedly common for a young person to choose a prefab subculture off the rack, wear it for a few years, then rejoin with the 'mainstream'[3] culture that they never really left at all. Perhaps the result of our autopsy will show that subculture (of the young, dissident, costumed kind) has become a useful part of the status quo, and less useful for harbouring discontent. For these reasons we can melodramatically pronounce that subculture is dead.

Yet still they come: goths, neo-hippies, and '77-ish mohawked punk rockers. And still people find solidarity, revolt, and individuality by inhabiting a shared costume marking their membership in a subculture. And still parents get upset, people gawk, peers shudder, and selves are recreated. Perhaps it is cruel or inaccurate to call these classical motifs dead, because they can be so very alive and real to the people who occupy them. Like squatters in abandoned buildings, practising subcultists give life to what seem to be deceased structures.

Or is subculture dead? The death of subculture – that is, the death of subcultural autonomy and meaningful rebellion – did not escape the notice of many. For decades people have decried the commercialization of style, the paisley without the politics. But such laments have not failed to produce strategies. There is something else – another kind of subculture, gestating and growing far below the classical subcultural terrain. For two decades thousands kept a secret: *punk never died.* Instead, punk had, even in its earliest days, begun to articulate a social form that anticipates and outmanoeuvres the dominance of corporate-capitalism. And as the Cold War finally disappears from decades of habit, and as the political and cultural hegemony of corporate-capitalism seems unrivalled, it suddenly becomes clear that the anarchist frameworks of punk have spread into all sorts of social groupings. The social forms punks began to play with in the early 1970s have penetrated subcultures across the spectrum. After the death of the classical subculture we

3. 'Mainstream' is used to denote an imaginary hegemonic centre of corporatized culture. It is used here as it is used by many people in dissident subcultures: to denote hegemonic culture. It is, in this sense, an archetype, rather than something with a precise location and character. It serves to conveniently outline a dominant culture for purposes of cultural critique and identity formation.

witness the birth of new practices, ideologies, and ways of being – a vast litter of anarchism.

For tribes of contemporary people who might be called *punk* (and who often refuse to label themselves), their subculture is partly in revolt from the popular discourse of subculture, from what has become, in punk eyes, a commercialized form of safe, affected discontent – a series of consumed subjectivities, including pre-fabricated 'Alternative' looks. Punk is, ironically, a subculture operating within parts of that established discourse, and yet it is also subculture partly dedicated to opposing what the discourse of subculture has become. As the century rolls over, punk is the invention of not just new subjectivities but, perhaps, a new kind of cultural formation. The death of subculture has in some ways helped to produce one of the most formidable subcultures yet: the death of subculture is the (re)birth of punk.

Part I. Classical Punk: The Last Subculture

Consumer voyeurism is much more offensive to punk sensibilities than song themes about addiction or slaughtering dolls onstage. (Van Dorston 1990)

At the heart of early punk was calculated anger. It was anger at the establishment and anger at the allegedly soft rebellion of the hippie counterculture; anger, too, at the commodification of rock and roll (Cullen 1996: 249). Its politics were avowedly apolitical, yet it openly and explicitly confronted the traditions and norms of the powers that be. Describing the cultural milieu for young people in 1975, Greil Marcus notes the centrality of cultural production: 'For the young everything flowed from rock 'n' roll (fashion, slang, sexual styles, drug habits, poses), or was organized by it, or was validated by it' (Marcus 1989: 53). But by the early 1970s, with commodification in full swing, with some artists said to have compromised their integrity by becoming rich stars, and with 'rock' having been integrated into the mainstream, some people felt that youth subcultures were increasingly a part of the intensifying consumer society, rather than opponents of the mainstream. Punk promised to build a *scene* that could not be taken. Its anger, pleasures, and ugliness were to go beyond what capitalism and bourgeois society could swallow. It would be untouchable, undesirable, unmanageable.

Early punk was a proclamation and an embrace of discord. In England it was begun by working-class youths decrying a declining economy and rising unemployment, chiding the hypocrisy of the rich, and refuting the notion of reform. In America, early punk was a middle-class youth movement, a reaction against the boredom of mainstream culture (Henry 1989: 69). Early punk sought to tear apart consumer goods, royalty, and sociability; and it sought to destroy the idols of the bourgeoisie.

At first punk succeeded beyond its own lurid dreams. The Sex Pistols created a fresh moral panic fuelled by British tabloids, Members of Parliament, and plenty of everyday folk. Initially, at least, they threatened 'everything England stands for': patriotism, class hierarchy, 'common decency' and 'good taste.' When the Sex Pistols topped the charts in Britain, and climbed high in America, Canada, and elsewhere, punk savoured a moment in the sun: every public castigation only convinced more people that punk was *real.*

> Damning God and the state, work and leisure, home and family, sex and play, the audience and itself, the music briefly made it possible to experience all those things as if they were not natural facts but ideological constructs: things than had been made and therefore could be altered, or done away with altogether. It became possible to see these things as bad jokes, and for the music to come forth as a better joke. (Marcus 1989: 6)

Punk was to cross the rubicon of style from which there could be no retreat. Some punks went so far as to valorize anything mainstream society disliked, including rape and death camps; some punks slid into fascism. When the raw forces and ugliness of punk succumbed to corporate-capitalism within a few short years, the music/style nexus had lost its battle of Waterloo. Punk waged an all-out battle on this front, and it wielded new and shocking armaments, but in the end, even punk was proven profitable. Penny Rimbaud (1998: 74) traces its cooptation:

> within six months the movement had been bought out. The capitalist counter-revolution-aries had killed with cash. Punk degenerated from being a force for change, to becoming just another element in the grand media circus. Sold out, sanitised and strangled, punk had become just another social commodity, a burnt-out memory of how it might have been.[4]

Profits serve to bandage the wounds inflicted by subcultures, while time and nostalgia cover over the historical scars. Even punk, when reduced to a neat mohawk hairstyle and a studded leather jacket, could be made into a cleaned-up spokesman for potato chips. Suddenly, the language of punk was rendered mean-ingless. Or perhaps – perhaps – the meaningless language of punk was made meaningful. Greil Marcus (1989: 438) records the collapse of punk transgression: 'the times changed, the context in which all these things could communicate not pedantry but novelty vanished, and what once were metaphors became fugitive footnotes to a text no longer in print.'

---

4. Penny Rimbaud is one of the founding members of Crass, an English punk band that helped to revitalize, de-stylize, organize, and politicize punk in the 1980s. In some ways latter-day punk is a direct outcome of the movement led by Crass and other self-described 'anarcho-punks'.

Like their subcultural predecessors, early punks were too dependent on music and fashion as modes for expression; these proved to be easy targets for corporate cooptation. 'The English punk rock rhetoric of revolution, destruction, and anarchy was articulated by means of specific pleasures of consumption requiring the full industrial operations that were ostensibly were the objects of critique' (Shank 1994: 94). Tactically speaking, the decisive subcultural advantage in music and style – their innovation, rebellion, and capacity to alarm – was preempted by the new culture industry, which mass-produced and sterilized punk's verve. With the collapse of punk's stylistic ultimatum, what had been the foundations for twentieth-century subcultural dissent were diminished - not lost, but never to completely recover the power they once had in music and style.

Part II. The Triumph of the Culture Industry

Gil Scott Heron is famous for the line, 'The Revolution will not be televised'. But in a way the opposite has happened. Nothing's given the change to brew and develop anymore, before the media takes hold of it and grinds it to death. Also, there's an instant commodification of everything that might develop into something 'revolutionary'. (Dishwasher Pete, quoted in Vale 1997: 17)

Having ostensibly neutralized early punk, the culture industry proved itself capable of marketing any classical youth subculture. All styles, musics, and poses could be packaged: seemingly no subculture was immune to its gaze. So levelled, classical subcultures were deprived of some of their ability to generate meaning and voice critique.

'Subculture,' in the discourse handed down to the present, has come popularly to represent youths who adorn themselves in tribal makeup and listen to narrow genres of music. Subcultures are, in this hegemonic caricature, a temporary phase through which mostly juvenile, mostly 'White,' and mostly harmless people symbolically create identity and peer groups, only to later return, as adults, to their pre-ordained roles in mainstream society.

The aforementioned idea of subculture is not without merit: it is often a temporary vehicle through which teens and young adults select a somewhat prefabricated identification, make friends, separate from their parents, and individuate themselves. As a social form, this classical breed of subculture is important, widespread, and diversely expressed. In this form 'subculture' is partly a response to prevailing political economies and partly a cultural pattern that has been shaped and reworked by subcultures themselves and by the mass media. As such it is an inherited social form, and one which is heavily interactive with capitalist enterprise. Thus, subculture is both a discourse that continues to be a meaningful tool for countless people and, at the same time, something of a pawn of the culture industry.

With its capacity to designate all subcultures, all youth, under a smooth frosting of sameness, the culture industry was capable of violating the dignity of subcultists and softening their critique. Implied in the culture industry's appropriation of subcultural imagery was the accusation of sameness, of predictability, of a generic 'kids will be kids.' To paste on any group a label of synchronic oneness is, in some way, to echo colonial tactics. 'Youths' or 'kids,' when smothered with a pan-generational moment of discontent, are reduced to a mere footnote to the dominant narrative of corporate-capitalism. Trapped in nostalgia and commercial classific-ations, subcultures and youth are merged into the endless, amalgamated consumer culture.

No wonder, then, that subcultural styles no longer provoke panics, except in select small towns. Piercings and tattoos might cause their owner to be rejected from a job, but they generally fail to arouse astonishment or fear.[5] Writes Frederic Jameson (1983: 124): 'there is very little in either the form of the content of contemporary art that contemporary society finds intolerable and scandalous. The most offensive forms of this art–punk rock, say . . . are all taken in stride by society'. So too, ideas of self-gratification are no longer at odds with the status quo. In the 'Just Do It' culture of the late twentieth century, selfish hedonism dominates the airwaves. Says Simon Reynolds (1988: 254): '"Youth" has been co-opted, in a sanitized, censored version . . . Desire is no longer antagonistic to materialism, as it was circa the Stones' "Satisfaction".' Instead young people often relate to the alienation of The Smiths or REM, who seem to lament that 'everyone is having fun except me'; the sense of failure at not having the 'sex/fun/style' of the young people in the mass media. Indeed, long before 'satisfaction' became hegemonic, the commodity promised to satisfy. But because it cannot satisfy it leaves a melancholy that is satisfiable only in further consumption. So notes Stacy Corngold (1996: 33) who concludes that 'Gramsci's general point appears to have been confirmed: all complex industrial societies rule by non-coercive coercion, whereby political questions become disguised as cultural ones and as such become insol-uble.' Youth subcultures, after the triumph of the culture industry, may perpetually find themselves one commodity short of satisfaction, and trapped by words that were once liberatory.

Or, as Grant McCracken (1988: 133) argues, commodities cannot be completely effective as a mode of dissent because they are made legible in a language written by corporate-capitalism. As he writes:

5. Subcultures arouse no fear, that is, so long as their members are 'White'. 'Gangs', a term that often refers to any gathering of young brown-skinned people (especially boys and young men) can frighten, alarm, and threaten straight society. The danger sometimes associated with non-White youth is the last vestige of subcultural fear. And that is one reason why 'White' youths are increasingly following the subcultural lead of their 'Black' agemates, and consuming and affecting what they believe to be is 'Black' culture.

when "hippies," "punks", "gays", "feminists", "young republicans", and other radical groups use consumer goods to declare their difference, the code they use renders them comprehensible to the rest of society and assimilable within a larger set of cultural categories . . . The act of protest is finally an act of participation in a set of shared symbols and meanings.

Though McCracken underestimates the efficacy of stylized dissent, he is able to locate a defining weakness in the emphasis that subcultures have historically placed in style. My contention is that style was far more potent as a mode of rebellion in the past, and that not until the demise of punk was subcultural style dealt a mortal wound. After the demise of punk's über-style, after a kind of terminal point for outrageousness, there is a banality to subcultural style. And it is for this reason that Dick Hebdige's (1979: 102) 'communication of a significant *difference*' can no longer serve as a cornerstone in the masonry of subcultural identity.[6] Following this logic, George McKay (1998: 20) comments on the 'Ecstasy Industry' of mass culture, which has seized control of style. Thus

the Ecstasy Industry, for its part, is doing only too well under contemporary capitalism and could easily absorb the techniques of lifestyle anarchists to enhance a marketably naughty image. The counterculture that once shocked the bourgeoisie with its long hair, beards, dress, sexual freedom, and art has long since been upstaged by bourgeois entrepreneurs.

We can say, too, that the economy for subcultural codes suffers from hyper-inflation. In other words, the value of subcultural signs and meanings has been depleted: an unusual hairstyle just can't buy the outsider status it used to. Stylistic transgressions are sometimes piled on one another like so many pesos, but the value slips away almost instantly. Thus, by the 1990s, dissident youth subcultures were far less able to arouse moral panics (Boëthius 1995: 52) despite an accelerated pace of style innovation (Ferrell 1993: 194). In the 2000s, subcultural style is worth less because a succession of subcultures has been commodified in past decades. 'Subculture' has become a billion-dollar industry. Bare skin, odd piercings, and bluejeans are not a source of moral panics these days: they often help to create new market opportunities. Even irony, indifference, and apathy toward styles and subculture have been incorporated into Sprite and OK Cola commercials: every subjectivity, or so it may seem, has been swallowed up by the gluttons of Madison Avenue (Frank 1996, 1997a, 1997b).

6. At the time of the publication of Hebdige's important book, I am arguing, the publicly symbolic expression of difference was easier to achieve.

Part III. The Discourse of Subculture, Plain for All to See

> We burrow and borrow and barrow (or dump) our trash and treasures in an endless ballet
> of making and unmaking and remaking. The speed of this process is now such that a
> child can see it. (McLuhan and Nevitt 1972: 104–5)

The patterned quality of youth subculture (innovate style and music Þ obtain a
following → become commodified and typecast) forms a discourse of subculture,
one that is recognized by academics and youths alike. That such a discourse is
identifiable over several decades, however, does not mean that it goes unchanged
or unchallenged. As a social form it undergoes change in its own right, but also
because it has become the discursive object of the mass media. In particular,
'subculture' has been in many ways incorporated as a set trope of the culture
industries which retail entertainment, clothing, and other commodities. Many
observers – academics, journalists, and culture industrialists – fail to recognize that
hegemonic appropriation of the discourse of subculture has had impacts for the
people in subcultures.

Observers may fall into a classic pitfall, wherein they typecast subcultures. Any
number of scholars are guilty of detailing the patterned quality of the discourse of
subculture, trapping subcultures in a kind of synchronic Othering.[7] One example
should suffice:

> Nowhere is the rapidly cyclical nature of rock-and-roll history more evident than in the
> series of events surrounding punk rock. Punk broke all the rules and declared war on all
> previously existing musical trends and rules of social behaviour. Rebelling against
> established musical trends and social mores, punk quickly became a tradition in itself –
> a movement with highly predictable stylistic elements. By 1981, just six years after the
> formation of the Sex Pistols, a new generation of performers had already begun to assert
> an identity distinct from the established punk style . . . Here we come full circle in the
> evolution of rock-and-roll as seen through the lens of punk. Emerging as the antithesis
> of the conservative musical climate of the 1970s, punk was quickly absorbed and
> exploited by the very elements against which it rebelled. Undoubtedly a new generation
> of performers will soon find an aesthetic and philosophical means of rebelling against
> the now commercial state of rock, just as punks did in [the 1970s]. (Henry 1989: 115,
> 116)

Henry, like so many other commentators, repeats serious errors in subcultural
studies: (1) she conflates well-known musicians with the subcultures that listen to
them; (2) rather than engage punk on its own terms she reduces punk to a type of
youth subculture and little more; (3) she assumes that the 'cyclical nature of rock-
and-roll' will continue to cycle, without considering the cultural effects of its

---

7. See Fabian (1983).

repeated rotations. Many witnesses fail to see the *dialectical* motion of the discourse of subculture.

Indeed, commodification and trivialization of subcultural style is becoming ever more rapid and, at the turn of the millennium, subcultures are losing certain powers of speech. Part of what has become the hegemonic discourse of subculture is a misrepresentative depolitization of subcultures; the notion that subcultures were and are little more than hairstyles, quaint slang, and pop songs. In the prism of nostalgia, the politics and ideologies of subcultures are often stripped from them.

For today's subcultural practitioners what does it mean when subcultures of the previous decades are encapsulated in commercials and nostalgia? Punks, mods, hippies, break dancers, 1970s stoners: all seem relegated to cages in the zoo of history, viewed and laughed at from the smug security of a television monitor. (The sign says, 'Please do not taunt the historical subcultures', but who listens?) Today's subcultural denizens are forced to recognize that yesterday's subcultures can quite easily be repackaged, made spokeswomen for the new Volkswagen.

One danger industrial pop culture poses to subsequent generations of dissident youth subcultures is that these youths may mistake style as the totality of prior dissent. Commercial culture deprives subcultures of a voice when it succeeds in linking subcultural style to its own products, when it nostalgizes and trivializes historical subcultures, and when it reduces a subculture to just another consumer preference. People within subcultures, for their part, capitulate when they equate commodified style with cooptation, when they *believe* that grunge, or punk, or break-dancing, is just another way of choosing Pepsi over Coke, when they believe that the entirety of subculture is shallow or stolen.

Dissident youth subculture is normal and expected, even unwittingly hegemonic. Where long hair and denim once threatened the mainstream, it has become mainstream and so has the very idea of subculture. Not only are deviant styles normalized, but subcultural presence is now taken for granted: the fact of subcultures is accepted and anticipated. Subcultures may even serve a useful function for capitalism, by making stylistic innovations that can then become vehicles for new sales. Subcultures became, by the 1970s, if not earlier, a part of everyday life, another category of people in the goings-on of society – part of the landscape, part of daily life, part of hegemonic normality.

But this fact did not go unnoticed by many people in the subcultural world.

Part IV. Long Live Punk: New Ways of Being Subcultural

Looking back at the 1980s one has to ask whether punk really died at all. Perhaps the death of punk symbolically transpired with the elections of Margaret Thatcher in England (1979) and Ronald Reagan in America (1980). The Sex Pistols broke up (1978), Sid Vicious died (1979), and – most damningly – too many teeny-boppers were affecting a safe, suburban version of 'punk'. For many people, spiked hair and dog collars had become a joke, the domain of soda pop ads and television dramas. But did punk disappear with the utter sell-out of its foremost corporate spokesband, the Sex Pistols? Did punk vanish when pink mohawks could be found only on pubescent heads at the shopping mall? If the spectacular collapse of punk was also the collapse of spectacular subcultures, what remained after the inferno? What crawled from the wreckage? In what ways can young people express their unease with the modern structure of feeling? A new kind of punk has been answering these questions.

After shedding its dog collars and Union Jacks, punk came to be: (1) an anti-modern articulation, and (2) a way of being subcultural while addressing the discursive problems of subcultures. In fact, these two courses prove to be one path. That is, the problems of contemporary punk subcultures, after the 'death' of classical subcultures, prove to be intimate with the characteristics of recent modernity. Punk, then, is a position from which to articulate an ideological position without accruing the film of mainstream attention.

Contemporary punk subcultures, may therefore choose to avoid spectacle-based interaction with dominant culture. Gone too is the dream of toppling the status quo in subcultural revolution. The culture industry not only proved louder than any subcultural challenge, it was a skilled predator on the prowl for fresh young subcultures. The power to directly confront dominant society was lost also with the increasing *speed* with which the commodification of deviant styles is achieved. It may be only a matter of months between stylistic innovation and its autonomous language of outsiderness, and its re-presentation in commercials and shopping malls.

Even the un-style of 1990s grunge (an old pair of jeans and a flannel shirt) was converted to the religion of the consumer; baptized and born-again as celebrations of corporate-capitalism. With such history in mind, new social movements such as punk attempt to forego style, shared music, and even names for themselves, for fear of being coopted by the market democracy. Tom Frank, speaking at a convention of zinesters addressed precisely this aspect of the structure of feeling in the 1990s:

> The real thing to do is get some *content*. If you don't want to be coopted, if you don't want to be ripped off, there's only one thing that's ever going to prevent it and that's politics. National politics, politics of the workplace, but most importantly politics of *culture*. Which means getting a clue about what the Culture Trust does and why, and saying what needs to be said about it. As culture is becoming the central pillar of our national economy, the politics of culture are becoming ever more central to the way our lives are played out. Realize that what the Culture Trust is doing is the greatest obscenity,

the most arrogant reworking of people's lives to come down the pike in a hundred years. Be clear from the start: what we're doing isn't a subculture; it's an *adversarial* culture. (Frank 1996)

To a certain extent, punk means post-punk – a nameless, covert subculture re-formed after punk. To recap: early punk was, in part, simulated 'anarchy;' the performance of an unruly mob. So long as it could convince or alarm straight people, it achieved the enactment. For its play to work, punk needed a perplexed and frightened 'mainstream' off which to bounce. But when the mainstream proved that it needed punk, punk's equation was reversed: its negativity became positively commercial. As mainstream style diversified, and as deviant styles were normalized, punk had less to act against. Punk had gambled all its chips on public outcry, and when it could no longer captivate an audience, it was wiped clean. Post-punk, or contemporary punk, has foregone these performances of anarchy and is now almost synonymous with the practice of anarchism.

Long after the 'death' of classical punk, post-punk and/or punk subcultures coalesce around praxis. For contemporary punks subcultural membership, authenticity, and prestige are transacted through action internal to the subculture.

> Greil Marcus' idea of punk's greatness is that the Sex Pistols could tell Bill Grundy to 'fuck off' on television. The real greatness of punk is that it can develop an entire subculture that would tell Bill Grundy and safe, boring television culture as a whole to fuck off directly, establishing a parallel social reality to that of boring consumerism. (Van Dorston 1990)[8]

Stripped nude, ideologies developed in the early years of punk continue to provide frameworks for meaningful subculture. Against the threatening purview of mass media and its capacity to usurp and commodify style, punk subcultures steer away from symbolic encounters with the System and create a basis in experience.

Punks, in my work among the anarchist-punks of Seattle, don't call themselves punks. Instead they obliquely refer to the *scene* in which they 'hang out'. They deny that they have rules, and claim that they are socially and ideologically porous. After three decades, here is what has become of many of the CCCS' spectacular subcultures. And yet, in their stead, vibrant, living subcultures remain, with sets of regulations, norms, and their own ideological turfs. Seattle's anarchist-punks, for example, disavow an orthodox name, costume, or music; yet in many ways they continue to live, or perhaps squat, within the classical structure of subculture.

---

8. Van Dorston is responding to Marcus (1989). Penny Rimbaud (1998: 79) makes much the same point: 'The pundits who now claim that punk grew out of bands like the New York Dolls, and then found its true expression in the Sex Pistols, have totally missed the point . . . The bands were secondary to an attitude, an attitude born on the street rather than manufactured in Tin Pan Alley.'

Although today's punks refuse to pay the spectacular rent, they find that a new breed of subculture offers them ideological shelter and warmth.

From whence did these latter-day punks come? In contemporary America, the relentless commodification of subcultures has brought about a crisis in the act of subcultural signification. Punk is today, in part, a careful articulation in response to the hyper-inflationary market for subcultural codes and meanings, an evasion of subcultural commodification, and a protest against prefabricated culture; and punk is a subculture that resists the hegemonic discourse of subculture. The public cooptation of punk has led some punks to disclaim early punk, while preserving its more political features. Having been forced, as it were, out of a costume and music-based clique, punk is evolving into one of the most powerful political forces in North America and Europe, making its presence felt in the Battle of Seattle (1999), Quebec City (2001), EarthFirst!, Reclaim the Streets, and in variety of anti-corporate movements.

Like the spectacular subcultures so aptly described by the CCCS in the 1970s, current punks are partly in pursuit of an authentic existence. However, now that stylistic authenticity has been problematized by the 'conquest of cool' (Frank 1997a), punks have found that the ultimate authenticity lies in political action. Where subcultures were once a steady source of freshly marketable styles for corporations, they now present corporations with a formidable opponent. *Punk* marks a terrain in which people steadfastly challenge urban sprawl, war, vivisection, deforestation, racism, the exploitation of the Third World, and many other manifestations of corporate-capitalism. The threatening pose has been replaced with the actual threat.

Perhaps that is one of the great secrets of subcultural history: *punk faked its own death.* Gone was the hair, gone was the boutique clothing, gone was negative rebellion (whatever they do, we'll do the opposite). Gone was the name. Maybe it had to die, so as to collect its own life insurance. When punk was pronounced dead it bequeathed to its successors – to itself – a new subcultural discourse. The do-it-yourself culture had spawned independent record labels, speciality record stores, and music venues: in these places culture could be produced with less capitalism, more autonomy, and more anonymity. Punk faked its own death so well that everyone believed it. Many people who were still, in essence, punk did not know that they were inhabiting kinds of punk subjectivity. Even today, many people engaged in what might be called punk think of punk only in terms of its classical archetype. Punk can be hidden even to itself.

Punk had to die so that it could live. By slipping free of its orthodoxies – its costumes, musical regulations, behaviours, and thoughts – punk embodied the anarchism it aspired to. Decentralized, anti-hierarchical, mobile, and invisible, punk has become a loose assemblage of guerrilla militias. It cannot be owned; it cannot be sold. It upholds the principles of anarchism, yet is has no ideology. It is called punk, yet it has no name.

References

Boëthius, U. (1995), 'Youth, the Media and Moral Panics', in J. Fornäs and G. Bolin (eds), *Youth Culture in Late Modernity*, London: Sage.

Clark, D. (2000), *Dancing on the Ruins: Anarchy and Subculture*. unpublished doctoral dissertation in anthropology, University of Washington, Seattle.

Corngold, S. (1996), 'The Melancholy Object of Consumption', in R. Bogue and M. Cornis-Pope (eds), *Violence and Mediation in Contemporary Culture*, Albany NY: State of New York Press.

Cullen, J. (1996), *The Art of Democracy: A Concise History of Popular Culture in the United States*, New York: Monthly Review Press.

Fabian, J. (1983), *Time and the Other: How Anthropology Makes its Object*, New York: Columbia University Press.

Ferrell, J. (1993), *Crimes of Style: Urban Graffiti and the Politics of Criminality*, New York: Garland Publishing.

Frank, T. (1996), 'Zines and the Global Economy,' talk given and tape recorded at the Center of Contemporary Art, Seattle, WA, 13 January.

Frank, T. (1997a), *The Conquest of Cool: Business Culture, Counterculture, and the Rise of Hip Consumerism*, Chicago IL: University of Chicago Press.

Frank, T. (1997b), (Untitled). Talk and book reading for *The Conquest of Cool*, from personal tape recording, Left Bank Books, Seattle WA.

Hebdige, D. (1979), *Subculture: The Meaning of Style*, New York: Routledge.

Henry, T. (1989), *Break All Rules! Punk Rock and the Making of a Style*, Ann Arbor MI: UMI Research Press.

Jameson, F. (1983), 'Postmodernism and Consumer Society', in H. Foster (ed.), *The Anti-Aesthetic: Essays on Postmodern Culture*. Seattle WA: Bay Press.

Marcus, G. (1989), *Lipstick Traces: A Secret History of the Twentieth Century*, Cambridge MA: Harvard University Press.

McCracken, G. (1988), *Culture and Consumption: New Approaches to the Symbolic Character of Consumer Goods and Activities*, Bloomington and Indianapolis IN: Indiana University Press.

McKay, G. (1998), *DiY Culture: Party & Protest in Nineties Britain*, New York: Verso.

McLuhan, M, and Nevitt, B. (1972), *Take Today: The Executive as Dropout*, New York: Harcourt Brace Jovanovich.

O'Hara, C. (1999), *The Philosophy of Punk*. 2 edn, San Francisco CA: AK Press.

Reynolds, S. (1988), 'Against Health and Efficiency: Independent Music in the 1980s', in A. McRobbie (ed.), *Zoot Suits and Second-Hand Dresses: an Anthology of Fashion and Music*, Boston MA: Unwin Hyman.

Rimbaud, P. (1998), *Shibboleth – My Revolting Life*, San Francisco CA: AK Press.

Shank, B. (1994), *Dissonant Identities: The Rock'N'Roll Scene in Austin, Texas*, Hanover NH: Wesleyan University Press.

Vale, V. (ed.) (1997), *Zines! Vol II.* San Francisco CA: V/Search Publications.

Van Dorston, A. S. (1990/2001), 'A History of Punk', *Fast N' Bulbous Music Webzine,* http://www.fastnbulbous.com/punk.htm (accessed September 2002).

Part VI
Gender and Post-subcultural Production

–16–

'Lady' Punks in Bands: A Subculturette?
Helen Reddington

There is perhaps no better example of male hegemonic control over popular cultural history than the rewrite of punk to exclude the very large and productive presence of young women in the subculture from its very beginning. Whether this presence was due to the high profile of a woman, designer Vivienne Westwood, at the epicentre of British punk's inception (the King's Road in London's Chelsea); or the impact of the 1975 Equal Opportunities Act, the year before punk 'officially' began; or whether it was due to the equalizing effect of mass unemployment on young people in Britain in the mid-1970s,[1] the collective memory of punk recalls young men as spitting, spiky yobs with the occasional nod in the direction of political commitment (until the obligatory signing ceremony with the major label), and young women as fishnet-clad dominatrixes.

While occasionally this attitude has been breached – see, for example, Laing (1985) – subcultural theory otherwise virtually ignored the involvement of young women. Angela McRobbie was the first scholar to identify the hidden subjectivity of male academics and the effect this had on the theoretical analysis of post-war youth subcultures. She noted that: 'the style of a subculture is primarily that of its men' (2000: 34). Punk was an exception here, for its women were visible not only in their fetishized form, but also in the asexual or even cross-dressing styles adopted by many girls (Miles 1997). Yet, from the writings of academics to the reports of the tabloid press, there is a whole history missing from accounts of punk during this period in Britain. As late as 1980, Stanley Cohen bravely claimed that there was nothing new to add to the subcultural history of the twentieth century:

1. As Virginia Caputo has written:

The decline in the material power of young people has led to a decline in their importance as consumers. Since so few jobs are available, 'adult' comportment and 'respectable' appearance become increasingly irrelevant . . . Not only are people increasingly disassociated from the culture of employment and from financial resources of their own, they are confined to the local street and family culture of their schooldays. This process of infantilization which has occurred over recent years has increased the relative importance of the informal activities and relations of the street, of leisure, the youth club and the domestic sphere. (Caputo 1995: 29)

To re-examine the subject of post-war British youth subcultures is not quite the same as constructing, say, a revised historiography of World War II: there are no new archives to be opened, no secret documents to be discovered, no pacts of silence to be broken. There are just the same (rather poor) sources of information from the same (often inarticulate) informants. The question is what new sense can be made out of this same data. (Cohen 1980: ii)

My research therefore began when I became aware that a phenomenon I had been conscious of in my early twenties had not been seriously documented any-where, and when it had been – for instance, Frith and McRobbie (1990); Reynolds and Press (1995) – it had not been analysed in any depth; nor had the reasons for the return to the status quo in British rock music been investigated. Yet elements of female punk subculture have been explored in the US (Roman 1988, 1993; Leblanc 2001), and as Caroline Coon has remarked: 'It would be possible to write the whole history of punk music without mentioning any male bands at all – and I think a lot of them would find that very surprising.'[2] What follows, then, is an examination of the confluence of events that facilitated the flow of young women into the hitherto male-dominated area of rock bands, and an analysis of the dist-urbance they caused when they got there. It examines three features excluded from the conventional image of punk in subcultural typologies: (1) female instru-mentalists; (2) a subculture of production, not consumption; and (3) a series of distinct micro subcultures.

Female Instrumentalists

This chapter is written by the ex-bass player of Joby and the Hooligans, a punk band that formed in Brighton in 1977 and existed for just over a year. Like many other bands at the time, they made no records, and therein lies one of the reasons for the 'forgetting' of female instrumentalists in this period of rock history. Both David Sanjek (1997)[3] and Dick Bradley (1992) relate recorded product to rock myth-making; Bradley observes the issue in Britain:

2. Personal conversation, 'No Future? Punk 2001' Conference, University of Wolverhampton, and Lighthouse, England, 21-23 September 2001.
3. According to Sanjek:

The inaccessibility of recordings by many if not most of the female rockabilly singers constitutes an even more effective silencing than their (in most cases) truncated careers in the late 1950s and early 1960s . . . The disappearance of a vast number of recordings from public circulation reminds one there is an acoustic component to the 'tree falling in the woods' conundrum of Philosophy 101: if a recording is made, but no one can hear it, the performer effectively has been silenced. (Sanjek 1997: 141)

I would argue very strongly that the view which sees the period 1955–63 in Britain as a mere 'background', to later Beat and other later styles, is heavily distorted by an almost fetishistic attention to the charts (i.e. the successes of The Beatles, etc.) and that, sales of records notwithstanding, the development of a 'youth culture' in Britain, and of a music of that youth culture, can only be understood by reversing that process. In a very real sense, there is an element of myth in the way rock histories skip from one commercial peak to another, or from one 'great artist' to another, ignoring almost totally the social roots of both the music making and the listening, which ought to be among their objects of study. (Bradley 1992: 12)

It is all the easier, therefore, since most writers (both journalists and sociologists) who focus on rock music are men, to completely ignore the fact that there was a notably high presence of women in rock bands at this time. An overlapping and parallel musical change also took place: women instrumentalists formed women-only bands that played to women-only audiences, with a deliberate avoidance of male approval.[4]

Naturally, this particular phenomenon was not reported in the male-orientated music press, being mainly documented in magazines such as *Spare Rib* that were targeted at women. Bayton (1999) has spoken to many women who took part in exclusively female music-making from the 1980s to the late 1990s. Her research reveals not only the variety of 'formats' that bands with female personnel might have, but also the variety of reasons for which young women might want to pick up instruments and make music.

What is interesting about the punk moment, however, is that many of the women to whom I spoke seemed to have fallen into the music-making part of the punk subculture almost accidentally. The experience of Lucy O'Brien, of the band The Catholic Girls, was typical:

> The first gig was sort of by accident as often happens with punk things. We'd just about scraped together all the instruments between us. I think Judith had just bought her bass guitar from Woolworth's really cheap. There were some male friends of ours who had heard that there's this all-girl band, we'll get them to support us, 'cos they had a gig . . . So they just rang us and said 'We've got a gig for you', and we thought, 'Oh shit we'd better write some songs!' So we just got about three songs together in as many days and just got up on stage and it was the most frightening experience of my life – but I was hooked from then on. (Lucy O'Brien)[5]

Once 'hooked', getting gigs was easy, partly because of the novelty of girls-with-guitars, but also because of the particular ethic within punk, described here by (male) punk poet Attila the Stockbroker:

4. Perhaps in a stage performance parallel of Roman's (1988: 153) 'safe pockets'.
5. Author's interview with Lucy O'Brien, 6 December 2001.

The unwritten law of punk was that if there was a little bit of space and someone wanted to do something you would let them do it. The most fundamental thing was not the music or the politics, it was that simple fact that everybody felt that they could get up and do something, and not just that; if you were denied the opportunity, then the people who were organising the gig weren't true punks. (Attila the Stockbroker)[6]

This meant that there was an enabling attitude towards young women who wanted to play in bands; they could literally build a set week by week as they became more prolific. There were also many opportunities to perform, with a thriving live band scene and a large variety of venues, a legacy of the pub-rock scene in the early 1970s. Many of the venues could guarantee an audience for bands because, in the words of bass-player Gaye Advert, talking about the London club, The Roxy, 'You didn't just go when there was a band you wanted to see, you just went there' (cited in Stevenson and Stevenson 1999: 84). If a band had a bad gig, there would always be an opportunity to redeem themselves within a week or so.

The willingness of band members to share equipment was another factor that encouraged girls to play in bands: there was a sort of 'chain of enablement'. Whether male or female, lack of funds meant that equipment was often worn out or improvised, and it was perceived as churlish not to lend guitars, drums, amps and so on; the anti-guitar-solo feeling was unanimous, a 'preciousness' about equipment was ridiculed. Siouxsie and the Banshees were lent equipment by New York band Johnny Thunders and the Heartbreakers until they signed a record deal; this was a common phenomenon across the country, as Rachel, from The Dolly-mixture, told me: 'I borrowed it off somebody and it was a Woolworth's guitar. It had a great name . . . it was a Thunder something or other. Every rehearsal I had to solder it back together again. This little wire inside it was getting shorter and shorter. We learnt quite a lot as we went along.'[7]

Because of the sharing of equipment, band members could try out their new roles while saving for instruments of their own. They did not have to justify the expense of buying top-notch equipment by trying to become financially successful. They had not invested in a 'career' as a musician.[8] The option was open to them

---

6. Author's interview with Attila the Stockbroker, 15 January 2001.
7. Author's interview with Rachel Dollymixture, 26 January 2002.
8. Old equipment was a badge of street-credibility:

After six months we thought 'Let's get our own gear then'. I remember I went from this really crap guitar to a Les Paul. I was kind of embarrassed to have a Les Paul, and that was 'cos I had a job, I was teaching and I had the money to do it. I had the definite impression that a Les Paul just wasn't very punk. So I put elastoplast all over the Les Paul and sort of stuck stickers on it so it looked a bit nasty cos I thought it looked too posh. (Author's interview with Mavis Bayton, 14 July 2000)

to reject the long-term opportunities to become a performer, to use the stage for an alternative means of communicating through music, (as for instance the Slits, the Au Pairs and The Raincoats did), or to sign with a major label and enjoy all the trappings (in both senses of the word) that such a deal would bring (as Siouxsie and the Banshees, X Ray Spex and The Dollymixtures did). I found it particularly interesting to talk to women punk instrumentalists who had not been convent-ionally successful in music business terms, because it was here that I felt the heart of the subculture lay. When asked what the purpose of her performing was, one of them told me:

> I had a really strong sense of not being in the straight world. I was listening to some punk record the other day and I was thinking [that] I really identified [it] as 'us' in some way. When I was on my own in my bedroom, I knew what I was against: my cousins, and the girls at my school. I went to an all-girls school, and they were so square I just thought they were awful. I had this real sense of the other world. I thought there'd be some kind of revolution in some way. I wanted to destroy it, I really wanted to destroy it.[9]

As she went on to say: 'my mum would say things like "why don't you go to secretarial college, shorthand is always useful". And I thought "I want to be Janis Joplin I don't want to go to fucking secretarial college"' Another woman, Mavis Bayton, told me: 'they kept dragging us round factories saying "This is your future" and I was getting quite upset because I hadn't envisaged my future working in a factory. I didn't know what my future was, but it wasn't working in a factory.'

There was a frustration with the idea of growing up to be a 'lady' with all the implications associated with such a destiny. Sheila Rowbotham observed that her 'own sense of self as a person directly conflicted with the kind of girl who was sung about in pop songs' (Rowbotham 1981: 13). As one woman bass-player, Gina Birch, said to me:

> I'm not sure when or why it all went pear-shaped, my behaviour, but I felt suddenly restricted by home life and the lack of emotional expression, the lack of creative outlet . . . I was desperate for this kind of aliveness of things . . . I wanted to be whacked over the head by alive! . . . I think I despised anything that wasn't what I was doing, because what I was doing was a revolution. We were revolutionaries as far as I was concerned, and we were on a mission, and what was going on outside was really just irrelevant. (Gina Birch)[10]

By no means all of the women I spoke to felt like this: some were just following up the original impulsive leap on to the stage, and were more interested in the fun of performing than anything else.

9. Author's interview, date 7 September 2001 (interviewee's name withheld).
10. Author's interview with Gina Birch, 23 June 2000.

The authenticity endowed on punk musicians by the audience perception of them as 'just like me', 'learning on stage' (and, in some cases, 'refusal of expertise')[11] could help the female instrumentalists greatly – although this was often misinterpreted by rock journalists. During my research I found that both Tina Weymouth (from US band Talking Heads) and Gaye Advert (from UK band The Adverts) were alternately patronized and scolded for the simplicity of their playing by rock newspapers; gradually, over a series of gigs by each of the bands, journalists began to realize that not only were the simple bass lines intentional, but they were an integral part of the music that the band was playing, and that the reviewer was enjoying. It is also interesting to follow the reassessment of musical skills according to the gender of the reviewer, (although sometimes female reviewers were tougher than males). For instance, the patronizing male reviewer:

> Gaye Advert – a far more appealing punkette than any of the Slits – provides point of visual attention (A). Oh to be gazed upon by those sultry, tempting eyes which Gaye fixes on the audience at least two or three times during every number. No more than two or three times mind you, because Gaye likes to look at her bass very hard because she doesn't know how to play it very well yet, and so it helps if she watches where she puts her fingers. Her playing is just about okay. (Salewicz 1977: 44)

Contrast this with the more thoughtful female reviewer: 'which brings me to my biggest realization of the gig – that Gaye's bass playing is far from the hilarious joke one has been led to believe, since she's graduated from her initially fearful and delicate finger placement to an adequately ballsy attack' (Errigo 1977: 7).

In order to retaliate, the female reviewer has had to pull Gaye into the male arena. Rather than discuss Gaye's musicianship, describing instead her playing style as 'ballsy' and using the word 'attack' she is praising the fact that Gaye has transcended her gender to achieve, through aggression, the status of honorary man! Lucy Green (1997: 26) has noted the advantages that punks' 'disdain for musical technicalities' has had for female instrumentalists; however, Gaye Advert was expected by reviewers to be technically better at playing bass than a male player in the same context, since she had the audacity to appear on stage alongside male musicians, to whom punk rock 'belonged'. She is described as a 'punkette' by the male reviewer in order to reinforce the impression that she is trespassing on male territory. As Dale Spender (1990: 20) has remarked, 'masculinity is the unmarked form: the assumption is that the world is male unless proven otherwise . . . [a woman] must signify that the norm, the positive, does not apply and so she becomes a lady doctor, a female surgeon, a woman lawyer, or else, in less prestigious occupations, a waitress, a stewardess, a majorette.' This point is reiterated

---

11. Reynolds and Press (1995: 307) use this term to describe the ornery behaviour of all-female band The Slits, who defiantly refused to learn to play their instruments well.

by Zillah Ashworth, who still performs with punk band Rubella Ballet, when articulating her feelings about press stereotyping of male and female roles in the punk scene:

> They changed the word 'punk rocker' to 'punkette' for girls. None of us were 'punk-ettes'. They tried to devalue the whole thing by trying to split it into punk girl and punk men, whereas everybody was just in the same scene . . .when I was becoming a punk in 1975 [there was] a sort of universal mind. (Zillah Ashworth)[12]

Whatever was happening 'on the street', the bands came up against mostly male gatekeepers in the form of music press journalists (see Davies 2001), or sometimes even female gatekeepers who wrote in 'malespeak' to impress their colleagues.

There was a continuous debate in the music press during the early years of punk rock in Britain (roughly from 1976 to 1979), in which both male and female reviewers adopted challenging stances regarding the 'girls in bands' issue. For instance, Julie Burchill (NME) was against the idea of girls using instruments in bands at all (except for Chrissie Hynde); Vivien Goldman (Sounds) was for; Phil McNeill (NME) was for: Gary Bushell (Sounds) was against. After 1979 the whole scene fragmented into a 'second wave' of proto-skinhead punk (dubbed 'Oi' by its champion, Gary Bushell), art-punk bands such as The Raincoats, Gang of Four and Scritti Politti, feminist separatist bands such as Jam Today, and the more main-stream 'new wave' bands such as Elvis Costello and the Attractions, and Squeeze. This fragmentation of subcultures had happened before; but in the case of punk, the separation of the different elements allowed the 'rock' part to be reclaimed by adolescent males.

Production

The major feature that differentiates punk from other subcultures is the issue of cultural production, rather than consumption. Undoubtedly an element of the acknowledged 'DIY' factor in the punk subculture was a direct legacy of the hippies, much as punks claimed to despise them; but whereas gender boundaries in the hippie subculture were marked along active-male/passive-female lines, these boundaries were harder to establish by the late 1970s. Previous visible post-war subcultures had looked outside the UK for purchasable products at their inception. For the teds, mods and, to some extent, the hippies, the US provided the musical soundtracks for their activities; while, in the area of dress, Italian style was the major influence on mod clothing and Indian fabrics the mainstay of hippy garb. These were subcultures defined by their consumption patterns, very much echoing

12. Author's interview with Zillah Ashworth, 8 September 2000.

the dominant culture at the time. Although Malcolm McLaren would have it that punk music in Britain was influenced by The New York Dolls and The Stooges (Savage 1991), my research reveals a much wider pool of reference and, among the female members of rock bands, this very much reflects an instant response to live band performances by contemporaries rather than a response to recorded material.

Mark Abrams (1959) closely linked purchasing power to the development of a separate 'teen' identity, and it is tempting to apply this factor retrospectively to punk because subsequent subcultures, especially those connected to dance music, have also had a strong consumer element. However, the DIY element of punk was born of necessity as much as fashion; furthermore, many young people at the time were inadvertently involved in a type of political revolution simply because as unemployed youth they *could not* conform and therefore had to improvise a daily existence out of their unemployed status. A corner of capitalism had temporarily collapsed. In 1973 Rowbotham had claimed that, 'antagonism between men and women is . . . actually built into the separation of the point of production from the point of consumption, which was a product of capitalism's organization of work . . . Women were oppressed before capitalism. But capitalism has changed the nature of female oppression' (see Rowbotham 1981: 57). But for one generation, for a short space of time, the status quo was disrupted enough to allow young women into adolescent males' space. Suzi Quatro has been critical of the female punk bands' lack of musical skills,[13] but there is a strong entrepreneurial flair involved in setting up a band, writing songs, organizing gigs, publicity and so on, as John Savage (1991) has noted, which presaged (and perhaps informed?) the 1980s focus on small businesses initiatives as the way out of economic recession.

Micro-Subcultures

From the perspective of 'now', post-twentieth century subculture, it is interesting to telescope spatially backwards from today's globalism and (alleged) multi-culturalism to what I will call the 'micro-subcultures' of local scenes in order to observe the facilitation process that enabled young women to pick up rock instruments and *produce* music. Although British punk arguably started in the Kings Road, Chelsea, the blueprint was taken to other urban centres and customized by local young people to become something quite different; this according to the local demography and aspects such as whether there was an art college in the vicinity, a local rock scene already in existence, an already active local women's centre, and

13. Interviewed on 'You and Yours', BBC Radio 4, 19 July 2000.

so on. Often, young people in these localities were uninterested in what was happening in London: once they had the blueprint, they could carry on with the activity of creating music without further reference to the original catalyst.[14] As Liz Naylor remarked to me: 'I never saw the Sex Pistols, I had no interest in them; London, The Clash, didn't interest me at the time. I didn't own a copy of the Sex Pistols album.'[15] In Manchester, the scene centred around Virgin Records, again according to Liz Naylor, who played in short-lived band The Gay Animals, in 1977. She says:

> Manchester at that time was really small, it was a tiny musical community and if you say to people, of course I knew Joy Division, it's nothing – they were just blokes you sat with. So we supported The Fall on lots of dates, it didn't mean anything to us. In a way we took it seriously because we thought we were great – I mean we were appalling but we didn't think of it as a career, it was just an experience, and we were there. Me and Cath thought we were kind of somebody in this tiny Manchester scene and our band was just the thing we did. (Liz Naylor)

Musicians would move on from one band to the other; members of The Passage, another Manchester band, had played in Property Of, whose personnel overlapped The Gay Animals.

The punk scene in Leeds, meanwhile, was centred much more around an Art College ethos, spawning Delta 5, Gang of Four and Scritti Politti; while Angela McRobbie, in a fascinating introduction to her book *Feminism and Youth Culture* (2000: 1–11), describes the atmosphere in Birmingham as DIY consciousness raising fed into the band scene. Birmingham band The Au Pairs contained two female instrumentalists, and their songs dealt directly with sexual politics in a way that credited their audience with a sophistication and daily relevance rarely heard since. Oxford punk band The Mistakes developed around a group of women who attended the Oxford Women's Centre, and who met a demand for a women's band to play at their social functions, thus directly addressing the problem of misogynist rock lyrics that Rowbotham had identified. As Mavis Bayton recalls in her interview, 'since the early 1970s the women's liberation movement had had women-only socials. They played records initially. I remember there was one when we were all having a jolly dance to the Rolling Stones and I remember thinking, "hold on, look at that stupid girl dancing to 'Under my Thumb'" . . . The contradictions of dancing to those lyrics!'

14. See, for instance, Paul Cobley's (1999: 170-185) description of the Wigan punk scene in north-west England.

15. Author's interview with Liz Naylor, 7 September 2000

So punk rock gigs had a different flavour according to what was needed, or wanted, by the local audience.[16] There were even local differences between various parts of London (for instance, the east-end scene was much more affiliated to football hooligans and the skinhead subculture), and it was not until Zillah Ashworth travelled into central London that she realized how politicized parts of the punk scene were:

> I was seventeen by the time I started driving, and I was at the Bridge House (in Canning Town, east London) and some guy had a badge and I asked him what it meant and he said it means 'Crass', and we drove to Conway Hall to see Crass . . . they were very arty, very friendly. There was a lot of rich people involved in that scene, very rich and very intelligent and very interesting. (Zilla Ashworth)

Crass later encouraged Zillah and her partner to form the band Rubella Ballet, who are still musically active to this day. West London, home of Rough Trade records, spawned bands such as The Clash and female bands The Slits, and The Raincoats, who were all greatly influenced by Jamaican reggae music, reflecting the cultural mix of Notting Hill. Much punk music was devoid of influences from what is recognized as Black culture, but these bands displayed an affinity with their local demography. Gina Birch, bass player and guitarist with The Raincoats, cites the clarity of production on reggae records, in particular those of Toots and the Maytals, as an ideal learning aid for her bass-playing.[17]

Undoubtedly, the ability to be a 'big fish in a small pond', with a small and loyal audience of friends and fellow band members, made it easier for young women to participate in rock music. In Brighton, for instance, the scene supported Poison Girls, fronted by female guitarist Vi Subversa who was in her early forties at the time, as well as several women's bands, and bands with mixed personnel. Vi Subversa was active in facilitating band activity not only involving young women but also young men; she had been instrumental in acquiring the Vault[18] underneath the Brighton Resource Centre as a venue. The Vault had no promoter, no bar, no lavatories, and a minimal PA system. It provided rehearsal facilities for almost fifty bands, and in order to arrange a gig there, one had to book the PA, carry it downstairs, move equipment from the rehearsal space in another burial arch in the Vault, set up, and start.

---

16. And also their social requirements as individuals: see Cartledge (1999: 150) on 'microclimates'.

17. Lecture given by Gina Birch to music students at the University of Westminster, London.

18. There is a Web site dedicated to the history of the Vault – see *The Punk History of Brighton*, www.punkbrighton.co.uk (accessed October 2002).

The rigmarole of recording demos (expensive and daunting) and sending them to a promoter (who may or may not like the songs) was thus completely removed; add to this the willingness of Poison Girls to lend equipment (not only amplification equipment but also, more unusually, guitars and drums), and anyone with a degree of bravery and enterprise could get up on stage and play.[19]

The scene was as volatile as it was encouraging; my personal experience included death threats graffitied on a hoarding outside a squat where it was believed that I lived: as many bands disliked each other as helped each other. However, it was the quantity of productive activity and the breadth of its spread that made the environment so encouraging for female musicians. As in London, there was a constant speculative audience in Brighton, encouraged partly by the 'buzz' and partly by the minimal entrance charges. Later, organizations such as Rock Against Racism, and Rock Against Sexism, provided further platforms, encouragement and impetus for those who would not normally see themselves as rock musicians to perform. The broadening of punk from its original thrashing guitars-and-drums format meant that women who had passed piano exams at school could, if lent a keyboard or synthesizer, provide a relatively strong musical foundation for any band they played with.[20]

The fact that these instrumentalists could not be stereotyped led to their erasure from the punk discourse; history delights in stereotypes, particularly female ones. There was no image of a spiky-haired woman playing a guitar because the phenomenon was ideological, not fashion-led. The mockery by punk women of sexual fetishism was an irony that was (deliberately) misinterpreted by the British tabloid press to emasculate (sic) them. The media and simplistic historians equate young women with fashion, not ideas. As John Shepherd (1991: 156) observes: 'women in pop and rock are isolated and objectified, decontextualized from the social relations often believed to be the woman's forte. In order to be "successful" in a male-dominated society, they must package themselves (or be packaged, as in advertising images) as objects amenable to control by men'.

Dale Spender (1990) describes the way that Victorian lady novelists were belittled and eased out of their place in history by the male reviewers who acted as gatekeepers for the literature of the day; the process in which creative women are continually re-placed in a passive and decorative sphere is not new. It seems that in a contemporary parallel to the women Spender writes about, once the quota of

19. Yet when I approached the local studies library in Brighton to seek information for my research, I was directed to a member of staff 'who had been to loads of Brighton punk gigs at that time'. He assured me that 'There were no women in punk bands in Brighton – if there were I would have known about it, because I went to see bands all the time.'

20. Several of the women who replied to the questionnaires I sent out in relation to this research used their musical keyboard skills as an entree into later punk and new wave bands.

acceptable female participants was met, young women's roles in punk bands have been reduced to the status of sub-subculture - or indeed, subculturette.

References

Abrams, M. (1959), *The Teenage Consumer*, London: The London Press Exchange Ltd.

Bayton, M. (1999), *Frock Rock*, Oxford: Oxford University Press.

Bradley, D. (1992), *Understanding Rock 'n' roll: Popular Music in Britain 1955-1964*, Buckingham and Philadelphia PA: Open University Press.

Caputo, V. (1995), 'Anthropology's Silent "Others", a Consideration of some Conceptual and Methodological issues for the study of Youth and Children's Cultures', in V. Amit-Talai and H. Wulff (eds), *Youth Cultures: A Cross Cultural Perspective*, London and New York: Routledge

Cartledge, F. (1999), 'Distress to Impress: Local Punk Fashion and Commodity Exchange', in R. Sabin (ed.), *Punk Rock: So What? The Cultural Legacy of Punk*, London and New York: Routledge.

Cobley, P. (1999), 'Leave the Capitol', in R. Sabin (ed.), *Punk Rock: So What? The Cultural Legacy of Punk*, London and New York: Routledge.

Cohen, S. (1980), 'Introduction to the New Edition', *Folk Devils and Moral Panics: The Creation of the Mods and Rockers*, Oxford: Martin Robertson.

Davies, H. (2001), 'All Rock and Roll is Homosocial: the Representation of Women in the British Rock Music Press', *Popular Music*, 20 (3): 295–313.

Errigo, A. (1977), 'Review of The Adverts', *New Musical Express*, 24 September.

Green, L. (1997), *Music, Gender, Education*, Cambridge: Cambridge University Press.

Laing, D. (1985), *One Chord Wonders: Power and Meaning in Punk Rock*, Milton Keynes and Philadelphia PA: Open University Press

Leblanc, L, (2001), *Pretty in Punk: Girls' Gender Resistance in a Boys' Subculture*, New Brunswick NJ and London: Rutgers University Press.

Frith, S. and McRobbie, A. (1990), 'Rock and Sexuality' in S. Frith and A. Goodwin (eds), *On Record: Rock, Pop and the Written Word*, London: Routledge.

McRobbie, A. (ed.) (2000), *Feminism and Youth Culture*, 2 edn, Basingstoke and London: Macmillan.

Miles, C. (1997), 'Spatial Politics: a Gendered Sense of Place', in S. Redhead, D. Wynne and J. O'Connor (eds), *The Clubcultures Reader: Readings in Popular Cultural Studies*, Oxford: Blackwell.

Reynolds, S. and Press, J. (1995), *The Sex Revolts: Gender, Rebellion and Rock 'n' Roll*, London: Serpent's Tail.

Roman, L. G. (1988), 'Intimacy, Labor and Class: Ideologies of Feminine Sexuality in the Punk Slam Dance', in L. G. Roman and L. K. Christian-Smith (eds), *Becoming Feminine: The Politics of Popular Culture*, London: Falmer Press.

Roman, L. G. (1993), 'Double Exposure: the Politics of Feminist Materialist Ethnography', *Educational Theory*, 43 (3) (Summer): 279–308.

Rowbotham, S. (1973/1981), *Woman's Consciousness, Man's World*, Harmondsworth and New York: Penguin.

Salewicz, C. (1977), 'Review of The Adverts', *New Musical Express*, 11 June.

Sanjek, D. (1997), 'The Wild, Wild Women of Rockabilly', in S. Whiteley (ed.), *Sexing the Groove: Popular Music and Gender*, London: Routledge.

Savage, J. (1991), *England's Dreaming: Sex Pistols and Punk Rock*, London and Boston MA: Faber & Faber.

Shepherd, J. (1991), *Music as Social Text*, Cambridge: Polity.

Spender, D. (1990), *Man Made Language*, London: Pandora.

Stevenson, N. and Stevenson, R. (1999), *Vacant: a Diary of the Punk Years 1976–79*, London: Thames & Hudson.

17

Resisting Subjects: DIY Feminism and the Politics of Style in Subcultural Production
Doreen Piano

> The day I quit punk rock was the day I found out that while the boys love to talk about how they aren't sexist and how oh-so-fucking-PC they are, it never seems cool to be a girl in the scene.
>
> Sarah, *The Day I Quit Punk Rock* (one-off zine, n.d.).

The influence of feminism on youth cultures is most vividly represented by the late 1980s riot grrrl movement in North America.[1] Disillusioned, bitter, angry, frustrated and excluded, women in punk banded together to make their presence known as something more than eye candy. The intense and magnetic spread of punk grrrl bands like L7, Bikini Kill, and Bratmobile into local clubs across the US brought the predominantly White male punk rock scene to its knees by highlighting its gender exclusions, thus underscoring what Nguyen (2001: 179) calls 'the foundation myth of punk egalitarianism'. Although women had been part of punk from its inception, many of them attracted to it by its acceptance of non-traditional gender roles (O'Brien 1999), they were often denied key roles in the scene or were subjected to physical and verbal harassment when they did take centre stage. Still, the inroads made by these early feminist punks in creating alternative positions for women within subcultures, as noted by O'Brien (1999), paved the way for the development of sustained feminist subcultural activities which the riot grrrl movement consolidated, both through its own communication network and through media attention. The result was innumerable young women donning combat boots and hooded sweatshirts, playing in bands and/or producing zines.[2]

---

1. For a comprehensive history of Riot Grrrl, replete with video interviews, articles, and chronologies, see 'Riot Grrrl Retro Retrospective', *emplive.com*, http://www.emplive.com/explore/riot_grrrl/index.asp (accessed September 2002).

2. For articles on DIY feminism and subcultures, see Comstock (2001), Garrison (2000), Gottlieb and Wald (1994), Kearney (1998), Leonard (1998), Piano (2002), Smith (1997), Soccio (1999), Sutton (1999), Wakeford (1997). For a recent ethnographic study of North American women in punk cultures who do not identify as riot grrrls, see LeBlanc (1999).

As a politically invested movement, riot grrrl helped enact a broad-based shift of women's subordinate position within punk subcultures from consumer or observer to that of producer. While this shift opened up subcultural spaces to include a variety of performers who were not predominantly young White men, its main result has been the creation of gendered subcultural spheres that contribute to, what Garrison (2000: 151) calls, 'oppositional technologics' – 'the political praxis of resistance being woven into low-tech, amateur, hybrid, alternative subcultural feminist networks that register below the mainstream'. More than ten years later, the effects of riot grrrl, particularly its use of DIY (do-it-yourself) as a feminist tool of communication and expression, can be seen in the emergence of a polymorphous infrastructure of grrrl-related cottage industries that include the production of not just music, but zines, stickers, crafts such as candle- and soap-making, mixed tapes, and alternative menstrual products. Distribution of these products through mail order or the Internet at women-run 'distros' such as Pander Distro, Grrrlstyle, and Pisces Catalog has resulted in a high-tech DIY scene where easier access to computers and Web software provides many women with opportunities to create sites online.[3] In addition, this 'subcultural infrastructure' has engendered activist groups as well as festivals and conventions such as the annual Southern Grrrls Convention, Mujerfest, and the various Ladyfests that take place all over Canada and the US.

These various and overlapping post-riot grrrl offshoots create informal networks that interface within a variety of subcultural environments that are geographically diverse and often virtual.[4] As Smith (1997: 238), an artist and activist in Olympia, Washington, observes, 'By connecting with one another in these different spaces, we both create and participate in the making of our identities and our communities.' Thus, it is in 'doing' (making zines, playing in bands, reading zines, organizing conferences) rather than in 'being' (viewed as a spectacle) that participants become group members, and consequently, where the potential for political intervention and group affiliation can take place. These spaces of cultural production 'far from being merely the commercial, low ebb of the subculture, as far removed from resistance as it is possible to imagine . . . can be seen as central to it' (McRobbie 1994: 161).

3. See Piano (2002) for a discussion of how electronic technologies have facilitated the growth of an informal feminist subcultural economy.

4. See Garrison (2000) for a theoretical discussion of the sophisticated feminist networking that youth subcultures engage in. Although network and networking are preferred terms for discussing feminist subcultures, I use the term 'subculture' in this paper as a way of engaging with earlier British 1970s work in subcultural studies, but with the understanding that, as Muggleton claims, 'the notion of a collective concept that "acts" is . . . a sociological fiction; only individuals have this ability' (Garrison 2000: 23).

In particular, the DIY production and distribution of zines has proved to be an enduring aspect of feminist subcultural production.[5] Ostensibly this may be because the technologies that go into making zines at its most basic – a glue stick, pen and paper, stapler, and a copy machine – are easy to come by. However, part of its attraction may be that riot grrrls' adaptation of the punk fanzine serves as both an individual space for identity construction and simultaneously as a 'safe space' for women to conscious-raise about their experiences. In other words, while zines have always played a role in disseminating information within punk subcultures, within the riot grrrl movement they became central to 'spreading the DIY feminist revolution' to young women in the US, Canada, and abroad.[6] As Leonard (1998: 107) explained it, 'By writing themselves into the text, through relating personal experiences and concerns, riot grrrls have expanded the discursive parameters of the fanzine.' Writing zines that focused on women's issues such as sexual assault, eating disorders, and sexism among punks was part of an intervention into male-dominated subcultural spaces where, as Leonard (1998: 107) claims, these issues were not necessarily prohibited, but 'there existed no rhetorical space for its articulation' (1998: 107). Similarly, Mimi Nguyen (2001) discusses the biting commentary she received from punk fanzine readers of *Maximumrocknroll* after criticizing a masturbatory fantasy about Asian women written by one of the zine's columnists. It was these kinds of exclusions and oversights that contributed to the growth of women-only subcultural spaces and activities where young women freed from male-dominant spaces can foreground their own issues.

Yet paradoxically these same safe spaces are vulnerable to class and race exclusions as the predominance of riot grrrl members who were middle class and White reproduced many of the same exclusions as their White, middle-class feminist elders. Thus, a more recent development in gender-specific subcultural spaces, and one that this chapter intends to analyse for its spectacular use of style, has been interventions by zine editors who fall outside of the White, middle-class paradigm that riot grrrl has come to represent. As Nguyen observes in her intro-duction to the compilation zine *Evolution of a Race Riot*,

5. The specific genre of zines that I focus on in this study are perzines. As opposed to fanzines, music zines, and political zines, perzines express the thoughts and experience of individuals (Duncombe 1997: 24). For specific articles on young women and zines, see Comstock (2000), Kearney (1998), Leonard (1998), Nguyen (2001), Sutton (1999). For a comprehensive analysis of zines and zine culture in the United States, see Duncombe (1997).

6. Although this chapter focuses predominantly on Third Wave feminist cultural production within current zine and punk subcultures, the type of zines discussed in this chapter can also be seen as linked to Second Wave feminism's creative and political uses of alternative media, such as pamphlets, newsletters and manifestos, to disseminate feminist theories and ideas. See Martha Leslie Allen's comprehensive 1988 study of Second Wave women's periodicals, 'The Development of Communication Networks Among Women, 1963-1983: A History of Women's Media', *The Women's Institute for Freedom of the Press*, http://www.wifp.org (accessed September 2002).

> The race riot has lagged years behind the grrrl one for reasons that should be obvious by
> now: whiteboy mentality became a legitimate target but whitegirls' racial privilege and
> discourse went unmarked . . . except among those of us who were never white. Like me
> . . . Zines are full of empty liberal platitudes like 'racism is a lack of love,' 'we're one
> race – the human race,' . . . and we are supposed to be satisfied with these . . . Whoop-
> de-doo: this does shit for me, how about you? (Nguyen, n.d.: 4)

The direct hit that Nguyen's comments create among zine editors parallels the
same debates over privilege and exclusion that currently rock North American
women's studies programmes across the US and Canada, at conferences, among
activist and politically progressive parties. In fact, the internal critique in which
Nguyen engages is an integral aspect of what is known as Third Wave feminism
whose most salient characteristic is its debates over differences among women.[7]
Thus, for many subculturalists who identify as feminists or have been exposed
to feminist theory, zines have become a medium for enacting what Thomas
McLaughlin (1996: 53) calls 'vernacular cultural criticism', their production
creating 'a space in which fundamental theoretical questioning of cultural systems
manages . . . to occur'. Viewed in this way, subcultures themselves are fraught with
conflicts over issues of representation and power, reflecting and reproducing
uneven power dynamics in mainstream dominant culture.

Nowhere are these tensions more obvious than in women-oriented zines where
the use of visual and verbal strategies reveal a dynamic and constantly evolving
subculture where style acts to form a collective identity at the same time that it
debates what the contours and shape of the community will be.[8] Therefore, the
study of their textual strategies can expand our understanding of how subcultural
production can engender possibilities for symbolic resistance as well as creative
and political expression. It can also illustrate how feminist thought and practice is
appropriated for very specific purposes outside academic and mainstream venues.

7. I use the term 'Third Wave' as a historical and social marker that frames key cultural and
theoretical influences on feminist subcultural production. These influences include the following:
debates among feminists about difference enacted by feminists of colour, such as Chela Sandoval,
Patricia Hill Collins, Gloria Anzaldua and Chandra Mohanty, and Anglo feminists such as Donna
Haraway, Teresa deLauretis and Adrienne Rich; the influence of anti-foundationalist and post-colonial
theories on women's studies; the feminist backlash of the 1980s; the cultural and economic consequences of global capitalism; and lastly, the emergence of new technologies. See Brooks (1997),
Garrison (2000), Heywood and Drake (1997) and Siegel (1997) for a good introduction to the various
definitions and positions that are implied in this term.

8. Although the perzines that I study are concerned with identity politics, many perzines are not.
Thus, as a group, the zines that I study were chosen for their particular emphasis on aspects of identity
politics that include gender, race, sexual orientation, class, disability, and nationality. Most, if not all,
of the zine editors that I interviewed have some exposure to feminist ideas, but may choose not to
identify as feminist.

I will do this first by examining how the feminist concept of embodiment alters the meaning of spectacular style, and secondly by illustrating several ways in which zine editors use style to engage in feminist critique about difference. Lastly, I want to consider what the implications of this study are in light of a post-subculturalist approach to analysing feminist subcultural production.

It's a Man's Man's Man's World – Embodying Subcultural Style

> Le style est l'homme même.
>
> Georges-Louis de Buffon

Since McRobbie's (1980) feminist critique of subcultural studies that pointedly criticized the absence of attention given to gender issues by leading male theorists, a growing body of scholarship in women's and subcultural studies has focused on analysing gender and sexuality issues found in subcultural sites and cultural production.[9] Despite, or because of, its seemingly male connotations, style has for many women zine editors become a site in which to contest dominant represent- ations of women, or what Jane Ussher (1997: 10) calls 'scripts of femininity' 'by telling their own stories of female adolescence' (Kearney 1998: 298). This chapter builds on this scholarship by mapping out the possibilities for reading an embodied subcultural style that is enacted at the level of textual production. As a term, embodiment has been used to convey the representational baggage, (much of it engendered by nineteenth-century racist and sexist scientific, colonial, and medical discourses) that positions as subordinate in Western culture those social groups who fall outside the White bourgeois male subject. A process achieved by defining them 'as different, as the Other . . . imprisoned in their bodies' (Young 1990: 123). However, despite essentialist discourses that attempt to situate bodies as Other to the White Western male subject, possibilities for resistance and agency exist. As Janet Wolff (1990: 122) observes, 'the body has been systematically repressed and marginalized in Western culture, with specific practices, ideologies, and discourse controlling and defining the female body. What is repressed, though, may threaten to erupt and challenge the established order.' Within feminist and social theories, embodiment takes on new meanings as it counteracts the effects of these master narratives by reading the body not 'as a fixed entity but . . . as having a plasticity or malleability [which] means that it can take different forms and shapes at different times' (McDowell 1999: 39). In this way, embodiment becomes perform- ative, its borders more fluid, and possibilities for reading the female body as transgressive multiply.

9. See Comstock (2001), Gottlieb and Wald (1994), Leonard (1998), McRobbie (1991), Miles (1997), Nguyen (2001), Roman (1988), Wakeford (1997).

In subcultural spaces the feminine body becomes a site of contestation over meaning as both its presence on stage or in the mosh pit, as well as its absence as in electronic and textual spaces, become sites of surveillance, violence, and voyeurism.[10] Paradoxically, however, these gendered spaces also create opportunities to explore and negotiate identities. As Miles (1997: 71) observes, 'for some women in punk there was a place to be angry and to celebrate the illicit and clandestine – for some a means of seeing critically into the mirror and of challenging the reflection.' By participating in subcultural practices such as slam-dancing, playing in bands, creating Web sites or journals and producing zines, women in punk subcultures actively resisted authorial and subcultural claims that positioned women as silent bystanders. This resistance was enacted not only by appropriating traditionally male roles, but also by foregrounding issues of gender and sexuality through the disruptive positioning of their bodies.

Examples of this are seen in the riot grrrl movement where performing punk as a woman was a direct intervention into oppressive patriarchal structures both within mainstream and subcultural spheres. However, as Gottlieb and Wald (1994: 26) note, this intervention in terms of musical production was not unproblematic, since women assuming such public roles as performers are often situated in two equally restrictive positions: 'the to-be-looked-at sex object, or the woman with balls'. Moving beyond these static representations entails using tactics that foreground sexuality in ways that dismantle these representations and open up alternatives. Hence, for example, the primal use of the scream – which is typically associated with women as 'a wordless protest against the overdetermined femininity that these performers . . . must occupy' (Gottlieb and Wald 1994: 262). This conveys bodily eruptions within subcultural spaces 'that voice not only rage, but rage as pleasure, the scream as orgasm . . . the scream replaces the pleasant, melodious and ultimately tame emotionalism traditionally associated with the female vocalist' (Gottlieb and Wald 1994: 262). In responding to already given representations of women's sexuality, behaviour, and representations within the space of a punk club, the scream challenges what a woman, a feminist, and a punk should be.

In the case of textual production, strategies of style that zine editors employ often locate the self as a starting point to explore issues of sexuality, gender identity, race, sexual orientation, and class. The performance of identity becomes addressed at the level of style where autobiographical testimonies, manifestos, visual representations that include self-portraits, city maps, pictures of role models, drawings and photographs as well as quotes from admired thinkers and intellectuals are patched together to form strategies of resistance, a method of what bell hooks describes as 'talking back'. As she explains it, 'in the world of the southern

---

10. See Nguyen (2001) for an exploration of the downside of cyberspace for online journals.

black community I grew up in, "back talk" and "talking back" meant speaking as an equal to an authority figure. It meant daring to disagree and sometimes it just meant having an opinion' (hooks 1989: 5). Thus, within feminist zine subcultures, 'talking back' becomes a method of theorizing the self and its relation to dominant and subcultural discourses. Hence, the body, particularly the female body, which normally is associated with materiality, emotion, irrationality, sexuality, becomes a site where questioning can take place, where identity, community, and dominant discourses can be negotiated and where possibilities for resistance occur.[11]

This form of producing knowledge is one that uses a 'politics of location'[12] to position itself as speaking from a very specific and partial point of view. As Celia Perez, a self-described twenty-nine-year-old Latina of Cuban and Mexican parentages, told me in explaining why she thought her zines were political: 'I deal with issues that are of a political/social nature the way I see them, the way they affect ME . . . the fact I am a Latina writing in a community(ies) that is over-whelmingly white influences what I write about . . . and brings to light a voice that may not otherwise be present'.[13] Because zines, or perzines as they are called among zine editors, are often subjective accounts of their producers' lives, they have the potential to re-envision the concept of style by addressing issues in which their identities are politically invested and have experience. Thus, many zine editors utilize experiences of racism, sexism, homophobia, and classism as a main part of their zine's content while simultaneously addressing these issues through a politics of style. Hence, the politicized nature of this subcultural production signals what McRobbie (1991) anticipated: that the influence of feminism and other social movements within subcultures would reconcile what Hebdige's (1979) account of style theorized as irreconcilable: politics and style.

The shift from reading style as a marker on the body to reading style as embodied in cultural production provides a new method of reading intentionality into sub-cultural presentation by acknowledging participants' subjectivities performed at the level of style. In other words, as LeBlanc (1999: 18) clearly states it, 'the person engaging in resistant acts must do so consciously and be able to relate that consciousness and intent'.[14] Thus, whereas Hebdige's (1979: 18) claim that 'Style is pregnant with significance' is meant to impute a subcultural resistance that is

11. For a discussion of the advantages and disadvantages of corporeality as a feminist strategy, see Wolff (1990), Chapter 8, 'Reinstating Corporeality: Feminism and Body Politics'. For a discussion of how corporeality functions in women's autobiographical writing, see Smith (1993).

12. For a more in-depth understanding of this term, see Rich (1986), Haraway (1991), Mohanty (1992).

13. Author's email interview with Celia Perez, 21 January 2002

14. In addition, levels of resistance vary from participant to participant and what and whom they are resisting may be as simple as parental authority, or as complex as multiple axes of oppression found in both subcultural and mainstream spheres.

read by 'us' (academics, outsiders) as an expression of 'a fundamental tension between those in power and those condemned to subordinate positions and second-class lives' (Hebdige 1979: 132), this re-gendered concept of style grants specificity of intent to subcultural participants by locating their textual performances in zines as direct challenges to specific forms of oppression. Hence, many women zine editors use style in various ways to address how both subculture and dominant culture excludes and overlooks specific kinds of bodies. It is to these strategies that I now turn to in illustrating, firstly, how an embodied subcultural style opens up space for the construction of alternative identities within mainstream and punk spheres and, secondly, how style also works as a marker of difference within a fractious and conflicted subcultural sphere.

Grrrls Like Us? The Embodied and Embattled Politics of Spectacular Style

> To make the liberated voice, one must confront the issue of audience – we must know to whom we speak. (hooks: 1989: 15)

Because of their ability to be used as tools of intervention, zines testify to the powerful influence of feminist thought in subcultural spaces, particularly in the contested site of representations where many feminist battles have been and continue to be fought. In riot grrrl zines, relationships among subculturalists were politicized through a variety of stylistic strategies, particularly the use of confession, manifestos, and testimonies that focused on 'their experiences of coming out as lesbian . . .; the disclosure of their traumas as rape or incest survivors, or as women struggling with eating disorders; and their gushy affirmations of girl-love and devotion to punk music' (Gottlieb and Wald 1994: 264).

Writing and exchanging life experiences, riot grrrls used the female body as a site for common experiences that engendered a style of representing grrrl. This became a central identifier within, and later outside of, punk subcultures as riot grrrl surfaced in the mainstream. Hence, covers of defiant, angry (usually White) punk girls, women power symbols, and manifestos that denounced sexism and promoted grrrl solidarity, signified both individual and collective discontent with the status of women in and outside of the punk club. Rectifying their status meant constructing alternative identities.

As both Kearney (1998) and Sutton (1999) point out, the importance of zines for young women lies in their possibilities for constructing alternative 'scripts of femininity' (Ussher 1997). Although the impact of these alternative identities may be limited in terms of enacting social change, constructing these narratives within subcultural spaces can be not only individually empowering for participants in terms of providing a means of self-representation, but more importantly they can work pedagogically in their ability to teach and to learn about difference. Currently, feminist zine production is undergoing another shift in style as the movement from single issue to multi-issue identity politics – a defining aspect of Third Wave feminism – is reflected in the commitment by many zine editors to construct more complex identities than those based on gender. The use of visible identity markers of race, disability, sexuality, body size, and transgender appear in titles such as *Bamboo Girl, Nappy Bush, Pussboy, The Making of a Femme Queen, Mala,* and *Hermana, Resist,* counteracting the universal White, middle-class subject of femininity that the riot grrrl movement came to represent. In addition, compilation zines such as Helen Luu's *Paint Me a Revolution* and *How to Stage a Coup,* as well as Mimi Nguyen's *Evolution of a Race Riot,* reveal collective critiques by persons of colour into the unrecognized race privilege that Anglo men and women in punk subcultures share.

Thus, style in zines is used to make visible the invisible. It works within feminist zine subcultures to highlight difference as a means of revealing exclusion. For Noemi Martinez, editor of *Hermana, Resist,* producing a zine was inspired by 'reading other zines that did not entirely identity with my experience; didn't express the feelings of a Chicana.'[15] For Martinez, membership in zine subculture is based more on making difference visible rather than attempting to join the crowd. Her experience of not seeing Chicana experiences reflected in the sub-cultural demographics of the zine world motivates her to produce her zine in order to find 'other Chicanas and mujeres to empathize with my sentiments . . . who share a common interest with me.' Martinez embodies her zine with images and words that designate her as a Latina, such as pictures of Frida Kahlo, cut-outs from the popular Mexican card game, Loteria, and definitions of Spanglish terms that only someone knowledgeable of the US/Mexico 'borderlands' would know.

Conversely, while Noemi Martinez marks her identity very clearly through choosing specific images and texts that perform a Latina identity, other zine editors such as Lauren Martin construct complex identities that refuse to be pigeonholed and thus easily consumed. In attempting to convey the complexity of her identity, Martin uses a variety of writing styles that are personal and expository, handwritten and typed, as well as picture essays, questionnaires, and quotes from activists and theorists. One page in her zine displays four photo booth self-portraits; each one labelled differently with the words: chink, kike, dyke, bitch. These racist, sexist, and homophobic epithets reveal the multiple oppressions that she experiences, yet at the same time combined with the pictures, they illustrate the inability of lang-uage to express and define who she really is.

15. Author's email interview with Noemi Martinez, 28 January 2002.

Using such an array of visual and verbal styles underscores Martin's commitment to multi-issue politics; in fact, an article in which she specifically critiques single-issue politics is aimed at those social movement groups that she has previously belonged to. Thus, it is not just the dominant culture but progressive cultures also that have not been able to acknowledge her complex identity. Thus, she writes

> It is impossible for me to be 'enough' of any one thing: can never be woman enough, dyke enough, colored enough, whatever, because I am not wholly any of those things. I am left open to attack by people within my own 'communities' because I cannot commit 100% of my energies to one single cause. Trying to do so only results in fragmentation. (Martin 2000: 33)

By having her identity reduced to one essential element, whether it is race, sexuality or gender, Martin is condemned to finding pieces of herself missing. Thus, it is the essentializing of her identity and not her occupancy of numerous subject positions that results in the possibility of fragmentation.

However, through constructing her zine, Martin defies both dominant and progressive cultures by arranging the various aspects of her identity in the way she chooses to be represented. She does this through layout, design, images, and content; in other words, her use of style. As Hetherington (1998: 138) suggests, 'identities . . . are forms of ordering. These orderings may not be stable or fixed but they are still ways of making sense of who one sees oneself to be and how one relates to others, both within a shared identification and with those outside'. The forms that identities take in zines can be marked by gender, race, class, nationality, and disability but they are also based on lifestyle politics in which choosing a position of marginality can be a marker of one's identity. As Hetherington (1998: 27) notes, 'Acts of resistance are choices, whether they be choices about fighting racist violence born out of one's own experiences or about trying to live a life in which one is responsible towards the environment . . .' Thus, similar to punks' use of *bricolage,* which reinvested already-made objects with new meanings, thereby subverting the objects' original meanings, women zine editors use stylistic guerrilla tactics that can be used individually and collectively to express difference, resistance, and solidarity.

What emerges from the shift from analysing subcultural appearance to analysing subcultural production is a new way of reading spectacular style as an embodied textual performance. In other words, the concept of a spectacular style in which subcultural participants enact resistance at the site of the body becomes less relevant when it is often the subcultural spaces themselves that serve as both sites of resistance and solidarity. Unlike earlier subcultural studies paradigms, what Muggleton (2000) calls 'the CCCS approach', in which theorists classified participants around specific factors, most notably race and class, within this broader subcultural movement, shared social affiliations such as age, class, sexual orientation, race, and even gender cannot be determining factors in defining a subculture.[16] Instead, what defines a subcultural identity within this particular formation is not similarity, but difference – where members may come from different backgrounds but may 'hold similar values that find their expression in shared membership of a particular subculture' (Muggleton 2000: 31).

An embodied politics of style assumes a conflicted and continually changing conception of subcultural participation in which differing attitudes overlap, converge, and conflict with one another. Yet it is the commitment to a politics of acknowledging difference that in a sense coheres the subculture's own identity, or in Maria Lugones' (1995: 142) words, 'If reality is complex, plural, then our bonding must honor this plurality. If our bonding misses the complexity of reality, then it will necessarily erase some of us.' Within feminist zine subcultures, debates about difference and exclusion are a central feature of the dynamic development of a spectacular style, one that is constantly adapting and evolving and that is influenced by those who come to zine production because their narratives are silenced, their bodies invisible.

Acknowledgments

I am indebted to Hosam Aboul-Ela, Dina Al-Sowayel, Ellen Berry, and Julia Good for helpful comments and feedback during the process of writing this chapter.

References

Brooks, A. (1997), *Postfeminisms: Feminism, Cultural Theory, and Cultural Forms*, New York: Routledge.

Comstock, M. (2001), 'Grrrl Zine Networks: Re-Composing Spaces of Authority, Gender, and Culture', *Journal of Advanced Composition*, 21 (2): 383–409.

Duncombe, S. (1997), *Notes from Underground: Zines and the Politics of Alternative Culture*, New York: Verso.

Garrison, E. K. (2000), 'U.S. Feminism—Grrrl Style! Youth (Sub)Cultures and the Technologies of the Third Wave', *Feminist Studies*, 1 (Spring): 141–70.

Gottlieb, J. and Wald, G. (1994), 'Smells like Teen Spirit: Riot Grrrls, Revolution and Women in Independent Rock', in A. Ross and T. Rose (eds), *Microfiends: Youth Music & Youth Culture*, New York: Routledge.

16. Within this subculture, gender is problematized through the recent emergence of gender ambiguous, transgender, transsexual, and intersex zines.

Haraway, D. (1991), 'Situated Knowledges: The Science Question in Feminism and the Privilege of Partial Perspective' in *Simians, Cyborgs, and Women: The Reinvention of Nature*, New York: Routledge.

Hebdige, D. (1979), *Subculture: The Meaning of Style*, New York: Routledge.

Hetherington, K. (1998), *Expressions of Identity: Space, Performance, Politics*, London: Sage.

Heywood, L. and Drake, J. (eds) (1997), *Third Wave Agenda: Being Feminist, Doing Feminism*, Minneapolis MN: University of Minnesota Press.

hooks, b. (1989), 'when i was a young soldier for the revolution: coming to voice', in *Talking Back: Thinking Feminist, Thinking Black*, Boston MA: South End Press.

Kearney, M. C. (1998), 'Producing Girls: Rethinking the Study of Female Youth Culture', in S. Inness (ed.), *Delinquents and Debutantes: Twentieth Century Girls' Cultures*, New York: New York University Press.

LeBlanc, L. (1999), *Pretty in Punk: Girls' Gender Resistance in a Boys' Subculture*, New Brunswick NJ: Rutgers University Press.

Leonard, M. (1998), 'Paper Planes: Travelling the New Grrrl Geographies', in T. Skelton and G. Valentine (eds), *Cool Places: Geographies of Youth Cultures*, New York: Routledge.

Lugones, M. C. in collaboration with P. A. Rosezelle. (1995), 'Sisterhood and Friendship as Feminist Models', in P.A. Weiss and M. Friedman (eds), *Feminism and Community*, Philadelphia, PA: Temple University Press.

Martin, L. (2000), *Quantify 2: Part vs. Whole* (Fall) (fanzine).

McDowell, L. (1999), *Gender, Identity, and Place: Understanding Feminist Geographies*. Cambridge: Polity Press.

McLaughlin, T. (1996), *Street Smarts and Critical Theory: Listening to the Vernacular,* Madison WI: University of Wisconsin Press.

McRobbie, A. (1980), 'Settling Accounts with Subcultures: A Feminist Critique', *Screen Education*, 34: 37–49.

McRobbie, A. (1991), *Feminism and Youth Culture: From Jackie to Just Seventeen*, Boston MA: Unwin Hyman.

McRobbie, A. (1994), *Postmodernism and Popular Culture*, London: Routledge.

Miles, C. (1997), 'Spatial Politics: A Gendered Sense of Place', in S. Redhead, D. Wynne, and J. O'Connor (eds), *The Club Cultures Reader: Readings in Popular Cultural Studies*, Oxford: Blackwell.

Mohanty, C. (1992), 'Feminist Encounters: Locating the Politics of Experience', in M. Barratt and A. Philips (eds), *Destabilizing Theory: Contemporary Feminist Debates*, Stanford CA: Stanford University Press.

Muggleton, D. (2000), *Inside Subculture: The Postmodern Meaning of Style*. Oxford: Berg.

Nguyen, M. (n.d.), 'Introduction', *Evolution of a Race Riot* (fanzine).

Nguyen, M. (2001), 'Tales of an Asiatic Geek Girl: *Slant* from Paper to Pixels', in A. Nelson and T. L. N. Tu with A. H. Hines (eds), *Technicolor: Race, Technology, and Everyday Life,* New York: New York University Press.

O'Brien, L. (1999), 'The Woman Punk Made Me', in R. Sabin (ed.), *Punk Rock: So What? The Cultural Legacy of Punk,* New York: Routledge.

Piano, D. (2002), 'Congregating Women: Reading Third Wave Feminist Practices in Subcultural Production', *Rhizomes.Net: Cultural Studies in Emerging Knowledge*, 4, Cyberfeminisms, http://www.rhizomes.net/issue4/piano.html (accessed September 2002).

Rich, A. (1986), 'Notes toward a Politics of Location', in *Blood, Bread, and Poetry: Selected Prose 1979-1985*, New York: W.W. Norton.

Roman, L. G. (1988), 'Intimacy, Labor, and Class: Ideologies of Feminine Sexuality in the Punk Slam Dance', in L. G. Roman and L.K. Christian-Smith (eds), *Becoming Feminine: The Politics of Popular Culture*, New York: The Falmer Press.

Siegel, D. (1997), 'The Legacy of the Personal: Generating Theory in Feminism's Third Wave', *Hypatia*, 12 (3): 46–75.

Smith, J. (1997), 'Doin' it for the Ladies – Youth Feminism: Cultural Productions/ Cultural Activisms', in L. Heywood and J. Drake, (eds), *Third Wave Agenda: Being Feminist, Doing Feminism*, Minneapolis MN: University of Minnesota Press.

Smith, S. (1993), *Subjectivity, Identity, and the Body: Women's Autobiographical Practices in the Twentieth Century*, Bloomington IN: Indiana University Press.

Soccio, L. (1999), 'From Girl to Woman to Grrrl: (Sub)Cultural Intervention and Political Activism in the Time of Feminism', *Invisible Culture: An Electronic Journal for Visual Studies*, 2, Interrogating Subcultures, http://www.rochester. edu/in_visible_culture/issue2/soccio.htm (accessed September 2002).

Sutton, L. (1999), 'All Media Are Created Equal: Do-It-Yourself Identity in Alternative Publishing', in M. Bucholz, A.C. Liang, L. Sutton (eds), *Reinventing Identities: The Gendered Self in Discourse*, Boston MA: Oxford University Press.

Ussher, J. (1997), *Fantasies of Femininity: Reframing the Boundaries of Sex*, New Brunswick NJ: Rutgers University Press.

Wakeford, N. (1997), 'Networking Women and Grrrls with Information/Communication Technology: Surfing Tales of the World Wide Web', in J. Terry and M. Calvert (eds), *Processed Lives: Gender and Technology in Everyday Life*, New York: Routledge.

Wolff, J. (1990), *Feminine Sentences: Essays on Women and Culture*, Berkeley CA: University of California Press.

Young, I. M. (1990), *Justice and the Politics of Difference*, Princeton NJ: Princeton University Press.

Part VII
New Technologies

18

'The X-Files', Online Fan Culture, and the David Duchovny Estrogen Brigades

Rhiannon Bury

In the past ten years the 'oral culture' identified by Fiske (1989) as surrounding and defining television has extended into cyberspace. Reliable numbers on Internet discussion forums are hard to come by, but suffice to say that talking about television is a popular online activity. In the context of the Usenet, for example, discussions on television are predominately clustered in the alt (alternative) section. A Google search indicated that *alt.tv* with 323 newsgroups was one of the largest subsections, dwarfed only by *alt.music* with 707 newsgroups and *alt.fan* with 1,107.[1] Based on visits to Web sites that serve as Internet television resources, I estimate that every American, British and Canadian television show broadcast has dedicated newsgroups and mailing lists, ranging from several to several hundred for popular series such as 'The X-Files'.[2] Indeed, soon after the series about FBI Agents Fox Mulder and Dana Scully was first broadcast in the fall of 1993 on the Fox network, *alt.tv.x-files* was created. By December some female fans had decided to turn their backs on this public online forum and form private mailing lists ostensibly named after the (former) lead actor of the series: The David Duchovny Estrogen Brigades (DDEBs). In 1996, I spent one year conducting ethnographic research with nineteen DDEB members in the context of a mailing list specifically set up for data collection.

My overarching argument in this paper is twofold. First, an online community does not simply exist because people join a mailing list or read/post messages to a newsgroup: it is created and maintained through the regular engagement of a specific set of practices by the majority of its members. Its status as an online community is therefore provisional, a collection of identities whose arrangement shifts with the ebb and flow of interaction. Second, contrary to claims that gender or other embodied identities no longer matter in cyberspace, online communities

---

1. A complete listing of all Usenet groups can be found at Google http://www. google.com by following the link to Groups (accessed 24 July 2002). There are also a few television discussion groups listed in rec (recreation) section, under *rec.arts*.

2. The source I accessed was the Usenet group *rec.arts.tv* FAQ (Accessed 24 July 2002).

are constituted along the fault lines of the gendered body in complex and some-times contradictory ways.

From Culture to Community

Criticism that the concept of culture is reductionist and reifying is not new. As Muggleton (2000: 24) puts it, 'individuals appear in the analysis only as epiphen-omena of essences, structures and totalizing theories' (quoted in Hills 2002: xv). The solution to the problem of 'culture' has typically been to make the term plural as in 'fan cultures' (Hills 2002) or 'cybercultures' (Bell 2001) or to use the term 'community', either in the singular, or the plural, as in 'interpretative communities' (Jenkins 1992) or 'virtual communities' (Rheingold 1993b). However, this solution fails to make the important distinction between the imagined and the local. By the former, I am drawing on Anderson (1983) to speak of a formation in which members share a set of identifications but, unlike a local formation, do not necessarily interact with one another, or perhaps more importantly, do not necessarily desire to interact with one another. I use 'culture' to describe the imagined, and 'com-munity' to describe the local formation. In drawing this distinction, I am not suggesting that a community is any more substantive or 'real' than a culture. Like the body, I understand community to be *performative*, having 'no ontological status apart from the various acts which constitute its reality' (Butler 1990: 139). What gives the community its substance is the consistent engagement of *communal practices* by a majority of its members. Similarly, I am not suggesting that the desire for community be naively celebrated. As Young (1990: 300) argues:

> community is an understandable dream, expressing a desire for selves that are transp-arent to one another, relationships of mutual identification, social closeness and comfort. The dream is understandable, but politically problematic . . . because those motivated by it will tend to suppress differences among themselves or implicitly to exclude from the political groups persons with whom they do not identify.

Singer (1991) goes a step further, claiming that the function of communal formations 'has largely been that of managing, consolidating, or overriding the dissembling effects of a *non*-regulated interplay of differences' (Singer 1991: 124). In other words, the creation of a group that uses the pronouns *we/us/our/ours* entails the establishment of sets of practices whose purpose is to create conformity and contain difference. In the context of my study, the name David Duchovny Estrogen Brigade overtly signals that membership involves an identification with a feminine heterosexual identity. While the naming of the lists was intended to exclude male fans and celebrate female desire (discussed below), it also had the effect of excluding female fans of the series who may have wanted to join a women-only list but identified as lesbian.[3]

If I make a distinction between culture and community, I collapse the one commonly made between virtual and RL ('real life') communities, one that allows for celebration of the former over the latter. Rheingold (1993a) implies that computer-mediated communication (CMC) is better suited than face-to-face communication for the job of community making, for the reason that we cannot 'form prejudices about others before we read what they have to say . . . In cyberspace, everyone is in the dark' (Rheingold 1993a: 66). In effect, he takes the inability to visually observe online interactants as evidence that the body, and the identities associated with it, have been 'left behind'. Yet reducing identities like race and gender to physical attributes is, to say the least, highly problematic. Identity must be understood as not only a product of discourse but as a process (Balsamo 1996), in other words as performative. Gender is thus an effect rather than a cause of 'words, actions and gestures' (Butler 1990: 136). The body's seeming invisibility in cyberspace should not be taken as a logical indicator that the body is no longer performing its gender; on the contrary, it continues to signify gender intelligibility, albeit *linguistically*, when it goes online. Certainly, the discourses that regulate the gender performances of the body seated at the keyboard have not magically vanished. What we do lack is access to visual practices with which to map gender onto subjects more or less instantaneously. Thus, online gender does not disappear but becomes akin to RL identities like class or sexuality not so easily pinpointed by the power of vision. The implication for virtual communities is that they cannot be celebrated as alternatives that circumvent the politics of exclusion.

The formation of the DDEBs is an empirical case in point:

> I was on alt.tv.x-files for awhile first, then as usually happens whenever a woman starts to express her appreciation for an actor on the net we started getting 'me toos' from women and flack from the men. (Why is it men can talk about actresses in public and not get flack, but let a woman talk about a man and we get jumped all over!) Anyway, that's why Julia and I started the original DDEB . . . I pretty much quit reading a.t.x. The signal to noise ratio got utterly unmanageable. (Kellie)[4]

---

3. After the formation of the DDEBs, the Gillian Anderson Estrogen Brigade (GAEB) was set up as a safe space exclusively for lesbian and bisexual women. Their Web site is http://gaeb.teatime.com (accessed July 2002).

4. Kellie and Julia are real names and I have used them with permission in the context of this particular quote as the information identifying them as the founders of the DDEB is available to anyone who visits their Web sites. All other names of the participants have been changed to protect confidentiality.

I decided as soon as I read Kellie's post. People think nothing of it if men talk about lusting after women, but if women discuss the sexual attractiveness of men, people act like were [sic] sluts. I wanted the freedom of being able to talk about lust without being exposed to condesension [sic] for it. (Hollis)

I think it was in February of 1994. I decided to join because I found the news groups to be a little hostile to women expressing their admiration of an actor. Also I thought it might be fun. I decided to stick around because the conversation was never limited to DD or to 'The X-Files' and because I met such interesting women from so many different parts of the world. (Moll)

As the above quotations indicate, the norms of the newsgroups were those of the male participants, who in 1993 would have been the overwhelming majority.[5] Some felt it necessary to dismiss women's talk about actors as 'drool', connoting a dirty and infantile act. Participants also described sexual come-ons or harassment in other online contexts like IRC (live 'chats') when identified as female by their names:

I consider the constant pestering by online Romeos to be harrassment. I swear I used to get talk requests once a day while I had a decidely [sic] feminine name on my account. (Hollis)

When I used to participate on IRC I got hit on a lot when guys figured out that I was a female. (Megan)

A number of participants also noted that they had not experienced any kind of harassment because of their gender-neutral names:

I've never had a problem with any guys – of course, the fact that my name is fairly non-gender specific may have something to do with that. (Ash)

Even this mis-recognition conforms to gender norms: If a woman is not identified as such by male participants, she is simply assumed to be male and treated as 'one of the guys'.

5. Researchers from the Georgia Institute of Technology reported that 94 per cent of those who responded to their first survey of Internet use in 1994 were male, the majority of whom worked as computer professionals. Survey data can be accessed at GVU's WWW User Surveys (2001) http://www.gvu.gatech.edu/user_surveys (accessed September 2002).

Community-making on the DDEBRP

The David Duchovny Estrogen Brigade Research Project (DDEBRP), the name of the research list set up with members of the three DDEBs, was a closed but unmoderated list, which meant that nobody was able to join and participate without the approval of the list owner (myself), but that posts were automatically sent to all list members without being vetted by a moderator. List 'traffic' ranged from 100 messages daily to no messages being posted for a week. All nineteen participants identified as White and had at least two years of post-secondary education. Seven had begun, and five had completed, master's degrees. Thirteen were between 30 and 40 years old. Drawing on feminist and critical approaches to research, I refused the position of 'the silent [observing] Other who is present in, while apparently absent from, the text' (Walkerdine 1990: 173). One way of marking my 'presence' was to participate actively in the community-making process. I joined and initiated discussion topics (often referred to as 'threads') and did not simply 'lurk' in the background, silently downloading data. I have included my own contributions in the analysis and therefore use the term 'DDEBRP members' to refer to both the participants and myself.

Despite the names of the lists and the reasons for which they were formed, interaction was not centred upon David Duchovny. Participants estimated that chat about the actor on the DDEBs comprised as little as 5 per cent to as much as 30 per cent of discussion.[6] Of the eighty-seven documents in my database, comprising several thousand messages, only 60 per cent contained messages explicitly referring to 'The X-Files', 56 per cent to Duchovny and 32 per cent to Gillian Anderson, Duchovny's co-star who played the role of Dana Scully.[7] As Moll indicated in the quotation in the previous section, she 'stuck around' on her DDEB list because a range of topics were discussed and because she enjoyed the company of the other female members. The community-making process was thus one that involved not only the creation and maintenance of a community of fans but a community of friends.

All in a Day's Work

Before examining the content of interaction, it is important to look at its timing and 'location' and understand these factors as imbricated with communal practices.

6. Email needs to be recognized as a hybrid form of communication. While it is obviously written text, it incorporates many features of speech. Hence my mixing of terms like chat and discussion as well as message and post is intentional.

7. I used the software package QSR NUD*IST to organize the data, search the database and generate reports based on the searches.

DDEBRP interaction almost entirely took place during the day and from the workplace, where members had relatively unrestricted access to email. Only four of the participants did not work in offices at the start of the project. Of the remainder, four worked in managerial/professional positions and remaining ten, over half the participants, worked in various administrative support positions. Using the office as a point of entry into DDEBRP cyberspace, however, was not just contingent upon easy Internet access at work, but restrictions at home. Although all the DDEBRP members had Internet access at home, the six who were single and lived alone were the ones who stated that they had no constraints limiting their time spent on line. Those who were in relationships and/or who were mothers cited social and domestic obligations:

> I have things to do with/for my family and non- virtual friends. I also write, so a lot of my free time is taken up doing that. I used to spend much more time on the net, but it was interfering with my life so I cut back some. (Drucilla)

> My daughter and my job must come before my net activities. That doesn't mean that there aren't times when I log on while she's awake or that I don't read mail while I'm sitting on hold waiting to talk with Microsoft support or something. (Liz)

This communal practice of posting at work and not at home is hardly surprising in light of the extensive work by feminist scholars on the gendering of space. The office is a veritable 'pink collar ghetto' even for university-educated women. Similarly, the home is a site of work for women, whereas it is more likely to be site of leisure for men (Wajcman 1992). Although anecdotal, the contrast between the experience of Drucilla and Liz quoted above and self-proclaimed cybernaut Howard Rheingold (1993b: 1) is instructive: "'Daddy is saying 'Holy moly!' to his computer again!" Those words have become a family code for the way my virtual community has infiltrated our real world. My seven-year-old daughter knows that her father congregates with a family of invisible friends who seem to gather in his computer.' Indeed, if we visualize the setting – the writer at his computer screen, his back to his daughter who seems to be calling out to another unidentified family member (the child's mother?) who is not even in the picture at all – it would seem that, for men, relationships with virtual friends *take precedence* over family.

It needs to be recognized, however, that this particular DDEBRP practice had consequences in terms of participation of those members who could not post during the day:

[From: Erin][8]
... People ... have 2 options: read through [the messages] and reply one at a time; read through them all and reply to certain chosen ones. I've done option one in the past and invariably, as I finish reading my email, I'll see that someone has already answered the question I was answering, expressed a similar opinion to what I was saying (and said it far better), or expressed something that made me change mine [sic] opinion (did I mention I'm indecisive?):) If I try option 2 and read through all of the messages before posting, I find I'm a bit exhausted :) and feel that so many great opinions and ideas have been expressed that some of my posts would mainly be me too's without a whole lot to add. I feel like I'm beating a dead horse or butting into other conversations ...

[From: Paula]
... by the time I get to read it, the topic has been discussed to death & I can't think of another original thing to contribute.

Although Erin ended up being one of the more active members for the six months that she was a participant in the project, the same was not true of Paula who posted less than ten messages over the year. Of course, there are other reasons for not posting messages, and one must be careful not to discount the act of reading messages as a communal practice in the way that listening is a form of participation in face-to-face interaction. In fact, Paula told me in a following email exchange that she had enjoyed 'reading the various messages, "listening" to the interesting opinions & getting X-Files tidbits'. Nonetheless, the practice that bound the majority together had the unintended consequence of marginalizing those unable or unwilling to engage in the practice.

Net Critics

In this section, I will highlight several key communal practices by presenting data from the discussion of the episode 'In the Field Where I Died' (3 November 1996). To contextualize, twenty-five new episodes were aired over the data collection period and nineteen were discussed to some degree. It is important to establish that such discussions were always framed by a critical discourse. Jenkins (1992) argues

---

8. In presenting data from the DDEBRP, I have tried to approximate the form of the original email messages. To save space and preserve confidentiality, I have removed or modified the lines from the message 'header', any lines from a previous message that were included in the body of the replies, as well as any 'signatures' or 'signature files'. In presenting list exchanges, I have 'threaded' the messages by subject and presented them sequentially, identifying them as [From: participant's name] *above* the extract. The participants also answered an email questionnaire, and data presented from these are distinguished from list-exchanges by giving the participant's name (in parentheses) at the *end* of the quotation.

that fans are often derided for their emotional attachments to a series and its actors, and as a result are assumed to be unable to pass 'objective' judgement on the 'quality' of the writing, acting, direction, camera work, and so forth. He draws on the work of Pierre Bourdieu (1984), who argues that aesthetics is not objective knowledge but rather a tactic or strategy used to justify the tastes of dominant groups. I would add that this derision is not only based on class, distinguishing consumers of mass culture from connoisseurs of high culture, but also gender. Female fans are often singled out as the worst offenders for letting their emotions cloud their judgement. According to Jenkins (1992), the term fan, an abbreviation of the Latin *fanaticus* was originally used playfully in reference to male sports enthusiasts but as a put-down by film and theatre critics of women who supposedly attended the performances for the sole purpose of admiring the actors. Mia Farrow played one such 'matinee girl' in the Woody Allen film, *The Purple Rose of Cairo,* whose romantic fantasy comes true when her idol walks off the screen and into her life. Beginning in the era of Frank Sinatra, the image of the swooning, besotted female fan was complemented by that of the hysterical, screaming teenager. The section on fandom in the Rock and Roll Fall of Fame in Cleveland, Ohio is dominated by huge blowups of such 'fangirls'. As the following quotation indicates, the DDEBRP members may have defended their right to express admiration for Duchovny and other actors but they firmly rejected the fangirl categorization:

> They assume I drool over him and think he can do no wrong. They assume that I am jealous of his girlfriend or that I stalk him. All of these assumptions are wrong and I find them offensive. (Mrs Hale)[9]

As middle-class women with post-secondary training in critical interpretation practices, the DDEBRP members clearly embraced 'bourgeois aesthetics'. On Monday 4 November 1996, I began the discussion of 'In the Field Where I Died', an episode that involved Mulder undergoing past life regression hypnosis to discover he had been a soldier in the American Civil War, and engaged to Melissa, a nurse with the battalion, who in her present incarnation is the wife of a Dooms-day cult leader under investigation by the FBI. I commented on the mood created by writers Glen Morgan and James Wong and the performance of the supporting actress (Kristin Cloke) playing Melissa the nurse. The only quibble I mentioned concerned the revelation during the hypnosis that Scully had been Mulder's Sergeant in his 'Civil War' life. I felt this detail strained the limits of credibility of their partnership. Pointing out strengths and weaknesses is a practice that demonstrates

---

9. This participant chose the pseudonym Mrs Hale as a playful reference to 'Little Green Men' (16 September 1994) in which FBI Agent Fox Mulder uses the name George E. Hale as an alias. She was very clear that 'in real life' she always uses her own last name and not that of her husband.

that one is familiar with and able to apply aesthetic 'standards' valued by the community. The first set of replies generally confirmed and expanded upon my critical comments. Although not preserved in the presentation of the data samples (in order to conserve space and avoid repetition) the respondents did not simply post a message with discrete comments but rather inter-cut their responses with relevant parts of the original message. This practice reinforced the process of collectively assessing and making sense of the episode.

[From: Drucilla]
I thought it was an excellent episode. One of DD's best performances ever. I hope I don't *ever* hear anyone call him 'wooden' again. And Kristin Cloke blew me away.[10]

I did get kinda confused during Mulder's hypnosis scene, didn't Mulder say something about two *different* people being Melissa in *this* lifetime? I need to rewatch it to figure that out. I'm not sure I heard that but I thought I did. Maybe he was talking about two different Melissa's. Melissa Scully, and Melissa R - I've forgotten her last name.

[From: Megan]
I really got into that episode . . . it really sucked me into the story. I can just see the relationshippers barfing up a lung over Mulder and Scully not being soul-mates (although I feel that they are, just of a different sort). I thought the acting and writing were excellent. So nice to have Morgan and Wong back!!![11]

Drucilla also pointed out a possible problem with the plot. Jenkins (1992: 278) points out that, unlike literary or film critics, fan critics do not simply compile a list of 'flaws' that take away from the text, but 'work to resolve gaps, to explore excess details and undeveloped potentials'. To this end, Drucilla suggested that the 'second Melissa' might be Scully's sister. Megan's disparaging remark about the reaction of 'relationshippers' is of particular significance because it serves to distance the DDEBRP members from those female fans who wanted the show's writers to offer them a Mulder/Scully romance, a development explicitly rejected at that time by series creator and executive producer Chris Carter. This position was confirmed indirectly by Daphne who felt 'it was entirely fitting that [Mulder and Scully] had been together beyond this life and were "comrades in war", in more than one lifetime.' At the end of her message, Daphne shifted from a discourse of aesthetics to one that can be labelled 'emotional realism' following Jenkins (1992):

10. Before Web-based email, asterisks were typically placed around words for emphasis in the same way that underlining or italics are used in traditional print media.
11. Glen Morgan and James Wong had left 'The X-Files' after the second season to write and produce their own short-lived Fox series, 'Space'.

[From: Daphne]
Was anyone else bugged by Scully's irritation during this ep? It just seemed as tho she kept yelling at Mulder but didn't have any better ideas. And if my partner was walking into sure death like that, I would have shot him in the leg.

Instead of criticizing the writers or the acting, Daphne criticized the *character's* behaviour, including her failure to protect Mulder from harm, literally by writing herself into the script. This vacillation between two competing discourses was typical of episode discussion and symptomatic of an uneasy alignment of normative middle-class and normative feminine identities. I responded in kind, moving from a justification of Scully's reaction as if she were a real person to pointing out another plot inaccuracy.

[From: Rhiannon]
I didn't like her lack of involvement in the case but I can understand her irritation with Mulder when he suddenly decided to get himself hypnotized when the cult leader is about to be released any minute, which will obviously have disasterous reprecussions [sic]: Skinner has already hinted at a new Jonestown. And speaking of the mass suicide, where did [Morgan and Wong] get the idea that drinking poison results in an instant and pleasant death. Anyone who has ever had a pet poisoned (thank goddess this has never happened to mine) will know how cruel and painful such a death is. Even using a gas (cynide [sic]pill sp?) is not instant, which is why the state of California finally gave up on the gas chamber for its state executions.

Moreover, I used knowledge of California penal practices to support my claim, drawing on a discourse of logical argumentation associated with a member of the university-educated middle class. In expressing disagreement, Ardis signalled that she was a member of the same class, providing a counterargument based on knowledge of aesthetics (editing processes and literature) and history:

[From: Ardis]
The editing gave that impression, not the story itself. Besides, it depends on the poison. I've never researched poisons, but I believe cyanide pills work pretty darn fast. I don't recall the Jonestown victims giving the impression they went in extended agony like Madame Bovary. And all the Goebbels children, who were given cyanide-laced chocolates by their mother, were described by the Russian soldiers who found them as looking like they were merely asleep. You can also factor in that the Seven Stars crowd went out in a religious high.[12]

12. Seven Stars was a religious cult based in California, and who had earlier, in 1996, committed mass suicide.

Until Mrs Hale joined the thread, there was consensus that the episode was well done overall:

[From: Mrs Hale]
Drucilla wrote:
> Maybe he was talking about two different Melissa's. Melissa Scully,
>and Melissa R--- I've forgotten her last name.

Reidel-Ephesian.

And there were more than a few major plot discrepancies in this one. But who cares, when we can wallow in poetry for an hour, dynamite the psychological basis of the ENTIRE GODDAM SERIES, and permit Duchovny to chew some scenery? We don't have to worry about no steenkin' details (like the fact that Cancerman, who would have been a BOY in the late thirties and early forties, was also supposed to be a Gestapo guard, and Melissa/Sarah was supposed to be a McCarthy era person who *also* knew what was going on at the compound, etc.) because we are Morgan and Wong and everyone loves everything we do. Sorry, but this is EXACTLY the kind of contempt for verisimilitude and blind emphasis on style over substance that killed off 'Space'. Too bad Morgan and Wong can't learn from experience.

Mrs Hale
really, really steamed

It is interesting that Mrs Hale did not simply insert her divergent views into the thread but first supplied a detail that Drucilla had forgotten, thus taking part in the collective interpretation process. Then, using sarcasm and non-standard speech ('no steekin' details'), she harshly criticized Morgan and Wong for their inattention to detail and their arrogance. Unlike the 'objective' critic of bourgeois aesthetics, though, she made no effort to hide her emotion, as indicated by the 'tag line' after her 'signature'. However, she was also indirectly insulting the other members who had previously complimented the writing. Perhaps recognizing the implication, she apologized before completing her attack.

Instead of resulting in a 'flame war', however, members, including Mrs Hale, worked to contain difference. According to Herring (1996), sending insulting or vitriolic messages to others is a violation of 'positive politeness', a term used in sociolinguistics to describe linguistic practices that establish solidarity with and connection to others. Her survey results indicate that women (61 per cent) are more concerned with observing positive politeness and avoiding violations than are men (39 per cent). Thus, the ensuing attempt at conflict resolution can be understood as a gendered practice. Drucilla was the first to respond by thanking Mrs Hale for providing Melissa's last name. Rather than baldly challenge her the claim that the writers had violated the psychology of the series, she implored, 'I wish you could explain exactly what damage you think has been done.' She then found common ground with Mrs Hale, agreeing that 'AM&W are *crappy* with continuity details . . . but then X-Files has always had that problem, no matter who's writing it. Their prideful insistence on "not having a bible" has become a problem.' With this statement the division between members shifts to one between critical fans like the DDEBRP members and the writers/producers of the show.[13] The exchange continued in the form of a debate, Drucilla and Daphne defending the episode premise and Mrs Hale providing counterarguments. Hollis again joined the thread, trying to reconcile her reaction (and by extension the rest of the participants in the thread) with that of Mrs Hale:

[From: Hollis]
I was so enrapt in the episode that I didn't notice the discrepancies until I was thinking about it later. That's sloppy writing to be sure. However, I don't consider such mistakes to be fatal unless they jolt me out of my comfortable suspension of disbelief while I'm still watching the show . . . You have a greater attention to detail than the average person, though, so I can see why you are reacting more strongly to it than I am.

Mrs Hale responded warmly, acknowledging that her investment in critical interpretative practices positioned her as a community outsider at that moment: '(grin) Hollis, my dear, you are *such* a diplomat. This is a polite way to say I nitpick too much! Well, you're right. :)'. In response, Hollis worked to protect Mrs Hale's positive face needs,[14] the effect being to bring Mrs Hale back into the community fold where critical reading is valued:

[From: Hollis]
I don't even consider that to be nitpicking. Nitpicking is whining over every petty detail. Things like the impossibility of Cancer Man being a Nazi but still being born in the US in time to be old enough to potentially be Mulder's father are fairly big errors regardless of whether most people notice them right off the bat or not. I also get the feeling that true nitpickers go out of their way to look for problems, just hoping to find a gaffe.

While a sense of community was restored for these members, it is important to keep in mind that this was not the case for everyone. In a private email exchange at the end of the data collection period, one member effectively told me that she equated these types of critical threads with 'nitpicking':

13. For a more extended discussion on the divisions between female fans and predominately male writers and producers, see Bury (1998).

14. A concept in sociolinguistics/pragmatics – need to maintain a positive face.

[From: Name Withheld]
Well, starting quite some time ago, I noticed how hypercritical my fellow . . . brigadiers were getting. They would rip apart every episode, not just in a good-natured analytical sort of way but with a certain jadedness and bad attitude that annoyed me. So I stopped reading their messages because they depressed me and made me think less of them! I'm more easily amused, I guess, and though I may see the same flaws in something that somebody else does, I don't think I take it so personally.

For her, too much criticism spoiled the pleasures of the text. This member's refusal not only to engage in the practice but even read the threads, resulted in her silent self-exclusion from the DDEBRP at the level of a critical fan community.

Conclusion

The DDEBs, and by extension the DDEBRP, are women-only online communities that deliberately marked themselves out as deviating from the unmarked masculinist norms of online fan culture in the mid-1990s. Once created, the process of maintaining the communities has involved engaging in practices that are both gendered and classed. In terms of posting practices, the majority of members experienced fewer constraints in accessing email during the day in the space of the office than in the space of the home. When new episodes aired, they engaged in critical discussions of aesthetics, politely debating acting abilities and the quality of writing without upsetting the apple cart of community. Although they also discussed the characters in terms of emotional realism, it is important to note that this practice was subsumed by the aforementioned critical practice: identifying too closely with characters on an emotional level is a dangerous practice for female fans who also identify as members of the larger educated middle-class. However, it is important not to romanticize alternative or oppositional communities. A minority of members still experienced marginalization at different moments as a consequence of being unable or unwilling to engage in the practices that gave the community its substance. This is not the fault of the other community members but rather is endemic to any formation based on a desire for unity and coherence.

Although I focused on fan practices in this paper, I wish to stress that the DDEBs and DDEBRP were also communities of female friends. Seeking and/or offering support and advice was a key practice that bound members together. When Hollis joined the 'In the field' thread, for example, she made reference to her husband's stroke as reason for her 'silence' on the list in recent days. Several members, including Mrs Hale and myself, sent our sympathies and good wishes in our replies to her message. This final point may partially answer the question that some may have about the relevance of women-only online communities in the early years of the twenty-first century. Most surveys on Internet usage show the number of women has increased dramatically. As of January 2002, women (52 per cent) now outnumber men in using the Internet in American homes (Nielsen NetRatings 2002). Yet, 'brigades' continue to form around actors, and lists dedicated to the reading and writing of fan fiction are *de facto* women only. As long as social identities matter IRL ('in real life'), they will continue to matter online.

References

Anderson, B. (1983), *Imagined Communities: Reflections on the Origin and Spread of Nationalism*, New York: Verso.

Balsamo, A. (1996), *Technologies of the Gendered Body: Reading Cyborg Women*, Durham NC: Duke University Press.

Bell, D. (2001), *An Introduction to Cybercultures*, London and New York NY: Routledge.

Bourdieu, P. (1984), *Distinction: A Social Critique of the Judgement of Taste* (trans. R. Nice), Cambridge MA: Harvard University Press.

Bury, R. (1998), 'Waiting to X-Hale: A Study of Gender and Community on an All-Female X-Files Mailing List', *Convergence: The Journal of Research into New Media Technologies*, 4 (3): 59–83.

Butler, J. (1990), *Gender Trouble: Feminism and the Subversion of Identity*, New York: Routledge.

Fiske, J. (1989), 'Moments of Television: Neither the Text nor the Audience', in E. Seiter, H. Borchers, G. Kreutzner and E.-M. Warth (eds), *Remote Control: Television, Audiences, and Cultural Power*, New York: Routledge.

Herring, S. (ed.) (1996), *Computer-Mediated Communication: Linguistic, Social, and Cross-Cultural Perspectives*, Philadelphia PA: J. Benjamins.

Hills, M. (2002), *Fan Cultures*, London and New York: Routledge.

Jenkins, H. (1992), *Textual Poachers: Television Fans & Participatory Culture*, New York: Routledge.

Muggleton, D. (2000), *Inside Subculture: The Postmodern Meaning of Style*, Oxford and New York: Berg.

Nielsen NetRatings (2002), 'More and more US women online', (21 January), *Nua Internet Surveys*, http://www.nua.ie/surveys/ (accessed 26 July 2002).

Rheingold, H. (1993a), 'A Slice of Life in my Virtual Community', in L. Harasin (ed.), *Global Networks: Computers and International Communication*, Cambridge MA: MIT Press.

Rheingold, H. (1993b), *The Virtual Community: Homesteading on the Electronic Frontier*, Reading MA: Addison-Wesley Publishing Co.

Singer, L. (1991), 'Recalling a Community at Loose Ends', in M. T. Group (ed.), *Community at Loose Ends*, Minneapolis MN: University of Minnesota Press.

Wajcman, J. (1992), 'Domestic Technology: Labour-Saving or Enslaving?', in G. Kirkup and L. Smith Keller (eds), *Inventing Women: Science, Technology, and Gender*, Cambridge UK: Polity Press in association with the Open University Press.

Walkerdine, V, (1990), *Schoolgirl Fictions*, New York: Verso.

Young, I. M. (1990), 'The Ideal of Community and the Politics of Difference', in L. J. Nicholson (ed.), *Feminism/Postmodernism*, New York: Routledge.

19

'Net.Goth': Internet Communication and (Sub)Cultural Boundaries

Paul Hodkinson

In the context of an increasingly all-encompassing culture of media and con-sumption, the notion of subculture is often regarded as inappropriate or irrelevant. The term's implication that the sphere of youth or popular culture can be divided into discreet, committed and clearly bounded groupings simply fails, it has been argued, to capture the cultural dynamism of a society where complex individual identities are always in transition and collective affiliations are partial, selective and temporary (see, for example, Muggleton 1997; Bennett 1999). Interestingly, such critiques have as yet tended not to include the impacts of the Internet in their analysis. In some respects, this may be deemed surprising, since 'virtual culture' has been argued by some of its most high profile commentators to intensify the kind multiplication of selves and crossing of boundaries emphasized by critics of subculture (Turkle 1995; Poster 1995). It may seem logical to suggest that the ability of anonymous Internet users to participate in limitless divergent cultural practices from the comfort of their homes adds further weight to the case of those who suggest we have now moved into 'post-subcultural' times (Muggleton 1997, 2000).

Developing an argument I have raised elsewhere (Hodkinson 2002), this chapter explicitly argues against such an interpretation of online technology. Without disputing the *potential* for Internet technology to enhance cultural fluidity in some circumstances, it will be suggested that online networks of communication can also function to enhance and intensify the boundaries that separate cultural groupings. The argument will be illustrated with reference to the impact of the Internet on the goth scene, a translocal youth grouping that emerged in the early 1980s and is most obviously identifiable by the interest in 'dark', melancholic styles of fashion and music shared by participants. I have previously argued that the substantive overall form of the goth scene – particularly in respect of its high levels of distinctiveness, identity, commitment and autonomy – warrants its conceptualization using a somewhat reworked notion of subculture (Hodkinson 2002). This conclusion resulted from extensive ethnographic research carried out on the subculture toward the end of the 1990s, a period during which the Internet had begun to establish itself as a significant part of the goth scene's infrastructure. What will become clear in the following pages, is that, far from eroding the substance of the grouping, the onset of the Internet served to consolidate and strengthen its subcultural boundaries.

Culture of Simulation and Fluidity?

Drawing heavily on post-modern theory in her analysis of the Internet, Sherry Turkle describes a 'culture of simulation' characterized by endless images and surfaces, none of which connected with substantive referents. The Internet, from this perspective, is the ultimate objectification of Baudrillard's emphasis on simulacra and of Jameson's focus on the triumph of surface over depth and play over seriousness (Turkle 1995: 44–5). According to Turkle, a 'new social and cultural sensibility' is being created by this technology, characterized among other things by the ability to 'invent ourselves', by moving freely – from the comfort of our own home – between an infinite number of potential online identities, and, indeed, playing out several at any one moment in time (Turkle 1995: 9–26). Post-modern theory need no longer be illustrated via appeals to the world of science fiction when the fluidities, multiplicities and decentred selves theorized by Jameson, Deleuze and Guttari and others are now being lived out everyday in the thoroughly rhizomic networks of the virtual (Turkle 1995: 15). Identifying the Internet as the central component of a 'second media age', Mark Poster has drawn comparable conclusions, emphasizing the constitution by a decentred on-line network, of unstable, multiple and diffuse subjects (Poster 1995: 32). In an explicit reference to the dissipation of collective forms of identity, he emphasizes that so-called 'virtual communities' are in fact associated with a fluidity of identity in a world where their participants are uninhibited by and liberated from the markers and boundaries associated with social life away from the Internet (Poster 1995: 34). Although he rejects many post-modernist claims about the Internet, Manuel Castells appears to concur with the notion of online communities as fluid, emph-asizing that they allow individuals to continually construct and reconstruct unique individual '"portfolios of sociability" in a number of networks with low entry barriers and low opportunity costs' (Castells 2001: 132; also see Wellman and Gulia 1999: 184).

The suggestion that selves on the Internet are decentred, multiple and fluid has clear consequences for those amalgamations of young people, music and style that have, until recently, been referred to as subcultures. Significantly perhaps, such interpretations of the Internet cohere with the more general conclusions of social theorists Maffesoli and Bauman, both of whom propose that rather than being divided into fixed, clearly bounded communities, contemporary consumer culture is characterized by complex and fluid patterns of individual movement between loosely knit 'neo-tribes' (Maffesoli 1996; Bauman 1992a, 1992b). Crucially, the boundaries of neo-tribes are loose, resulting in extensive internal diversity, external overlap and continual flows of multi-affiliated individuals between one group and another (Maffesoli 1996: 76). While for Maffesoli, neo-tribes represent something of a revival of the importance of the social, Bauman interprets them as evidence of an essentially individualistic society where community is an ideal, sought but never found. Society merely consists of insecure individuals negotiating their own fickle privatized routes through the superficial elective points of identity on offer (Bauman 1992a, b).

As well as corresponding with such general theoretical visions, post-modern oriented interpretations of the Internet such as those described appear to provide further weight to the case of those who have specifically applied such an emphasis on fluid, loosely bounded collectivities to the terrain previously occupied by subcultural theory. If we accept interpretations such as those of Turkle and Poster, for example, the instantaneity of access and anonymity created by the Internet would surely facilitate and even enhance the existing 'neo-tribal' tendency identified by Bennett for young people to reject communal norms or categories in favour of a process of drawing upon various styles and traditions in the construction of highly individualized identities (Bennett 1999: 610). The apparent enhancement of inter-group movement on the Internet invites the conclusion that the technology may encourage and enhance an ongoing playful process of the trying on and casting off of multiple styles and selves. The extra instability and diversity of membership created by such fluid individual patterns would have the effect of intensifying the dissolution of group boundaries, rendering notions such as subculture obsolete (see Leonard 1998). Indeed, such erosion of collective distinctiveness and group autonomy by the Internet might surely be taken as a defining characteristic of so-called *post-subcultural* times (Muggleton 1997, 2000).

Internet as Plurality of Media

The notion of the Internet as a medium conducive to the kind of fluidity and multiplicity of identity described above tends, however, to be premised on a mistaken belief that the technology brings together an infinite array of information and culture into one singular 'space' shared by a diverse, free-floating and intensely curious mass of users. In practice, the Internet rarely functions to expose each user to a diversity of culture or to encourage them to broaden their horizons. It operates as a singular mass medium or space no more than does a magazine rack in a newsagent store. Let us consider the latter for a moment. Multitudes of publications invite the attentions of a diverse readership. Some cover issues of 'general interest' aimed at large, mixed audiences, whilst most address the more specialist interests of smaller and smaller audience groups. Crucially, the technical possibility, created by the technology of the rack, of everyone reading all of them and continually diving between the infinitely different cultural pursuits which they offer, does not mean this is the way in which most consumers behave. Instead, most individuals utilize the largely decentralized nature of the display to ignore the vast majority of magazines and focus in on one or more titles that are familiar to them as a result of existing interests and established reading habits.

Similarly, the Internet consists of a mixture of widely used mass media forms – such as those associated with established media and commercial corporations – alongside a multitude of niche and micro media, in the form of more and more specialist, subject specific Web sites and discussion facilities. As with the magazine rack, the technical potential to explore, move between and affiliate oneself to many such specialisms does not mean that most people are likely to do so. Indeed, in an exploration of politics on the Internet, Hill and Hughes (1998) suggest the opposite is true – that the Internet tends to encourage the specialist pursuit of existing interests and beliefs, resulting in the withdrawal of each grouping and faction into its own autonomous and clearly bounded virtual space. Far from increasing external recruitment, or cross-group contact, the technology often reinforces existing ties (Diani 2001: 123), something liable to prompt a great deal of preaching to the converted (Hill and Hughes 1998: 73). In light of this, the Internet is perhaps no more a singular culture without boundaries than is society off the screen. Indeed, it may be suggested that the way in which we are required as users of the Internet to culturally align ourselves may even serve to exaggerate offline tendencies to cluster in those spaces in which we feel most comfortable.

Searching and Selecting

Consistent with this reasoning, the vast majority of users of those Internet facilities associated with our case study grouping, the goth scene, are liable to have already been goths. Primarily, this is because, in contrast to centralized and pre-filtered traditional broadcast or print media, use of the Internet is dominated by the selections and choices of the consumer. Whether through entering a keyword into a search engine or inputting an exact Web address into their browser, the user is required to decide, to adapt a famous Microsoft slogan, where they want to go today. While it certainly enhances the ability to explore existing areas of interest in depth, this compulsion to choose is not conducive to the continual discovery and adoption of brand new pursuits or roles. One is unlikely, then, to decide to search for sites or discussion groups associated with a specialist interest group such as the goth scene without having an initial interest of some kind. Conversely, for those already highly involved and committed to such a group, there is a considerable likelihood that the tastes and practices with which it is associated will have some bearing upon the content the user opts to view.

Sure enough, most goths I spoke to said that the first thing they ever entered into a search engine was either the name of a goth band or the word 'goth' itself. Meanwhile, others bypassed search engines completely, preferring directly to access goth Web sites or discussion groups whose location they learned about through subcultural channels of word of mouth. Furthermore, in the same way that magazine readers often read one or two favourite titles regularly, most goths said that their Web use was dominated not by continual exploration and the discovery of new phenomena, but by the continual revisiting of exact same Web sites. As one respondent put it:

> I don't usually go on a two hour random search – very rarely these days . . . in my case it tends to be things I already know are there. (Caroline)

The inclusion of 'favourites' or 'bookmarks' facilities on Web browsers in order to make such repeat viewing easier, does little to persuade users to discard their current interests in favour of new ones. Far from encouraging movement, discovery or exploration, such tools explicitly encourage the individual to stick with existing tastes and affiliations.

Subnetwork

While most used a variety of non-goth online resources from time to time, all those I asked said that the majority of their leisure-time use of the Internet involved Web sites and discussion groups related to the goth scene. While the ability and requirement to initially decide upon a specific site or search topic played a crucial role in this, the concentration of their net-use within such a specialist area was further enhanced by the way goth sites, discussion groups and chat facilities were clustered together via webs of hyperlinks. One might suggest, perhaps, that the continual movement from one virtual space to another enabled by never-ending webs of hyperlinks is precisely what makes the Internet essentially rhizomic and fluid. In practice, however, links can sometimes be patterned into relatively discreet subnetworks – after all, they usually connect together sites or other facilities which are similar to one another in their content or subject matter. Goth sites, then, were often linked to and from one another, creating between them a subnetwork, unlikely often to be stumbled upon unwittingly. The ability of goths effectively to navigate between their highly specialist Web sites was greatly enhanced by the numerous direct connections between them. But because there were far more links from goth site to goth site than there were between the subnetwork they formed and subjects or cultures external to it, the technology did little to encourage virtual immigration or emigration.

The cohesiveness of the goth subnetwork on the Internet was further enhanced by the gradual development of central or nodal points, in the form of well established Web sites that had generated for themselves a high subcultural profile. Among other things, these usually contained extensive databases of links to other subcultural resources on the net. The most important node for goths based in Britain during the late 1990s and early 2000s, was a server based at *www.darkwave.org.uk*, which contained numerous interactive resources. Involving management and filtering by a variety of trusted volunteers in order to keep it up to date, relevant and running smoothly, *Darkwave* housed the *Net.Goth Site*, which offered its numerous regular goth visitors an extensive A-to-Z of goth related links, including Web sites connected with bands, shops, promoters, clubs, articles and e-zines (*Net.Goth links page,* accessed 1999–2002). While the ability of surfers to submit their own suggested links made the resource participatory, the centralized filtering of these by site managers and, in particular, their selection of a limited number of popular sites for inclusion on the site's main introductory page, functioned to provide a degree of order and structure to the goth subnetwork. The site was used by many goths as a continually revisited entry point for their subcultural surfing and, as such, it played a role in structuring their virtual journeys. In spite of offering considerable choice for those willing to investigate for long enough, the way in which the content was organized encouraged the pursuit of particular routes and therefore contributed to internal subcultural coherence.

Goth discussion facilities also tended to play the role of nodal points in the subnetwork, containing a variety of hyperlinks – this time in the content of messages posted directly by users. *Slashgoth* (accessed 1999–2002), a Web-based participatory 'news' facility housed on the *Darkwave* server, had become an important example for British goths, as had the longer established Usenet group *uk.people. gothic*. Such resources, in a more interactive and, hence, less structured fashion than centrally produced or filtered pages of links, allowed users themselves directly to advertise their own and other people's sites to a large number of subcultural readers. Nevertheless, it is worth emphasizing that while some sites were mentioned only in one-off occasional advertisements from an individual producer, others were referred and linked to repeatedly by a variety of subscribers – something that reintroduced an element of predictability through encouraging the pursuit of established popular routes.

Most significantly, perhaps, accessing Web sites having been prompted by links posted on subcultural discussion groups, as with doing so via the other methods described, implies a clear prior involvement and interest. Although hard to prove beyond doubt with empirical evidence, simple logic would suggest that, as a result of the clustering of hyperlinks, their organization around nodal points and the more general need on the Internet for users to select their own destination, goth Web sites and discussion groups were relatively exclusive subcultural spaces. Rather than encouraging goths to dilute their subcultural commitment and involve themselves more in other kinds of affiliation, the Internet effectively placed them next to one another on the net, enabling and encouraging them to intensify their subcultural knowledge, friendships and commitment, at the same time as insulating them from outsiders in a way every bit as effective as the pubs and clubs they frequented (see Hodkinson 2002: 85-108).

Defending Boundaries

Thus far we have discussed the ways in which the workings of the Internet and the linkages between subcultural sites seemed to encourage coherent subcultural use of the net by insiders and to mitigate against accidental discovery of the subnetwork by outsiders. But this is not to say that there was no chance whatever of individuals without prior interest coming across the occasional link to goth material on the net. Keywords shared with other cultures, such as 'clothes' or 'music', for example, might sometimes bring them into the results of Web searches. Goth sites were also occasionally linked to from non-goth sites as a result of elements of their content that cross-cut with the interests of other groups. The Web site of one of my interviewees, while unambiguously oriented to the goth scene, contained a poetry section that he had advertised on general literature Web sites outside the subculture:

> It's obvious that the goth stuff is going to be hit by goths, but I know that the poetry stuff has got hit by . . . just people searching for poetry would find it because I posted it around the web on a few places. (Phil)

However, in those relatively unusual circumstances whereby links to goth Web sites or discussion groups were 'stumbled upon' in this way, the chances of an individual without an initial interest deciding to investigate their contents also seem somewhat slim. The author of the Web site mentioned above felt that non-goths who had reached his material via poetry sites were fairly unlikely to spend much time or thought engaging with the majority of his overtly subcultural Web site:

> But then again, how many people are going to actually bother to read it . . . someone could follow a link about poetry . . . and suddenly think 'shite, it's a bloke that wears make-up – ahhhhh – run away!!'(Phil)

The likelihood of significant investigation of subcultural material through curiosity was perhaps even lower in the case of goth discussion groups, whose highly specialist status tended to be immediately and unambiguously denoted by titles such as *uk.people.gothic*, *Lexgoth* and *Slashgoth*.

Furthermore, the content of the interactions within goth discussion groups provided a second line of boundary defence. In a manner possibly more concentrated than has been identified on Usenet discussion groups by Baym (1995, 1997, 1998) and Watson (1997), the specialist and exclusive nature of discussions and a distinct normative environment made goth forums far from ideal for cultural 'ski-jumping'. A highly committed learning process was necessary in order effectively to participate, something liable to induce a hasty exit on the part of those unprepared to exert such effort. In contrast to suggestions discussed earlier that 'virtual communities' are characterized by cultural fluidity, the relative stability of goth discussion groups tended to be protected by internal normative pressures and external boundaries of exclusion. While in some ways the discussions were fairly diverse in subject matter, effective participation required sophisticated knowledge and experience about what kinds of opinions, topics and forms of behaviour were liable to be deemed worthwhile or acceptable by other subscribers. Furthermore, far from being dominated by anonymity and the invention of online selves, it tended to be obvious on goth discussion groups that many existing subscribers had got to know one another face-to-face as well as online – something that further enhanced the exclusive atmosphere. Until 'newbies' had demonstrated a degree of insider status, through successful interaction with other subscribers, they were liable to be treated with caution and suspicion. 'Inappropriate' posting by the subculturally naïve often resulted in their being completely ignored, and in some cases it even provoked what McLaughlin and colleagues have termed 'conduct-correcting episodes' – including aggressive rebuttals from other subscribers (McLaughlin *et al.* 1995: 95). While the substantive and distinctive nature of the subculture of which they were a part may have made their normative environments particularly strict, goth discussion groups were far from alone in generating and protecting a distinctive environment. According to Baym, forums of various kinds 'create unique normative standards' and 'continually reinforce the norms by creating structural and social sanctions against those who abuse the groups' systems of meaning' (Baym 1998: 60).

The notion of individuals effortlessly moving into and out of lifestyle groupings seems inconsistent with the need, in order to feel accepted, to gain such levels of subject-specific knowledge, group-specific etiquette and acquaintance with other subscribers. The considerable effort and commitment needed from would-be recruits suggests that only those with the most substantive interest would wish to persevere long enough to successfully cross the boundaries of goth discussion groups. It also invites the conclusion that having made such an effort and finally gained the rewards associated with being an insider, such individuals would tend to be motivated to remain involved rather than to move swiftly on. Here too, then, we demonstrate the potential for Internet technology to allow the enforcement and maintenance of (sub)cultural boundaries, rather than their disintegration.

Linking Online and Offline Goth

Thus far we have illustrated the ways in which the workings of the Internet functioned to enable goth Web sites, discussion facilities and their users to operate relatively independently from those facilities and users on the Internet that lay outside the remit of the subculture. In respect of the reinforcement of subcultural boundaries by the Internet, however, the links which joined goth online facilities with one another were no more important than the equally extensive if less instant-aneous 'links' between this online subnetwork and the predominantly offline world of goth events, music and style. In the form of information and influence, such online to offline links demonstrated that, rather than connecting goths with the rest of society in a singular 'virtual culture', the Internet's most important function tended to be as an enhancer and concentrator of their existing 'real life' subcultural participation. By way of example, the following respondent emphasized that the Internet was invaluable for finding out about goth events and, in the process, meeting other goths face to face.

> I see the net as a means to an end, and I suspect that most people feel the same . . . the net is a very good source for finding out what's going on where, and . . . I've certainly used it a great deal in that way. In fact, that's probably how I've met many of the people that I now know . . . (Richard)

Through reading discussion group threads and accessing relevant Web pages, one could obtain details not just of forthcoming goth events, but also bands, CD releases, specialist retailers of music and clothing and printed subcultural fanzines. Whether or not the initial destination of such 'links' was an online outlet, the eventual result was often to enhance offline involvement, whether in the form of ownership of consumables, or attendance at gigs and clubs. Although some Web sites contained only limited and somewhat out-of-date information, others had developed particular reputations for the range and reliability of their information.

In addition to its database of links to other online locations, the *Net.Goth* pages on the *Darkwave* server contained extensive information about the goth scene off the net. For example, it contained a translocal listing of goth or 'goth-friendly' events taking place across Britain in the coming months, viewable in linear or calendar form (*Net.Goth Events Page*, accessed 2002). The site also contained a more expansive and specialist resource known as the *Net.Goth Map*, which consisted of a map of Britain and Ireland, split into different regions (*Net.Goth Map*, accessed 2001–2). Clicking on any of the regions resulted in a screen full of information about goth-friendly pubs, clubs, shops and individual participants in that area. While much of the information originated from users of the site, subcultural boundaries of acceptability, as with the *Net.Goth Links Page*, were protected by filtering and moderation. As well as being a valuable local resource for goths residing in the area in question, the region-specific pages of the map enhanced the ability of individuals to take part in the goth scene in areas outside their own.

In spite of the highly reputed accuracy of high profile Web sites such as those housed by *Darkwave*, newsgroups and email lists were often the most important online source of information about the goth scene. Event promoters, bands, record labels or retailers themselves frequently made announcements at appropriate times to an already subscribed specialist audience. The advantage this means of promotion had over Web sites was that the large group of subscribers would be guaranteed to see the message as soon as they collected their mail or read their newsgroups – there was no need to rely upon people taking the proactive decision to visit a Web site. Discussion groups also constituted a useful link to the offline goth scene, from the point of view of participants, because it was possible specifically to ask questions and request information – something that invariably resulted in a positive reply. By way of illustration I reproduce below a reply posted in response to a specific request for information about goth clubs in the city of Plymouth made on the Usenet group, *uk.people.gothic*:

Subject: Re: Plymouth
> Anything going on there, or nearby, this Sunday or Monday night?

There is the well cool Goth night at Charlies on a Monday night 10 till 2 quid to get in, Charlies is in the city centre, the good companion isn't a bad pub to go in before hand usually with a live band (North, *uk.people.gothic*, 1999).

The interactive conversations on discussion groups also tended to generate a collective enthusiasm about events, bands or products. The respondent below suggested that a goth event held in Sheffield in the late 1990s gained a significant amount of its translocal clientele as a result of a individuals picking up a sense, from reading newsgroup conversations, that lots of others were going to make the trip:

The first time people went was because everyone else who they knew on-line was raving about it – it's this thing that people want to get together, and Epitaph . . . was an ideal thing for this. (Jamie)

As well as increasing social enthusiasm in general terms, online communications often helped to cement individuals to the subculture through establishing and maintaining specific social bonds and friendships. In this respect, using the net as a means to establishing an offline social life was often more important than friendships which were exclusively 'virtual'. The following respondent, for example, explained that he regarded the Internet as a valuable 'ice-breaker' that enabled shy individuals such as himself to get to know people a little via the Internet prior to meeting up face-to-face:

> It's a lot easier to make friends (the first time) on the net than it is in real life. At least it is for me. I don't find it easy to meet and mix with people in real life (Richard).

Establishing new offline friends and keeping in contact with existing ones, then, was another example of the ways in which online subcultural resources were linked together with the 'real life' goth scene, off the screen. The relationship between the Internet and subcultural friendships was particularly important as it functioned to provide participants with social incentives to keep returning to the same online subcultural forums *and* to regularly go to real life goth events that would be attended by fellow subscribers.

In addition to their role in facilitating social participation in the goth scene, *Darkwave* and many of the sites it linked to, served to construct the distinctive values and tastes of the subculture. In so doing, they helped prevent possible excessive growth in the breadth of interpretations from leading to the complete breakup of goth. Construction of stylistic boundaries on the Web took place in various ways, from the photographs individuals posted of themselves on homepages to the kinds of music recommended by e-zines, to the definitions of goth offered by those who produced and maintained high-profile 'frequently asked questions' sites about the subculture.[1] While there remained some room for differential versions of the goth scene's style, roots, history and *raison d'être*, there was a remarkable amount of consistency in the styles and definitions exhibited. The fact that such resources were liable to be accessed by a translocal audience meant that they played a particular role in maintaining the consistency of the distinctive goth style from place to place. In particular, nodes such *Darkwave* enhanced the coherence and stability of the goth scene as a result of clear and high profile subcultural status and due to the way in which content was filtered for suitability by gatekeepers. Whether or not it was the intention, such sites played a particularly important role in reinforcing the boundaries between the subculture and external society.

In the same way, then, that the organization of online-to-online hyperlinks connecting goth Web sites functioned to cement rather than to dissolve boundaries,

---

1. Examples of goth frequently-asked-questions sites included the *uk.people.gothic FAQ* (accessed 2000) and the *alt.gothic FAQ* (accessed 2000).

the online to offline links discussed here tended to enhance collective distinctiveness, as well as to facilitate and encourage the participation of existing participants, rather than to expose goth events, music or fashion to the outside world. The Internet provided practical information and resources, helped maintain a consistent and distinctive set of norms and offered social incentives for individuals to take an active part in the subculture. As well as demonstrating the capacity of online communications to strengthen subcultural involvement rather than to induce cultural ephemerality, this demonstrates a more general point, recently emphasized by Castells (2001: 118), that online communications are more frequently used as an extension of 'life as it is' than as tools for explorative identity building and the continual living out of personal fantasies (also see Castells 2002: 393; Baym 1998: 55). Rather than replacing existing interests and affiliations, the Internet often allows individuals to pursue them in greater depth.

Conclusion

It is not the intention of this chapter to suggest that notions of fluidity and multiplicity of identity are incompatible with the technological attributes of the Internet. The potential for anonymity and the ability instantly to gain contact with a diversity of lifestyle groupings may enhance possibilities for identity experimentation for those wishing to use the medium for such purposes. Meanwhile, the possibilities on the Internet to participate simultaneously in several different lifestyles may make it a highly valuable resource for those whose identities are already split relatively equally between a variety of interests and concerns. What the medium seems to have less capacity to do, however, is *either* to broaden the horizons of those already committed to a particular subcultural grouping *or* significantly to open up the boundaries of such a distinct grouping to an influx of fickle outsiders. On the contrary, the way in which specialist materials can be interlinked into relatively discrete subnetworks functions to bring together those motivated enough to find them, without inducing significant exposure to the rest of virtual culture. Depending upon circumstance and context, then, the Internet may be every bit as effective in the reinforcement of subcultural boundaries as in their dissolution.

References

Bauman, Z. (1992a), *Intimations of Postmodernity*, London: Routledge.
Bauman, Z. (1992b), 'Survival as a Social Construct', *Theory, Culture and Society*, 9 (1): 1–36.

Baym, N. (1995), 'The Emergence of Community in Computer Mediated Communication', in S. Jones (ed.), *Cybersociety: Computer Mediated Communication and Community*, London: Sage.

Baym, N. (1997), 'Interpreting Soap Operas and Creating Community: Inside an Electronic Fan Culture', in S. Kiesler (ed.), *Culture of the Internet*, New Jersey: Lawrence Erlbaum Associates.

Baym, N. (1998), 'The Emergence of On-Line Community', in S. Jones (ed.), *Cybersociety 2.0: Revisiting Computer Mediated Communication and Community*, London: Sage.

Bennett, A. (1999), 'Subcultures or Neo-Tribes? Rethinking the Relationship Between Youth, Style and Musical Taste', *Sociology* 33 (3): 599–617.

Castells, M. (2001), *The Internet Galaxy: Reflections on the Internet, Business and Society*, Oxford: Oxford University Press.

Castells, M. (2002), *The Rise of the Network Society*, 2 edn, Oxford: Blackwell.

Diani, M. (2001), 'Social Movement Networks: Virtual and Real', in F. Webster (ed.), *Culture and Politics in the Information Age: A New Politics?* London: Routledge.

Hill, K. and Hughes, J. (1998), *Cyberpolitics: Citizen Activism in the Age of the Internet*, Oxford: Rowman & Littlefield.

Hodkinson, P. (2002), *Goth. Identity, Style and Subculture*, Oxford: Berg.

Leonard, M. (1998), 'Paper Planes: Travelling the New Grrrl Geographies', in T.Skelton and G. Valentine (eds), *Cool Places: Geographies of Youth Cultures*, London: Routledge.

Maffesoli, M. (1996), *The Time of the Tribes: The Decline of Individualism in Mass Society*, London: Sage.

McLaughlin, M., Osborne, K. and Smith, C. (1995), 'Standards of Conduct on Usenet', in S. Jones (ed.), *Cybersociety: Computer Mediated Communication and Community*, London: Sage.

Muggleton, D. (1997), 'The Post-Subculturalist', in S. Redhead, D. Wynne and J, O'Connor (eds), *The Clubcultures Reader: Readings in Popular Cultural Studies*, Oxford: Blackwell.

Muggleton, D. (2000), *Inside Subculture. The Postmodern Meaning of Style*, Oxford: Berg.

Poster, M. (1995), *The Second Media Age*, Cambridge: Polity Press.

Turkle, S. (1995), *Life on the Screen: Identity in the Age of the Internet*, London: Phoenix.

Watson, N. (1997), 'Why We Argue About Virtual Community: A Case Study of the Phish.Net Fan Community', in S. Jones (ed.), *Virtual Culture: Internet and Communication in Cybersociety*, London: Sage.

Wellman, B. and Gulia, M. (1999), 'Virtual Communities as Communities: Surfers Don't Ride Alone', in M. Smith and P. Kollock (eds), *Communities in Cyberspace*, London: Routledge.

Web Site References

alt.gothic FAQ (accessed 2000), http://www.Darkwave.org.uk/faq/ag
Darkwave main page (accessed 2002), http://www.Darkwave.org.uk
Net.goth Links Page (accessed 1999-2002), http://www.netgoth.org.uk/links
Net.goth Map (accessed 2001-2002), http://www.netgoth.org.uk/gothmap
Slashgoth (accessed 2002), http://slashgoth.org/
Events Page (accessed 2002), http://www.netgoth.org.uk/events
uk.people.gothic FAQ (accessed 2000), http://www.Darkwave.org.uk/faq/ukpg

Discussion Group References

North, M. (January 1999), 'Re: Plymouth', *uk.people.gothic*.

−20−

Internet Subcultures and Oppositional Politics

Richard Kahn and Douglas Kellner

Subcultures traditionally represent alternative cultures and practices to the dominant culture of the status quo. They are often to be found acting within the governing culture from which they are born, but their comparatively smaller population size, their associations with emergent youth culture and the cultural novelties of the day, and their occasionally politically resistant and activist temperaments all serve to ensure that subcultures are constructed so as to be more than mere reproductions of the grander cultural forms, themes, and practices. If the dominant culture provides the semantic codes by which cultures attempt to transmit and reproduce themselves then subcultures represent a challenge to this symbolic order in their attempt to institute new grammars and meanings through which they interpret the world, and new practices through which they transform it. In this sense, alternative subcultures strive to capture media attention, and in so doing become involved in the Janus-faced process of attempting to transform dominant codes even as they become appropriated, commodified, and redefined by the dominant culture that they contest.

Our present moment, however, is far from simply traditional and is better characterized as a 'post-modern adventure' in which traditional forms of culture and politics are being resurrected, imploded into and combined with entirely new cultural and political modes in a global media culture that is becoming increasingly dominated by the corporate forces of science, technology, and capital (see Best and Kellner 2001). To speak of post-subcultures, then, is to recognize that the new emerging subcultures are taking place in a world that is saturated with media awareness and being propelled into new global configurations by technological advances such as the Internet and multi-media.

Thus, whereas many traditional subcultures, like the Beat Generation, could aspire to the spirituality of 'immediate' experience and intimate face-to-face communal relations, this is increasingly difficult for the post-subculture generation. Instead, the new subcultures that are arising around the evolving Internet appear as wholly mediated and committed to the medium of network communication that they correctly recognize as their foundation.

However, as with previous generations of subcultures, Internet subcultures are desirous of a certain immediacy of experience that seeks to circumvent dominant codes in the attempt to access a wealth of global information quickly and directly, as well as an immediacy in the production and transmission of the same. The new subcultural immediacy, then, centres around flows of information, and post-subcultures can be seen to be using the Internet as an environment that supports their attempts to gain and provide access to information that exists beyond the means of control of the dominant media culture. In other words, there is reason to believe that subcultures associated with the Internet are involved in the revolutionary circulation and democratization of information and culture. In as much as this information is also part of the media process by which people come to identify and define themselves, the new mediated post-subcultures are also involved in the attempt to allow people the freedom to redefine and construct themselves around the kind of alternative cultural forms, experiences, and practices which radical deployments of the Internet afford (see Witheford-Dyer 2001; Best and Kellner 2001).

The Evolving Subcultures of the Emerging Online Global Network

While there are a plethora of alternative cultures at work on the Internet today, it would, of course, be a mistake to categorize them all as concerned strictly with either democracy or progressive politics. Rather, akin to the complexity of the post-modern era at hand, the subcultures of the Internet would be better represented as multiplicitous, with the Internet being used for both progressive and reactionary causes by an abundance of groups whose politics range from the far left to the far right.

Indeed, while the overall tenor of the revolution that is being brought about by the Internet is toward the proliferation of new information and forms of culture and subjectivity, many voices affiliated with both hate and violence have also found ready homes amidst the new technology. The Internet allows a myriad of groups to propagate and propagandize for their cause outside the media and norms traditionally instituted by pre-Internet society. Our point here is certainly not to valorize the gains made by such subcultural groups but rather to note that the use of the Internet as a media tool has allowed for the construction of a wide variety of non-mainstream identities and communicative practices. Much like the hyper-textual nature of the Web itself, the identities of Internet subcultures are often hybridic and complex themselves, revealing a tendency to evolve through constant reorganization and affiliation with other Internet subcultural groups. In this sense, many post-subcultures of the Internet can be seen as dissolving classical cultural and political boundaries that appear too rigid and ideological for Internet life. Still, groups also exist that have clearly defined political orientations.

At work within all of these Internet subcultures is also the question of how they stand in relation to the dominant culture. During the late 1980s, major Internet subcultures such as BBS (bulletin board systems) hubs represented the leading edge of the technology fringe. Populated mostly by an underground network of technically sophisticated professional users and computer literate youth, the bulletin boards proffered a veritable 'gift economy' of pictures, simple games, and message boards over extremely slow networks. There was little or no discussion of service charges and most BBSs relied upon users to develop online reputations through which proven community service would garnish greater access from friendly SYSOPs (system operators). With the advent of the 1990s, many success-ful bulletin boards, such as The Well, transferred protocols onto the emerging World Wide Web of hypertext. Within only a few years, corporate and government culture would begin colonizing the Web too, and by the time of the dot-bomb tech crash of 2000, early Web pioneers such as Yahoo!, Amazon, and NCSA (National Center for Supercomputing Applications), would be joined by a huge influx of companies selling everything from advertising to zoo animals.

As the Internet went corporate and online service providers like America Online (AOL), Compuserve, Prodigy and Earthlink sought to brand and sell the Internet experience, many subcultures formed around the new online corporate behaviours with service providers becoming a key to one's online and offline identity. Histor-ically, similar subcultures had formed around hardware computer manufacturers like Apple, Kaypro, and IBM, but during the 1990s factions erupted within comp-uters as well over software domains such as Web browsers (Microsoft versus Netscape) and search engines (Yahoo! versus Alta Vista). Still, the strongest user bonds seem to have solidified around service providers, with AOL providing a sort of cultural benchmark for the movement. During this time of relative infancy for the Internet, AOL helped to bring millions of new Internet users online with its graphical user interface (GUI), 'you've got mail' aesthetic, and limitless user chat-rooms wherein people could find love, local gossip, trans-sexual vampires and anything else available to the user's imagination!

However, behind the corporate branding and growing of the Internet during the 1990s, non-corporate subcultures thrived too. Multi-user Dungeons (MUDs) and their relatives, the MOOs, sprung up along side the WWW, allowing people to explore basic virtual environments and interact with one another in real time. Newsgroups became a rage and an important source of information, debate, and file sharing, as people freely formed topical groups on the Internet's Usenet platform. Then, as emailing grew readily popular, an equally large number of listserves became housed upon the Web and available for free user subscription. Large, popular listserves like Nettime-L, or the Spoon lists housed at University of Virginia, allowed a variety of diverse subcultures to form themselves through group email discussions and opinion postings. And eventually, the WWW itself, though rapidly transforming under the 'tech revolution's' pay-to-play capitalist ideology into a mainstream cultural movement, continued to support a veritable carnival of alternative voices and cultures as well. Far beyond the provocative Web antics of Church of the Subgenius or Terence McKenna, the late 1990s revealed a Web that people were actively helping to create and not simply experience.[1]

The rise of the Internet, then, as cultural and subcultural force, has been multi-faceted, and socially and politically complex. While corporate forces rapidly built a larger and speedier Internet for the new millennium, subcultural forces equally rapidly sought to borrow the new online environment for their own socio-political intentions. Thus was the case, infamously, with the peer-to-peer (P2P) client Napster, which allowed approximately sixty million users at one point to share and trade a variety of files directly with one another freely. However, when users began sharing large volumes of copyrighted audio material, because the newly formed broadband networks made such files easily accessible, corporate forces intervened and fractured the movement. Yet a movement had been started that publicized the utopian potential of the Internet as subcultural community and bearer of a gift economy. Hence, despite Napster's fall, many continued to believe that the idea of the P2P network signalled a form of cultural revolution and a number of new P2P communities arose within the Internet space previously dominated by Napster.[2]

The music industry, however, has made every attempt to block P2P trading of music online and there is now intense interest in Hollywood's response to circulating videos and films. Less maliciously, but equally exemplary of how mainstream corporate culture has resituated subcultural movements on the Internet, is the case of early online 'zines like *Suck*, *Feed*, and *Salon*. As these online cultural spaces grew in popularity, corporate culture was quick to import and copy elements of their style and reinterpret and reposition them. Suddenly, the trendy use of neon colours like *Feed*'s orange became an industry standard, which, as tech became 'cool', lent itself equally as well to sneakers, clothing and record posters as it had to Web sites. Further elements of zine style such as written and visual language became equally replicated and repositioned as advertising norms. Under such intense corporate pressure many of the successful online zines of the past decade have folded, unable to demonstrate or innovate a particular cultural niche in the face of countless impostors. Even the widely read and discussed *Salon* was rumoured to face the possibility of insolvency in 2002, and only Microsoft's online journal *Slate* appears financially secure.

---

1. On MOOs, MUDs, Internet chat rooms, and new forms of identity, culture, and community produced by new technologies, see Turkle (1996, 1997).

2. For a solid journalistic account of the Napster and P2P story see Alderman (2001); for an optimistic account of the continuing potential of P2P potentiality, see Barbrook (2002).

Globalization and Internet Politics

The present Internet moment remains a complex assemblage of a variety of groups and movements, both mainstream and oppositional. However, following the massive hi-tech sector bust at the start of the new millennium, and with economic sectors generally down across the board with the global economic recession and the Terror War erupting in 2001, much of the corporate colonization of the new media has also waned. Following '9/11', however, the politicization of the Internet again emerged as a major cultural issue and new oppositions are forming around the online rights to freedom of use and information, as well as user privacy, that groups like the Electronic Frontier Foundation (EFF), Computer Professionals for Social Responsibility (CPSR), and the Center for Democracy and Technology (CDT) have long touted. Such online political oppositions directly pit post-subcultural groups, many that did not previously have an obvious political agenda, against the security policies of government. In this scenario, Internet corporations are often left 'in the middle' with the choice to either side with the users whom they would court as consumers or with the political administrations. The latter are capable of making business either easy or difficult depending upon which laws are enacted and prosecuted (for example, Microsoft's anti-trust battle under the Clinton administration and then again under Bush).

Still, as the culture of the Internet becomes more highly politicized, it is becoming harder for corporations to portray themselves simply as 'neutral' cultural forces. Using the very online means that these corporations helped to popularize against them, users are globally beginning to portray for each other a maturing political awareness that perceives corporate and governmental behaviour as intertwined in the name of 'globalization'.[3] As part of the backlash against globalization over the past years, a wide range of theorists have argued that the proliferation of difference and the shift to more local discourses and practices define significant alternatives to corporate globalization. In this view, theory and politics should shift from the level of globalization and its accompanying often totalizing and macro dimensions in order to focus on the local, the specific, the particular, the heterogeneous, and the micro level of everyday experience. An array of discourses associated with post-structuralism, post-modernism, feminism, and multiculturalism focus on differ-ence, otherness, marginality, the personal, the particular, and the concrete over more general theory and politics that aim at more global or universal conditions.[4]

3. On globalization, see Cvetkovich and Kellner (1997), Best and Kellner (2001), and Kellner (1998, forthcoming).

4. Such positions are associated with the post-modern theories of Foucault, Lyotard, Rorty, and have been taken up by a wide range of feminists, multiculturalists, and others. On these theorists and post-modern politics, see Best and Kellner (1991, 1997, 2001), and the valorization and critique of post-modern politics in Hardt and Negri (2000) and Burbach (2001).

Likewise, a broad spectrum of Internet subcultures of resistance have focused their attention on the local level, organizing struggles around identity issues such as gender, race, sexual preference, or youth subculture.

However, it can be argued that such dichotomies as those between the global and the local express contradictions and tensions between crucial constitutive forces of the present moment, and that it is therefore a mistake to reject a focus on one side in favour of an exclusive concern with the other (Cvetkovich and Kellner 1997). Hence, an important challenge for the emerging critical theory of globalization is to think through the relationships between the global and the local by observing how global forces influence and even structure an increasing number of local situations. This requires analysis as well of how local forces mediate the global, inflecting global forces to diverse ends and conditions, and producing unique configurations of the local and the global as the matrix for thought and action in the contemporary world (see Luke and Luke 2000).

Globalization is thus necessarily complex and challenging to both critical theories and radical democratic politics. But many people these days operate with binary concepts of the global and the local, and promote one or the other side of the equation as the solution to the world's problems. For globalists, globalization is the solution, and underdevelopment, backwardness and provincialism are the problem. For localists, globalization is the problem and localization is the solution. But, less simplistically, it is the mix that matters, and whether global or local solutions are most fitting depends on the conditions in the distinctive context that one is addressing and the specific solutions and policies being proposed.

Specific locations and practices of a plurality of post-subcultures constitute perhaps what is most interesting now about oppositional subcultural activities at work within the Internet. Much more than other subcultures like boarders, punks, mods, or followers of the New Age, Internet subcultures have taken up the questions of local and global politics and are attempting to construct answers both locally and globally as a response. Importantly, this can be done due to the very nature of the medium in which they exist. Therefore, while the Internet can and has been used to promote capitalist globalization, the current configuration of online subcultures are interested in the number of ways in which the global network can be diverted and used in the struggle against it.

Technopolitics and the Anti-globalization Movements[5]

One of the more instructive examples of the use of the Internet to foster movements against the excesses of corporate capitalism occurred in the protests in Seattle and throughout the world against the World Trade Organization (WTO) meeting in

---

5. On technopolitics see Kellner (1997) and Armitage (1999).

December 1999. Behind these actions was a global protest movement using the Internet to organize resistance to the WTO and capitalist globalization, while championing democratization. Many Web sites contained anti-WTO material and numerous mailing lists used the Internet to distribute critical material and to organize the protest. The result was the mobilization of caravans from throughout the US to take protestors to Seattle, many of whom had never met and were recruited through the Internet. There were also significant numbers of international participants in Seattle, which exhibited labour, environmentalist, feminist, anti-capitalist, animal rights, anarchist, and other groups organized to protest aspects of globalization and form new solidarities for future struggles. In addition, protests occurred throughout the world, and a proliferation of anti-WTO material against the extremely secret group spread throughout the Internet.

Furthermore, the Internet provided critical coverage of the event, document-ation of the various groups' protests, and debate over the WTO and globalization. Whereas the mainstream media presented the protests as 'anti-trade', featured the incidents of anarchist violence against property, while minimizing police violence against demonstrators, the Internet provided pictures, eyewitness accounts, and reports of police brutality and the generally peaceful and non-violent nature of the protests. While the mainstream media framed the protests negatively and privil-eged suspect spokespeople like Patrick Buchanan as critics of globalization, the Internet provided multiple representations of the demonstrations, advanced re-flective discussion of the WTO and globalization, and presented a diversity of critical perspectives.

The Seattle protests had some immediate consequences. The day after the demonstrators made good on their promise to shut down the WTO negotiations, Bill Clinton gave a speech endorsing the concept of labour rights enforceable by trade sanctions, thus effectively making impossible any agreement and consensus during the Seattle meetings. In addition, at the World Economic Forum in Davos a month later there was much discussion of how concessions were necessary on labour and the environment if consensus over globalization and free trade were to be possible. Importantly, the issue of overcoming divisions between the infor-mation rich and poor, and improving the lot of the disenfranchized and oppressed, bringing these groups the benefits of globalization, were also seriously discussed at the meeting and in the media.

More importantly, many activists were energized by the new alliances, solid-arities, and militancy, and continued to cultivate an anti-globalization movement. The Seattle demonstrations were followed by April 2000 struggles in Washington DC, to protest against the World Bank and IMF, and later in the year against capitalist globalization in Prague and Melbourne; in April 2001, an extremely large and militant protest erupted against the Free Trade Area of the Americas summit in Quebec City and in summer 2001 a large demonstration took place in Genoa.

In May 2002, a surprisingly large demonstration took place in Washington against capitalist globalization and for peace and justice, and it was apparent that a new worldwide movement was in the making that was uniting diverse opponents of capitalist globalization throughout the world. The anti-corporate globalization movement favoured globalization-from-below, which would protect the environment, labour rights, national cultures, democratization, and other goods from the ravages of an uncontrolled capitalist globalization (see Brecher, Costello and Smith 2000; Steger 2002). Similar demonstrations had taken place in Monterrey, Mexico two months earlier and, more recently, two more occurred during June 2002 at Calgary and Ottawa to protest against the G8 Summit meeting in Canada. Each of these demonstrations was comprised of people hailing from many locations and intent on using the venue as an opportunity to promote their voice, and fight in common cause against what is perceived to be the oppression of a dominant mono-culture.

Initially, the incipient anti-globalization movement was precisely that: anti-globalization. The movement itself, however, was increasingly global, was linking together a diversity of movements into global solidarity networks, and was using the Internet and instruments of globalization to advance its struggles. Following the Battle for Seattle, the Internet witnessed the rise of the Indymedia network, with major global cities receiving Web portals in which to document, organize and proliferate information that would not otherwise be readily available through the major media. Countless other organizations and sites have developed similar Web sites and networks since, turning the Internet from a valuable tool in the anti-globalization struggle into the driving engine for a new global cultural vision.

Through the practice of the type of large-scale organization and assimilation of information afforded by the Internet, many opponents of capitalist globalization evolved from a simple subcultural nihilism to recognize the need for a global movement with a positive vision. Such alternative and oppositional globalizations stand for such things as social justice, equality, labour, civil liberties, universal human rights, and a healthy planet on which to live. Accordingly, the anti-capitalist globalization movements began advocating common values and visions, and started defining themselves in positive terms such as the social justice movement.

Thus, technopolitics became part and parcel of the involvement of Internet subcultures, a mushrooming global movement for peace, justice, democracy, rights, and other positive values. In particular, the subcultural movement against capitalist globalization used the Internet to organize mass demonstrations and to disseminate information to the world concerning the policies of the institutions of capitalist globalization. The events made clear that protestors were not against globalization *per se*, but were against neo-liberal and capitalist globalization, opposing specific policies and institutions that produce intensified exploitation of labour, environmental devastation, growing divisions among the social classes and the undermining of democracy. The emerging anti-globalization-from-below movements are contextualizing these problems in the framework of a restructuring of capitalism on a worldwide basis for maximum profit with zero accountability and have made clear the need for democratization, regulation, rules, and globalization in the interests of people and not profit.

The new movements against capitalist globalization have thus placed the issues of global justice and environmental destruction squarely in the centre of important political concerns of our time. Hence, whereas the mainstream media had failed to debate vigorously or even report on globalization until the eruption of a vigorous anti-globalization movement, and rarely, if ever, critically discussed the activities of the WTO, World Bank and IMF, there is now a widely circulating critical discourse and controversy over these institutions. Stung by criticisms, representatives of the World Bank, in particular, are pledging reform and pressures are mounting concerning proper and improper roles for the major global institutions, highlighting their limitations and deficiencies, and the need for reforms like debt relief from overburdened developing countries to solve some of their fiscal and social problems. Nonetheless, others like the world leaders involved in the G8 and related summits are resorting to hold their meetings in ever more remote regions, their inaccessibility thereby conveying a political reality that new subcultures are eager to reveal to ever-wider audiences.

From Hackers to Terrorists: Militant Internet Culture

To capital's globalization-from-above, the subcultures of cyberactivists have thus been attempting to carry out globalization-from-below, developing networks of solidarity and propagating oppositional ideas and movements throughout the planet. To the capitalist international of transnational corporate-led globalization, a Fifth International, to use Waterman's phrase (1992), of computer-mediated activism is emerging, that is qualitatively different from the party-based socialist and communist Internationals. Such networking links labour, feminist, ecological, peace, and other anti-capitalist groups, providing the basis for a new politics of alliance and solidarity to overcome the limitations of post-modern identity politics (see Dyer-Witheford 1999; Best and Kellner 2001; Burbach 2001).

Of course, as noted previously, right-wing and reactionary forces can and have used the Internet to promote their political agendas as well. In a short time, one can easily access an exotic witch's brew of Web sites maintained by the Ku Klux Klan, and myriad neo-Nazi assemblages, including the Aryan Nation and various militia groups. Internet discussion lists also disperse these views and right-wing extremists are aggressively active on many computer forums, as well as radio programs and stations, public access television programs, fax campaigns, video and even rock music productions. These organizations are hardly harmless, having carried out terrorism of various sorts extending from church burnings to the bombings of public buildings. Adopting quasi-Leninist discourse and tactics for ultra-right causes, these groups have been successful in recruiting working-class members devastated by the developments of global capitalism, which has resulted in widespread unemployment for traditional forms of industrial, agricultural, and unskilled labour. Moreover, extremist Web-sites have influenced alienated middle-class youth as well (a 1999 HBO documentary on 'Hate on the Internet' provides a disturbing number of examples of how extremist Web-sites influenced disaffected youth to commit hate crimes).

A recent twist in the saga of technopolitics, in fact, seems to be that allegedly 'terrorist' groups are now increasingly using the Internet and Web sites to promote their causes. An article in the *Los Angeles Times* (8 February 2001: A1, A14) reports that groups like Hamas use their Web site to post reports of acts of terror against Israel, rather than calling newspapers or broadcasting outlets. A wide range of groups labelled as 'terrorist' reportedly use email, listserves, and Web sites to further their struggles, causes including Hezbollah and Hamas, the Maoist group Shining Path in Peru, and a variety of other groups throughout Asia and elsewhere. The Tamil Tigers, for instance, a liberation movement in Sri Lanka, offers position papers, daily news, and a free email service. According to the *Los Angeles Times*, experts are still unclear 'whether the ability to communicate on-line worldwide is prompting an increase or a decrease in terrorist acts.'

Currently, there have been widespread discussions of how the bin Laden Al Qaeda network used the Internet to plan the September 11th terrorist attacks on the US, how the group's members communicated with each other, received funds and purchased airline tickets via the Internet, and used flight simulations to practice their hijacking (see Kellner 2002). Since 'Operation Enduring Freedom', news stories have documented how many pro-Al Qaeda Web sites continue to appear and disappear, serving as propaganda conduits and potential organization channels for remaining terrorist cell members. By encrypting messages within what appear to be simple Web pictures, Al Qaeda (or any group or person) can transfer sensitive information that only requires the receiving party to download the picture and then decrypt it in order to reveal the secret message. The sheer volume of video and still picture information on the Internet helps to ensure that the information can be circulated even when perused by such powerful governmental surveillance systems as Echelon and Carnivore. But, apparently in response to the threat posed to the US 'war on terror' interests, the Bush administration has begun the attempt to discontinue Web sites that it suspects terror cells are frequenting to gain information that could be used in terrorist attacks.

In fact, despite the expectation that any governmental administration would target the information channels of its enemy, it is exactly the mammoth reaction by the Bush administration and the Pentagon to the perceived threats posed by the Internet that have the subcultural forces associated with the battle against global-ization-from-above fighting in opposition to US security policies. Drawing upon the expertise of a subculture of politically minded computer hackers to inform oppositional groups of security threats and to help defend against them, a technical wing has become allied to those fighting for globalization-from-below. Groups like Cult of the Dead Cow and Cryptome and the hacker journal *2600* are figureheads for a broad movement of exceptionally computer literate individuals who group together under the banner of HOPE (Hackers On Planet Earth) and who practice a politics called 'hacktivism' (on hacker culture, see Himanen 2001). The hack-tivists have been widely responsible for allowing oppositional subcultures to understand how they may maintain online privacy and how their privacy may be easily jeopardized by anyone seeking to do so.

Additionally, hacktivists have been especially influential in educating the public about governmental and corporate protocols that have been developed in order to survey the habits and attitudes of those active online. Perhaps most importantly, some of the hacktivists are involved in creating open source software programs that can be used freely to circumvent the intervention of government and corporate control into Internet experience. Notably, and somewhat scandalously, the hack-tivists have released programs like Six/Four (after Tiananmen Square), that combines the peer-to-peer capabilities of Napster along with a virtual private networking protocol that makes user identity anonymous, and Camera/Shy, a powerful Web browser stenography application that allows anyone to engage in the type of secret information storage and retrieval that Al Qaeda allegedly uses to combat the Pentagon. Moreover, associated with the hacktivist cause are the 'crackers' who create 'warez', pirated versions of commercial software or passwords. While anathema to Bill Gates, there is no software beyond the reach of the pirate crackers and to the delight of the alternative Internet subculture, their often otherwise expensive programs are freely traded and shared over the Web and peer-to-peer networks across the globe.

Hacktivists are also directly involved in the immediate political battles being played out around the dynamically globalized world. Hacktivists like the German hacker, 'The Mixter', who authored the 'Tribe Floodnet' program that shut down the Web site for the World Economic Forum in January 2002, routinely use their hacking skills to cause disruption of governmental and corporate presences online. On 12 July 2002, the home page for the *USA Today* news site was hacked and altered content was presented to the public, leaving the *USA Today* to join such other media magnets as the *New York Times* and Yahoo! as the corporate victims of a media hack.

While a revolutionary subculture of hackers has formed online, those involved in the fight for an alternative globalization are far from comprising the totality of the hacker population. The US government and Al Qaeda, as well as an increasing number of different political groups, are all engaging in cyberwar as an important adjunct of their political battles. Indeed, Israeli hackers have repeatedly attacked the Web-sites of Hezbollah, while pro-Palestine hackers have reportedly placed militant demands and slogans on the Web-sites of Israel's army, foreign ministry, and parliament. Likewise, in the bloody struggle over Kashmir, Pakistani and Indian computer hackers have waged similar cyberbattles against opposing forces' Web sites, while rebel forces in the Philippines taunt government troops with cell-phone calls and messages and attack government Web sites as well.

Blogging: A Vision of the Democratic Future of the Internet?

On an entirely different note, but equally political and contested in nature, a vibrant new Internet subculture has erupted around the phenomenon of 'blogging'. A blog, tech slang for 'Web log', is an extension of the World Wide Web of hypertext pages. A blog differs from other Web pages, however, in certain key ways. Firstly, most blogs are created using a relatively easy-to-use automated software interface, provided freely (or for a small fee) by companies like Blogger or Radio Userland. Some blog subcultures like NetDiary, however, disdaining any tinge of capitalism, provide their own interface freely, but by invite only. Whichever is chosen, the interfaces load like any other Web page in a user's web browser, but provide a template for users to fill in with their blog's name, style, and features. Additionally, spaces for blog entries exist that incorporate all of the standard features associated with hypertext. When users fill in the information that they would like to post to their Web log and hit 'publish', the blog interface automatically formats and posts the user's information to the desired blog. This ease of use has made blogging a popular sensation in 2002, with hundreds of thousands of new bloggers con-structing blogs since April alone.[6]

Another feature relatively unique to blogs is their ability to integrate a variety of Internet features into their pages. Thus, a typical blog will not only provide postings from a blogger (or a team of bloggers) but it will also provide readers the opportunity to reply to postings and begin discussions with each other and the blog author(s) as would a messageboard. Blogs will also often permit users to subscribe to them, like a listserve, thereby allowing readers to receive new blog postings directly to their email address. Blogs, and bloggers, are also doing interesting things with the hyperlinks that link Web pages together. From the first, blogging

6. For examples, see our two Web sites: BlogLeft: Critical Interventions (2002), http://www.gseis. ucla.edu/courses/ed253a/blogger.php (accessed August 2002); Vegan Blog: The (Eco)Logical Weblog (2002), http://getvegan.com/blog/blogger.php (accessed August 2002).

has been about community, with bloggers eager to read one another's entries, post comments about them on their own blogs, and provide lists of links to the blog cartels that identify who particular bloggers think is 'who' in their blog world.

This has led to interesting networks of links, with dynamic maps of the most popular blogs and the news stories that these blogs discuss being provided in real-time by such sites as *Blogdex* (of MIT) and *Daypop.com*. Another result of bloggers' fascination with networks of links has been the subcultural phenomenon known as 'Google Bombing'. Documented in early 2002, it was revealed that the popular search engine Google had a special affinity for blogs because of its tendency to favour recently updated Web content in its site ranking system. With this in mind, bloggers began campaigns to get large numbers of fellow bloggers to post links to specific postings designed around desirable keywords that Google users would normally use to search. A successful Google Bomb would then rocket the initial blog that began the campaign up Google's rankings to No. 1!

Thus, while those in the blog culture often abused this trick for personal gain (for example, to get their own name and blog placed at the top of Google's most popular search terms), many in the blog subculture began using the Google Bomb as a tool for political subversion. Known as a 'justice bomb', this use of blogs serves to link a particularly distasteful corporation or entity to a series of keywords that either spoofs or criticizes the same. Hence, thanks to a Google Bomb, Google users typing in 'McDonald's' might very well get a blog link entitled 'Lies About Their Fries' as the top entry.

Blogs have not always been political, but post '9/11' the phenomenon of Warblogging appears to be trumping the simple diary format. More blogs than ever are being created to deal with specific political positions and alternative media sources than ever before and group-style blogs like Fark, Metafilter and Slashdot, wherein community users post and discuss information of the day, have become extremely popular. But, it is perhaps the new ability to syndicate one's blog that truly marks the blog subculture as a democratic and oppositional culture with which the mainstream must reckon. News blogs like Google, NewsIsFree, and Syndic8 daily log syndicated content and broadcast it globally to a diverse audience. This has resulted in a revolution in journalism in which subcultures of bloggers are continually posting and commenting upon news stories of particular interest to them, which are in turn found, read, and re-published by the global media.

The examples in this section suggest how technoculture makes possible a reconfiguring of politics, a refocusing of politics on everyday life, and the use of the tools and techniques of emergent computer and communication technologies to expand the field of politics and culture. In this conjuncture, the ideas of Guy Debord and the Situationist International are especially relevant with their stress on the construction of situations, the use of technology, media of communication, and cultural forms to promote a revolution of everyday life, and to increase the realm of freedom, community, and empowerment.[7] To a meaningful extent, then, the new technologies *are* revolutionary, they *do* constitute a revolution of everyday life being presently enacted by Internet subcultures. Yet, it has often been a revolution that also promotes and disseminates the capitalist consumer society, individual and competition, and that has involved new modes of fetishism, enslavement, and domination yet to be clearly perceived and theorized.

The Internet is thus a contested terrain, used by left, right, and centre of both dominant cultures and subcultures to promote their own agendas and interests. The political battles of the future may well be fought in the streets, factories, parliaments, and other sites of past struggle, but politics is already mediated by broadcast, computer, and information technologies and will increasingly be so in the future. Those interested in the politics and culture of the future should therefore be clear on the important role of the new public spheres and intervene accordingly, while critical cultural theorists have the responsibility of educating students around the cultural and subcultural literacies that ultimately amount to the skills that will enable them to participate in the ongoing struggle inherent in cultural politics.

References

Alderman, J. (2001), *Sonic Boom. P2P and the Battle for the Future of Music*, London: Fourth Estate.

Armitage, J. (ed.) (1999), Special Issue on Machinic Modulations: New Cultural Theory and Technopolitics, *Angelaki: Journal of the Theoretical Humanities*, 4 (2) (September).

Barbrook, R. (2002), 'The Napsterization of Everything,' *Science as Culture*, 11 (2) (June): 277–85.

Best, S. and Kellner, D. (1991), *Postmodern Theory: Critical Interrogations*, London and New York: Macmillan and Guilford Press.

Best, S. and Kellner, D. (1997), *The Postmodern Turn*, New York and London: Guilford Press and Routledge.

Best, S. and Kellner, D. (2001), *The Postmodern Adventure*, New York and London: Guilford Press and Routledge.

Brecher, J., Costello, T. and Smith, B. (2000), *Globalization From Below*, Boston MA: South End Press.

Burbach, R. (2001), *Globalization and Postmodern Politics: From Zapatistas to High-Tech Robber Barons*, London: Pluto Press.

7. On the importance of the ideas of Debord and the Situationist International to make sense of the present conjuncture see Best and Kellner (1997: Chapter 3), and on the new forms of the interactive consumer society, see Best and Kellner (2001).

Cvetkovich, A. and Kellner, D. (1997), *Articulating the Global and the Local: Globalization and Cultural Studies*, Boulder CO: Westview.

Dyer-Witheford, N. (1999), *Cyber-Marx. Cycles and Circuits of Struggle in High-Technology Capitalism*, Urbana and Chicago IL: University of Illinois Press.

Hardt, M. and Negri, A. (2000), *Empire*, Cambridge MA: Harvard University Press.

Himanen, P. (2001), *The Hacker Ethic*, New York: Random House.

Kellner, D. (1997), 'Intellectuals, the New Public Spheres, and Technopolitics', *New Political Science*, 41–2 (Fall): 169–88.

Kellner, D. (1998), 'Globalization and the Postmodern Turn', in R. Axtmann (ed.), *Globalization and Europe*, London: Cassell.

Kellner, D. (2002), 'September 11 and Terror War: The Bush Legacy and the Risks of Unilateralism', http://www.gseis.ucla.edu/faculty/kellner/papers/sept11kell.htm (accessed August 2002).

Kellner, D. (forthcoming), 'Theorizing Globalization', *Sociological Theory*.

Luke, A. and Luke, C. (2000), 'A Situated Perspective on Cultural Globalization', in N. Burbules and C. Torres (eds), *Globalization and Education*, London and New York: Routledge.

Steger, M. (2002), *Globalism. The New Market Ideology*, Lanham MD: Rowman & Littlefield.

Turkle, S. (1996), 'Virtuality and its Discontents', *The American Prospect*, 7 (24) (December), http://www.prospect.org/print/V7/24/turkle-s.html (accessed September 2002).

Turkle, S. (1997), *Life on the Screen: Identity in the Age of the Internet*, New York: Touchstone Press.

Waterman, P. (1992), *International Labour Communication by Computer: The Fifth International?* Working Paper Series 129, The Hague: Institute of Social Studies.

Index

Index

Bourdieu, Pierre, 5, 28, 31–3, 38
  developed by Jenkins, 276
  developed by Thornton, 4, 9–10, 12, 32
  on pop culture, 43, 44
  on *sens pratique*, 45, 47
  versus essentialism, 11, 45–6
Bradley, Dick, 240–1
Brah, A., 153, 170
Brake, M., 211
Bratmobile, 253
Brecher, J., 306
bricolage, 127, 173, 188, 216, 220, 262
Brooks, A., 256n
Brotherton, D. C., 134
Brown, Andy, 7, 212
Brown, I., 76
Brulard, I., 199
BSE (bovine spongiform encephalopathy), 71
Buffon, Georges-Louis de, 257
Burbach, R., 303n, 307
Burchill, Julie, 245
Bury, Rhiannon, 19, 280n
Bushell, Gary, 245
Butler, Judith, 5, 10, 11, 107, 270, 271
  versus essentialism, 45–6
Buzzacott, Kevin, 76

Cachin, O., 203
Cagle, M. Van, 214, 215
Califia, Pat, 129
Calvo Ospina, H., 153, 154
Camphausen, R. C., 119, 121
Cannon, S., 203
capital, subcultural, 5, 7, 31–2
  Thornton on, 9–10, 11, 12–13, 31–2, 43,
    102–3
Caputo, Virginia, 239n
Carey, James, 36
Cartledge, F., 248
Cashmore, E., 212–13
Castells, M., 72, 286, 296
Cathus, O., 196
CCCS (Centre for Contemporary Cultural
    Studies), 167, 178, 188
  as masculinist, 18
  critique by Stahl, 27–33
  critique by others, 84–5, 169, 176, 204, 213,
    215–16, 262–3

gender and, 18–19
ignores heavy metal, 211–12
politics of youth culture and, 14–15
rave and, 101–2
semiotics and, 54
subcultural 'heroism' of, 4–6, 6–13, 83, 85
Cepeda, M. E., 152
Chambers, I., 3–4, 220
Chan, S., 73
Cheesman, T., 202
Childs, P., 199
Chirac, Jacques, 200
Chow, Rey, 170
Clark, Dylan, 8
Clark, Gary, 215
Clarke, John, 14, 88, 127, 175, 188, 214
  Resistance Through Rituals, 215–17
class, 211, 213–14, 217–18
Clifford, James, 108, 110–11, 125
Cloke, Kristin, 276
clubbing, 68
'clubculture', 6
CMCs (computer-mediated communications),
    36, 38, 71–2, 271
Cobley, Paul, 247n
Cohen, E., 67, 168
Cohen, Phil, 136, 144, 168
Cohen, Stanley, 168, 239–40
Collins, Patricia Hill, 256n
Comstock, M., 253n, 255n, 257n
consumption, shift from, 245–6, 254
'contact zone', 110, 114
Cooley, C. H., 124
Coombes, A. E., 153, 170
Coon, Caroline, 240
Corbiscello, G. V., 134, 139
Cornershop, 195
Corngold, Stacy, 228
Costello, Elvis, 245
Costello, T., 306
counter-tribes, 71–2
Couturier, B., 196
Crass, 226n
Criminal Justice Act (1994), 73, 110
Critical Mass, 70
Cross, B., 200, 203
Crossroads Conference (Birmingham 24 June
    2000), 83n

Index

Index

Index

'machismo', 136–7
Maffesoli, Michel
 limitations of, 77
 on neo-tribes, 5, 6, 12, 65–7, 286–7
 on 'orgiasm', 74
 on 'tribus' 11–2
 The Time of the Tribes, 129
Malbon, Ben, 12, 67, 105, 106
 on clubbing, 68, 103, 104, 171, 176
Malraux, André, 114n
Manchester Institute for Popular Studies, 4
Manuel, P., 153
Marchart, Oliver, 8, 13, 16, 94
Marcus, G. E., 109, 125
Marcus, Greil, 225, 226, 233
Martin, G., 4n, 10, 15n, 68, 74, 83n
Martin, Lauren, 261–2
Martinez, Noemi, 261
Marxism, 60
masculinity, 220
masochism, 51–5
Massey, Doreen, 37
Maximumrocknroll, 255
Maxson, C. L., 142
MC Solaar, 197, 198, 202
McCarthy, C., 158
McCracken, Grant, 228–9
McCron, R., 215
McDonald's, 311
McDowell, L., 257
McGuigan, J., 89
McKay, G., 14, 65, 70
McKay, George, 229
McKinney, M., 196
McLaren, Malcolm, 246
McLaughlin, M., 292
McLaughlin, Thomas, 256
McLuhan, Marshall, 230
McNeill, Phil, 245
McNeish, W., 70
McRobbie, Angela, 5n, 18, 175n, 257, 259
 critique of Laclau, 84
 Feminism and Youth Culture, 247
 on clubbing, 176
 on 'cockrock', 220, 240
 on micro-politics, 103
 on moral panics, 168

 on Riot Grrrl, 254
 on riots, 174
 on subcultures, 8, 210, 239
Mead, G. H., 124
Melly, George, 215
Melucci, A., 70
Mercer, Kobena, 172, 173
Mercury, M., 123
Mercury, Maureen, 129
micro-politics, 83–4, 90, 93
Miklitsch, R., 106
Miles, C., 239, 257n, 258
Miles, L. G., 18
Miller, W. B., 136
mimesis, 11, 46–8
mind/body problem, 52
Ministère AMER, 197
Mitchell, T., 203, 204
Mizrach, S., 127
Modern Primitives, 17, 119–29
Mods, 6
Mohanty, Chandra, 256n, 259n
Moore, Joan, 136
'moral panics', 168
Morales, Willie, 139
Moreiras, A., 151n, 152
Morely, D., 203, 204
Morgan, Glen, 276
Morley, D., 7, 185
Mouffe, Chantal, 13, 16, 84, 90–2, 95
Mouri, Y., 102n
Muggleton, D., 4, 6n, 7, 10, 18, 158n, 162
 on CCCS, 167
 on class decomposition, 15
 on culture as reifying, 270
 on individualism, 53, 56
 on method, 213
 on post-subcultures, 29, 58, 77, 173, 176, 183
 on punk, 209
 on shifting identities, 169–70, 218, 285
 on subcultures, 262–3
Mungham, G., 4n, 211, 214
Muñoz, J. E., 153
Münz, R., 182
Murdock, G., 215
Musafar, Fakir, 119–120, 123

Index

Index

Index